BILINGUAL AND
ESL CLASSROOMS

BILINGUAL AND ESL CLASSROOMS

Teaching in Multicultural Contexts

Carlos J. Ovando
University of Alaska, Anchorage

Virginia P. Collier
George Mason University, Fairfax, Va.

McGraw-Hill Book Company

*New York   St. Louis   San Francisco   Auckland   Bogotá   Hamburg
London   Madrid   Mexico   Montreal   New Delhi
Panama   Paris   São Paulo   Singapore   Sydney   Tokyo   Toronto*

Library of Congress Cataloging in Publication Data

Ovando, Carlos Julio.
   Bilingual and ESL classrooms.

   Bibliography: p.
   Includes index.
   1. Education, Bilingual—United States. 2. Inter-
cultural education—United States. 3. English language
—Study and teaching—Foreign students. 4. Community
and school—United States. I. Collier, Virginia P.
II. Title.
LC3731.096   1985   371.97'0973   84-20107
ISBN 0-07-047951-8

      5 6 7 8 9 0 DOC/DOC 9 0

ISBN 0-07-047951-8

The editors for this book were Tom Quinn and Jim Bessent,
the designer was Elliott Epstein, and the production
supervisor was Sally Fliess. It was set in Times Roman
by Achorn Graphics.

Printed and bound by R. R. Donnelley & Sons Company.

CONTENTS

Preface   ix

ONE: STUDENTS   1
The range of students, 3
The home background, 4
   The role of culture, 5
   The social context, 6
   Previous schooling experience, 7
What happens at school, 9
   The emotional challenge, 9
   The linguistic challenge, 11
Discovering the student, 15
   Literature and inservice training, 15
   Taking a fresh look, 16

TWO: POLITICS, PROGRAMS, AND RESOURCES   21
Historical background, 23
   English as a second language, 25
   Bilingual instruction of the 1960s, 25
   Federal legislation: Title VII, 26
   Related federal legislation, 29
   State legislation, 31
   State certification, 32
   Court decisions, 34
Program models, 37
   Transitional bilingual education, 38
   Maintenance bilingual education, 39
   Two-way enrichment bilingual education, 40
   Eliminating the transitional-maintenance dichotomy, 42

Immersion bilingual education, 42
"Structured immersion," 44
English as a second language, 44
Other programs for teaching second languages, 45
Resources in bilingual education and ESL, 46
  Title VII support services, 46
  Professional organizations, 50

THREE: LANGUAGE   57
Research in language acquisition, 58
  Child first- and second-language acquisition, 58
  Acquisition-learning distinction, 59
  Input hypothesis, 62
  Socioaffective filter, 63
  Cognitive-academic language proficiency (CALP) and
  basic interpersonal communicative skills (BICS), 63
  Additive versus subtractive bilingualism and the threshold
  hypothesis, 64
  Influence of L_1 on L_2, 65
  Definitions of bilingualism, 66
Native language arts, 67
  Teaching first language, 67
  Standard, dialects, and language variety, 68
  Language arts curricular materials, 70
Methods of teaching second language, 70
  Approach, method, and technique, 71
  Older methods, 71
  Innovative approaches, 74
  Second-language methods for primary school, 77
  Second-language syllabus organization, 77
Methods of teaching in a bilingual classroom, 80
  Bilingual program models, types, and designs, 81
  Classroom design: Balance of the two languages, 82
Teaching language skills, 90
  Relationships among the four skills, 90
  Listening and speaking, 91
  Reading in L_1 and L_2, 92
  Writing, 98

FOUR: CULTURE   101
Perspectives on the concept of culture, 102
  The anthropological view of culture, 102
  Popular views of culture, 105
  Biculturalism and cultural pluralism, 107

Concepts related to culture and education, 113
  Cultural deprivation and cultural deficit, 114
  Marked and unmarked languages and cultures, 117
  Ethnocentrism and cultural relativity, 119
  Stereotypes, 121
  Socioeconomic status and cultural background, 124
  Cultural transmission and acquisition of ethnicity, 126
  Language variation and home-school mismatch, 129
Research on culture and education, 133
  Cognitive styles and cultural background, 133
  Social interaction, 138

FIVE: **SOCIAL STUDIES, MUSIC, AND ART**   153
A framework for social studies, 153
Bilingual and ESL classroom structures, 155
  Elementary-level bilingual self-contained classrooms, 155
  Secondary-level bilingual social studies, 156
  ESL social studies classes, 157
Instructional approaches to cultural awareness, 158
  The interdisciplinary framework, 159
  Teachers and students as cultural researchers, 164
Resources for social studies, 169
  Maps, 170
  Periodicals and the media, 171
  Resources in consumer education, 171
  Resources for a problem-posing curriculum, 172
  Electronic media and films, 173
Music, 175
  Including music in classroom events, 176
  Caveats, 177
  Learning objectives for musical experiences, 179
  Music in extracurricular activities, 182
  Resources on music, 183
Art in the bilingual and ESL classroom, 184
  Building acceptance of the individual, 186
  Art appreciation in cross-cultural context, 186
  Art and language learning, 187

SIX: **MATHEMATICS AND SCIENCE**   189
Achievement status of students in math and science, 191
Cognition and cross-cultural research, 195
  The cognitive deficit framework, 196
  Developmental universals and cross-cultural research, 196
  Inferences for teaching, 200

Language and culture in mathematics and science
classrooms, 206
    Use of language, 207
    An interdisciplinary framework, 216

SEVEN: ASSESSMENT   223
Purposes of assessment in bilingual and ESL programs, 224
    Testing implications of Lau remedies, 225
    Placement testing, 229
    Diagnostic-prescriptive process, 232
    Exit criteria, 235
    Program evaluation, 236
Issues in assessment of language-minority students, 239
    Language assessment, 239
    Bilingualism, intelligence, and IQ tests, 243
    Assessment for bilingual special education, 246
    Cultural bias, 248
Assessment instruments, 251
    Tests of oral language proficiency, 251
Teacher-constructed tests, 256
    Measures in language assessment, 257

EIGHT: SCHOOL AND COMMUNITY   263
Development and types of ethnic communities, 265
    Chronology of the status of ethnic communities, 266
    *Characteristics of immigrant and indigenous ethnic
    communities*, 267
Legal cases and community organization, 271
    Legal cases, 271
    Community organization efforts, 274
Community profiles, 276
    Language use in the community, 277
    Social relationship between school and community, 280
    Informal community description and reflection, 283
Community involvement, 289
    Legislation for community participation, 291
    Parents as mutual partners, 295
    Models and suggestions for community involvement, 300

References   311

Index   345

PREFACE

Designed for bilingual and English as a second language (ESL) teachers (K-12), *Bilingual and ESL Classrooms* combines theory and research with practical classroom applications. It addresses the needs of all teachers who work with limited English proficient students of all language backgrounds. In addition, there is information for teachers on working with English-dominant students with a minority language background, bilingual bicultural students, and English-speaking students in bilingual classes. Transitional, maintenance, two-way, immersion, and ESL-only programs receive in-depth treatment, addressed to both teachers and administrative staff in bilingual and ESL settings. For administrators, the text is useful for its discussion of politics, federal regulations and resources, assessment issues, and school-community relations.

Bilingual and ESL Classrooms is authored rather than edited. As such, it bypasses the internal contradictions often encountered in edited texts. It is also one of the first teacher training textbooks to emphasize the integration of bilingual education and ESL. Bilingual and ESL staff serve the same student population, coordinate programs and resources jointly, and often receive comparable professional training. This book can be used as a textbook for teacher training courses in methods of teaching, curriculum development, language acquisition, content area instruction, multicultural awareness, assessment, and administration for all bilingual and ESL settings. And it contains a wealth of useful references and recommended readings for teachers and administrators who wish to examine the issues raised in greater depth.

In this book we have emphasized that language and culture are integral components of the instructional process in bilingual and ESL classrooms and that, as such, they are important foundations upon which cognitive and affective development are based. Our chapters on Language and Culture describe this foundation. Another major theme which permeates the entire volume is that bilingualism and the accompanying intercultural awareness is a source of great human richness. All of the students whom we serve, regardless of the type of bilingual or ESL program, are learning formally and informally how to deal with the multiple worlds they live in at home and at school. Educators, through the quality of education which they provide, represent an important bridge to students' success in benefitting fully from the multiple languages and cultures which they are experiencing. For all students, teachers, administrators, and community members who have the opportunity to participate in interculturally sensitive bilingual and ESL programs, their world is opened to many new possibilities.

The text is organized into eight chapters:

1. *Students.*   Special characteristics of students in bilingual and ESL classes are the main focus of the first chapter, including variations in personality, educational background, social class, ethnicity, national origin, language, and culture. Here, we survey the broad range of students found in bilingual and ESL classrooms: English-dominant students with a minority language background, bilingual bicultural students, limited-English-proficient students, and English-speaking students.

2. *Politics, Programs, and Resources.*   Following an overview of the historical development of bilingual education and ESL in the United States, this chapter examines federal and state legislation and court decisions which have had a strong impact on the field. The second section discusses major program models for bilingual education and ESL, including transitional, maintenance, two-way, immersion, and ESL-only programs. A third section examines resources available in the field.

3. *Language.*   Chapter 3 focuses on the integral role of language in bilingual and ESL classes, including definitions of bilingualism, use of the two languages in a bilingual classroom, code-switching, dialect variation, recent findings in second language acquisition research, methods of teaching first and second languages, and some pointers on teaching listening, speaking, reading, and writing.

4. *Culture.*   Integral aspects of culture in bilingual and ESL classrooms are discussed through perspectives on the concept of culture and research related to culture in the classroom. The anthropological view of culture, popular views of culture, biculturalism and cultural pluralism, cultural deprivation, marked and unmarked languages and cultures, ethnocentrism and cultural relativity, stereotypes, socioeconomic status, cultural transmission, and language variation are among the concepts discussed. Research on learning styles and social interaction is also examined.

5. *Social Studies, Music, and Art.*   Suggestions provided for social studies lessons for bilingual and ESL classrooms weave together the fields of anthropology, sociology, geography, history, music, and art. We encourage teachers to develop problem-posing, interdisciplinary activities and to work together with students as cultural researchers. Activities emphasize continuing cognitive development through first and second languages—in an acquisition-rich context.
6. *Mathematics and Science.*   Chapter 6 explores concepts in mathematics and science methodology as these relate to first and second languages. It investigates the cross-cultural transferability of mathematical and scientific concepts and points to the need to ground such concepts to the linguistic and sociocultural realities of the students. The chapter offers both conceptual and practical guidelines for bilingual and ESL teachers.
7. *Assessment.*   The Assessment chapter examines federal guidelines and the purposes of assessment for placement, diagnosis, exit, and evaluation in bilingual and ESL programs. Special issues which receive attention are language assessment, including a section on teacher-constructed tests and a discussion of a few specific assessment instruments; bilingualism and intelligence; assessment for bilingual special education; and cultural bias in tests.
8. *School and Community.*   Finally, Chapter 8 analyzes and recommends approaches by which parents and other community members can be made to feel a strong sense of ownership in bilingual and ESL education. The learning community is one which includes a strong partnership of parents, teachers, students, and school administrators. The chapter comprises both a conceptual and a practical view of the ethnic community in relation to schooling, with discussions of immigrant, indigenous, and majority communities involved in bilingual and ESL education.

Bilingual and ESL Classrooms is the product of mutual effort throughout all of its eight chapters. Each author took primary responsibility for specific chapters—Dr. Ovando: Chapters 1, 4, 6, and 8; and Dr. Collier: Chapters 2, 3, and 7. We share equally the responsibility for Chapter 5.

We wish to thank Tom Quinn and Jim Bessent, our editors, for their patience, encouragement, insightful suggestions and trust in us throughout the gestation period of the manuscript. Our thanks also to the anonymous reviewers, whose comments and suggestions were extremely useful. To our loved ones, who endured the long process, we thank you.

Carlos J. Ovando
Virginia P. Collier

Chapter One

STUDENTS

The passage in 1968 of the federal Bilingual Education Act* brought to the attention of educators throughout the United States an exciting yet controversial approach to educating students of non-English-language background. Educators and linguists in the area of English as a second language (ESL) had developed over the years a substantial knowledge base in their field, and various forms of bilingual education were experimented with in the United States since at least the early 1800s, but it was not until the 1970s that bilingual and ESL programs were widely implemented throughout the United States. These programs were initiated primarily in an effort to provide equal educational opportunities for students of non-English-language background.

BASIC DEFINITIONS

A bilingual-education program, defined in its most basic form, is one which is organized with the following three aims in mind:

1. The continued development of the student's primary language (L_1)

2. Acquisition of the second language (L_2), which for limited-English-proficient (LEP) students is English

3. Instruction in the content areas utilizing both L_1 and L_2 (California State Department of Education, 1981, p. 215)

---

*The federal Bilingual Education Act of 1968 is Title VII of the Elementary and Secondary Education Act.

1

Because one cannot totally separate language from culture, bilingual programs include historical and cultural components associated with the languages being used.* Furthermore, because both language and culture are integral to a person's self-identity, the inclusion of culture in the bilingual curriculum is believed to promote students' self-esteem.

> [Bilingual education is] . . . the use of two languages, one of which is English, as mediums of instruction for the same pupil population in a well-organized program which encompasses all or part of the curriculum and includes the study of the history and culture associated with the mother tongue. A complete program develops and maintains the children's self-esteem and a legitimate pride in both cultures. (U.S. Office of Education, 1971)

English as a second language instruction has been succinctly defined as "a structured language-acquisition program designed to teach English to students whose native language is not English" (Brière, 1979a, p. 201). English as a second language is an important component of all bilingual programs. In addition, there are many schooling contexts in which LEP students may be immersed in monolingual English instruction in all content areas but also may participate in regularly scheduled ESL classes to facilitate their acquisition of English. The choice to use such monolingual instruction, including an ESL component, may be made because there are not enough LEP students in the school to justify a bilingual program; or because there are many languages represented, which makes English, as the lingua franca, the only feasible choice for instruction; or because a community or school considers this approach, regardless of the number of LEP students or languages involved, to be the one best suited to local desires and educational objectives (Schorr, 1983, p. 1).

Teachers of English to Speakers of Other Languages (TESOL), the major organization representing ESL instructors in the United States, has taken the position that bilingual instruction is the best approach to the education of LEP students. As mentioned before, however, it is not always feasible to implement such a program, depending on the number of LEP students and languages involved. When the number of LEP students is insufficient, monolingual instruction with an ESL component is recommended. Monolingual instruction without an ESL component, however, does not provide LEP students with the specialized instruction needed for the acquisition of English-language skills (TESOL, 1976).

These brief definitions just begin to hint at the myriad issues to be

---

*While the literature sometimes refers to "bilingual-bicultural" education, in this book we use the term "bilingual education" as a comprehensive one to include culture as well.

considered in the implementation of such programs. In later chapters we take a detailed look at the program models and teaching process itself. In this first chapter we examine the reason for our professional existence: our students. Who are the learners in bilingual and ESL classrooms? What particular and diverse needs do they have, and how can teachers be sensitive to all of their variations in personality, educational background, social class, ethnicity, national origin, language, and culture? We examine the range of students in bilingual and ESL classrooms, the backgrounds the students bring with them, what happens when such backgrounds are mixed into the culture of the schools, and how teachers can use this information to know their students better.

THE RANGE OF STUDENTS

As of 1980 there were approximately 2.4 million limited-English-proficient students aged 5 to 14 in schools in the United States. It is predicted that their numbers will increase by about 40 percent to 3.4 million by the year 2000. These numbers do not include language-minority students who are bilingual or English-dominant, who also may benefit from placement in a bilingual program. The total population of students of non-English-language background (aged 5 to 14, limited-English-proficient, bilingual and English-dominant) was estimated for 1976 at 3.8 million and was projected to increase to 5.1 million by the year 2000. The entire 4- to 18-year-old school-age population of LEP students was estimated to be 3.6 million in 1978 (Oxford et al., 1981, pp. 1–2).

Such figures, although important, do not unveil the rich mix of students found in bilingual and ESL classrooms. Students range from indigenous minorities such as Native Americans to very recent immigrants and represent both the oldest and newest members of American society. Through the nation's history, assimilative and acculturative factors have impacted powerfully on the lives of such students to produce many different configurations of language and culture. In terms of language skills and ethnicity, students in bilingual and ESL classrooms may include English-dominant students with a language-minority background; bilingual, bicultural students; limited-English-proficient students; and English, monolingual students with no language-minority background.

A closer look at these groupings reveals that English-dominant students who have a home language other than English may be involved in a bilingual program to improve academic achievement and, perhaps additionally, to develop their home language skills. An English-dominant minority student, for example, may be a Hispanic or Native American child who speaks English predominantly or exclusively and yet is exposed to the family's other language through parents or grandparents. English-dominant language-minority students often come from stigmatized eth-nolinguistic groups who because of societal pressures, historical circum-stances, or geographical location have not maintained their ancestral languages and cultures. Although considerably acculturated into the En-glish-speaking milieu, they may be socioeconomically or socioculturally marginal. While some members of such groups are now undergoing lin-guistic and cultural revitalization, other members question the value of such a linguistic and cultural renaissance.

Besides those ethnolinguistic students whose parents want them to be reexposed to their ancestral languages through bilingual instruction, there are bilingual, bicultural students who are enrolled in bilingual classes because of the desire to continue learning in two languages and living in two cultures. Because such students are already considerably fluent in two languages, bilingual instruction constitutes enrichment of the stu-dent's academic experience and an affirmation of the family's ethnolin-guistic identity.

The students most often associated in the public eye with bilingual and ESL instruction are the limited-English-proficient students who on school entry lack the necessary English skills for immediate success in an all-English curriculum. Bilingual instruction for such students is a way of providing educational equity and quality. Through bilingual instruction, including instruction in ESL, limited-English-proficient students can be-gin to develop the linguistic and academic skills appropriate to their level of cognitive development.

Because it is illegal to school students in volitionally segregated con-texts, bilingual classrooms also have a proportion of English, monolingual students with no language-minority background for whom exposure to a second language is an academically and personally enriching experience. Moreover, such students play a socializing role in schools within cultur-ally plural societies. Thus, understanding how such students fit into the teaching and learning configuration is also crucial.

THE HOME BACKGROUND

Very few educators would argue against the value of being familiar with the students' cultural background, socioeconomic status, and previous schooling experience. While such information about any student is valu-able, it becomes even more important when the student population in-cludes children of ethnic and language-minority groups. Without suffi-cient knowledge in such situations, there may be a greater risk of failure in school adjustment and cognitive growth.

The Role of Culture

Ethnic visibility is usually associated with such salient features as language and racial background, name, clothing, and food. While such obvious cues are just the tip of the cultural iceberg, many of the negative attitudes found in society toward minority ethnic groups are rooted in fairly simplistic interpretations of items in those categories. Beyond these obvious markers of being "different" are many more subtle but important aspects of ethnicity which contribute to a student's identity. For example, there is much cultural variation in the roles which are assigned to individuals within and outside the family. Lines of authority and socialization expectations as manifested in birth order, sex roles, and division of labor are powerful agents in molding children's social relationships.

Values and religion, as expressions of belief systems, serve as windows to the interior of cultural structures. The things that we believe in—democracy, socialism, capitalism, extended family, independence, cooperation, competition, education, magic, horoscopes, Buddhism, pantheism, secular humanism, agnosticism, Judaism, Catholicism, Protestantism—provide a powerful synthesis of how we as humans attempt to make at least partial sense of the world surrounding us. The new linguistic and cultural environment of the school may intentionally or unintentionally play an affirming or negating role regarding the values of students and their families. A child who has been taught to be quiet and unquestioning when dealing with adults, for example, may find that his or her idea of the "good student" is not rewarded in an open, child-centered classroom.

Styles of nonverbal communication are also an important aspect of cultural identity. In communicating with each other, humans draw from many paralinguistic actions as well as from the verbal message. Cultural groups attach different meanings to types of body movements, spatial distance, eye contact, and emotional tone (Birdwhistell, 1970; Cazden, John & Hymes, 1972; Hall, 1959; Philips, 1983). The significance of a laugh, a pat on the shoulder, or a hug can be quite different depending on the cultural background of the person interpreting it. What message, for example, does a Chamorro student convey with the up-and-down motion of the eyebrows? (Among the Chamorros of Guam, raising the eyebrows and tilting the head back slightly indicate recognition of a person's presence. It is a silent hello.) Knowledge of such nonverbal codes strongly affects the outcome of intercultural communication between the subculture of the home and the subculture of the school.

Students from immigrant families have usually had some type of exposure to the popular version of "American" culture before immigration. For some the United States is everything that Hollywood projects through the movies. Others may have a more accurate vision of particular characteristics of life in the United States. Many have impressions of the country filtered through the interpretations of friends or relatives who have gone to the United States. Indigenous language-minority children also encounter cultural patterns which are alien to behavior and communication fostered at home, often through internal migration to urban centers or simply through entry into the school system. How students and their families react to the differences which they find in their new community depends partially on the impressions and attitudes toward the mainstream culture which they bring with them.

The Social Context

Many students in bilingual and ESL classrooms come from sociocultural groups which have been and continue to be the recipients of varying degrees of socioeconomic marginality and racial or ethnic discrimination. However, students served through bilingual instruction are not uniformly from lower socioeconomic backgrounds. A volunteer in a secondary-level ESL class was somewhat surprised to discover the educational level of the family of one of her students:

> Edwin and I talked some today about where he is from—the Philippines. He told me a little about his family's background. I learned that his mother and father are well-educated people. His mother was a science and botany teacher at the high-school level and his father worked for an insurance company. His oldest brother is attending the University of Manila, studying electrical engineering.

How language-minority groups are perceived by mainstream citizens to fit into the social texture of the nation has a strong impact on both immigrants and indigenous minority populations. Some research indicates that the positive or negative perceptions of the host population can affect the academic performance of language-minority students as they internalize these perceptions (Ogbu, 1978; Skutnabb-Kangas & Toukomaa, 1976).

> Having just received a large federal grant for Cuban refugees, eager teachers in a new adult education center watched their enrollment drop in just 3 weeks from full classes to a trickle of students. Why? "I need a job more." "I'm not a welfare case; I'm proud of myself." "The government treats us like babies."

Is such behavior imprudent, or is it a way of holding on to a positive self-image?

LEP students often bring with them to the schools a change in their socioeconomic status. Sometimes such students come from relatively well-educated middle-class families who have to undergo some alterations economically and socially until they get themselves on their feet in the United States. Many language-minority students, depending on the economic conditions, undergo social adjustments because of the change in the way in which they fit into society. This can be the case whether the family has moved from a higher socioeconomic status in the country of origin to a lower status in the United States or is experiencing upward mobility.

Tied in with the social class of language-minority students is the fact that much of what they represent is strongly linked to their geographical region of origin. Very often immigrants from rural areas have considerably different values and customs from their urban counterparts from the same country. The urban resident, for example, may have been more exposed to the popular cultural version of the United States portrayed through the mass media, which serves as a powerful assimilator worldwide.

Previous Schooling Experience

Embedded in indigenous language-minority and immigrant language-minority children's sociocultural background are their families' attitudes toward formal schooling and, in some cases, the students' previous academic experiences. The nature of an immigrant child or family's previous school experience will depend on socioeconomic status, country of origin, and the circumstances of the geographical move. Some students have had a sound base of knowledge which can be transferred to the English curriculum, while others have had almost no schooling. Beto and Mee represent the extremes:

> Beto, a teenager who spent his childhood in the Dominican Republic, never had a chance to attend school regularly there and learn how to read. Now, in lessons in Spanish, he has made three grades' progress in reading and math in 1 year.

> Mee, a Korean-born student, is already literate in her native language due to her previous education. Her literacy in Korean is helping her to understand materials in English, and she is excelling in mathematics because of previous exposure to the concepts.

Even for children who come to the United States at a preschool age or who are born in the United States of recent immigrants, the parents' schooling experiences in the country of origin affect the way the child's schooling is perceived. Information about schooling background is valuable not only for making curricular adjustments but also for taking an affirmative posture toward the learner. It may enable the teacher to see that a student or a student's family is responding to the school environment in a way which, based on past experiences, is rational.

Of course language-minority students and their parents come from myriad schooling backgrounds. Some, for instance, arrive from countries which stress an authoritarian style within the school: the adult commands and the children play a strictly subordinate role. Placing a child from such a setting into one in which there is a degree of academic and physical freedom often creates predictable confusion on the part of the learner. In some countries children are exposed to a fairly standardized curriculum nationwide, and there is a high degree of uniformity in pedagogic methods. To families from such backgrounds, the variety of options available in most American school systems today seems quite puzzling.

A predominant approach to instruction in some countries emphasizes memorization of information rather than problem-posing or open-ended learning activities. Students accustomed to such pedagogy may feel uncomfortable initially with the critical thinking and discussion format often encountered in the new school environment. The student may have been rewarded previously for taking a passive learning role, or the family may have expected her or him to assume that role; accommodation to a more active role may be facilitated if the teacher is aware of the different traditions which have enabled the student to survive in the previous academic environment. Whether students have experienced small- or large-group instruction, whether time schedules and attendance requirements have been strict or lax, whether there has been an emphasis on oral or written work, and whether there has been a cultural bias toward cooperation or competition and independence—all have an effect.

While some immigrants are middle- and upper-class people whose children have attended private schools in the country of origin, other immigrant families are from less affluent social classes. Some of the latter students and their parents may have experienced very limited schooling opportunities in their country of origin. Immigrant parents from *any* social-class background may be unprepared for the design and value systems of schools in the United States. Standardized tests, varied grading systems, ability or achievement grouping, and individualized instruction—all may be unfamiliar concepts.

On the other hand, parents of indigenous minority students may be familiar with the operation of local school systems, but may have experienced chronic failure in those systems themselves. This in turn will influence what they want for their children as they are educated in those same systems. The frustration with past school experiences is reflected in this language-minority college student's explanation of why she has chosen to become a bilingual teacher: "I thought I could do a better job than some of the teachers I was working for [as an aide]."

WHAT HAPPENS AT SCHOOL

If language-minority students, whatever their sociocultural background and whatever the previous schooling experiences of their families, did not have to relate reciprocally with the subculture of the school, there would be no reason to focus on this theme. But conventional wisdom and research suggest that much of the difficulty experienced by language-minority children in school can be attributed to the apparent mismatch between the world of the home and the world of the classroom (Jordan, 1984; Trueba, Guthrie & Au, 1981).

The Emotional Challenge

Basic to analyzing the level of integration of LEP or bilingual students into the life of the school are their emotional needs and experiences. Combining the variation in cultural patterns with the individual personality of each student, there are many different ways in which language-minority children react to the classroom situation. The following sketches illustrate just a few behaviors from the wide range exhibited by these students.

Reserved, silent, seated in a corner, Lan prefers the isolation and comfort of written exercises. She refuses to respond orally to the teacher or to Vietnamese peers. Who knows what are her innermost thoughts with family gone, her familiar world taken away?

Pedro, full of energy, acts out his aggression in class. An Ecuadorian Indian, short for his 13 years, he alternately is eager for lessons and teases classmates. He drives his teacher crazy.

A handsome and bright new student, José, arrives from Venezuela. He is immediately popular and highly social, adjusts well to the new school context, and picks up English extremely fast. He attends school faithfully and follows all the rules. Then the bilingual counselor discovers that he is a drug peddler in the back corner of the school yard.

> Yuki, an elementary-level Japanese student, has always spoken only in a whisper. Today she is playing an ESL game in which she acts out sentences such as "I am jumping." She becomes so involved in the game that she forgets her self-consciousness and speaks in an easily heard tone of voice for the first time.

Sensitizing oneself to the emotional needs of LEP students sometimes requires careful tuning in on the part of the teacher. A desire to express one's cultural or personal identity may come in very subtle ways:

> Using Cuisenaire rods, the ESL teacher modeled an activity which reinforced color, direction, and prepositions. He sat with his back to a student, who gave directions as to how to place the rods. If the student communicated her directions clearly, the teacher would end up with the same configuration of rods that she had formed. Kyun Sun did a great job, and her teacher ended up with the targeted design. The girl then informed him that it was the symbol for her name in Korean.

Unfortunately, whether actual or perceived, subtle or blatant, some form of racial and ethnic discrimination is a reality of life in most culturally plural environments. And the school may be one of the first places in which language-minority children discover that they are perceived by the mainstream culture as being different. An American-born language-minority student from a rural background recalls: "When we came to this city I first experienced prejudice in school and that really cut me down. I wanted to go back where we came from, but my parents wanted me to stay here with them."

As they mature, students, like their adult models, unconsciously assess the sociocultural texture of society to see what is valued and what is denigrated. The direct impact which discrimination or prejudice can have on a person is a feeling of not being in control of the environment, which in turn can lead to low self-esteem.

Students' and families' academic aspirations vis-à-vis their view of the school's expectations of them are a barometer of the level of trust between the students, the community, and the school. Regardless of whether or not they are justified, feelings on the part of some language-minority students that less is expected of them are real and have to be faced. Here, for example, is a quotation revealing a high degree of resentment:

> I want to be a doctor and I want to go to some third-world country because they need a lot of doctors there. What motivates me is when the white man tells me that I can't do it. It's up to me to prove that I can. It really makes me angry.

A college-bound senior who entered the school system as a LEP student reflects on the expectations she thought teachers had of her:

> When I first came here to grade school the teachers thought I would have a lot of problems and they ended up putting me in a reading class a couple of grades below what I could read. I think it was a Dick and Jane book. In high school now, some of the teachers talk real slow, like I don't understand or something, but then others . . . Well, it seems like it's always either below my knees or above my head! I don't relate to my school counselor very well. I've done all the financial-aid stuff for college pretty much myself.

The nature of the ethnic identity which children establish for themselves may depend partially on the ethnic composition of the school they attend. Although there are many other factors involved in a student's self-concept, a school with a large proportion of language-minority students may sometimes provide a supportive environment for positive self-identification (Ovando, 1978b). Conversely, schools in which a small number of students receive bilingual or ESL instruction may create the possibility of feelings of stigmatization. It is not unusual for children to feel uncomfortable in receiving any "special" academic assistance, but the fact that language-minority youth are filtering their experiences through a different culture and language background may tend to make them particularly vulnerable. An ESL tutor wonders about the psychological impact of a pullout program on a LEP student:

> I am concerned about María Angela's feelings as to why I was asked to work with her. I don't want her to think, "I am an especially poor student, so they've assigned me a special tutor."

Finally, for LEP students the process of acquiring English itself can be an emotion-laden experience. Research by Krashen (1982) and Dulay, Burt, and Krashen (1982) suggests that affective factors play a powerful role in the acquisition of a second language. As Mettler (1983) puts it, in learning a second language the "chances for success seem to be lodged as firmly in the viscera as in the intellect" (p. 1).

The Linguistic Challenge

Language is usually the most salient challenge to LEP students as they establish their role within the classroom. It is the dominant theme in the instructional process and the driving force behind the organization of bilingual and ESL classrooms. In addition to coming to the classroom with a different oral base, LEP students also come with different literacy traditions: different writing systems; different concepts of sound-symbol relations; and different thought patterns, modes of normal discourse, and story patterns. Also, finding the appropriate balance in the development of the first and second languages becomes a challenge: we must learn the extent to which each language dominates the student's face-to-face communication and academic language skills. It is often difficult for teachers, who have mastered the English language, to maintain a realistic perspective on the amount of time it takes a child to become academically fluent in the second language. After students have mastered the basics of informal, conversational English, for example, it is easy for teachers to assume incorrectly that they comprehend the many forms of expression, vocabulary items, and sentence structures encountered in content-area class work. The amount of language information for students to absorb becomes particularly striking past the primary grades, which rely on a simpler language base and many concrete cognitive operations. Two university students' log entries on classroom observations suggest the difficulties which students can face:

> The directions on Jaime's worksheet would be confusing even to a native English speaker, and the vocabulary was quite advanced: architects, aqueducts, soldiers, canals. The worksheet lessons focused on punctuation and sentence structure. They were clearly designed for native English speakers needing remedial work.

> Several idiomatic expressions were really unfamiliar to Ounalom, such as "John Doe" and a "Dear John letter." "John Doe" was surprisingly difficult to explain. It makes you realize what is involved in English content mastery for a LEP student.

> Patricia has not yet decided what her report topic will be. Time lines are a possibility. She expresses some anxiety over this oral presentation. She is better able to communicate with pen and paper than verbally, and she admits to being embarrassed to speak in front of others.

LEP students acquire communicative competence in English from peers, other family members, sports activities, and the media, in addition to the formal classroom. The type of language that is learned, standard versus nonstandard, varies in such contexts. Yet, as teachers we sometimes become frustrated when LEP students use so-called incorrect English despite our efforts to instill in them the standard version of the language. Students, however, learn to speak English not only to get good grades and please their teachers but also to survive socially and fit in with the sociolinguistic structure of their communities and peer subcultures.

Another linguistic issue is the nature of the LEP student's primary language. As in any linguistic community, LEP students are likely to represent a wide range of standard and nonstandard language variations. Such students also may receive primary language signals in the classroom which differ from the language they are familiar with at home. Therefore, in coming to know the student's background, the bilingual or ESL teacher is not just dealing with standard English and, when appropriate, the standard form of the home language. In the context of the classroom, variation in language may be represented in English as well as in the other languages used by students.

Another facet of the language variation found among bilingual and ESL students is the existence of varying levels of proficiency in the first as well as the second language. It is easy to think of students in terms of three simple categories: non-English-speaking, limited-English-proficient, and English-proficient. But another layer must be added to the construction of language categories: there are also students who have, relative to their age, linguistic deficiencies in both the home language and English. Such linguistic deficiencies may be the result of schooling experiences with "subtractive bilingualism" in which the first language is lost as the second language is learned (California State Department of Education, 1981, pp. 217–218). There are many circumstances under which this can occur, and the following is just one example:

> Somsouk, a Laotian student, arrived in the United States at the age of 6. He is now 7½. His school district has neither enough students nor sufficient resources for instruction in his first language, but he is receiving ESL instruction. He is doing well in his class work, but his English is limited. One day, to illustrate some point, his teacher asked him how to say "dog" in Laotian. He stopped, thought hard, and then exclaimed, "I don't remember!" He seemed surprised and puzzled that he could not recall the word.

There are also children in bilingual classrooms who speak only English but who come from a language-minority background that is experiencing language revitalization. Although grandparents, adapting to the demands of the social environment, might have suppressed their ancestral languages, some parents today want to restore such languages and cultures for their children. In areas such as Alaska and Guam, which have strong oral traditions but little written literature, this has prompted the development of curricular materials in native languages. An Iñupiak (Eskimo) college student compares her elementary school language development, which included only English, with that of a younger niece:

> When I go back home from college I'm trying to tell my dad everything that has happened to me at school in our language [Iñupiak], and he'll be really

exhausted because he corrects me and tries to understand what I'm saying, so finally he says, "Why don't you tell your mother instead!" I started learning how to read and write my native language in college, but I have a niece in third grade who first learned how to read and write in Iñupiak. We used to write letters to each other in Iñupiak, and it was funny because we were both learning to write the language, I in college and she in first grade.

Finally, in surveying the linguistic identity of students in bilingual classrooms, it is important not to forget the English-proficient students who are not from language-minority homes. Under present federal guidelines, up to 40 percent of the students in bilingual classrooms may be fluent English speakers. The English-language-background students in bilingual classes may come from homes in which parents value the learning of a second language and the exposure of their children to the multicultural reality of our society. These students may also represent the same socioeconomic class as lower-income LEP students in urban ethnically mixed neighborhoods. In inner-city low-income schools, for example, many bilingual classrooms are composed predominantly of language-minority students and English-language-background black students, with perhaps a few English-language-background white students.

The ethnic and linguistic mix in bilingual classrooms helps to keep them from becoming isolated linguistic and cultural enclaves and makes it possible for many children to be exposed to different languages and cultures. For example, a two-way bilingual classroom, one which provides second-language learning for all children, enriches the academic experience of both language-minority and mainstream students. How the participation of English, monolingual children in bilingual education can be beneficial to the individual and to the nation is colorfully illustrated in the following statement by a fourth grader of Japanese ancestry:

American people should study two languages. When you travel to another country you can make friends easier by speaking their language. When you grow up if you work for the government and the government wants to have a meeting with another country, if you can speak their language you can talk to them and you will know what they are saying. If you grow [up] and become a teacher and a new student is Japanese and you can speak Japanese, if the student doesn't know a word you can talk to them in Japanese and tell what the meaning is. When you go shopping in another country and there's a hamburger shop, if you want to buy two hamburgers you can. If you can't speak another language you don't get any hamburgers. In Japan most people study English and Japanese. In Canada most people speak French and English. In America most people do not speak two languages. It would be a good idea for Americans to learn two languages.

DISCOVERING THE STUDENT

"I think it would have helped me a lot if the teachers just *knew* more about me." Reflecting on her total school experience, a bilingual student accentuates, in the preceding quotation, the importance of having more than an illusion of knowledge about our students and making time in our schedules to obtain objective data about their lives. Knowing more about the student enables the teacher to relate with empathy.

One of the most pervasive characteristics of human behavior is that we rarely ignore each other. As teachers, for instance, we are constantly monitoring the quality and quantity of our students' intellectual and social development. Usually, the intellectual perceptions we acquire are based on objective achievement criteria. The social or cultural profiles we develop of our students, however, more often than not are based on stereotypic or assumed data about their worlds. While it is only natural for us to continue to develop positive, neutral, or negative perceptions of persons based on subjective, impressionistic data, teachers of language-minority students can benefit from a somewhat more systematic and rational approach to the gathering of information. Notwithstanding the rigorous demands of the classroom, it is useful to pause and examine the cultural detail students unintentionally bring to our lives, which has an important impact on the learning process.

Literature and In-Service Training

Out of the necessity to come to a conclusion, some of the information on language-minority students found in the education literature tends to overgeneralize. Thus it is possible for the teacher to acquire reductionist information about a cultural group, which provides him or her with a sense of security but also perpetuates stereotypes. Writers on education, like other social science researchers, are bearers of their own cultural and social blinders and may therefore develop points of view about ethnolinguistic minorities which are colored by their own background. Because teachers want to discover who their students are, they may receive information packets or take part in in-service training programs which provide them with lists of characteristics, language overviews, historical outlines, and sketches about holidays, customs, and foods. While not denying that there may be some congruence between this kind of information and the actual lives of students, teachers are not always sufficiently exposed to the ever-changing and internally heterogeneous characteristics of cultural groups.

As we take time to focus on individual student variables which may affect teaching strategies, it is important to seek out the available information bases, but also to be open to variations and surprises. This is particularly true when working with information about traditional cultural groups which may in some ways project an image that time has stood still. Overemphasis on descriptions of the traditional culture may lead to somewhat static or romanticized views which overlook the subtle or glaring changes that students, as members of contemporary cultural groups, are undergoing (Schafer, 1982, pp. 96–97). A teacher learning about Japanese culture may be interested in kimonos and the tea ceremony, but his or her Japanese students may be more interested in sharing their comic books and robot toys.

Taking a Fresh Look

Almost immediately within the first days of school, teachers are absorbed in time-consuming tasks which take them away from careful attention to who each student is. These can be a combination of demands from the principal, regular paperwork, handling student discipline, following curricular objectives set by the district, supervising standardized testing, and meeting the expectations of fellow teachers. Many teacher duties interfere with the philosophical ideal of positive, caring student-teacher relationships.

Yet we all want very much to show care and concern for the success of all of our students. When everything seems to be going right—students are on task, classroom activities are varied and stimulating, behavior problems are minimal—then a teacher can feel fulfilled. But we rarely feel that we have accomplished that ideal. There are always students who seem hard to reach, who continually demand our attention but rarely settle down to accomplish a task, who would progress much better with one-to-one help that is not available, and who are obviously underchallenged by the tasks the class as a whole needs to master.

Getting away from preconceived notions about language-minority students and making a deliberate effort to take a fresh look is not always easy. Teachers, like anyone, are subject to the limitations associated with their own interpretations of and inferences about the world. Therefore, one way to start is by examining our image of our own role vis-à-vis these students: "Do I see myself as a facilitator of student learning, a cultural and academic agent with the key to success in the mainstream culture, or an exploited cog in the bureaucratic machine of the school district?" The way we see ourselves will affect the way we see our students. One's own ethnic or language background can serve as a starting point. Members of our own families—our grandparents or our great-grandparents—may have had experiences parallel to those of some of our students today. How did our parents and members of our local communities interact with people of other cultural backgrounds when we were growing up? As adults, what positive and negative experiences have we had dealing with persons from cultural or language backgrounds different from our own? Also, what positive and negative experiences have we had in learning a second language ourselves?

Given the increasing presence of language-minority students in schools throughout the country, many teachers—whether trained in ESL and bilingual methods or not—will at some time in their career be wholly or partially responsible for the education of such students. Working with students whose language and cultural heritage are enigmas can be perplexing, but openness to their backgrounds can result in a mutual learning experience and enhanced communication. A bilingual teacher comments on the positive reaction of another teacher to such an experience:

> Following a New Year's celebration shared by Chinese students and their monolingual, English peers, students from Taiwan animatedly chattered in Cantonese in the corridors. One teacher not involved in the bilingual program observed to a bilingual teacher, "I really thought the extra Cantonese I heard in the halls these days would mess up their English, but my Chinese students are doing even better in their class work. They've been so excited recently."

We have examined thus far a wide variety of themes to be considered in exploring the identity of students in bilingual and ESL classrooms, but almost any experienced teacher reading this discussion would question the practicality of expecting instructors to keep carefully prepared written ethnolinguistic profiles on each student. It is not unreasonable, however, for teachers to keep a running file of mental notes. We say "running" because it cannot be assumed that the child will remain static or that our perceptions at a given moment are completely accurate. Therefore, a valid student profile will reflect changing perceptions and changing behavior as the year goes on. Getting reliable information about a student will depend on the use of a variety of sources: cumulative records; registration forms; student compositions; discussions; role-play; informal classroom and playground observation; journal writing; talks with parents; and the local ethnic media, which frequently reveal the nature of the community and thus some of the forces impacting on language-minority students. Silent language (eye contact, facial expression, physical space) and style of verbal communication (softness or loudness of voice, for example, or willingness to take risks) are also useful keys in arriving at a profile of what is happening to the student in the school context.

In sum, beyond the assessment of language-minority students' proficiency in English and the home language, the following topics can be used as an initial guide in getting to know our students.

1. Students' family background

    a. Immigrant or native-born status; length of residency in the United States

    b. Existence of relatives in the home country; frequency of visits

    c. Position within family and responsibilities

    d. Socioeconomic profile and families' aspirations for themselves and their children

    e. Rural versus urban tradition

    f. Nature of students' and families' previous academic experience

    g. Parents' expectations of schools

    h. If immigrants, reasons for emigration

2. Observations of students' behavior in school

    a. Activities which students enjoy, as a reflection of cultural values

    b. Activities which students dislike or avoid, as a reflection of cultural values

    c. Students' nonverbal communication

    d. If immigrants, students' comments on life in the United States

    e. Signs of positive and negative adjustment in peer relationships

    f. Comments which indicate a desire to share something of the home background

3. Knowledge about the students' cultural and linguistic backgrounds: cross-checking and relating what has been learned through reading, classes, and in-service training with the learners' and the families' own experiences.

4. Students' own notions of bilingual or ESL instruction: students' understanding of the purpose of bilingual or ESL instruction as it relates to their own education.

Sylvia Ashton-Warner, a creative and experienced multicultural educator from New Zealand, captured quite forcefully the importance of discovering and linking the life of the student with that of the school:

> The method of teaching any subject in a Maori infant room may be seen as a plank in a bridge from one culture to another, and to the extent that this bridge is strengthened may a Maori in later life succeed. (1963, p. 28)

Education, as a bridge, should enhance communication, understanding, and human potential for language-minority and language-majority students alike. Be open to all the possibilities of your students!

Chapter Two

POLITICS, PROGRAMS
AND RESOURCES

Wall Street Journal (Ricklefs, December 15, 1972)
Bilingual Instruction for Minority Pupils Grows, Stirs Dispute.

Washington Post (MacKenzie, January 22, 1974)
The Supreme Court ruled unanimously yesterday that public school systems are required by federal law to take positive action to help children who do not speak English.

Newsweek (Sheils, McGee, Harper & Boyd, February 7, 1977)
Bilingual education, the wide-ranging network of programs that offer all or part of the public-school curriculum in a language other than English, is now a firm part of U.S. educational policy. From coast to coast, and especially in areas where large minorities do not speak English as a mother tongue, bilingual projects are proliferating at an extraordinary rate.

Washington Post (Epstein, June 5, 1977)
The Bilingual Battle: Should Washington Finance Ethnic Identities?

Washington Star (Porter, August 11, 1978)
Bilinguality Is Job Insurance. . . . Learn a foreign language. With a language skill added to your other skills, you might double your chances of getting the job you want.

Philadelphia Inquirer (Associated Press, August 25, 1978)
Crisis in Quebec Cited as Hayakawa Opposes U.S. Bilingual Program.

Washington Post (Pope, November 7, 1979)
Can a State Learn French? Mais Oui, a Louisianan Believes.

Wall Street Journal (Labor Letter, September 2, 1980)
¿HABLA ESPAÑOL? A shortage of bilingual teachers worsens in many areas.

Washington Star (Muscatine, September 19, 1980)
Hispanic Leaders Cheer as Carter Defends Bilingual Education.

Washington Post (Reid & Epstein, February 3, 1981)
Reagan administration scraps controversial regulations that would have required schools to teach non-English-speaking students in their native languages while they also learn English.

Los Angeles Times (Savage, January 7, 1982)
For the last 2 years, Houston has paid an $800 bonus to teachers in the shortage areas—math, science, bilingual education, and special education. This year, the bonus will jump to $2000.

Richmond Times-Dispatch (Grimsley, May 13, 1983)
Bilingual education in the United States is discriminatory and fosters illiteracy. It ought to be scuttled. So says the Twentieth Century Fund, an independent research organization.

Washington Post (Hoffman & Rich, August 14, 1983)
President Reagan, seeking the political support of Hispanic American voters, today endorsed "effective bilingual programs" for Hispanic schoolchildren. But White House officials said no substantive changes in programs or new funds for bilingual education were planned by the administration. . . . "You could say he has a growing sensitivity on the issue based on the discussions he's had with Hispanics in recent weeks," a White House official said of Reagan's praise for bilingual education.

Given the ups and downs of the politics of bilingual education, as portrayed by the media, it is no wonder that the public feels angry, concerned but confused, misinformed, and resentful. Bilingual and English as a second language (ESL) teachers need to know and understand fears and uncertainties expressed by parents and to have some sense of clarity as to what has happened in federal and state legislation and court decisions. This chapter provides an introductory overview to the major developments which have influenced bilingual and ESL education in the United States over the last several decades.

There are many sources which go into much greater detail on this topic, as there is more written material concerning the politics of bilingual education than there are resources for teachers in the classroom. Therefore, this chapter highlights only major issues that the authors feel teachers should be aware of, with the understanding that more detail is available on these issues in other sources, such as those recommended at the end of this chapter.

Information on the politics of bilingual education is most readily accessible through public documents produced by the federal government. Because laws and court decisions are constantly changing, however, the reader is cautioned to proceed through this introduction with the understanding that the United States will witness continuing changes in federal and state funding and court decisions which influence the way bilingual and language education is implemented over the years to come. Sources for this chapter, in addition to the references listed, include many interviews with federal and Title VII support staff; documents from federal offices; and articles from *Forum* (published by the National Clearinghouse for Bilingual Education), *NABE News,* and the *TESOL Newsletter.*

At the time this is being written, there are some gloomy predictions that, owing to a political trend of less concern for social programs, bilingual education will become just another educational experiment to lose support at the federal level before having a chance to mature. However, many supporters are hopeful that as a nation we have passed our period of less tolerance for cultural pluralism and have recognized the importance of cultural flexibility in educating citizens who are capable of functioning in at least two languages. During the past 16 years of federal and state legislation for bilingual education, the laws and court decisions have focused on improving educational services for students of minority status. Those who have seen the enrichment value of bilingual education hope in the near future to broaden the constituency of bilingual education supporters to include English speakers learning other languages in addition to the goal of providing a meaningful education for children of limited English proficiency (cf. National Advisory Council for Bilingual Education, 1980–81, 1981–82; Pifer, 1979; Tucker, 1983). The following overview highlights some of the major events which have influenced services to students of limited English proficiency in the United States up to the present time.

HISTORICAL BACKGROUND

Contrary to the belief prevalent among adults who grow up in the first half of the twentieth century, the United States has not always been a nation with English as the only language of its schools and with a prevalence of Anglo cultural patterns. During the eighteenth and nineteenth centuries, different groups with varied national and language backgrounds settled across the country. As long as some sense of geographical and psychological openness existed, varied linguistic and cultural groups generally co-existed successfully. Some communities were self-sufficient and agrarian-based; others were ethnic pockets in urban areas (Ovando, 1978c, p. 102).

Historical records show that during the nineteenth century many public and private schools offered courses in languages other than English, not only as foreign-language classes but as content-area instruction as well. In the Midwest in 1900, for example, records show that at least 231,700 children were studying in German in public elementary schools (Tyack, 1974, p. 108). At the turn of the century in New Mexico, either Spanish or English or both could be the language of a school's curriculum (Leibowitz, 1971, pp. 51–52). During the second half of the nineteenth century, bilingual or non-English-language instruction was provided in some form in some public schools as follows: German in Pennsylvania, Maryland, Ohio, Indiana, Illinois, Missouri, Nebraska, Colorado, Oregon; Swedish, Norwegian, and Danish in Wisconsin, Illinois, Minnesota, Iowa, North and South Dakota, Nebraska, Washington; Dutch in Michigan; Polish and Italian in Wisconsin; Czech in Texas; French in Louisiana; and Spanish in the Southwest (Kloss, 1977, pp. 85–161).

Toward the end of the 1800s, however, European nationalism began to exert its influence on the United States, with increasing fears resulting in the call for all immigrants to be assimilated into one cultural and linguistic mold. The new immigrants arriving in largest numbers during that time were coming from southern, eastern, and central Europe. Those northern and western European immigrants already established in the United States clamored for power to control institutions, and one solution to the power struggle focused on schools. Thus schools were charged with the task of "Americanizing" all immigrants, and many state laws were passed calling for English-only instruction. This push for English-dominant cultural and linguistic homogeneity became established as a pattern within schools during the first half of the twentieth century. It was spurred by many factors, such as the standardization and bureaucratization of urban schools (Tyack, 1974), the need for national unity during the two world wars, and the desire to centralize and solidify national gains around unified goals for the country (González, 1975).

After several decades of all-English instruction, the Second World War dramatically demonstrated the lack of foreign-language skills among the populace of the United States. Eventually, as the cold war mentality increased the need for the United States to compete for international status and power, the National Defense Education Act (NDEA) of 1958 provided federal money for the expansion of foreign-language teaching. Although this step represented an improvement in foreign-language policy, it did not resolve the two conflicting philosophies prevalent in U.S. policy which remain to this day. On the one hand, the federal government has recognized the need to develop and support foreign-language instruction for the sake of improved international relations and for national security purposes. On the other hand, a natural resource which new immigrants bring to this country is lost as U.S. schools encourage the loss of native languages of linguistic minorities through insistence on English instruction exclusively. At the present time, even transitional bilingual education programs sponsored by federal and state governments are designed as remedial instruction to be carried out only until students can function exclusively in English.

English as a Second Language

During the 1950s and 1960s, the profession of teaching English as a second language began to expand in response to increasing numbers of immigrant and refugee children entering the United States, as well as the growing numbers of international students coming from countries around the world to attend universities in the United States. The professional organization TESOL (Teachers of English to Speakers of Other Languages) was established in 1966, development of ESL textbooks expanded, and courses in linguistics and ESL methodology were in increasing demand (Paulston, 1976).

With specialized classes in which students received instruction at their level of English proficiency, ESL instruction represented a significant change in school policy. In the early twentieth century the approach had been immediate immersion in all content-area classes taught in English, in which new immigrants had to compete throughout their school day with native English speakers. For linguistic-minority groups, Cohen (1976) calls the sink-or-swim immersion approach "submersion." Some immigrants survived the submersion process, but many others suffered low educational attainment and school achievement. ESL instruction greatly improved the process of the teaching of English, but it did not yet focus attention on the cultural mismatch between home and school nor on the importance of the development and maintenance of the native language for linguistic minorities.

Bilingual Instruction of the 1960s

The Cubans' arrival in Miami following the revolution of 1959 reintroduced bilingual instruction into U.S. schools. The occurrence was a response to very specific local conditions—to meet the educational needs of the Cuban refugees as they poured into Miami. Cubans quickly established private schools taught in Spanish, with the hope that they would eventually return to their island; but as they recognized that the political situation would not be easily changed, they began to influence the public schools to establish bilingual classes. The first bilingual program was thus begun at Coral Way Elementary School in Miami, and its success soon led to the establishment of other bilingual schools in Dade County, Florida, and eventually in other states in the United States. González (1975) suggests that many special factors influenced the Cubans' success in establishing bilingual schools, such as their middle- and upper-middle-class status; the presence of trained Cuban teachers among those who resettled; the aid of the Cuban Refugee Act in providing special training and jobs for the refugees; special sympathy for the refugees, who were seen as victims of their political situation; and a lesser degree of racism practiced against them because of the predominance of European stock among the first groups to arrive.

In 1964 following Florida's example, Texas began to experiment with some bilingual instruction in two school districts. By 1968 bilingual education was being provided in at least fifty-six locally initiated programs in thirteen states. The large majority were Spanish-English programs, but six other languages were represented (Andersson & Boyer, 1970, appendix V).

Federal Legislation: Title VII

The first federal legislation for bilingual education, passed by Congress in 1968 under Title VII of the Elementary and Secondary Education Act, created a small but significant change in policy for linguistic minorities. The civil rights movement and the climate of social change of the 1960s had spurred the passage of legislation, such as the Civil Rights Act of 1964 and the Elementary and Secondary Education Act of 1965, which focused on special needs of minorities. The Bilingual Education Act of 1968 represented the first national acknowledgment of special educational needs of children of limited English proficiency.

Starting from a humble beginning of $7.5 million appropriated for Fiscal Year (FY) 1969,* with seventy-six basic projects funded under Title VII, the Bilingual Education Act was reauthorized in 1974 and 1978, with

*A current federal fiscal year (e.g., FY 1984) refers to the period from October 1, 1983, to September 30, 1984.

appropriations increased each year until FY 1980, when $166.9 million was spent and 564 basic projects were funded. The lower appropriations figures for FY 1981 ($161.4 million) and FY 1982 ($138 million) reflect cuts in spending in all areas of education, as requested by the Reagan administration. Funding has remained at the same level for FY 1983 ($138 million) and FY 1984 ($139.4 million). The Bilingual Education Act was scheduled to be reauthorized in FY 1983, but has been extended through FY 1984 under the Omnibus Budget Reconciliation Act. New legislation will be proposed in 1984 (Lyons, 1983).

The 1968 law specified that services were to be provided to "children who come from environments where the dominant language is other than English" and from families with incomes below $3000 per year. The 1974 amendments changed the law to include all children of "limited-English-speaking ability" (LES), ending the low-income requirement, and the 1978 law expanded the definition additionally to include children of limited English proficiency (LEP). The last change allows students to remain in a program until they reach full proficiency in English rather than requiring that they be tested and exited solely on the basis of oral skills (Leibowitz, 1980, p. 17).

The three purposes of the 1968 act were to "(1) increase English-language skills, (2) maintain and perhaps increase mother-tongue skills, and (3) support the cultural heritage of the student" (Leibowitz, 1980, p. 24). The reauthorizations in 1974 and 1978 placed increasing emphasis on the importance of mastery of English-language skills as the main purpose of the bill. The 1978 bill also allows participation of English-speaking children in bilingual programs funded by Title VII, as long as the number does not exceed 40 percent. This was an important step toward recognition of the value of two-way, integrated programs. The inclusion of English speakers was a small beginning toward addressing the conflict in federal language policy; it provided funding for both English-language instruction for linguistic minorities and foreign-language education for majority students. The main intent of the legislation, however, was to solve the problem of segregation of students of limited English proficiency.

Provisions were made in the 1968 Bilingual Education Act and expanded in 1974 and 1978 for training of bilingual personnel through grants, contracts, and fellowships to local educational agencies (LEAs), state educational agencies (SEAs), and institutions of higher education (IHEs). In addition, beginning in 1975 the federal Office of Bilingual Education began to fund a network of institutions designed to provide resources and services to state and local school districts. In recent years, these support services have consisted of three Evaluation, Dissemination, and Assessment Centers (EDACs); between fourteen and nineteen Materials Development Centers (MDCs); and fifteen to twenty Bilingual Education Service Centers (BESCs). For FY 1984, sixteen new Bilingual Education Multifunctional Support Centers (BEMSCs) have been established. These were intended to replace the EDACs, MDCs, and BESCs, but Congressional support has allowed some of the EDACs and MDCs to continue to function. In addition, the National Clearinghouse for Bilingual Education (NCBE) was begun in 1977 to analyze, synthesize, and disseminate information on bilingual education and related subjects. NCBE is now authorized through FY 1985.

Funds for research were not included until 10 years after the Bilingual Education Act was first passed. Designated as Part C of the 1978 amendments to the Bilingual Education Act of 1978, the research studies were charged with the task of providing answers to Congressional questions for reauthorization in FY 1983. Research results from these studies are now beginning to be made available. In addition to the Part C research, the National Center for Bilingual Research was established in 1979 as a part of the total research effort.

During 1983, as in other years, Congressional committee hearings were conducted on proposed amendments to the Bilingual Education Act. No proposed changes were acted on, but it is expected that a significantly different piece of legislation will be proposed in 1984, the next year of reauthorization. The Reagan administration has been in favor of reducing federal appropriations for bilingual education while at the same time allowing school districts to apply for Title VII funds for any type of instructional program for limited-English-proficient students. If Title VII program types are to be expanded to include ESL-only programs, then federal funds for Title VII must also be increased significantly to serve all those who qualify for the funds. There will probably be considerable discussion of this and other issues, such as inclusion of English speakers in two-way bilingual programs for developing better foreign-language skills, and whether to continue a discretionary program for those who apply for Title VII funds or to move to a formula grant program, in which funds are distributed to states based on their LEP population.

While the Reagan administration originally opposed bilingual education, Congressional support for bilingual education has helped to moderate the administration's position. The reauthorization process will probably receive considerable political attention, even though the Bilingual Education Act receives an extremely small portion (roughly 1 percent) of the total federal funds spent on education. This is a reflection of the continuing state of political uncertainty regarding national language policy.

Related Federal Legislation

During the Reagan years, there have been many changes in the federal education legislation. It is predicted that there will continue to be many more changes in the near future, depending on the 1984 election results. Therefore, this review will only briefly mention several other bills besides the Title VII legislation that presently provide funding for ESL and bilingual programs. The reader is again cautioned that this information is constantly changing.

As of January 1984, programs funded by the Elementary and Secondary Education Act (ESEA) of 1965 have been reorganized into two divisions. Chapter I programs of the Education Consolidation and Improvement Act (to replace ESEA) are former Title I ESEA programs. Since this money is for disadvantaged students, there are many ESL programs funded through Chapter I. In 1981–82, an estimated 24 percent of all limited-English-proficient students received support from Chapter I services, while 7 percent of all limited-English-proficient students received support from Title VII (Evans, 1984). Also under Chapter I, migrant education money is distributed directly to the states. Approximately 70 percent of the students served in migrant education programs are limited-English-proficient students. Chapter II has incorporated almost all other former ESEA programs into block grants, in which the money is distributed by the states. Under Chapter II are laws such as the Ethnic Heritage Act, which funded projects to encourage the preservation of ethnic groups' history and culture, and the Emergency School Aid Act, which has in the past funded some bilingual programs that tackled the issue of desegregation. The only two ESEA programs which were exempted from block granting and which operate separately from Chapters I and II are bilingual education (Title VII) and special education (Public Law 94-142). Under P.L. 94-142, there is funding for programs for students of limited English proficiency with special needs, such as those who are specific learning disabled, seriously emotionally disturbed, mentally retarded, physically or otherwise health impaired, visually impaired, hearing impaired, severely or profoundly handicapped, or gifted and talented.

Other important pieces of legislation include the Refugee Act of 1980 and the Refugee Assistance Amendments of 1982, which are administered by the federal Office of Bilingual Education and Minority Languages Affairs (OBEMLA). This legislation provides funds for educational programs and other services for refugees, and local education agencies must apply for grants based on the number of eligible refugees enrolled in their school district (National Clearinghouse for Bilingual Education, 1982b). A recently passed immigration act is also expected to provide funding for ESL instruction.

The Vocational Education Act provides funds for special training programs for students of limited English proficiency, including bilingual vocational training. This funding is administered by OBEMLA. Federally supported adult education programs also serve adults with limited English proficiency, who represented 26.5 percent of the total adult education attendance in 1981 (Evans, 1984).

There are federal services provided specially for Native Americans, such as Title IV of the Education Amendments of 1972, the Indian Education Act. This legislation and other services are described in a publication produced by the National Clearinghouse for Bilingual Education, *Guide to U.S. Government Departments and Agencies, States, and Private Foundations that Provide Information and Assistance to American Indians* (1982a). One of the sixteen new Bilingual Education Multifunctional Support Centers funded by Title VII is the National Indian Bilingual Center at Tempe, Arizona. This center is responsible for providing training and technical assistance to all Title VII Native American projects in a thirteen-state area, in cooperation with the other BEMSCs assigned to the same service areas.

Title IV of the Civil Rights Act provides training and technical assistance to school personnel for problems in school desegregation with regard to sex, race, color, religion, and national origin. The National Origin Desegregation Assistance Centers (more commonly called Lau Centers), funded by Title IV, cannot provide direct services to students, but they do provide considerable assistance to school district personnel serving limited-English-proficient students.

There are still other pieces of federal legislation which provide funding for foreign-language instruction, international education, and training in multicultural sensitivity for English speakers, such as the National Defense Education Act (NDEA) of 1958, Title V of the Higher Education Act, which has funded the Teacher Corps, and the National Security and Economic Growth through Foreign-Language Improvement Act of 1983 (Osman, 1983). The Joint National Committee for Languages (JNCL), located in Washington, D.C., is the national organization which oversees all language legislation.

Most of the federal funding described is available to local educational agencies by application, following guidelines available from the federal offices. Some of the federal funding is distributed by state education agencies. For additional information, teachers should first contact the administrators in their local school districts and discuss the possibility of applying for funds.

State Legislation

In addition to federal support for bilingual and ESL education, a number of states have adopted statutory provisions to assist local school districts in the implementation of bilingual and ESL programs. Over the last decade there has been a marked increase in state support for bilingual education. For example, in 1971 thirty states permitted or required some form of bilingual instruction, while twenty states prohibited such instruction (National Advisory Council for Bilingual Education, 1978–79, p. 99). In 1983 bilingual education was permitted in all fifty states, even at times in those seven states in which statutes or constitutional provisions limit the language of instruction to English: Alabama, Arkansas, Delaware, Nebraska, North Carolina, Oklahoma, and West Virginia. Twenty-one states have passed legislation explicitly permitting bilingual instruction: Arizona, Colorado, Florida, Idaho, Illinois, Indiana, Iowa, Kansas, Louisiana, Maine, Maryland, Minnesota, New Hampshire, New Mexico, New York, Ohio, Oregon, Pennsylvania, Rhode Island, South Dakota, and Utah. In addition, nine states *mandate* some form of bilingual instruction for students of limited English proficiency: Alaska, California, Connecticut, Massachusetts, Michigan, New Jersey, Texas, Washington, and Wisconsin (Gray, 1983; Gray, Convery & Fox, 1981; Predaris, 1982).

All of the thirty states permitting or mandating bilingual education encourage some form of special instruction for all students of limited English proficiency, with options including ESL-only instruction, transitional bilingual classes, language maintenance, and two-way bilingual instruction. (For a detailed discussion of the differences between these programs, see the section Program Models in this chapter.) Some states mandate ESL instruction if bilingual instruction cannot practically be provided. Recent changes in Colorado and Rhode Island state legislation permit local program options, including ESL-only instruction. All state legislation requires the inclusion of ESL instruction in all bilingual programs.

Ten states explicitly permit the inclusion of monolingual English speakers in two-way bilingual classes: California, Illinois, Indiana, Iowa, Massachusetts, New Jersey, New Mexico, Texas, Utah, and Wisconsin. Other state laws prohibit the segregation of LEP students. Most of the state laws permitting bilingual education stipulate transitional bilingual programs, but five states have provisions for language maintenance programs as well: Alaska, California, Louisiana, New Mexico, and Utah (Gray, 1983; Gray, Convery & Fox, 1981; Predaris, 1982).

While either federal or local support is provided for many bilingual and ESL programs, states also provide funds for many bilingual and ESL

TABLE 2-1   State-Funded Bilingual Education Programs (FY 1981)

State	State funds	Number of programs	Number of students
Alabama	$ 210,000	3	165
Alaska	7,678,134	29	8,618
Arizona	3,500,000	36	*
California	*	*	*
Colorado	*	*	*
Connecticut	1,620,000	14	9,600
Hawaii	3,326,005	*	6,652
Illinois	16,900,000	75	37,028
Iowa	*	*	*
Kansas	480,000	36	3,200
Massachusetts	18,839,824	50	14,950
Michigan	3,150,000	67	18,700
Minnesota	3,270,000	117	7,800
New Jersey	10,967,239	176	35,000
New Mexico	2,800,000	43	32,000
New York	4,400,000	174	97,000
Rhode Island	205,999	9	*
Texas	8,637,500	201	198,872
Utah	*	*	*
Washington	2,100,000	130	10,000
Wisconsin	1,900,300	14	3,729

*Figures not available.
SOURCE: Predaris, 1982.

programs. For example, in FY 1981, the bilingual programs shown in Table 2-1 were state-funded.

State Certification

Another indication of considerable state support for both bilingual education and ESL instruction is the increasing number of states with bilingual and/or ESL teacher certification standards. As of March 1982, twenty-eight states had developed certification standards for bilingual teachers and twenty-six for ESL teachers, and the District of Columbia had developed both. Table 2-2 gives a state-by-state breakdown.

TABLE 2-2   Bilingual and ESL Teacher Certification Standards

State	Bilingual certification	ESL certification
Alaska	x	x
Arizona	x	
California	x	x
Colorado	x	
Connecticut	x	
Delaware	x	x
Florida	x	x
Hawaii		x
Idaho	x	x
Illinois	x	
Indiana	x	
Iowa	x	x
Kansas	x	x
Kentucky		x
Louisiana	x	x
Massachusetts	x	x
Michigan	x	
Minnesota	x	
Nebraska		x
Nevada		x
New Hampshire	x	x
New Jersey	x	x
New Mexico	x	x
New York	x	x
North Carolina		x
Ohio	x	x
Pennsylvania	x	
Rhode Island	x	x
Tennessee		x
Texas	x	x
Utah	x	x
Vermont	x	x
Virginia		x
Washington	x	
Wisconsin	x	x
D.C.	x	x

SOURCES: Blatchford, 1982; Predaris, 1982.

Blatchford (1982) lists bilingual and ESL certification requirements for each state and the universities which provide training in bilingual education and ESL as of March 1982.

Court Decisions

An increasing array of court decisions has had serious influence on the implementation of bilingual education, especially in the decade of the 1970s. The landmark U.S. Supreme Court decision, *Lau v. Nichols* (January 1974), has had by far the most significant impact. From 1900 to 1944, the few court decisions which issued rulings related to language policy were mainly concerned with preserving and promoting English as one of the key elements in the formation of U.S. national identity (Teitelbaum & Hiller, 1977b, p. 2). Three decades later, *Lau v. Nichols* did not deny the importance of learning English, but the Supreme Court justices ruled unanimously, on the grounds of the Civil Rights Act of 1964, that 1800 Chinese students in San Francisco were not being provided an equal educational opportunity compared with their English-speaking peers:

> There is no equality of treatment merely by providing students with the same facilities, textbooks, teachers, and curriculum; for students who do not understand English are effectively foreclosed from any meaningful education.
>
> Basic English skills are at the very core of what these public schools teach. Imposition of a requirement that, before a child can effectively participate in the education program, he must already have acquired those basic skills is to make a mockery of public education. We know that those who do not understand English are certain to find their classroom experiences wholly incomprehensible and in no way meaningful. (*Lau v. Nichols,* 1974)

The Supreme Court did not require one specific remedy to provide a more meaningful education for students of limited English proficiency; however, *Lau v. Nichols* had a direct and immediate impact on the growth of the bilingual education movement:

> Although it did not expressly endorse bilingual education, the Lau decision legitimized and gave impetus to the movement for equal educational opportunity for students who do not speak English. Lau raised the nation's consciousness of the need for bilingual education, encouraged additional federal legislation, energized federal enforcement efforts, led to federal funding of nine regional "general assistance Lau centers," aided the passage of state laws mandating bilingual education, and spawned more lawsuits. (Teitelbaum & Hiller, 1977a, p. 139)

In August 1974, Congress passed the Equal Educational Opportunities Act, which gave legislative backing to the Lau decision and extended its scope to apply to all public school districts, not just those receiving federal financial assistance. Additional pressure on school districts to implement some kind of meaningful instruction for students of limited English proficiency came from the Office for Civil Rights (OCR), which jointly with the Office of Education issued the 1975 *Lau Remedies*. An important precedent to the *Lau Remedies* was an OCR memorandum of May 25, 1970, which stated OCR's concern about discrimination in schools based on national origin. Like the Supreme Court decision and the 1970 memorandum, the *Lau Remedies* did not specifically mandate bilingual education, but they encouraged school districts to implement bilingual education whenever feasible, especially at elementary and intermediate levels, in schools which have at least twenty students of the same (non-English) language group. The *Lau Remedies* were designed to be quite flexible, but they represented a new level of federal requirements when none had existed previously. School districts were now required to demonstrate that they had some kind of effective educational program for students of limited English proficiency. If a school district was found to be out of compliance, it could be threatened with loss of federal funds (Teitelbaum & Hiller, 1977a).

In August 1980, a new set of Lau regulations was proposed. Written in substantial detail, these regulations specified identification and assessment procedures and proposed alternative methods of instruction for LEP students, such as transitional, maintenance, or two-way models of bilingual education; compensatory education (combining LEP students with underachieving English speakers); or ESL-only instruction. During the period of public hearings, there was so much negative reaction to the proposed Lau regulations that the secretary of education withdrew the proposed regulations. Therefore, the 1975 *Lau Remedies* remain in effect. They have not been enforced by OCR during the Reagan administration, but merely serve as a guideline for school systems. Nine Lau Centers (officially titled National Origin Desegregation Assistance Centers) are operated by OCR to provide advice and assistance to school districts in the planning and implementation of educational programs for LEP students. For a more detailed description of the May 25, 1970, OCR memorandum and the *Lau Remedies*, see Chapter 7.

Since *Lau v. Nichols,* several other court decisions have affected the implementation of programs of bilingual education in specific school districts. Even before Lau, the judicial trend of mandating some form of bilingual instruction had begun with cases such as *United States v. Texas* (San Felipe del Río School District, 1971), *Arvizu v. Waco Independent*

School District (Texas, 1973), and *United States v. Texas* (Austin, 1973). Soon after Lau, in *Serna v. Portales* (1974), the school officials of Portales, New Mexico, were ordered by the Tenth Circuit Court of Appeals to implement bilingual instruction for 30 to 60 minutes per day for all students at the elementary level. *Aspira of New York v. Board of Education of the City of New York* (1974) was a decision with far-reaching implications for bilingual education. The consent decree mandated a system of identification of Hispanic students in need of special instruction, described necessary teacher qualifications, and set standards for instruction in English and Spanish. Bilingual instruction was required as part of the overall desegregation plan in the three desegregation cases of *Morgan v. Kerrigan* (Boston, 1975); *Bradley v. Milliken* (Detroit, 1975); and *Evans v. Buchanan* (Wilmington, Delaware, 1976) (Teitelbaum & Hiller, 1978, p. 43).

In *Cintrón v. Brentwood Union Free School District* (1977), the court ordered this New York school district to keep recently hired bilingual teachers who were being dismissed because of declining enrollment in the district. Two plans submitted by the school district were rejected by the court as violating desegregation guidelines and the *Lau Remedies*. The school district was ordered to submit to the court a new plan for bilingual instruction in compliance with the *Lau Remedies*.

In *Ríos v. Read* (1977), a district court ruled that the school district of Patchogue-Medford, New York, was obligated under Lau to provide a *quality* program for students of limited English proficiency. The court rejected the school district's practice of providing mostly ESL instruction with 40 to 50 minutes of subject matter instruction in Spanish for kindergarten and first grade only. The school district was ordered to identify language-minority students, validly assess their abilities, and provide English language acquisition and bilingual instruction by competent bilingual personnel.

In *Castañeda v. Pickard* (1981), the school district in Raymondville, Texas, was charged with inappropriate ability-grouping practices, discrimination against Hispanics in employment as teachers and administrators, and inadequate bilingual instruction. The court did not find the school district guilty of segregation or discrimination, but it applied a three-part test to judge the adequacy of the school program. First, the educational theories of the school system were examined; second, actual practice was compared to the theoretical base; and third, after an appropriate trial period, the effectiveness of the program was examined. The court found the school district's plan conceptually sound but ordered improvement of the Spanish-language ability of teachers and more appropriate assessment of students' achievement in both Spanish and English.

In another well-publicized case, *U.S. v. the State of Texas,* in January 1981 a federal district judge ordered bilingual instruction in grades K through 12 for all Mexican-American students in Texas with limited English proficiency. At the time, Texas had state-mandated bilingual education for grades K through 3 only. The ruling was based on the equal protection clause of the Fourteenth Amendment and on the Equal Educational Opportunities Act. However, this decision was later overturned by the Fifth U.S. Circuit Court of Appeals on July 13, 1982 (Leibowitz, 1982).

In summary, in the United States over the last two decades, dramatic changes have taken place at federal, state, and local levels with regard to provision of educational services for students of limited English proficiency. School systems across the country are now required by law to identify all LEP students by language and national origin, and to state the kinds of services they are providing for these students. Many schools are at least providing classes in English as a second language, rather than relying on sink-or-swim submersion for linguistic minorities. Increasingly large numbers of bilingual programs are being implemented across the country in a wide variety of languages and program designs, and are supported by federal, state, or local funds.

PROGRAM MODELS

The literature on bilingual education is extremely confusing when it comes to naming and defining the multiple variations in bilingual program designs which have been implemented across the United States over the last 20 years. Researchers, politicians, journalists, and school administrators have used a wide variety of sometimes conflicting terms to refer to program differentiation, with little sense of continuity or clarity. This synthesis is written in the hope of clarifying the terms frequently found in writings on bilingual education.

The terms and descriptions which follow have been chosen as those most widely accepted by authors and researchers. This discussion also is limited to those terms which best represent major differences in overall program design. There are many ways to implement bilingual education, and each major model carries with it very different social and political implications which may affect students' performance in school. Thus, identification of the needs of each community is a necessary prerequisite to choosing a model appropriate for that community.

Transitional Bilingual Education

In transitional classes, students of limited English proficiency receive instruction in their native language in all subject areas as well as instruction in English as a second language, but only for a limited period of time. Native-language instruction is provided to avoid loss of grade-level skills while mastery of second language is taking place. As soon as students are considered proficient enough in English to work academically in all-English classes, they are moved from the bilingual program into monolingual classes with English-speaking students. Most transitional programs exit students into all-English classes after a maximum of 2 years in bilingual classes. In such a short-term program there is less opportunity to mix English-speaking students with LEP students in academic tasks; thus it is generally a segregated model. The highest priority of a transitional bilingual program is the teaching of English, with the goal of mainstreaming LEP students as soon as possible.

There are many problems with the transitional model. One criticism frequently mentioned by both researchers and teachers involves the social status of its members within schools because it is viewed as a remedial program. Transitional classes tend to be perceived by regular staff and students as a lower track for slow students. It is sometimes thought of as another form of segregated, compensatory education, which has had limited success in raising students' achievement scores. Some researchers and vocal minority groups criticize transitional bilingual instruction as another means of perpetuating the status quo of the society; it keeps language-minority students in separate groups which are often perceived as having low ability, thus maintaining their lower-class status (Hernández-Chávez, 1977; Kjolseth, 1972).

Another major problem with the transitional model is the common misconception that 2 years is sufficient time to learn a second language. All research findings in studies that have been methodologically well done show that the longer students remain in a quality bilingual program, the more successful they are in school achievement in both first and second languages. According to studies done in the United States, students in a bilingual class may, during their first 2 years, score below a comparable group of students schooled monolingually in English when both groups are tested in English. Generally, the bilingually schooled children begin to catch up and outperform their monolingually schooled peers in the third or fourth year and continue to perform as well as and frequently better than the comparison group (cf. Legarreta, 1979; Troike, 1978).

Cummins (1980, 1981a) explains this phenomenon with reference to his distinction between basic interpersonal communicative skills (BICS) and cognitive-academic language proficiency (CALP). BICS are generally acquired to a level of relative fluency within about 2 years of arrival in the host country, whereas academic aspects of second-language proficiency —CALP—may not develop to a level of full proficiency until as many as 5 to 7 years of schooling have elapsed (Cummins, 1980, p. 53). Proficiency in CALP is believed to transfer from first to second language when it is fully developed in first language; thus it is wise, whenever feasible, to provide language-minority students with a good solid school base in their first language. For these reasons, the research thus far has found that the short-term transitional model encompasses an insufficient length of time to aid language-minority students in successful school achievement.

The one clearly useful function of transitional bilingual education is found in transitional classes for fourth- through twelfth-grade recently arrived immigrants. Older immigrants who have had a good educational background have well-developed cognitive-academic skills in their first language, which automatically transfer to their second language when BICS proficiency in the second language is achieved. Thus classes in content areas (e.g., math, science, social studies) taught in the first language help a student master course content without losing time while second-language proficiency is developing. Transitional classes can keep students at grade level while learning a second language and can aid those below grade level to catch up with their peers through intensive instruction in a language the student fully understands.

Maintenance Bilingual Education

In the maintenance model, there is less emphasis on exiting students from the program as soon as possible. Students in bilingual classes receive content-area instruction in both languages equally throughout their school career, or for as many grades as the school system can provide the service. The large majority of bilingual school programs across the United States are designed for elementary grades only. Thus kindergarten through sixth-grade bilingual instruction is generally recognized as "maintenance" in the United States, even when there is only English instruction available at the secondary level. Ideal maintenance bilingual education would include classes taught in both languages in a multicultural curriculum from kindergarten through twelfth grade, with continuing dual language offerings at the university level.

The maintenance model has prompted a controversy over how federal money should be spent, with some concern raised that native-language maintenance is not the task of the federal government (Epstein, 1977b). However, maintenance bilingual education has become an issue of great political and economic significance for local communities that wish to maintain their ethnic heritage and has created new pride and dramatic improvement in achievement in some bilingual Native American schools in the Southwest (Rosier & Farella, 1976; Rosier & Holm, 1980). In addition to new political awareness and increased community control of the school, this model creates a new source of income for bilingual teachers and aides hired by the school and thus is an economic incentive to upward mobility for the community. At the same time, it presents a threat to present personnel in the school system (Read, Spolsky & Neundorf, 1976).

Maintenance does not necessarily imply, however, that the school system can fully maintain a minority language for a community, since bilingual instruction in U.S. models frequently is not continued at the secondary level. The most important concern in U.S. maintenance bilingual programs is that students receive a solid academic curriculum with support for reaching full English-language proficiency without negating their first language in the process. The advantages of the cumulative effect of more than 2 years in a bilingual program are obvious when the growing body of research studies on bilingual education is examined seriously. The studies show that benefits expected in school evaluations, such as higher achievement scores and higher IQ test scores, are not apparent until the fourth, fifth, or sixth year of bilingual instruction (Cummins, 1980). Another advantage of maintenance bilingual education is that the program can last long enough for English speakers to be included in two-way bilingual classes; as explained in the next section, this involves an integrated setting in which both groups work together academically in both languages.

Two-Way Enrichment Bilingual Education

The distinction between one-way and two-way bilingual instruction was first made by Stern (1963). In one-way bilingual education one language group is schooled bilingually. Two-way bilingual education refers to an integrated model in which speakers of both languages are placed together in a bilingual classroom to learn each others' language and work academically in both languages.

"Enrichment bilingual education" is a term used by Fishman (1976, p. 35) to refer to bilingual instruction for all members of society, rather than for minorities alone. Two-way enrichment bilingual education can be seen as an effective means of teaching a second language to English-dominant students in the United States as well as providing an integrated class for language-minority students. It is the only model which places both groups at the same starting point and thus sensitizes English speakers to the complex process of learning a second language and becoming more aware of other systems of thought. Parents of English-speaking children in bilingual classes frequently become advocates of bilingualism when they see the unique intellectual, social, and commercial advantages it provides their children. Furthermore, young children's natural acquisition of the language through content-area instruction, rather than focusing on the language itself (as in foreign-language classes), provides a context in which children can develop and retain complete fluency in the second language.

Two-way bilingual instruction is difficult to implement in the first year of a program because it involves multiple grouping of students, depending on the tasks to be carried out and the relative level of proficiency required for each of those tasks in each language. The most efficient method of instruction is to team one native English-speaking teacher with a teacher who is a native speaker of the other language, both of whom have at least some knowledge of the second language. The two teachers can organize activities which separate students into groups according to the tasks to be carried out. As the students become increasingly proficient in their second language during the first and second years, they are increasingly mixed together until they are able to work together on all tasks in either language. The two-way enrichment model probably has the most potential for proficient second-language acquisition for both language groups, in addition to satisfying integration requirements. Many program evaluations in recent years have included English-speaking students, and both language groups in the bilingual programs were scoring at or above the levels of comparison groups schooled monolingually (Troike, 1978).

Predictions are that the 1984 reauthorization of the Bilingual Education Act will be more successful if it can address this issue of foreign-language instruction for English-speaking students. The greatest difficulty in using bilingual programs to provide second-language instruction for English speakers is to convince parents of the value to their children of learning the particular minority language(s) spoken in their community. Former Secretary Hufstedler of the Department of Education strongly encouraged the implementation of more two-way bilingual programs, because of the significant difference that they seem to make in English-speaking students' attitudes toward language-minority students, which in turn leads to increased positive self-concept and better achievement of language-minority students (Biascoechea, 1980).

Eliminating the Transitional-Maintenance Dichotomy

The transitional, maintenance, and two-way enrichment models represent general patterns of bilingual programs practiced in the United States up to the present time. A lot of the political battles have focused on creating a dichotomy between transitional and maintenance programs. The distinction between the two might more appropriately be eliminated, with the focus placed on *quality* of program rather than quantity of time spent in a program. The most important point that teachers need to get across to parents and school personnel is that the total amount of exposure to English within the school is less important than providing students with a solid cognitive-academic base (González, 1979b, 1980).

Immigrant parents are sometimes afraid that their children will not learn English when provided with both ESL and native-language instruction. However, most students very quickly receive the message sent loudly and clearly that English is necessary for survival in this country.* Students succeed in English, even with less exposure to English in school, if they are given the chance to feel good about themselves as human beings and to develop their cognitive-academic skills in both first and second languages. It is unnecessary to establish an arbitrary time limit by which all students should exit from a bilingual program. It is more appropriate to provide bilingual instruction and promote additive bilingualism for as long as it is practically feasible for the school system. Two-way enrichment is the most attractive option for mixed-population schools, as it integrates a mixture of students into one classroom and addresses the issue of teaching foreign languages to English-speaking students.

> We are a bunch of monolinguistic bumpkins and American education is to blame. (U.S. Secretary of Education, Terrel Bell, *Forum,* October 1981)

> Americans' incompetence in foreign languages is nothing short of scandalous, and it is becoming worse. (President's Commission on Foreign Language and International Studies, 1979)

Immersion Bilingual Education

Less practiced in the United States but used extensively in Canada is immersion bilingual education, mainly designed for speakers of the dominant language. A general description of early immersion is that students

*Two exceptions may be (1) isolated linguistic-minority communities which have their own socioeconomic autonomy and therefore are less motivated to participate in the broader society, and (2) Puerto Rico, where Spanish is the dominant language, but proficiency in both Spanish and English provides access to the better jobs.

are taught in a second language from the first year of school, with first-language instruction introduced possibly as late as second or third grade. First-language instruction may be increased in the upper grades or it may be limited to 1 or 2 hours per day. There are other variations, such as partial or late immersion, which vary the time of introduction of first language (L_1) or second language (L_2) and the amount of L_1 instruction. This model has been used successfully and tested extensively in Canada, in areas in which speakers of the dominant language (English) receive their schooling largely in French (Cummins, 1979b; Swain, 1978; Swain & Lapkin, 1981). Immersion bilingual education has been successfully used with English-speaking children in several U.S. schools, such as in the Culver City, California, Spanish-immersion program (California State Department of Education, 1984; Cohen, 1976; Plann, 1977).

Immersion bilingual education works very well for speakers of the dominant language, but it is not to be confused with submersion (Cohen, 1976, p. 73) of language-minority children, a common practice in schools in the first half of this century. Submersion provides no native-language support or structured ESL instruction and may unconsciously place minority students in a position subordinate to monolingual English-speaking students and teachers; it may lead to low achievement and high dropout rates, especially among minorities who sometimes perceive their status as low relative to the majority, such as Native Americans, Mexican-Americans, Puerto Ricans, and blacks in the United States. While "submersion" is a widely accepted term among linguists, most U.S. school personnel, including ESL administrators, still use "immersion" to refer to schooling exclusively in English (including ESL). The program type commonly termed "immersion" in the United States is very different from an immersion bilingual program.

A good discussion of the differences between Canadian immersion bilingual education and U.S. bilingual programs is available in two *Focus* papers from the National Clearinghouse for Bilingual Education (Lambert, 1980; Tucker, 1980). Immersion bilingual education as implemented in Canadian programs has not yet been tried extensively in the United States. The California State Department of Education is encouraging more experimentation with immersion bilingual education through a new publication, *Studies on Immersion Education: A Collection for U.S. Educators* (1984). After presentation of papers by Genesee, Lapkin, Cummins, and Swain on the Canadian experience, the publication explains the possible use of immersion for English-speaking students in the United States and the reasons it does not work for language-minority students. Campbell, Hernández-Chávez, and Lambert describe possible applications of immersion in the United States.

"Structured Immersion"

Beginning in 1983–84, some federal bureaucrats began referring to and stimulating publicity for a program model called "structured immersion." This model provides language-minority students with instruction totally in an ESL format, with native-language tutoring support as needed during the first year or two. Teachers in such a program are bilingual and accept students' responses in first language but respond only in English. The materials used are highly structured to introduce students step-by-step to the second language. Politically, this model is popular with the Reagan administration and is being promoted as something new. The reality is that this model is very similar to many transitional bilingual and ESL-only programs that have been implemented throughout the United States. It is not at all new but has just been given a new label.

English as a Second Language

ESL is an integral component of transitional, maintenance, and two-way bilingual education; however, it is not by itself a form of bilingual instruction. ESL instruction in a bilingual classroom includes English taught from a second-language point of view in language arts classes and content-area instruction in English, provided at the students' level of English proficiency. In a team-teaching situation, the English-speaking teacher should be knowledgeable in the latest findings of applied linguistics and ESL methodology.

A variety of ESL-only programs have been developed in public schools to meet the needs of international students who have no common language. When there are just a few LEP students in each school of a district, itinerant ESL teachers may have to travel to several schools in 1 day to meet the needs of students. ESL pullout programs, in which students receive from 1 hour to a half day of instruction in segregated ESL centers or classes, may involve the same stigma as transitional bilingual programs—being perceived as compensatory, remedial classes for students with "problems." Bilingual and ESL staff can help to lessen this image somewhat through encouraging active participation in all aspects of school life with monolingual students and staff.

Some school systems have developed all-day or half-day intensive ESL classes which introduce content-area subjects to LEP students at their level of proficiency in English. These special ESL classes may be called High-Intensity Language Training (HILT), ESL clusters, or alternative ESL programs. Content-area ESL instruction is a very effective method of teaching English, through less focus on language itself and more emphasis on hands-on, motivating tasks in math, science, and social studies, which encourages natural acquisition. As LEP students increase their mastery of English, they are gradually moved into academic classes with native speakers of English.

Other Programs for Teaching Second Languages

English as a Foreign Language   EFL instruction is similar to ESL instruction. The main distinction between the two is in how much English the students are exposed to outside of their English class. EFL is taught in countries in which English is not generally spoken, or in educational situations in which instruction in other subjects is not normally given in English. In EFL classes, the teacher is the main and sometimes only English-language model. In contrast, in an ESL context students generally acquire large portions of their second language outside an ESL classroom, thus accelerating the process of second-language acquisition.

Foreign Languages in the Elementary School   FLES was introduced extensively in U.S. elementary schools in the 1960s as a means of exposing younger English-speaking children to foreign languages. Typically, FLES has been an add-on program, considered a nice but unimportant extra in the school curriculum, with lessons of 15 to 30 minutes 2 to 3 times per week. There is little evidence that FLES has had any success in bringing about a significant amount of foreign-language acquisition among English-speaking children; in contrast, dramatic acquisition of a second language has been achieved with English speakers in two-way and immersion bilingual classes (Cohen, 1976; Gray, 1984).

In summary, the program models outlined here represent some of the major types used in the United States for teaching second languages. Part of the confusion in the literature comes from attempts to enter many variables into an overall typology (e.g., Mackey, 1970; Valencia, 1976). While these typologies present the complexity of the multiple variables which must be taken into consideration in establishing a bilingual program, they do not leave the practitioner with a clear understanding of the major differences among options actually used in U.S. bilingual programs. In this analysis we have attempted to clarify those differences.

Another problem is sometimes created in the literature when overall program models are confused with specific differences in program design, such as the balance of use of the two languages in a bilingual classroom. This book deals with issues of classroom organization, such as balance of the two languages (concurrent, alternate-language, and preview-review approaches), team teaching, and grouping of students, in chapter 3. The dual-language model (González & Lezama, 1976), for example, is one form of classroom organization for a two-way enrichment program; it is discussed in detail in chapter 3. For the purposes of this book, the major program models used in bilingual education in the United States up to the present time are the transitional, maintenance, and two-way enrichment models.

RESOURCES IN BILINGUAL EDUCATION AND ESL

The review of political developments and program models in this chapter points out the many resources which may be tapped for aid in implementing and sustaining a quality bilingual or ESL program. For those preparing to become bilingual or ESL teachers or to improve their skills, this section gives an overview of some very important services and resources.

The first level of services is your local school system. Many school districts have established resource centers staffed by specialized bilingual personnel to help in transcript evaluation, social services, counseling, special education, curriculum development, textbook selection, testing, and other special needs. If the school district or county has few resources, the next level of assistance may be your state department of education. Most states have either a bilingual education director or a Title VII coordinator, or they combine bilingual services with foreign languages and English as a second language. The contact persons for each state are listed in a publication of the National Clearinghouse for Bilingual Education compiled by Theodora Predaris, *Guide to State Education Agencies*, which is updated each year.

Title VII Support Services

Clearinghouse   At the federal level, a wide variety of valuable assistance is available. The most up-to-date and immediate source of information is the National Clearinghouse for Bilingual Education, located at 1555 Wilson Blvd., Suite 605, Rosslyn, VA 22209. (Toll-free phone: 800-336-4560.)

The Clearinghouse functions as "an information center gathering, analyzing, synthesizing, and disseminating information—to promote the improvement of educational opportunities and practices for minority-language persons in the U.S." The free monthly newsletter, *Forum*, provides the most current information on bilingual education. Other publications from the Clearinghouse include resource guides, bibliographies, and short books and information packets on current topics in bilingual educa-

TABLE 2-3   Bilingual Education Funding

Program	FY 1981	FY 1982	FY 1983	FY 1984
Grants to school districts	$ 98,917,000	$ 79,222,000	$ 84,126,000	$ 89,567,000
Bilingual desegregation grants	8,100,000	7,356,000	2,400,000	—
Training grants	32,075,000	28,836,000	31,288,000	32,610,000
Support services	18,375,000	18,957,000	16,557,000	13,502,000
Bilingual vocational training	3,960,000	3,686,000	3,686,000	3,686,000
Total	161,427,000	138,057,000	138,057,000	139,365,000

SOURCE: *Forum*, April 1982; November/December 1982; December/January 1984.

tion and ESL. Other services provided by the Clearinghouse are its bibliographic databases, abstracts of current bilingual education research, a list of courseware/software computer programs for bilingual and ESL classes, and an on-line electronic job bank. During 1984–85, the Clearinghouse will focus on twelve priority/scope areas for gathering and disseminating information: bilingual education history and legislation; bilingual programs; culture; curriculum and instruction, including educational technology; English as a second language; ethnic and linguistic minority groups; international education; languages and linguistics; parent and community involvement; special populations; teacher and administrator education; and tests, measurement, and evaluation (*Forum,* October/November, 1983, p. 1). The Clearinghouse is funded jointly by the National Institute of Education (NIE) and the U.S. Department of Education.

OBEMLA   The federal Office of Bilingual Education and Minority Languages Affairs, within the U.S. Department of Education, administers all Title VII funds. OBEMLA is the source of information on issues related to federal policy and on rules and regulations regarding Title VII grants. Table 2-3 provides a general breakdown of services administered by OBEMLA and actual expenditures for FY 1981, 1982, 1983, and 1984.

EDACs   The three Evaluation, Dissemination, and Assessment Centers are located in Los Angeles, California; Cambridge, Massachusetts; and Austin, Texas. One of the main tasks of the EDACs has been to publish bilingual materials for classrooms. Their free annual catalogues give bilingual teachers a sampling of materials recently developed specifically for U.S. public schools by bilingual personnel. These centers were scheduled to be replaced by the new Bilingual Education Multifunctional Support Centers as of 1984, but Congressional support may allow one or more of the EDACs to continue.

MDCs   The Materials Development Centers were established to develop the materials which the EDACs publish. There have been as many as nineteen MDCs funded under Title VII, but these centers have been reduced in number because of administrative decisions connected with budget cuts. Congressional lobbying may allow some of the MDCs to continue operating in 1984–85. Materials development is being emphasized as one outcome of basic grants for local education agencies that apply for Title VII funds. To get an idea of the variety of languages in which materials have been developed, the following list indicates locations and languages of the MDCs funded in FY 1981:

1. *Anchorage, Alaska:* Iñupiaq, Alutiig, St. Lawrence Island Yupik, Central Yupik, Tlingit, Haida, Tsimshian, Eastern Aleut, Western Aleut, Ahtna, Dena'ina, Gwich'in, Central Koyukon, Lower Koyukon, Upper Kuskokwin, Upper Tanana

2. *Tucson, Arizona:* Spanish/English

3. *Berkeley, California:* Chinese, Japanese, Korean, Pilipino

4. *Los Angeles, California:* Chinese, Japanese, Korean, Vietnamese, Cambodian, Laotian

5. *Pomona, California:* Korean, Vietnamese

6. *San Francisco, California:* Chinese, Pilipino

7. *Miami, Florida:* Haitian Creole, Spanish/English

8. *Tallahassee, Florida:* Greek

9. *Honolulu, Hawaii:* Carolinian, Chamorro, Ilokano, Korean, Marshallese, Palauan, Samoan, Trukese, Ulithian, Woleian, Yapese

10. *Oakdale, Iowa:* Cambodian, Laotian, Vietnamese

11. *Ann Arbor, Michigan:* Arabic

12. *Bedford, New Hampshire:* French

13. *South Orange, New Jersey:* Chinese, Japanese, Korean

14. *Albuquerque, New Mexico:* Navajo

15. *Brooklyn, New York:* Greek, Italian, Russian, Spanish

16. *Providence, Rhode Island:* Portuguese

17. *Dallas, Texas:* Spanish/English

BESCs and New BEMSCs   The nineteen Bilingual Education Service Centers, which were funded through FY 1983, have been responsible for providing training and technical assistance to their assigned service areas by responding to the immediate concerns of instructional personnel, parents, community members, university students, and professors on issues related to bilingual education and ESL. For example, BESCs provided assistance with conferences, workshops, in-service training, materials, student assessment, program planning, and library resources.

The BESCs are being replaced by sixteen Bilingual Education Multifunctional Support Centers, beginning in FY 1984. These new centers will continue to provide training and technical assistance to school districts as the BESCs have done, and in addition may take over some of the dissemination functions of the EDACs, along with state education offices.

IHEs   As of FY 1984, there are thirty-three Institutions of Higher Education that have fellowship programs at the doctoral level, 25 IHEs with dean's grants to schools of education, and 42 IHEs with teacher training programs at the bachelor and master degree levels, supported by Title VII funds. These programs are designed to train teachers, upgrade professional skills in bilingual education and ESL, or develop skills in specialized areas such as bilingual special education. Financial assistance is generally available to students who qualify for these programs. For the current list of IHEs, BEMSCs, MDCs, and EDACs, contact the Clearinghouse.

NCBR   The National Center for Bilingual Research, located in Los Alamitos, California, was established in November 1979 to coordinate research and disseminate findings in the area of bilingual education. In addition to the work carried out at NCBR, there are many research studies currently funded through Part C of the 1978 Bilingual Education Act. These studies, along with a compilation of research data collected at NCBR, will be a part of the package presented to legislators for study of reauthorization of Title VII in 1984.

NACBE The National Advisory Council for Bilingual Education was established in 1975 to serve in an advisory capacity to the federal offices responsible for the administration of Title VII. Appointed by the Secretary of Education, NACBE produces an annual report on the current status of bilingual education and makes recommendations for future policy. These annual reports are full of valuable information and are available from the Clearinghouse.

Lau Centers While the National Origin Desegregation Assistance Centers (NODACs), more commonly called Lau Centers, are not a part of the Title VII network, they serve a function similar in level to that of the BEMSCs. Operating with funding from the Office for Civil Rights under Title IV of the Civil Rights Act, the Lau Centers were designed to assist school districts out of compliance with the Lau decision and the Civil Rights Act (on which the Lau decision was based) to formulate and implement a compliance plan. With the Reagan administration's nonenforcement of the *Lau Remedies*, the Lau Centers now assist school districts with identification of LEP students, choice of assessment instruments, training of teachers, curriculum development, and other needs. Their main goal is to help school district personnel find the optimal solution to meet the varied educational needs of linguistic minorities. Funding for the Lau Centers varies from year to year.

Professional Organizations

NABE Teachers will find it extremely worthwhile to join the professional organizations closest to their interests. Membership in the National Association for Bilingual Education provides a very lively stimulus to full understanding of the scope and depth of the field. Annual NABE conferences stimulate an exchange of ideas among those involved in bilingual education and ESL: teachers and other bilingual personnel, parents, students, local and state administrators, researchers, evaluators, university professors, lawyers, and federal bureaucrats. Activities especially designed for teachers are workshops, teacher demonstrations, displays of teacher-made materials, minicourses, and commercial exhibits. The exhibits are worth the cost of the conference, as many commercial publishers give free examination copies of or discounts on textbooks and materials. NABE also provides a good taste of the politics of bilingual education. Membership includes a bimonthly newsletter and subscription to the *NABE Journal*. NABE headquarters are located at Room 405, 1201 16th Street, N.W., Washington, DC 20036.

TESOL   The other large professional organization in this field is Teachers of English to Speakers of Other Languages. TESOL membership includes a newsletter, subscription to *TESOL Quarterly,* access to a job-bank file, and reduced rates at the annual convention, at which a teacher can learn about the latest theories, methods, and techniques of teaching second languages, new discoveries in second-language acquisition, and other issues related to applied and theoretical linguistics. The special-interest group on bilingual education sponsors many sessions on this subject at each annual convention. TESOL also publishes many important books and monographs on ESL and bilingual education.

It is also wise to join the local affiliates of NABE and TESOL for their regular meetings on current topics of interest. These regional meetings provide you with the opportunity to meet other professionals with similar interests and concerns and exchange ideas. The national headquarters of TESOL are located at 202 D.C. Transit Building, Georgetown University, Washington, DC 20057.

NAAPAE and Others   There are many other professional organizations that specialize in various aspects of bilingual and ESL education or closely related issues, such as the National Association for Asian and Pacific American Education (NAAPAE) (which focuses on the education of Asian and Pacific American students), the National Association for Vietnamese-American Education (NAVAE), the National Indian Education Association (NIEA), and the American Council on the Teaching of Foreign Languages (ACTFL).

Two other organizations that focus on intercultural awareness are the Council on Anthropology and Education of the American Anthropological Association (with a special-interest group on bilingual education) and the Society for Intercultural Education, Training, and Research (SIETAR). A large professional organization for educators and educational researchers with a sizable special-interest group on bilingual education is the American Educational Research Association (AERA). A more exhaustive listing of professional organizations can be found in the calendar of events in *Forum.*

Private, Nonprofit Organizations

Several private organizations carry out contract research in bilingual education and ESL, including the Center for Applied Linguistics (CAL). CAL was established in 1959 as "an independent, nonprofit professional organization dedicated to the application of the findings of linguistic science to the solution of educational and social problems" (*The Linguistic*

Reporter, 1981). CAL has served over the last 20 years as an important support organization for the development of appropriate educational environments for linguistic minorities. Publications from CAL include several series on bilingual education and applied linguistics. CAL staff members are helpful in giving advice on program planning and evaluation; CAL also serves as the Educational Resources Information Center (ERIC) Clearinghouse on Languages and Linguistics. The Center for Applied Linguistics is at 3520 Prospect Street, N.W., Washington, DC 20007.

This list is not exhaustive but provides an overview of the variety of resources available to you in bilingual education and ESL. The final section of this chapter is an annotated listing of sources which provide information in greater detail on the topics covered in this chapter.

RECOMMENDED READING

1. *Historical Background of Bilingual Education*

    a. For histories which provide detailed information on the education of linguistic minorities in the United States, works by Heinz Kloss are considered classics. His most recent publication, which summarizes his other work, is *The American Bilingual Tradition* (1977).

    b. Another classic is Joshua Fishman's, *Language Loyalty in the United States* (1966b).

    c. David Tyack's history of the development of public urban education in the United States, *The One Best System* (1974), includes the efforts for education of various religious, ethnic, and linguistic minorities and their struggles for power to control or influence schools.

    d. Arnold Leibowitz has written a historical monograph on the educational experiences of Japanese-Americans, Mexican-Americans, Native Americans, and Puerto Ricans in the United States, entitled *Educational Policy and Political Acceptance: The Imposition of English as the Language of Instruction in American Schools* (1971).

    e. Three brief overviews of the history covered in this chapter are Josué González' "Coming of Age in Bilingual/Bicultural Education: A Historical Perspective" (1975); Carlos Ovando's "Political Issues in Bilingual/Bicultural Education" (1978c);

and Gary Keller and Karen van Hooft's "A Chronology of Bilingualism and Bilingual Education in the United States" (1982).

f. A source with substantial information from a historical point of view is *A Better Chance to Learn: Bilingual-Bicultural Education,* produced by the U.S. Commission on Civil Rights in 1975. Some sections on federal policy in this book are now out-of-date, but it is a good historical reference.

g. For a detailed history of bilingual education in Dade County, Florida, see William Mackey and Von Nieda Beebe's *Bilingual Schools for a Bicultural Community: Miami's Adaptation to the Cuban Refugees* (1977).

h. A historical and sociological analysis of the complications of implementation of one bilingual program is found in Virginia Collier's study of the Washington, D.C. Bilingual Program (1980).

2. *Federal Policy and Legislation*

a. A reference on the history of bilingual schooling in the United States, including federal policy through 1974, is Theodore Andersson and Mildred Boyer's second edition of *Bilingual Schooling in the United States* (1978). This includes the texts of the Bilingual Education Acts of 1968 and 1974, the OCR memorandum of May 25, 1970, and the *Lau v. Nichols* decision.

b. Federal and state policy analysis is the main focus of Raymond Padilla's (ed.) *Bilingual Education and Public Policy in the United States* (1979). This book is packed with articles which describe in substantial detail various pieces of federal and state legislation and court decisions that have affected bilingual education.

c. The annual reports published by the National Advisory Council for Bilingual Education (1976–1983) and available through the National Clearinghouse for Bilingual Education summarize federal and state policy for language-minority students.

d. Analysis of the Title VII legislation is provided by Susan Schneider in *Revolution, Reaction, or Reform: The 1974 Bilingual Education Act* (1976) and by Arnold Leibowitz in *The Bilingual Education Act: A Legislative Analysis* (1980).

e. Three articles that examine federal policy in bilingual education and U.S. language policy implications include Carlos Ovando's "Bilingual/Bicultural Education: Its Legacy and Its Future" (1983); Ricardo Otheguy's "Thinking About Bilingual Education: A Critical Appraisal" (1982); and Iris Rotberg's "Some Legal and Research Considerations in Establishing Federal Policy in Bilingual Education" (1982).

f. A collection of papers on language policy issues is provided in the publication of the National Clearinghouse for Bilingual Education, *Exploring Strategies for Developing a Cohesive National Direction toward Language Education in the United States* (1983).

g. Periodically, the Title VII legislation requires a report from the secretary of education summarizing the activities under Title VII. The report by Secretary Bell, *The Condition of Bilingual Education in the Nation, 1982,* is available from the National Clearinghouse for Bilingual Education.

3. *State Legislation*

a. The Clearinghouse provides a quick overview of Title VII state directors, Title VII resources for each state, state funding for bilingual education, a brief summary of state legislation on bilingual education, and the status of state bilingual teacher certification in *Guide to State Education Agencies,* compiled by Theodora Predaris. This volume is updated each year.

b. *The Current Status of Bilingual Education Legislation,* compiled by Tracy Gray, Suzanne Convery, and Katherine Fox (1981), includes the text of all federal and state legislation through 1980, as well as excerpts from some federal court decisions. Gray (1983) updates this book, with information on changes in state legislation in Colorado, Illinois, Rhode Island, and Texas.

4. *Court Decisions*

a. Herbert Teitelbaum and Richard Hiller, who are lawyers with the Puerto Rican Legal Defense and Education Fund, have written several thorough articles on legal developments which have influenced bilingual education, such as "Bilingual Education: The Legal Mandate" (1977a).

b. Another article which gives a brief overview of legal decisions is Perry Zirkel's "The Legal Vicissitudes of Bilingual Education" (1977).

c. Arnold Leibowitz has summarized and printed the text of major legal decisions that have affected political, legal, economic, and educational access for language minorities in *Federal Recognition of the Rights of Minority Language Groups* (1982).

5. *Program Models*

a. For a discussion of two-way enrichment bilingual education, see Josué González' explanation of this model as the solution to legal desegregation requirements in *Bilingual Education in the Integrated School* (1979a).

b. Immersion bilingual education in Canada and the United States is the topic of a new book issued by the California State Department of Education entitled *Studies on Immersion Education: A Collection for U.S. Educators* (1984).

Chapter Three

LANGUAGE

Once upon a time there was a grown-up who loved children. One child who came to know this person was eager to find out about many things. Together they discovered the intimate secrets of time and space and nature and the way things work. They played with language. They both grew in wisdom and they learned how infinite and mysterious knowledge is.

Don't we as teachers wish that somehow we could capture that special vision—romanticized—of what learning is all about? Why does twentieth-century technological society have to be so complicated, politics so confused, education so bureaucratized and standardized? How do we prepare students to face this complicated world we have created to live in and yet allow them to retain their love of learning?

Being a bilingual teacher seems to multiply the complications of teaching. One must teach in two languages, affirm the cultural values of both home and school, teach standardized forms of the two languages but respect and affirm the multiple varieties and dialects represented among students in class, be a creative and flexible teacher, serve as a catalyst for discovery as students learn to operate effectively in their multiple worlds, be able to mediate and resolve intercultural conflicts, keep students on task, and on and on. An ESL teacher is expected to teach English at breakneck speed, provide meaningful content-area instruction in all subject areas, solve all problems of limited-English-proficient students, and serve as a mediating link between home and school. In other words, bilingual and ESL staff are to be superpeople! But let's get back to the reality. Somewhere, in between the ideal vision and the complicated school world of proposals and administrative superplans, we as teachers have to deal with day-to-day working relationships with the group of live human beings who have been assigned to us.

As you read through these pages, try to keep in mind a vision of your ideal—where the magic happens—as well as one of the reality as you see it daily. Teaching is complicated, but it is also rewarding in ways that many other jobs can never be. You have the chance to interact daily with live, growing, thinking, maturing human beings, and that time is special, despite the complications of managing a late-twentieth-century, bureaucratized, overcrowded classroom of overtested, underchallenged students.

This chapter focuses on the teaching of language. Both this and the chapter on culture are designed to be read carefully, for the concepts and methods elaborated touch and influence every other aspect of teaching and learning discussed throughout the book. In this chapter we discuss (1) recent findings in first- and second-language acquisition; (2) issues in the teaching of native language arts, including teaching the standard language with an appreciation of dialect differences; (3) methods of teaching a second language; (4) second-language curriculum design: grammatical, situational, and notional-functional syllabuses; (5) patterns of classroom organization for bilingual and ESL teachers; (6) balance of use of the two languages in a bilingual classroom: concurrent, preview-review, and alternate-language approaches; (7) concerns about code-switching; and (8) the teaching of basic language skills: listening, speaking, reading, and writing.

RESEARCH IN LANGUAGE ACQUISITION

Since the revolution in linguistics generated by Noam Chomsky's ideas, we have learned a lot about the processes of first- and second-language acquisition. Today the field is replete with studies which refine theories and test new hypotheses about how language is learned or acquired. Because a short review cannot begin to synthesize this growing body of literature, we will instead highlight some of the major hypotheses presently being tested which seem to have implications for bilingual and ESL educators.

Child First- and Second-Language Acquisition

Studies in child L_1 (first-language) acquisition have served as a stimulus for research in L_2 (second-language) acquisition. For example, studies such as Brown's (1973) analysis of the L_1 acquisition order of fourteen grammatical morphemes in English in three children initiated a long series of studies and a still-continuing debate on morpheme order in L_2 acquisition. When the L_2 morpheme studies are examined together, we see enough similarity in the order of acquisition of morphemes across all types of learners to hypothesize that natural developmental stages are more powerful factors than influences from first language, at least in morpheme acquisition. That is, children seem to use L_1 acquisition strategies for learning or acquiring L_2.

The picture which has emerged thus far from L_1 acquisition research is that children actively engage in a gradual subconscious and creative process of discovery through which they acquire the rule system of the language. There are predictable stages, or universal strategies, in this process, which all L_1 acquirers go through. It is thought that one possible key to the language acquisition process is the kind of input provided by the models of language available to the acquirer. This type of input, called "caretaker speech," will be discussed shortly. (See Clark & Clark, 1977, chaps. 8–10 or de Villiers & de Villiers, 1979, for an overview of first-language acquisition in the child.)

Strategies of the young L_2 acquirer that are similar to those of the L_1 acquirer involve

> the identification of patterns; attempts to simplify and use words and phrases even if the meanings and structures are only partial approximations; the finding of ways of figuring out socially embedded language not only as a means of gaining confirmation of meaning but also as a way of learning culturally appropriate patterns; and the flexibility and risk-taking behaviors of trying to use analogies with his first language, knowing that these analogies may be only partially correct in meaning and structure. (Guskin, 1976, p. 241)

Differences between L_1 and L_2 acquisition in children come from variables such as the child's age, place and time of L_2 acquisition, individual learning style, the broader society's social perceptions of the status of the child's identity group, and the child's desire or need to understand and/or identify with speakers of the new language. (See Dulay, Burt, & Krashen, 1982, for additional reading.)

Acquisition-Learning Distinction

Krashen (1981) has developed his "Monitor theory" around the hypothesis that adults have two independent systems for development of a new language: subconscious language *acquisition* and conscious language *learning*.

Acquisition is the natural process young children use for picking up first and second languages with little or no formal instruction. Acquisition requires meaningful, natural interaction in the new language with the focus on understanding the message rather than on its form. In acquisition, native speakers modify (e.g., simplify) their speech to aid the acquirer, with the focus on meaningful communication.

On the other hand, error correction and explicit teaching of rules are associated with formal, conscious language *learning*. Krashen posits that the learned system operates in the form of a monitor, which the learner uses only when (1) there is enough time to think about and consciously apply grammatical rules, (2) the learner is focused on form, or correctness, and (3) the learner knows the rule. Given these limits, a new adult learner may depend on formal instruction in the early stages to provide both conscious learning and an acquisitionlike context (since adults do not naturally simplify their speech with other adults). Increasingly, as an adult develops more proficiency in L_2, acquisition becomes more important than learning, with some of the formal learning subsumed into the body of acquired knowledge of L_2.

The acquisition-learning distinction has several implications for teaching L_2:

1. Young children acquire language naturally; therefore, their environment at school for learning and acquiring L_2 should be acquisition-rich. Dulay and Burt (1973, 1978a) recommend that younger children *not* be taught syntax of L_2 in the classroom, nor be corrected, but recommend that the focus be on the message rather than the form of the message. Activities should include visually demonstrable subject matter such as science experiments, role playing, story telling, problem solving, games, arts and crafts, music, and physical movement; in other words those activities which teachers of young children do naturally in the classroom. Children acquiring L_2 will self-correct their own utterances over time as they progress through the various stages of L_2 development, which are similar to those experienced by a child learning her or his first language.

2. Older children and adults, who are more mature cognitively and whose L_1 proficiency is more fully developed (provided the learner has had formal schooling in L_1), acquire cognitively demanding aspects of L_2 faster than younger children, contrary to the popular myth that children always learn L_2 faster than adults. For example, an abstract word such as "democracy" requires concept development for a 6-year-old, whereas a 14-year-old immigrant with formal schooling may have some L_1 concept of democracy. The older child needs only the vocabulary item in L_2 to transfer and continue expanding his or her understanding of the concept (Cum-

mins, 1981b, p. 30). The one skill in which older learners do not have an early advantage over young learners is pronunciation. Adults may be more heavily influenced by socioaffective factors that inhibit the learner (to be discussed shortly). Because of this, younger acquirers tend, overall, to attain higher levels of proficiency in second languages than adults (Krashen, Long & Scarcella, 1979).

3. If acquisition is an extremely important part of the acquiring-learning process, then teachers need to find ways to create more acquisition-rich classrooms for all ages. We must provide an appropriate balance of both acquisition and formal learning for older learners, depending on their perceived needs and the cognitive objectives of the school system. In addition to the suggestions outlined above for young learners, older learners and adults can also benefit from:

a. Classroom activities which focus on tasks to be carried out rather than on language itself (e.g., schoolwork in the content areas, such as math, science, and social studies; role playing, problem solving; consumer education, real-life activities)

b. Humanistic techniques in which language exercises are personalized, and affective growth as well as cognitive growth is a goal (e.g., Moskowitz, 1978)

c. Techniques adapted from some of the more recent innovative methods of teaching L_2, many of which focus on attempting to create a childlike, acquisition-rich environment for learning and acquiring L_2

All the above will be discussed in more detail later in the chapter.

4. The acquisition-learning distinction is especially relevant when one considers the difference between teaching a foreign language and teaching a second language. In a foreign-language class the teacher may be the only model for the students' exposure to the new language. It is in this context that all the formal methods of teaching language developed. But in a bilingual or ESL classroom, students may be acquiring the language outside of the formal class at a tremendous pace, through interaction with people on the street, other subject areas taught in L_2, listening to the media, and so on. In a second-language context, it is not so crucial for a teacher to control carefully the structures introduced in class or to follow the strict order of a grammatical syllabus.

Input Hypothesis

If acquisition plays a central role in second-language performance, then we need to understand how students acquire. The "input hypothesis" (Krashen, 1981) posits that the key to acquisition is a source of L_2 input (perhaps you the teacher) which is understood, natural, interesting, and meaningful to the student (i.e., used for real communication) *and* is roughly one step beyond the student's present level of competence in L_2. The term "intake" refers to that subset of input which the acquirer actually internalizes. For example, a lot of input in L_2 from TV, movies, or science and social studies lessons taught to native speakers may go in one ear and out the other. Intake is that subset of input which the acquirer actually absorbs and which eventually becomes part of his or her performance in L_2. Even in formal L_2 classes, neither free conversation nor mechanical drills provide optimal input for maximum intake. Instead, according to this hypothesis, we acquire structures through understanding messages containing new structures, rather than being taught them directly. (See Krashen, 1981, chap. 8, for a more detailed discussion of input.)

In child L_1 acquisition, adults and older children provide natural input through what is called "caretaker speech"—a simplification of vocabulary and structures to enable meaningful communication with the child (not baby talk, but acceptable adult language in a form comprehensible to the child). It is thought that caretaker speech may provide clues as to helpful forms of L_2 input for the L_2 acquirer. Some common characteristics of caretaker speech are as follows:

1. Parents talk about what is going on here and now. The child is actively involved in the immediate context, rather than dealing with abstractions or artificialities.

2. Sentences are short and simple. As the child moves from one stage of acquisition to the next, sentences become longer and more complex. Sentences are on the level that the child controls or the next higher level.

3. Speakers repeat themselves using the same syntactic patterns, not through exact repetition, but through rephrasing.

4. When speakers find they must slow down, they insert pauses; they do not distort words and intonation.

5. Speakers provide models to acquirers by saying for them what the acquirers seem to want to say.

6. When they do any kind of correcting, speakers focus attention not on the error, but on trying to communicate better with the child. Focus of the whole conversation is on communication, not on grammatical form or pronunciation. (See Snow & Ferguson, 1977, for a discussion of caretaker speech.)

Socioaffective Filter

Dulay and Burt (1978a, pp. 554–557) use the term "socioaffective filter" to describe all social and emotional factors which affect the learner's acquisition of L_2. All teachers know that students do not learn or acquire everything in L_2 to which they are exposed. Some input may be incomprehensible or nonmeaningful. Other input may be missed by the student because of conscious or unconscious emotional or social factors which keep the student from taking in maximum input at that time. Many attitude studies in L_2 acquisition have shown a positive influence on L_2 acquisition of low anxiety, self-esteem and self-confidence, an outgoing personality, and high motivation for instrumental (practical use) or integrative (identity with another group) purposes. (See Krashen, 1981, chap. 2, for a review of attitude studies.)

In addition to affective variables which influence or interfere with day-to-day acquisition, there are more complicated sociocultural factors such as the learner's preferences for certain input models over others (e.g., peers over teachers, peers over parents, own ethnic group members over nonmembers [Dulay & Burt, 1978b, p. 556]); amount of social interaction with speakers of the target language; ambivalence or hostility toward the majority cultural group (Cummins, 1981b, p. 35); or perceived expectations of the broader society (Ogbu, 1974, 1978).

Cognitive-Academic Language Proficiency (CALP) and Basic Interpersonal Communicative Skills (BICS)

Cummins (1979a, 1980, 1981b) has proposed a model that offers theoretical insight into the influence of L_1 and L_2 in a bilingual school setting. His model should be examined in detail by all bilingual and ESL teachers. Briefly Cummins suggests that school personnel often test LEP students and assume full proficiency in English on the basis of context embedded face-to-face communicative proficiency (or BICS). This level of English proficiency includes the ability to handle complex conversation (one might call it ability to get along in the outside world) using contextual cues such as paralinguistic feedback from the other speaker (e.g., gestures and intonation) and situational cues to meaning. This level of nativelike proficiency generally takes students 2 years to master. Tasks at this end of the continuum between BICS and CALP are not very demanding cognitively.

Moving to the opposite end of the continuum, CALP involves language which is context-reduced and highly demanding cognitively. Context-reduced communication relies heavily on linguistic cues alone and involves abstract thinking. It is what we think of as traditional academic instruction at secondary and adult levels. Cummins has found that when language-minority students work academically only in L_2, it takes them from 5 to 7 years to master commonly accepted age-grade norms in context-reduced aspects of English proficiency. Furthermore, skills in context-reduced language developed in the first language automatically transfer to the second language. All current linguistic research supports the theory that there is a common underlying proficiency (CUP) for both languages (Cummins, 1981b).

For this reason, choice of language in which the student works academically is less important than success in mastering school skills, or cognitive-academic language proficiency. Minority students who have ambivalent feelings toward the majority culture may achieve fuller proficiency in English through spending more time developing solid CALP in L_1. This seems contrary to the commonsense notion that more instruction in English will bring about greater English proficiency, but the research evidence clearly supports L_1 and L_2 instruction for language-minority students (Cummins, 1981b, pp. 25–29; Dulay & Burt, 1978b; Troike, 1978). Language-majority students who have self-confidence in their native language, however, may do fine developing all CALP skills in L_2 in the early grades, as the skills automatically transfer to L_1. Cummins (1981b, p. 28) summarizes these findings:

> The results of research on bilingual programs show that minority children's L_1 can be promoted in school at no cost to the development of proficiency in the majority language. . . . The data clearly show that well-implemented bilingual programs have had remarkable success in developing English academic skills and have proved superior to ESL-only programs in situations where direct comparisons have been carried out.

Additive versus Subtractive Bilingualism and the Threshold Hypothesis

A corollary to Cummins' model regarding CALP and BICS is his "threshold hypothesis" (Cummins, 1976), which has been confirmed by many continuing research studies. It is parallel to Lambert's concept of additive versus subtractive bilingualism, identified in the 1970s (Lambert, 1984). There seems to be a minimal "threshold" level which students must reach in cognitive development in L_1 to succeed in full development of proficiency in L_2. "Subtractive bilingualism," which is the loss of or development of only limited proficiency in L_1, may lead to cognitive deficiency in L_2. "Additive bilingualism," or continued cognitive development in L_1 while mastering L_2, provides the greatest potential for successful development of full proficiency in L_2.

Influence of L_1 on L_2

During the 1950s and 1960s, the "contrastive analysis hypothesis" was the most commonly used explanation for errors in L_2, thought to come from "interference" from L_1. Studies over the last decade and a half have increasingly shown that L_1 has a predominantly positive influence on L_2 (such as Cummins' research), rather than the negative impact implied in the term "interference." In many studies using error analysis, it has been shown that only 4 to 12 percent of the errors in grammar made by children are traceable to L_1, as are 8 to 23 percent of errors made by adults. The large majority of these are errors in word order rather than morphology (Dulay, Burt & Krashen, 1982, p. 102).

The one strong area of L_1 influence is pronunciation. Children process the new sound system through L_1 phonological patterns in early stages of acquisition of L_2, but they gradually rely on the L_2 system and their accent disappears. Many adult learners, on the other hand, process the L_2 sound system through their L_1 system and retain the accent for the rest of their lives. Very little research has been done on this phenomenon, but it is a common pattern with which most teachers are familiar.

L_1 is also known to have increased influence on L_2 when the student is expected to produce L_2 before he or she has had enough exposure to the new language. In this case, the student relies on L_1 structures in an attempt to communicate. Another activity which can cause excessive reliance on L_1 structures is translation. Most language teaching methods today avoid translation tasks, except for individual vocabulary items.

L_1 influence is also evident in the interaction which occurs between a bilingual person's first and second languages. Linguistic borrowing and code-switching are two phenomena that occur naturally in any situation in which two languages come in contact in multilingual societies or regions. These will be discussed in the section on code-switching in this chapter.

There are many other interesting issues being examined in research into first- and second-language acquisition; this review merely touches on a few important findings. An excellent summary of recent research in child and adult second-language acquisition, *Language Two* by Dulay, Burt, and Krashen (1982), is very readable and useful for teachers.

Definitions of Bilingualism

Before discussing methods of teaching first and second languages, it is important to comment on the varying definitions of the term "bilingualism." Goals of a bilingual program differ, depending on the amount of proficiency in the two languages desired by the community. The methods of language teaching you choose depend on the goals of your program. In this book we have encouraged acceptance of the strong version of bilingualism, or nativelike proficiency in two languages, proposed by Bloomfield (1933). There is, however, a wide range of other definitions, forming a continuum from strong to weak bilingualism. For example, a bilingual is one who:

1. Can use two languages alternately (Weinreich, 1953)

2. Can produce meaningful sentences in L_2 (Haugen, 1969)

3. Can use two languages alternately; but the point at which a person actually becomes bilingual is arbitrary or impossible to determine (Mackey, 1962)

4. Can engage in communication in more than one language (Fishman, 1966a)

5. Possesses at least one language skill (listening, speaking, reading, or writing) in L_2 to a minimal degree (Macnamara, 1967)

6. (An "incipient bilingual") can use a passive knowledge of L_2 and a little lexical competence to transact business in L_2 (Diebold, 1961)

7. Speaks only one language but uses different language varieties, registers, and styles of that language (Halliday & Strevens, 1964)

There are reasons for these widely differing definitions of bilingualism. Fishman (1966a) and other sociolinguists believe strongly that the purposes of using two languages vary greatly from one region to another and from person to person, according to the topic, listener, and context. It is therefore unrealistic to require that bilingualism always be defined as the complete mastery of two languages in all contexts. School planners should take into consideration language-use patterns in the community in choosing goals for the appropriate level of mastery of first and second languages. For a good summary of these definitions and other concepts in bilingualism, see McCollum (1981).

While we encourage adoption of the strong version of bilingualism, we are aware that it is an idealistic goal, not always realistically attainable.

Clearly, all public school programs in the United States have as one of their goals students' full proficiency in English. Transitional bilingual programs tend to be less concerned with development of complete proficiency in L_1, because L_1 instruction is gradually phased out. Maintenance and two-way bilingual programs, however, strive for full proficiency in both of the languages taught.

NATIVE LANGUAGE ARTS

Teaching First Language

A bilingual teacher, it often seems, needs to be all things to all people. Regarding the teaching of language alone, a bilingual teacher in a two-way Spanish-English classroom, for example, must know something about teaching English language arts to native speakers, teaching standard English as a second dialect, and teaching English as a second language. The same teacher, or team teacher or aide, must understand the teaching of Spanish language arts, standard Spanish as a second dialect, and Spanish as a second language. One teacher may indeed be given all these responsibilities—a tough assignment!

A first step in the teaching of native language arts can be to study the overall goals of your school system for English language arts objectives. Many goals will be the same, whatever language you are teaching. Do not think of yourself as a remedial teacher expected to correct "deficiencies" of your students. Instead, whether in English, Korean, Central Yupik, Navajo, Greek, or Portuguese, you are working to develop language power as an effective instrument of cognitive growth for your students. In a two-way bilingual class, English-speaking parents demand that the English-speaking team teacher know English language arts objectives for that grade level and expect their children to stay at or above grade level. The same kind of expectations can be assumed for Vietnamese, Spanish, Arabic, or Choctaw language arts lessons. You are helping your students to build a solid cognitive base in which they will feel confident and take pride. For example, native language arts objectives in any language may include the following:

1. Listening, observing, and speaking skills

2. Basic reading skills

3. Language [skills] through experiences with books

4. Spelling abilities

5. Competence and creativeness in oral and written communication

6. Effective language skills for use in daily life

7. Habitual and intelligent skills in use of mass modes of communication

8. Competent use of language and reading for vocational purposes (Valdés, 1981, pp. 11–13)

Standard, Dialects, and Language Variety

In a first-grade bilingual classroom, composed primarily of children of very recent immigrants from rural Mexico, the assignment is to write about something that happened in the story "Jack and the Beanstalk." Marta's sentence reads as follows: "Jack jue ne ca la giganta." "Ne" is a spelling error for "en," but the rest of the sentence is written correctly according to the Spanish that the child speaks. The "translation" to standard Spanish would be: "Jack fue a la casa de la giganta."

The difficulty with teaching languages to native speakers is that many teachers have been trained to teach them as *foreign* languages. Not only are second- or foreign-language methods inappropriate with native speakers, but also a foreign-language teacher on first assessing his or her students may see the particular dialect represented in class as in need of remediation, to be eradicated in favor of a standard variety. It takes special sensitivity to understand the full complexity of the relation of all the language varieties represented in class and the appropriate varieties to teach (Valdés, 1981).

The first step is to recognize that spoken languages are constantly in a process of change. While strict English grammarians complain, spoken English continues to split infinitives, place prepositions at the ends of sentences, and accept incomplete sentences as legitimate, complete thoughts. Other changes occur when a language is moved to a geographical location separate from its origin, or when its speakers are socially isolated. Geographical or social isolation in the new setting ensures the development of a new language variety. Languages also change when they come in contact with other languages. As members of one language community interact with members of another and, as a result of the contact, some members begin to use aspects of both languages for different tasks, each language influences the other. Most bilingual teachers must deal with some form of language contact, raising the issue of which variety to teach: Standard? If so, from which country or region? Local dialect? What to do with a mixed variety? There are never any easy answers.

First, a teacher cannot learn a new version of the standard. Let us use

Spanish as an example because there are so many standard varieties. A Spanish-speaking teacher from Spain, Argentina, Cuba, Mexico, Puerto Rico, California, Colorado, . . . has a vocabulary and pronunciation unique to that particular area, which may vary quite a bit from that of her or his students. The teacher models her own variety, making it clear to the students where she is from and helping them to become aware of language differences between countries and regions. She can affirm the varieties represented by students in class, and as students become older and more cognitively aware, they can benefit from understanding the contrasts and affirming them as language differences not to be looked down on.

Dialects get even more complicated when one considers that there are clearly stigmatized varieties. Students who speak these varieties tend to be those who experience the most failure in school. Educators have tended to blame the language variety and/or home environment for the child's lack of success. The solution proposed in the past has been eradication of the stigmatized variety:

> Eradication . . . , which may be said to be the traditional view of the English-teaching profession as a whole, looks upon dialects other than standard as deficient in themselves, as deserving of the stigma they have attracted, and as the causes of severe problems in the total learning process including the acquisition of reading and writing skills.

> Educators who hold this view look upon the educational process as a means by which one is made to distinguish "right" from "wrong." They see themselves as the tools by which a particular student can rid himself of stigmatized dialect features and become a speaker of the "right" type of English—well known to be a passport to achievement, success, and acceptance. They insist that as educators they have a solemn duty to their students, which includes the total eradication of nonstandard dialects. (Valdés, 1981, pp. 14–15)

Eradication, applied for the last half century, has not significantly altered the school achievement of minority students.

Another strategy used in a few inner-city schools has been to affirm and teach the variety of black English spoken in a particular city, assuming that students will be able to function more effectively in that community and attempting through the schools to give more affirmation to acceptance of that variety. This position of appreciation of dialect differences is a very positive way to affirm local varieties, but it does not deal effectively with the real world, in which minorities are held back from jobs they might wish to get on the basis of the language variety they speak.

A third position, which is perhaps the most popular current view among linguists and bilingual educators, is the acceptance of "bidialectalism." This position affirms the importance of home dialect and its appropriate use within the community in which it is spoken while at the same time students are taught the standard variety. Affirming home language means that students may produce utterances in the classroom in native dialect without being told that they are wrong or that what they say is vulgar or bad. Instead, the teacher analyzes with the students the differences between their dialect and the standard variety: grammatical patterns, pronunciation differences, vocabulary items, varying social contexts, and so on.

Language Arts Curricular Materials

There are few textbooks that will help with this process of comparison of standard with other language varieties represented in the classroom. Although there are some linguistic analyses of language varieties within the United States, these vary a great deal from region to region (see Floyd, 1981, for a literature review of studies of language variation in southwestern U.S. Spanish; and Barkin, Brandt & Ornstein-Galicia, 1982, for analyses of Spanish and Native American language variations along the U.S.-Mexican border). Thus the teacher generally must embark on this type of analysis with his students without special curricular aids. However, it is a worthwhile venture in which you will likely be rewarded by your students' deeper understanding of the whole process of language. Overall, your goal is to help your students master the language used in formal schooling (cognitive-academic language proficiency) and at the same time give your students language tools for use in all contexts in the outside world.

Bilingual and ESL teachers have been creating their own materials with students for many years now, using the language experience approach in which students talk and write about their own personal knowledge and experiences. Language arts texts developed in Materials Development Centers in a wide variety of languages can never completely replace homemade materials that reflect the day-to-day life of the student and the changing nature of language itself. Books written for third graders in Spain may be inappropriate to meet the curricular needs of Central American children in Washington, D.C. Each reality is different and teachers have to adapt to those differences.

METHODS OF TEACHING SECOND LANGUAGE

This section is rather lengthy because so much change has taken place in second-language teaching over the last several decades. The methods to be discussed here can apply to teaching English as a second language or

Mandarin, French, Arabic, Spanish, or any language, as a second language. We refer to second language rather than foreign language, even though our setting is the United States, in which English is the dominant language, for the following reasons. If you are teaching a two-way Vietnamese-English bilingual class and your English-speaking students receive some instruction in math, science, and social studies in Vietnamese, then they are acquiring Vietnamese outside of a formal class focused on learning the language. They also acquire Vietnamese through informal contact with Vietnamese-speaking peers at school. This context of formal classes in Vietnamese as a second language is not precisely a foreign-language context, even though Vietnamese is not spoken in the broader society. This distinction between teaching foreign and second language continues and expands the concept presented on pages 45 and 61.

Approach, Method, and Technique

The terms "approach," "method," and "technique" are frequently confused in the literature on language teaching. Although sometimes they are used interchangeably, there are subtle differences between approach and method and large differences between approach and technique. An "approach" to teaching language generally involves a set of assumptions about the nature of learning and teaching. Clearly distinguishable from a method or approach is a "technique," which can be defined as an instructional activity carried out at one particular time in the classroom. The term "method" falls somewhere in between an approach and a technique. A method is a set of techniques that seem to work well together and share some explicit or implicit assumptions. Some methods use the term "method" in their name, while others are called approaches. For the sake of simplicity we will call all methods and approaches "methods" of teaching second language.

Older Methods

The overview which follows touches on the historical development and some of the basic distinctions among language teaching methods. There are extensive readings available elsewhere on each of these methods. Methods chosen for discussion are those which have received the most attention in the literature.

Grammar-Translation   In use during the first half of this century, grammar-translation is best understood as a way to teach classical languages such as Greek or Latin. Emphasis is on the teaching of reading and writing skills, with little or no concern for the oral language. The method involves memorizing long vocabulary lists out of context, deductive instruction of grammar in which rules are taught explicitly and long verb conjugations are memorized, and reading difficult literature passages through translation. There is extensive use of L_1 to explain, discuss, and translate L_2. Most foreign-language courses in the United States were taught from texts organized around this way of teaching language until the early 1960s, when audiolingual methods became popular in reaction to the lack of emphasis on oral skills. The method of grammar-translation has little or no basis in experimental research in linguistics. This method is seen as extremely inappropriate for teaching modern second languages, given our concern today for full communicative competence in languages.

Direct Method   One reaction to grammar-translation, the direct method has been in existence for centuries as a natural way to learn language through acquisition. Sometimes called immersion, the direct method is not to be confused with immersion bilingual programs such as those in Canada, in which there is always some form of native-language support in school. The direct method focuses on total immersion in L_2 with no use of L_1 allowed in the classroom. Presentation of new material is frequently done through films, tapes, and readings which are situational or organized around topics rather than by the sequencing of grammar structures to be taught. Grammar and culture are taught inductively, through experiences with the language. All discussion takes place in the second language.

ESL classes with students from mixed language backgrounds automatically become immersion classes taught completely in second language. But not all ESL classes can be classified as using the direct method. ESL teachers vary in their choice of sequencing by grammar or by situation and in the types of classroom activities chosen. The direct method does not focus on manipulative drills as does the audiolingual method. Instead, it involves an open-ended response to the materials brought into the classroom by the teacher, which are less carefully sequenced, more natural, and oriented toward real-life activities in the culture(s) in which the language is spoken. Since no L_1 is used in a direct-method class, teachers must demonstrate and role-play language through active use of realia, pictures, films, tapes, and other visual aids.

Audiolingual Method   Sometimes called the aural-oral approach, this method also was developed in reaction to the lack of emphasis on oral skills of the grammar-translation method. Experimentation with the method was accelerated during World War II, when U.S. military personnel were in need of crash courses in communicative skills in foreign languages. The audiolingual method peaked in popularity during the 1960s. Even with heavy criticism from cognitive linguists during the 1970s, however, many public schools still rely heavily on audiolingual textbooks, and many university foreign-language courses are still taught using audiolingual methods.

The audiolingual method is based on theories from structural linguistics and behavioral psychology. Second or foreign language is taught through mimicry and memorization—"mim-mem"—and through repetitive, manipulative drills. Grammar structures are carefully sequenced and taught inductively with great care taken to structure drills to prevent student errors. All four skills are considered important, but the sequence of teaching listening, speaking, reading, and writing is carefully followed, with early emphasis on accurate pronunciation. Tapes, language labs, and visual aids are considered crucial. Minimal use of L_1 is permitted for instructions and explanations, although some writers recommend that all instruction be only in L_2. Most audiolingual foreign-language textbooks are based on a contrastive analysis between L_1 and L_2 for choice of teaching points.

The audiolingual method has been heavily criticized for producing students who could model perfect sentences in L_2 with nativelike pronunciation but could not use the language in a real communicative situation with native speakers. Student graduates of the method criticize it for its militarylike drills; its boring repetitions, which do not encourage students to focus on meaning; and the long dialogues to be memorized, which have little transfer to real language use. Cognitive linguists criticize the method for the structural linguistic principles on which it is based, such as language learning as habit formation.

Cognitive Approach   The cognitive approach was developed from Chomsky's theories about how language is learned. Language learning is seen as a creative cognitive process rather than a patterned, predictable one that can be manipulated with conditioning, as the behaviorists assert. The cognitive approach received the most attention throughout the 1970s. Curiously, few ESL texts have been written which call themselves cognitive in approach; however, several foreign language textbooks for teaching Spanish, French, and German in the United States have been written making use of cognitive principles.

Cognitive methods emphasize language acquisition as rule rather than habit formation; thus it again became acceptable to teach grammar deductively. All four language-learning skills are considered equally important, and more emphasis is given to vocabulary building. The teacher is viewed as a facilitator, and classroom organization can vary from total-group to small-group, paired, and individualized instruction. Errors are acceptable and used for teaching purposes, and use of L_1 is permitted for explanations and some translation. Most important are the types of exercises, which focus on meaningful, natural language and real communication. The catchword is teaching for "communicative competence," which includes proficiency in listening, speaking, reading, and writing through knowledge not only of the syntactic and semantic rules of the language but also of social and psycholinguistic factors which influence use of the language in varying contexts. Among the objectives included in the affective domain are increased positive self-concept of students and quality student-teacher and student-student interactions. In the acceptance and use of L_1 in teaching L_2, bilingual-bicultural proficiency is seen as an ideal goal.

Innovative Approaches

The remaining methods to be discussed are more recent, innovative experiments that have received increasing attention in professional language-teaching conferences. Silent Way, Suggestopedia, and Community Language Learning are commercially based and have some limits as to their applicability for teaching ESL. Nevertheless, there are techniques used in each which may be applicable to bilingual and ESL classes for students in all grades. We encourage all bilingual and ESL teachers to examine each method in enough detail to glean ideas appropriate for use in classes. For additional reading, Blair's *Innovative Approaches to Language Teaching* (1982) provides an extensive review of the following methods and many others.

Silent Way   Caleb Gattegno is the proponent of this method, which forces the teacher to be silent at least 90 percent of the time and let students generate language on their own. There is no use of L_1. Students begin with childlike experimentation with sounds. In the first hour of class, the teacher points to color-coded graphemes on charts which cover all visual representations of phonemes in that language. As students discover the sounds, precision with phonemes, stress, and intonation is reinforced through repetition and teacher direction, but without teacher talk. Later, Cuisenaire rods (rods color-coded by size, traditionally used for teaching math), word charts, wall pictures, and worksheets are used to increase vocabulary and provide topics for conversation and composition. Students initiate experimentation and naturally generate language. No judgment is expressed by the teacher, and social interaction, with students helping other students, is more important than the process of imitation and drill itself. The process is intense and encourages increasing student confidence and independence. Silent Way encourages natural language acquisition through sequenced exercises which are understood, meaningful, and focused on communication rather than on form. (See Gattegno, 1976, and Stevick, 1980, for additional reading.)

Suggestopedia, or Suggestology Developed in Bulgaria by Georgi Lozanov, this method also emphasizes childlike experimentation with L_2. In contrast to Silent Way, in Suggestopedia the teacher takes a much stronger role as guide and authority figure in deciding what takes place in class; however, students also initiate and generate language, with the guidance of the teacher. The setting for lessons must be relaxing and aesthetically pleasing; carpeted floors, easy chairs, music, art, and theatre are used to encourage informal, natural communication. On entering class, students accept a surrogate identity for role playing. Long dialogues are presented in phases, with long spaces of silence and classical music. Later, students engage in interaction activities based on the dialogue. The teacher is expected to be lively, cheerful, efficient, and competent, and to uphold the overall goal of reducing the tensions and anxieties of students. Error correction is minimal. L_1 is used for explanations and discussion. The method seems to encourage lack of inhibition and, consequently, to lead to natural language acquisition. (See Lozanov, 1979, and Stevick, 1980, for additional reading.)

Community Language Learning Developed by Charles Curran, Counseling-Learning is a general approach to education which builds on principles in humanistic psychology. Community Language Learning (CLL) is the name given to the Counseling-Learning method for teaching second or foreign languages. Goals and principles include learner security, assertion, attention, reflection, retention at a "deep" memory level, and discrimination (learner-initiated analysis of the language). The most important goal is creation of a cooperative learning community, in which students are responsible for each other (similar to that of Silent Way).

On the first day, learners are seated in a closed circle (a maximum of six students is ideal), with the resource person (the teacher, called the "knower") outside the circle. The learners initiate conversation in L_1 and the knower provides translation in L_2, close to the student's ear, in a clear, gentle, supportive voice. The sentences generated are taped. After eight to ten sentences, the students and knower work with this material, guided by the knower through occasional short silent periods followed by questions (e.g., "Do you remember anything we said?"). Students may ask anything they desire, and discussion may flow freely in L_1 and L_2.

There is cooperative community support with student-initiated activities; the knower serves as facilitator rather than dominant authority figure and engages in minimal error correction.

Group problem solving is somewhat like that of a therapy group, with lessons generated by students. Since the material generated is personal, there is high retention of L_2. Anxieties are lowered; natural L_2 acquisition is encouraged; and a learning community is created in which the students actively support, counsel, and motivate each other. The use of L_1 in the early stages for generating utterances and explanations is very gradually phased out as L_2 acquisition expands; eventually, all discussion takes place in L_2. (See Curran, 1976, and Stevick, 1980, for additional reading.)

Total Physical Response   This method, developed by Asher (1977), cannot be considered a complete method, but it is very useful for both adults and children in the early stages of second-language learning. The teacher gives a command and models the physical movement to carry out the command. In the first stages, students focus only on listening comprehension by responding to the commands with the appropriate physical movement. As students are ready for the production stage, they begin speaking and, eventually, move to reading and writing. Adding body movement to the acquisition of structures and vocabulary expands the potential for storage in long-term memory; touch and movement are added to the stimulants of sight and sound. (For additional reading, see Bancroft, 1978.)

Natural Approach   Terrell (1977, 1981) has proposed a method of teaching second language which recognizes the centrality of the acquisition process. Techniques in this method focus on providing a context in the classroom for natural language acquisition to occur, with acquirers receiving maximum "comprehensible input," and establishing the best conditions possible for lowering students' socioaffective filters. This is done through a teacher's simplification of his or her speech, similar to modifications in caretaker speech (see p. 62), and through the creation of low-anxiety situations. Other factors include (1) a focus on the student's needs and desires, (2) little overt error correction, (3) avoidance of forcing production until acquirers are ready, and (4) a positive acceptance of the children's native language (while modeling the second language). Traditional drills that are focused on a specific grammar point fail as a source for acquisition and thus are not used.

· In the early stages, the Natural Approach uses Total Physical Response techniques, allowing the acquirer as long a silent period as needed. As the acquisition process expands, through pictures, manipulatives, games, problem solving, and humanistic activities (Galyean, 1977; Moscowitz, 1978), students' attention is focused on the content of language rather than on form. As basic interpersonal communicative skills (Cummins' BICS) are developed, cognitive-academic language proficiency (CALP) is increasingly taught. (For additional reading, see Terrell & Krashen, 1983.)

Second-Language Methods for Primary School

All the methods just described were originally developed for teaching foreign or second languages to teenagers and adults. Terrell's Natural Approach has been adapted and described for use with young children (Terrell, 1981), but no other method has been described in detail as an approach to use with children. Students in the early grades can benefit most from the same kinds of tasks that native speakers are given. All second-language learning can be incorporated into active, meaningful, hands-on tasks which stimulate the senses of touch, taste, smell, sight, and sound. Music, art, and physical movement should be an integral part of language, math, science, and social studies lessons.

Students in grades 4 through 6 may have second-language lessons which focus more specifically on language arts objectives, but natural, acquisition-rich activities lead to better long-term memory storage than does reliance solely on pencil and paper tasks that focus on grammar. Active learning through interesting and meaningful manipulatives, games, puzzles, and problem-solving tasks which clearly teach the language arts objectives provides students with the solid cognitive-academic language base they need to achieve in school.

A very insightful source for elementary school bilingual and ESL teachers is by Ventriglia (1982). This book summarizes the natural strategies which children use to acquire their second language and provides many practical suggestions for classroom activities based on the natural acquisition process. Ventriglia introduces "bridging" (from L_1), "chunking," "creating," "listening in and sounding out," "follow the phrase," "socializing," "cue me in," "peer prompting," "wearing two hats" (bicultural), "copycatting," "putting it together," and "choosing the way" as strategies that children naturally develop through play and classroom activities to acquire their second language.

Second-Language Syllabus Organization

As formal second- and foreign-language teaching for older learners has expanded over the last several decades, three basic types of syllabus design have received increasing attention in the literature: structural (grammatical), situational, and notional-functional. In writing a textbook, an author must choose not only the method to be followed, which affects the types of exercises to be written, but also the content of those exercises. The material chosen by a textbook writer inevitably reflects the author's philosophy and objectives of second-language teaching and learning. The following provides a very brief overview of the three most common patterns of textbook organization for second-language teaching for older students.

Structural   The most common organizational scheme is the structural syllabus, which is focused on the sequencing of grammar points to be taught. The grammar structures may be chosen on the basis of simplicity (simple forms are taught early with increasingly complex forms added as the course progresses), regularity (the most useful structures are taught first), frequency (structures that occur most often are taught first), or contrastive difficulty with the students' first language (Wilkins, 1976, p. 6). The structural, or grammatical, syllabus is the most conventional approach to syllabus design, but other ways of organizing material have received increasing attention in recent years.

Situational   The situational syllabus centers each lesson around a context (situation and topic) in which the learner will need to communicate in the target language. Included in a situation could be a chosen location, the types of people involved and relationships between them, and the activities to be carried out. For example, a lesson might be built on "a trip to the supermarket" or "buying tickets to the baseball game." In this type of syllabus, grammar structures may be limited in each lesson by the vocabulary introduced but not sequenced according to simplicity and complexity. For example, a first-week ESL lesson situated "in the classroom" might include verbs such as "open," "close," "pick up," "put," and "write," conjugated in present progressive, future with "going to," and past tenses (Hall & Costinett, 1971).

Notional-Functional   This approach to syllabus design has received increasing attention in recent years, and many new ESL texts are being written following the ideas of its proponents in Europe, such as D. A. Wilkins, Jan van Ek, and Henry Widdowson. A notional-functional syllabus incorporates grammatical sequencing with situations and topics, adding to both of these the deeper dimension of communicative competence. Such syllabi are much more complex to teach than a grammatical syllabus and require that the teacher be fully fluent and proficient in the second language.

From the development of notional-functional syllabus design, we now know that grammatical competence is only a small part of the total range of language skills a student must master. Communicative competence requires knowledge of a wide range of additional sociolinguistic, cultural, and contextual factors, such as why someone is talking, what that person wants, relationship of two speakers to each other (e.g., age, sex, race, dialect differences), appropriateness of style (e.g., formal, informal, polite, impolite, positive, negative, sarcastic), medium of communication (spoken or written), nonverbal communication, and paralinguistics. A notional-functional syllabus combines function(s) to be examined (e.g., apologizing, persuading, agreeing) with a notional category (a situation, a topic, and ideas related to both), and teaches the appropriate grammatical points which occur within the chosen context and functions.

Wilkins (1976) devised one of the first lists of categories for a notional-functional syllabus, in the form of a taxonomy with 339 categories of notions and functions. An excellent list of functions to be taught in an ESL class is available in *The ESL Miscellany* by Clark, Moran, and Burrows (1981, pp. 133–143). These authors have organized functions into five general types:

1. Basic needs. Using the language to satisfy basic physical requirements of food, shelter, and clothing.

2. Socializing. Using the language to forge social links with native speakers. At its lowest level it satisfies basic emotional needs.

3. Metalinguistic. Using the language to deal with the language. Also includes certain fundamental linguistic labels and functions.

4. Professional. Using the language to make a living.

5. Cultural. Using the language to deal with the social and cultural milieu.

The ESL Miscellany also includes a comprehensive listing of grammatical structures, situations, topics, and functions, and of cultural, metalinguistic, and paralinguistic aspects of American English. It is designed for curriculum developers and ESL teachers who wish to develop their own supplementary materials from a grammatical, situational, and notional-functional perspective.

A notional-functional concept of syllabus design requires some radical changes in teaching techniques and methods. Although no one, as of this writing, has yet proposed a complete accompanying methodology, there are some beginning suggestions from notional-functional proponents. Brumfit (1982) suggests that teachers pay close attention to recent findings in second-language acquisition, such as the importance of natural acquisition over formal learning (Krashen, 1981) and the influence of affective variables (Moskowitz, 1978; Stevick, 1976). Wilkins (1976) stresses the importance of using authentic language materials, written for or spoken by native speakers, so that natural language is used. The newspaper, magazines, radio, TV, tape recordings, and video cassettes are sources of natural language for second-language classes. Another technique found in a notional-functional syllabus is based on the concept of recycling or spiraling the notions and functions to be taught, so that as students reach more advanced levels they return to notions and functions studied previously and learn increasingly complex subtleties in language. An example of an ESL notional-functional text with a spiraling curriculum is *Lifelines* (Foley & Pomann, 1981). Also important with use of a notional-functional syllabus is the style of classroom organization. Teaching to communicative competence includes moving away from a traditional teacher-centered classroom to one in which there is varied work for individuals, pairs, small groups, and the total class, with many tasks to be performed in a natural, acquisition-rich classroom.

For teachers who want a very readable, nontechnical discussion of second-language teaching which combines all old and new methods and is based on recent second-language acquisition research, Stevick's *Teaching and Learning Languages* (1982) is hard to beat. This book is full of practical advice from an experienced teacher.

METHODS OF TEACHING IN A BILINGUAL CLASSROOM

On first hearing about bilingual education, everyone immediately wants to know the method of teaching. In some ways, a bilingual classroom is just like any other classroom. A bilingual teacher learns how to become a teacher first of all. Methods of teaching language arts, reading, second language, math, science, and social studies are the same as for any other teacher. Differences, however, are created by the two major variables of language and culture. How the two languages are used in the classroom is one aspect of methodology. A second aspect, discussed in chapter 4, concerns culture. Here we address issues regarding the use of two languages in a classroom: program design, balance of use of the two languages, factors influencing language choice in the classroom, and code-switching.

Bilingual Program Models, Types, and Designs

In our discussion of bilingual program models in chapter 2, we used the term "model" to refer to basic broad classes of bilingual programs, and described what we consider to be the three major models in actual practice in the United States at the present time: transitional, maintenance, and two-way enrichment. Trueba (1979, pp. 72–73) states, "it is obvious that the status quo of the art in model building for bilingual education is at a very crude and initial stage." He proposes a distinction between program models, types, and designs. We do not examine in detail here the middle category, types, which are variations of the three major models. The typologies of Fishman and Lovas (1970), Mackey (1970), Cohen and Laosa (1976), and Valencia (1976) can be examined in summary in Trueba (1979, pp. 54–73). In actual implementation of bilingual programs within the United States, most of the variations among programs occur at the third level—program design at the classroom level. To clarify the relations among the various levels, we first take a brief look at the process of establishing models, moving from overall design to the level of classroom organization.

Once the overall philosophical-political goals of a bilingual program are determined, the model(s) of bilingual instruction for a school district can be chosen. Ideally, the models are based on detailed examination of community needs—which in turn are based on factors such as the psychological, sociological, economic, political, religious, cultural, geographical, demographic, historical, and linguistic makeup of the community (Spolsky, 1978a, p. 268). Each school would then operate its program based on the needs of the total population attending that school. Some school districts bus students to a special school for a portion of a day or a full day for their bilingual or ESL classes. Others have a sufficiently large population of multilingual students to offer a special program at each school. Rarely does one school district organize one model for all schools within its boundaries. The more common pattern is for each school district to have many administrative models, from pullout ESL classes to transitional, maintenance, and two-way bilingual classes, depending on the student population of each school. The administrative model your school superintendent and building principal choose will determine to a large extent your pattern of classroom organization.

As you become familiar with your students' needs, you may see better ways to organize the program. Changes should be negotiated among all program staff, who may be aided greatly by a process evaluator—someone who looks at the overall model and the progress of students and proposes changes in the structure to create the most effective learning environment for all. (See Cohen, 1980a, to examine ways in which teachers can participate actively with evaluators of bilingual programs to create ongoing, constructive change.)

Classroom Design: Balance of the Two Languages

Whether you teach a transitional class, a maintenance class, or a two-way bilingual class, the main difference from a monolingual class is the balance in use of the two languages. A second variable which affects the process of classroom organization is who teaches: a team, a teacher and an aide, or one teacher alone. The third variable comes from the structure of your program model. In transitional bilingual and pullout ESL classes, the students are probably not with the bilingual teacher for a full day. Maintenance and two-way bilingual instruction involve a comprehensive, full-day program.

The following discussion provides an overview of the three major variations in classroom design which affect use of the two languages in a bilingual classroom: the concurrent, preview-review, and alternate-language approaches. It must be kept in mind that these three strategies are used only for teaching the content areas. Overt language development is taught monolingually in a bilingual classroom: ESL is taught in English only, Navajo language arts in Navajo only, and so on.

Concurrent Approach   Concurrent teaching is probably the most common pattern of language use in bilingual classrooms throughout the United States, yet very little has been written describing the approach in detail. A teacher using the concurrent approach may use both languages interchangeably in teaching a content area, or two teachers may team teach one lesson, each modeling a different language.

The concurrent approach has received a lot of criticism from researchers. One problem cited is that a teacher's interchangeable mixing of the languages will produce "compound bilinguals," who mix the two languages together, rather than "coordinate bilinguals," who have the two codes clearly separated and can operate fluently in either linguistic context (Cohen, 1975b; Mackey, 1972). Another criticism of the concurrent approach is that, even though teachers are supposed to avoid direct translation, so much translation actually takes place that the students tune out the language they do not understand and simply wait for the translation into their dominant language (Gaarder, 1978; Wong-Fillmore, 1980). A third criticism is that teachers using the concurrent approach assume that they are using a fifty-fifty balance of English and the other language, whereas in reality the teacher frequently uses English (the dominant language) much more than the other language, and students receive the implicit message that English is the more important language (Legarreta-Marcaida, 1981; Milk, 1982).

Rodolfo Jacobson (1981) has proposed a "*new* concurrent approach" to solve some of these problems. After serving as evaluator of the Laredo, Texas, bilingual program for 4 years, Jacobson provides a detailed look at the concurrent approach and suggests a scheme for helping teachers to modify their own patterns for the most effective use of a new concurrent approach. The following are some of the modifications he proposes:

1. No intrasentential (inside a sentence) code-switching should occur with children still in developmental stages of language competence (therefore, for both L_1 and L_2 development, at least until postpuberty).

2. Language switches must achieve pedagogically sound objectives.

3. Through taping of classes, a teacher can monitor and eventually modify the balance of use of the two languages until achieving a ratio closer to fifty-fifty.

4. Code-switching at the ends of sentences for appropriate reasons is acceptable, but translation is to be avoided.

Jacobson (1981, p. 19) lists the following classroom factors as appropriate cues for initiating switches to the other language:

1. Classroom strategies
   a. Conceptual reinforcement
   b. Review
   c. Capturing of attention
   d. Praise/reprimand

2. Curriculum
   a. Language appropriateness
   b. Topic
   c. Text

3. Language development
   a. Variable language dominance
   b. Lexical enrichment
   c. Translatability

4. Interpersonal relationships
   a. Intimacy/formality
   b. Courtesy
   c. Free choice
   d. Fatigue
   e. Self-awareness
   f. Rapport

It seems particularly appropriate to teach bilingual classes using a con-current approach in areas of the United States in which there is a substantially large bilingual community and language use among bilinguals within that community involves natural code-switching. Discussion of this issue continues in the section on code-switching, which follows shortly.

Preview-Review   This approach involves three steps in a team-teaching situation: (1) An introduction to the lesson is first given by one instructor in one language. (2) The lesson is then presented in the other language by the second instructor. (3) Review and reinforcement of the lesson takes place with the whole class using the two languages interchangeably in a concurrent approach, or the class is divided into dominant-language groups, led by each teacher separately. González and Lezama (1976) first described this approach as part of their "dual-language model" for bilingual teaching. (According to our distinctions between program models, types, and designs, the González-Lezama model is not an overall program model, but a classroom design.)

Ideally, this design works best in an integrated, two-way bilingual program with English-speaking students included. Each of the teachers teamed together provides a consistent model for only one of the two languages. For example, the English-medium teacher understands and shows great respect for the other language but speaks only in English in response to students. If the two teachers who are teamed together wish to help students keep the two languages clearly separated, they can handle the third step of review and reinforcement with the total class through allowing students to ask questions in either language, but responding only to the questions in the language for which he or she serves as model.

Brisk and Wurzel (1979) describe an "integrated bilingual curriculum model" for kindergarten-level instruction in Boston which is based on the González-Lezama classroom design. Some bilingual schools in Dade County, Florida, have used similar patterns of classroom design in their two-way classes, with instruction in the alternate-language approach (Mackey & Beebe, 1977). The Washington, D.C., public school system operates a two-way bilingual school similar to the González-Lezama design, with both preview-review and alternate-language approaches (Collier, 1980).

Alternate-Language Approaches   The basic philosophy behind this approach to organization of a bilingual class requires complete separation of the two languages. There are several possible variations:

1. In the alternate-day approach, all classes are taught in one language on Monday, the second language on Tuesday, and back to

the first language on Wednesday. This model is less often used in the United States.

2. A more common model in the United States is the alternate half day, in which students receive half the day's instruction in English and half in the second language. Care must be taken to alternate the schedule so that both languages receive an equal number of morning hours, the time when students are more alert.

3. Alternating by subject area is a third form of separation of the two languages. For example, science might be taught in English and social studies in Arabic. During the students' first year in a bilingual class, they are separated into language-dominant groupings and taught each subject area in the language they best understand. As students become increasingly proficient in the second language, alternate-subject-area instruction should include half a day in each language.

All of these variations—alternate-day, half-day, or alternate-subject-area instruction—encourage a fifty-fifty balance of the two languages once students are fully proficient in both. Alternate-language approaches are administratively structured to force the balance through clearly delineated times for instruction in each language. Legarreta (1977, 1979) makes a strong case for the alternate approach on the basis of two studies comparing monolingual instruction in English with no ESL training, monolingual instruction with ESL, concurrent bilingual approaches, and alternate-half-day bilingual instruction. Students in the alternate-half-day programs made the most signficant gains in both English and Spanish. Legarreta also found that teachers in the concurrent programs spoke in English 72 percent of the time and in Spanish only 28 percent of the time, even though they thought they were providing a fifty-fifty balance of the two languages. Wong-Fillmore (1980) found similar positive gains among children taught with the alternate-subject approach compared with those in concurrent bilingual classes.

The strongest criticism of all three patterns of language use in a bilingual classroom centers around the amount of time spent in direct translation and in repetition of lessons that are presented in both languages. Dulay and Burt (1978a, p. 558) describe the problem:

When core subject matter is taught to LEP students in two languages at once (as in the concurrent method), or in one language after another (as in the preview-review method), students probably filter out the language they do not understand in favor of the language they do understand. In other words, much of the English used to present the same content a second time is probably tuned out, as it has no real function in the communicative situation. There would appear to be little motivation to exert the extra effort to attend to information presented in a new language when students have either just heard it in their native language, or know that the same content will soon be presented in their native language.

The solution is for a teacher to modify the pattern of language use, whatever approach is used. The new concurrent approach as described by Jacobson (1981) pushes teachers to avoid direct translation and to develop a natural flow from one language to the other at appropriate times without boring repetition. The preview-review approach has the same potential danger, but teachers aware of the problem can plan introductions to and reviews of lessons which do not repeat material but reinforce and expand the concepts presented. The alternate approach automatically provides the structure for avoiding repetition or translation, although some theoretical descriptions of alternate-day approaches state that lessons are repeated in the second language. Clearly, repetition of the exact lesson should be avoided.

Code-Switching   When two languages are used in the school curriculum, both lesson plans and spontaneous events influence the language to be used. A teacher may plan the precise times for use of each of the two languages through a theoretical model using the concurrent, preview-review, or alternate approach, but natural, spontaneous patterns of code-switching, or language alternation, may play a stronger role in language choice for both teachers and students. It is very important for bilingual teachers to examine the functions of code-switching in a bilingual setting to determine how best to respond to it in the classroom.

Code-switching, the alternate use of two languages, can occur at the word, phrase, clause, or sentence level. Code-switching is considered by linguists to be a creative use of language by bilinguals who know both codes (languages) well. It is not to be confused with L_1 interference, which is now referred to by the less pejorative term "L_1 influence." For example, first-language influence might affect a student's pronunciation or word order in the second language. In code-switching the items inserted in the second language represent a "clean break" between the two phonemic and morphologic systems. Code-switching is also not to be confused with language borrowing, in which vocabulary items from one language are borrowed and incorporated into the sound system of the second language. For example, in the sentence "Los muchachos están puchando la troca" (The boys are pushing the truck.), the verb "puchar" and noun "la troca" have been borrowed from English (Valdés-Fallis, 1978, pp. 1–2).

When two languages come in contact with each other, it is inevitable that code-switching, language influence, and language borrowing occur. Code-switching, the most creative and dynamic process of the three, seems to be rule-governed. Rather than indicating language weakness, it shows a high degree of sophistication in the understanding of the uses and functions of both languages. Code-switchers use both languages only with speakers who know both codes. "Bilingual speakers are aware that each of their languages has certain strengths and that two languages can be used simultaneously to convey the most precise meaning" (Valdés-Fallis, 1978, p. 7).

Research studies on code-switching have shown a wide variety of reasons for the switches from one language to the other. An excellent summary of these is found in Table 3-1, taken from Valdés-Fallis (1978, p. 16). The examples given are in Spanish/English.

Although sociolinguists emphasize the positive aspects of code-switching, González and Maez (1980) discuss what they call "regressive code-switching," which occurs when a student who is losing a first language leans on the second language to provide the missing lexical items or structure. This occurs most often in within-sentence code-switching. It is difficult but nevertheless important for a bilingual teacher to develop a linguistic profile of each student's growing competence in both languages and to recognize the appropriateness of code-switching within a student's linguistic repertoire. One way to make sure code-switching is not a crutch for avoiding structures forgotten in one language is to use the alternate approach, in which the times for use of each language are clearly separated. Unfortunately, this may be an artificial method of instruction in a bilingual community in which code-switching is the general style of communication for many transactions at home, work, and leisure activities.

González and Maez (1980), Jacobson (1981), and Valdés-Fallis (1978) all recommend that, if any code-switching is used in the classroom, intersentential code-switching (switching after the ends of sentences) is best. Intrasentential (within a sentence) code-switching by students should be accepted but not used by the teacher.

> The natural phenomenon of code-switching should not be forbidden in a maintenance program. . . . Conversational switches may be signals that the students feel a common bond among themselves and a teacher. Permitting the expression of this feeling may increase students' motivation and promote learning. Acceptance of the functions that different languages serve might produce better academic results than a constant preoccupation with maintaining a single language. (Genishi, 1978, pp. 189–190)

TABLE 3-1 Principal Code-Switching Patterns

Patterns	Definitions	Examples
	SWITCHING PATTERNS THAT OCCUR IN RESPONSE TO EXTERNAL FACTORS	
Situational switches	Related to the social role of speakers	Mother uses English to chat with daughters but switches to Spanish to reprimand son.
Contextual switches	Situation, topic, setting, etc., linked to the other language	Students switch to English to discuss details of a math exam.
Identity markers	In-group membership stressed	*Ese bato, órale, ándale pues* used in English conversations, regardless of actual Spanish fluency.
Quotations and para-phrases	Contextual: related to language used by the original speaker	Y lo (luego) me dijo el Mr. Johnson que *I have to study.* (Remark was actually made in English.)
	SWITCHING PATTERNS THAT OCCUR IN RESPONSE TO INTERNAL FACTORS	
Random switches of high-frequency items	Unpredictable; do not relate to topic, situation, setting, or language dominance; occur *only* on word level	Very common words, such as days of the week or colors. Function like English synonyms: gal-girl, guy-fellow, etc. Fuimos al *party* ayer y estuvo tan suave la fiesta.

Switches that reflect lexical need	Related to language dominance, memory, and spontaneous versus automatic speech	Include the "tip of the tongue" phenomenon; item may be momentarily forgotten.
Triggered switches	Due to preceding or following items	Yo lo vi, you know, *but I didn't speak to him.* (Switch is triggered by the preformulation.)
Preformulations	Include linguistic routines and automatic speech	*You know, glad to meet you, thanks for calling,* no te molestes, qué hay de nuevo, etc.
Discourse markers	But, and, of course, etc.	*Este . . . este . . .* yo sí quería ir.
Quotations and paraphrases	Noncontextual: not related to language used by original speaker	He insisted *que no me fuera.* But I did anyway. (Remark was originally made in English.)
Stylistic switches	Obvious stylistic devices used for emphasis or contrast	Me tomé toda la cafetera, *the whole coffee pot.*
Sequential switches	Involve using the last language used by the preceding speaker	Certain speakers will always follow the language switches of other speakers; others will not.

SOURCE: Valdés-Fallis, 1978, p. 16.

The decision to switch or not to switch will vary according to the goals of the community, the type of bilingual program design, the specific classroom structure, the bilingual competence of the teacher(s), and the formality or informality of the specific classroom tasks. Code-switching is generally considered appropriate in informal, casual, or intimate speech among bilingual speakers (Valdés-Fallis, 1978, pp. 17–19). A teacher's acceptance and use of code-switching may be a very appropriate strategy for a particular setting. If code-switching is used in the classroom, caution must be taken to ensure that the languages are given a fifty-fifty balance, unless the goals of the program are other than equal maintenance of the two languages. Since the tendency in concurrent bilingual classrooms, according to many observational research studies, is to use more switches to English than to the other language (Ramírez, 1980), one possible solution would be to monitor language use in your classroom according to Jacobson's (1981) new concurrent approach, until the balance is achieved.

TEACHING LANGUAGE SKILLS

Relationships among the Four Skills

Because of the many excellent references available on teaching the four language skills of listening, speaking, reading, and writing, this section covers just a few important points involved in the teaching of first and second languages in bilingual and ESL classrooms. Sometimes materials on the teaching of these four skills tend to isolate the skills, whereas in reality each skill is intimately related to the others. Here are several reminders for teachers.

In the literature on teaching second or foreign languages, the main reason the four skills have been isolated and emphasized has been to point out to teachers the importance of providing a balanced approach to the four skills. The grammar-translation approach was rightfully criticized for its emphasis on the teaching of reading and writing skills while neglecting oral skills. The audiolingual method in its early years overemphasized listening and speaking by holding students back from reading and writing in the second language for the first 6 to 8 weeks of a course. The cognitive approach emphasized a return to a balance of the four skills beginning with the first lessons, and most audiolingual texts published more recently have modified the approach to provide a balance from the beginning.

Another misconception sometimes seen in the literature is the idea, extended from the audiolingual method, that oral skills must be mastered by young children before written skills are taught. It is very important for students to use the oral base they have in reading, but it is not at all necessary for young learners to achieve complete fluency in the spoken language before moving on to written language. Listening and reading are receptive skills, which always exceed the productive skills of speaking and writing. In other words, children can comprehend a great deal more (through listening *and* reading) than they demonstrate on speaking and writing tasks. Students of limited-English proficiency should not be held back in their development of cognitive-academic language proficiency (Cummins, 1980), which includes the addition to oral skills of all the reading and writing objectives required in a formalized educational setting.

Listening and Speaking

One important point in teaching oral skills is to help students recognize the major differences between spoken and written language. For example, spoken English is much more informal in grammatical expectations: there is no differentiation between who and whom; prepositions occur at ends of sentences; verb contractions are assumed. Understanding sandhi-variation is an important skill to master in listening comprehension; this is natural variation in sound patterns, such as contractions and omissions, when native speakers speak at normal speed (e.g., Whatcha gunna do?: What are you going to do?).

One of the best ways to teach sandhi-variation and other aspects of spoken language is to use samples of live language, spoken by native speakers, from a variety of natural sources such as the radio, TV, newspapers, magazines, commercials, video cassettes, telephone recordings, and live recorded events. Live language demonstrates variations in intonation, emotional overtone, redundancy, pauses, fillers, false starts, colloquialisms, and register (intimate, casual, informal, consultative, and formal) (Joos, 1962). Herschenhorn (1979) has some good suggestions for use of live language, involving teachers' relating of personal experiences, telephone conversations, students' interviews with native speakers, and short taped conversations between native speakers. Proponents of notional-functional and communication-based approaches to teaching languages strongly support the use of live language for teaching listening and speaking skills, rather than formal, contrived classroom exercises. For a balanced approach, however, students also need to understand formal classroom language in order to succeed in all their classes.

The audiolingual method encouraged the use of language labs, but after many schools installed this expensive equipment, most of the labs sit idle today. Whether or not you have a fancy lab in your school, you can think of a simple cassette tape recorder as your lab. This is all you need, and it is a very effective teaching tool. You can bring in tapes of music, speech, or sounds for class activities, or your students can produce cassettes for class use. You can set up a learning center with individualized listening activities, or you can work with small groups or the whole class.

Teaching listening and speaking skills should include the whole range of activities, from manipulative, structured exercises, needed especially for beginning students, to open-ended, communicative activities with student creativity influencing the outcome. Paulston and Bruder (1976) recommend the use of social formulas, community-oriented tasks, problem-solving activities, role-play, and games as means of developing full communicative competence. Variations in social formulas are frequently taught in notional-functional texts. Community-oriented tasks involve students in activities outside the classroom, such as the telephone, housing, shopping, media, the library, bank, social services, and other consumer-oriented activities. Many good examples of problem-solving and role-play activities are suggested in books on values clarification and humanistic techniques. (For a detailed bibliography, see Moskowitz, 1978.)

Music and art are integral parts of many listening and speaking activities and should be included as a regular part of the curriculum. Many suggestions for music and art activities are provided at the end of chapter 5. Games are highly motivating and should be included not merely for entertainment but also to encourage long-term retention of language skills. Games for the primary grades can be designed by teachers and students to teach the senses, colors, shapes, numbers, sounds, measures, and many other objectives of the school system. For upper elementary and secondary students, communication games are the best for teaching language. Whereas traditional and commercial games tend to emphasize competition and guessing and need to be closely monitored by a teacher, communication games emphasize cooperation, open-ended communication, and interaction, and use the teacher as a facilitator. Some excellent examples of communication games for teaching language in bilingual and ESL classes are available in Winn-Bell Olsen (1978) and Nielson (1981).

Reading in L₁ and L₂

Reading and writing are probably the most crucial skills for school success. Yet an amazing number of transitional bilingual and ESL programs for primary school children consider competence in English oral skills only as the exit criterion for placing students in regular classes. Some students who miss developmental stages in reading and writing skills are able to acquire those skills on their own, but many more do not fill in the gaps and stay behind in academic preparation. The teaching of reading and writing skills in both L_1 and L_2 provides the backbone for any school program, for full development of cognitive-academic language proficiency. This does not mean that students need 3 or 4 hours per day of native language arts and second-language lessons; in fact, too much formal language instruction can be deadly. Many of the language objectives are taught through science, math, and social studies lessons as well. (See chaps. 5 and 6.)

The first question asked when addressing issues of teaching beginning reading to students of multiple language backgrounds frequently concerns the issue of first-language literacy. Is it important to be able to read the mother tongue before beginning to read in a second language? Several literature reviews that lumped all studies together found the results inconclusive (e.g., Engle, 1975). However, a more careful reading of the literature indicates there is a significant distinction to be made between majority- and minority-language students. All studies of students whose dominant language is the majority language and who are taught to read first in L_2 show positive results (such as English-speaking students in immersion bilingual programs). In contrast, language-minority students are much more successful in school when L_1 is used as the initial language of literacy. Cummins (1981b), Tucker (1980), and Skutnabb-Kangas (1979) explain that in contexts in which the language-minority group feels ambivalence or hostility toward the majority group, the insecurity and confusion results in low academic performance. Use of the minority language in instruction builds students' identity and feelings of self-worth and reduces feelings of ambivalence toward the majority language and culture.

> The case for native-language reading instruction for language-minority students is strong. The rationale can be defended on logical grounds and empirical evidence. . . . Once language-minority students have learned to read well and have understood the strategies for obtaining meaning from print, these abilities provide a solid foundation for literacy skills in the second language. (Thonis, 1981, p. 178)

Many studies show that many skills in reading transfer from one language to another. Even when the two languages do not use the same writing system, researchers have found that general strategies, habits and attitudes, knowledge of text structure, rhetorical devices, sensorimotor skills, visual-perceptual training, cognitive functions, and many reading readiness skills transfer to L_2 reading (Chu, 1981; Mace-Matluck, 1982, pp. 14–15; Thonis, 1981, pp. 150–154). Students who are literate in L_1

generally progress much faster in L_2 reading than those who are nonliterate in their mother tongue. This means that parents should be encouraged to continue the use of L_1 at home with children for development of full proficiency, including reading and writing if possible, especially if the school does not have the resources to provide bilingual personnel for all language groups.

Reading experts differ on the issue of simultaneous development of reading in two languages. Some have maintained that L_1 literacy should be developed before introducing L_2 literacy. Studies of language-minority students (especially those who belong to a group which seems to have subordinate status in the region) indicate better gains when L_1 literacy has a firm base before the introduction of L_2 literacy. It is a more common pattern of bilingual schooling worldwide to start students in the first language and introduce the second language in the third or fourth grade, after an academic base has been established in the first languge. On the other hand, students who are confident about their first language have had great success when introduced to literacy in L_2 first or when taught literacy in L_1 and L_2 simultaneously.

When reading is taught simultaneously in both languages, there must of course be some oral base in L_2 on which to build literacy skills. However, many theoretical descriptions have overemphasized the necessity for holding students back in reading in L_2 until a complete oral base is established. Recent studies show that students do not need to wait to begin reading in L_2 until oral proficiency is achieved (Goodman, Goodman & Flores, 1979; see previous discussion on pp. 90–91). Students of limited English proficiency are fully aware that other students in the school are learning to read, and they want to learn the written form of each English word and phrase mastered in oral form.

In the United States, teaching L_1 literacy is not always possible for all students before introducing reading in L_2. We have managed to hire bilingual staff for only the largest language groups in some school districts. More important than the time to introduce reading in L_2 is the way that reading is taught. Reading is more likely to be successful if the curriculum and goals are culturally relevant, meaningful, and sensitive to the needs of the child.

Recent developments in preschool biliteracy hold some exciting possibilities. Robert Lado, Theodore Andersson, and others have spearheaded a movement to introduce reading in two languages before entering first grade. In addition to highly successful case studies in which middle-class parents have taught reading in two languages to their preschool children (Andersson, 1981), a very successful preschool project has been in operation at the Spanish Education Development Center in

Washington, D.C., since 1978 for children of low-income families. These children are taught to read first in Spanish and later in English, through play experience with sight words, and later, through phonics (Lado, 1982; Lado, Hanson & D'Emilio, 1980). On entering first grade, these students have the advantage of additive bilingualism through biliteracy, and they feel confident about their ability to succeed in school.

Beginning Reading Methods   It is assumed that for certification, all bilingual and ESL teachers have had at least one course in the teaching of reading. For purposes of synthesis, we attempt only to summarize what has been written about extensively in many sources. One of the best overall summaries of reading methods for language-minority students is by Thonis (1981). She groups all methods into three major categories: synthetic, analytic, and eclectic:

> Reading methods for language-minority students are often debated from the viewpoint of whether the code or the meaning approach is the better. The synthetic method in which the letters, sounds, syllables, and smaller segments of the written language are introduced may lend itself well to certain languages that offer reasonably dependable speech-print correspondence. The analytic methods in which whole words or utterances are presented may stress meaning at every level. How the parts of the writing system go together is not considered of great importance. Making sense of the written material and comprehending the ideas and events are the important goals of the reading instruction. For languages with many irregularities in the speech-print correspondence, like French or English, the analytic approach has worked well for some students. Eclectic methods offer the opportunities both to learn the code and to obtain meaning. Regardless of the method, to read is to comprehend and to comprehend is to think. (p. 167)

Synthetic approaches, which break the elements of reading into segments, include the onomatopoeic method (everyday sounds are associated with visual symbols), alphabetic method (criticized for not teaching the sounds of the letters), phonics methods (which teach sound-symbol associations), syllabic method (which teaches units of syllables rather than sounds), and linguistic method (which teaches frequently occurring patterns in words). In contrast, analytic approaches stress whole words and comprehension of meaning, such as the global method (look-say memorization of whole words and phrases), generative word method (whole-word memorization plus analysis of the parts), and language experience approach (students produce their own personalized materials for reading). The language experience approach has received a lot of attention as an especially appropriate method for language-minority children,

given the difficulty of finding suitable reading materials which are culturally and linguistically relevant. An excellent summary of the language
experience approach is available in Hansen-Krening (1981, 1982).

Eclecticism involves taking the best of all methods and individualizing
to meet the varied needs of all students in each class. Many urban school
systems, frustrated with low scores in reading achievement, have in-
stituted a strict back-to-basics approach with a very structured program
for teaching reading. These programs frequently overemphasize the elements of reading at the expense of holistic skills in reading comprehension, when instead comprehension should be the ultimate goal. Whenever
teachers deviate from overly structured materials and teach all skills,
including creativity and thinking skills, students surely benefit. As an
illustration of eclecticism, Thonis describes possible combinations of
methods for teaching literacy in English to language-minority students:

> Good choices for the transitional stage might be the language experience
> approach supported by a cautious program of phonic skills based on sounds
> pupils can *hear* and *say*. Another method might be a *linguistic* program,
> which presents short written patterns on the basis of a regular sound-symbol
> correspondence (*man—Dan—ran—fan,* etc.) and support this somewhat
> sterile, artificial written language by rich oral English in poems, storytelling,
> choral speaking, and dramatizations. Still another might be a carefully paced
> basal reader approach augmented by pictures, news events, and descriptions
> of life in the language-minority community as written in English. In this
> manner, the content of the basal stories could be enlivened by content of
> cultural relevance to learners. There are many combinations of methods that
> could well support the second-language-literacy plan in English. (1981,
> p. 173)

Preliterate Students in the Upper Grades   In recent years, increasing numbers of immigrants or refugees arriving from war-torn countries have gaps
in their educational background, and some of these older students have
low levels of L_1 literacy or have never been to school before. Since it is a
general policy in U.S. schools to place students according to their age,
bilingual and ESL teachers are faced with the overwhelming task of bringing these older students up to grade level. These students have special
needs, but it is not appropriate to place them in special education classes
unless they have some type of learning disability or impairment. Yet these
students can make rapid progress with individualized teaching.

Bilingual and ESL staff can arrange for special one-to-one instruction
in literacy in L_1 and L_2 through the use of teacher aides, student teachers,
and college volunteers. If there are enough preliterate students of one
language background in adjacent grades, a special L_1 literacy class can be

organized for these students. Assuming these students have a fully developed oral base in L_1, teaching them to read in L_1 is worth the time commitment, as students will experience success in school skills (CALP) which will transfer to reading in L_2. The greatest challenge these students present is in finding ways to integrate them socially with students of their own age and at the same time present meaningful lessons at both their level of maturity and their level of cognitive development. Unfortunately, there are no easy answers. ESL teachers of preliterate secondary students might examine recent ESL materials for teaching preliterate adults. There are a number of new textbooks coming out which look promising, such as *Passage to ESL Literacy,* published by Delta Systems; *Impact!* from Addison-Wesley; and *A New Start,* published by Heinemann Educational Books.

Reading Strategies   Many books and articles have been written describing techniques for teaching reading; we mention just a few points to keep in mind when working with students of limited-English proficiency.

In a literate society, children become aware very early of the importance of written language in their world through books, the media, signs, printed containers, logos, instructions, and letters in the mail. Reading is a natural process which most students can readily acquire when they are given a classroom environment for learning to read that makes full use of the natural reading activities surrounding the child (Goodman & Goodman, 1976). For example, materials which students learn to read can include stories that the children dictate to the teacher (language experience approach), directions the class creates for use of different learning centers (e.g., "Feeding our gerbils"), exchange of personal letters, a teacher-student dialogue journal, games, recipes, instructions to make things, and a class newspaper; all of these can incorporate the cultural and linguistic backgrounds of all the students in the class.

As students begin to make the leaps from decoding skills to reading comprehension, and they move from class-made materials to books, poems, and stories written by other authors, both teacher and students can search for books that are humorous, exciting, of high interest, and culturally relevant to the students. Children's literature of recent years in many languages is phenomenal in its excitement, beauty, and pure fun. An excellent, thorough annotated bibliography of reading materials in English for children from multiple cultural backgrounds is available in Tiedt and Tiedt (1979).

Above all, it is important in early reading to stress strategies which promote understanding the meaning of the written word as opposed to those that focus extensively on isolated parts of words. Phonics is a useful tool, especially for languages with close sound-symbol correspondence, but too much focus on mastering all the separated parts before moving to an activity which is meaningful to students can slow students' progress toward confidence in their ability to read.

A final point involves achieving some reasonable balance between natural, acquisition-oriented activities in reading and fulfilling the requirements of the school system necessary for helping students to pass tests designed to measure grade-level skills mastered. In general, middle-class children in the United States tend to develop test skills very early, from regular exposure to a variety of testing activities. Students coming from other countries and those from lower social-class backgrounds may have initial difficulty with test-taking skills and can improve their scores a great deal by activities which teach, for example, following directions, categorization, analogy, definition (Martin, 1982), and other concepts which involve complex levels of cognitive development.

Writing

To help students develop confidence in their writing ability, writing activities which focus on acquisition-oriented tasks are important. Excessive focus on form with exclusion of writing tasks which are meaningful, personalized, or culturally relevant to students can slow down growth in writing skills. Some examples of acquisition-focused activities which teach writing skills are dialogue journals, freewriting, and development of consumer skills.

Dialogue journals have been used by many language teachers to develop writing skills as well as to enhance personal communication and mutual understanding between teacher and student. Using this technique, each student keeps a bound composition notebook in which a private written conversation is carried on between teacher and student. The writing style is informal, conversational language, and each student is free to write about anything of interest to him or her. No error correction is done by the teacher other than modeling correct form through the response given. A teacher's comments should be warm, supportive, and responsive to the student's attempt to communicate. Research on dialogue journal writing has found that

> . . . interactive writing does not lead to dependence on the teacher, but to greater independence in communication. A student who might write very brief entries at the beginning learns the strategies for elaborating on a topic by observation and participation, and gradually takes on the teacher's role in discussing a topic by writing more complex, elaborate, and independent entries. (Staton, 1983, p. 1)

While the main focus of dialogue journal writing is on functional, personal, interactive use of the language, teachers report that students also improve in grammar, spelling, form, and content as the year goes on, without direct error correction, and students are extremely proud of their progress when they compare early entries with their writing at the end of the year.

Another useful tool for upper elementary and secondary students is freewriting. Each time students are assigned a writing task, they are encouraged to write without correcting themselves, just as the words come. The first step of this process is prewriting, which involves topic selection and may include brainstorming and jotting down words which come to mind related to the topic chosen. The writer then starts writing about this personalized topic without concern for the form of the language she or he is producing. The message is more important at this stage. The writing should be as open and honest as possible. At later stages the students revise for content and organization, and at the last stage they correct errors in grammar and mechanics which might get in the way of understanding the writer's message. In freewriting, all kinds of writing are encouraged; the overall purpose is to communicate a personal, meaningful message.

A third strategy for teaching reading and writing to older students centers around consumer skills for survival in the world outside of school. Units can be developed in areas such as budgeting (Ashton, 1979), health care services, nutrition (excellent practical school materials are available from the Center for Science in the Public Interest, Washington, D.C.), consumer-wise shopping, or anything students express keen interest in. Reading and writing tasks of practical help to students are self-motivating and generate student self-confidence.

In choosing materials for reading and writing tasks for all students, another powerful source can be myths and folktales from all the cultures represented in the classroom. Students can experience the power and magic of language through the oral and written words passed on through the generations. They can study the multitude of ways people have interpreted reality, varying cultural values, the depth of cultural traditions, environmental reasons for varying behavior, and the changes occurring in the world now as a result of technology. Through writing tasks based on studies of folklore and myths, students can recreate the stories which have power for them personally.

Language is enchanting, powerful, magical, useful, personal, natural, all-important. We as teachers serve as catalysts for our students to make the best use of their two (or more) languages. Language is the most powerful tool they have.

RECOMMENDED READING

These sources are recommended for interesting and informative reading to expand the concepts presented in this chapter.

1. On child and adult second-language acquisition: *Language Two* by Heidi Dulay, Marina Burt, and Stephen Krashen (1982).

2. For summaries of Jim Cummins' and Stephen Krashen's theories; Tracy Terrell's Natural Approach; and Eleanor Thonis' work on the teaching of reading: *Schooling and Language-Minority Students: A Theoretical Framework* (1981), developed by the Office of Bilingual Bicultural Education of the California State Department of Education.

3. On teaching Spanish language arts in bilingual classes: *Teaching Spanish to the Hispanic Bilingual: Issues, Aims, and Methods,* edited by Guadalupe Valdés, Anthony Lozano, and Rodolfo García-Moya (1981).

4. For methods and techniques of teaching ESL, with detailed information on teaching listening, speaking, reading, and writing: *Teaching English as a Second or Foreign Language,* edited by Marianne Celce-Murcía and Lois McIntosh (1979).

5. For teaching second languages to children: *Conversations of Miguel and María: How Children Learn a Second Language: Implications for Classroom Teaching* by Linda Ventriglia (1982).

6. On innovative language teaching methods: *Innovative Approaches to Language Teaching,* edited by Robert W. Blair (1982).

7. For a combination of old and innovative methods of language teaching: *Teaching and Learning Languages* by Earl W. Stevick (1982).

8. For ESL curriculum development: *The ESL Miscellany: A Cultural and Linguistic Inventory of American English* by Raymond C. Clark, Patrick R. Moran, and Arthur A. Burrows (1981).

9. On code-switching: *Code-Switching and the Classroom Teacher* by Guadalupe Valdés-Fallis (1978).

10. On the language-experience approach to teaching reading: *Language Experiences for All Students* by Nancy Hansen-Krening (1982).

Chapter Four

CULTURE

Bicultural education, multicultural education, culture conflict, culture shock, cultural assimilation, cross-cultural communication, cross-cultural studies, cultural pluralism, and biculturalism—these are just a few of the culture-related terms that teachers of language-minority youth repeatedly come across. Specific definitions are not easy to find. As Spolsky observes, "the term 'culture' has come to be very important in the rhetoric of the bilingual-education movement, but its meaning is seldom explained or defined precisely" (1978b, p. 20). Such vagueness, however, can be useful. Culture is a deep, multilayered, somewhat cohesive hodgepodge of language, values, beliefs, and behaviors that pervades every aspect of every person's life, and it is continually undergoing minor—and occasionally major—alterations. When it is studied, it becomes an abstraction—albeit a useful one—for giving meaning to human activity. What it is *not* is an isolated, mechanical aspect of life which can be used to directly explain phenomena in a multiethnic classroom, or which can be learned as a series of facts. For this reason teachers often find curricular suggestions regarding cultural awareness to be unrealistic when viewed against the day-to-day events of the classroom. With respect to culture there should be an uneasy tension between theory and practice to reflect the elusive and impermanent nature of cultural knowledge.

Despite Spolsky's lament, there are more definitions of culture than could possibly be included here. To establish a basis for what we mean and do not mean by the word "culture," the first section of this chapter provides an analysis of anthropological and popular views of the term. Focusing more specifically on multiethnic schooling environments, we subsequently explore the meanings of biculturalism and cultural pluralism. The second section draws on the conceptual framework developed in

101

the first section to delineate some of the explicit and implicit ways in which culture touches the actual instructional process. Examples of culture-related research in education furnish glimpses of the understanding which such studies can provide, but they also demonstrate the need to avoid casting cultural conclusions in concrete.

PERSPECTIVES ON THE CONCEPT OF CULTURE

The Anthropological View of Culture

The concept of culture has been an enigma for social scientists. There is, to begin with, disagreement as to how culture should be defined. A common point of departure for discussion, however, is the definition formulated in 1871 by one of the earliest anthropologists, E.B. Tylor: "Culture . . . is that complex whole which includes knowledge, belief, art, law, morals, custom, and any other capabilities and habits acquired by man as member of society" (Kroeber & Kluckhohn, 1963, p. 81). Such broad, listlike definitions of culture have served as natural seedbeds for cultural analysis and intellectual enrichment for many years; however, if one views culture as an enumerable, although complex, set of traits, values, beliefs, and customs—as suggested by Tylor's definition—anthropological analysis runs the risk of limiting itself to what Geertz (1973, p. 29) refers to as:

> turning culture into folklore and collecting it, turning it into traits and counting it, turning it into institutions and classifying it, turning it into structures and toying with it.

For this reason, many anthropologists suggest that a less segmented and more conceptually intricate definition is needed (Geertz, 1973; Moore, 1967). As a proponent of a deeper view of culture, Geertz (1973, pp, 5, 29) offers the following interpretation:

> Believing, with Max Weber, that man is an animal suspended in webs of significance he himself has spun, I take culture to be those webs, and the analysis of it to be therefore not an experimental science in search of law but an interpretive one in search of meaning.

> Cultural analysis is intrinsically incomplete. And, worse than that, the more deeply it goes the less complete it is. It is a strange science whose most telling assertions are its most tremulously based, in which to get somewhere with the matter at hand is to intensify suspicion, both your own and that of others, that you are not quite getting it right. . . . Anthropology, or at least interpretive anthropology, is a science whose progress is marked less by a perfection of

consensus than by a refinement of debate. What gets better is the precision with which we vex each other.

Despite conceptual disagreement (with deep philosophical underpinnings) over a specific definition of culture, anthropologists do tend to agree on three of its most basic traits (Hall, 1976, p. 13): (1) Culture is shared and in effect defines the boundaries of different groups; (2) the various facets of culture are interrelated; and (3) culture is not innate, but learned. Let us consider these three points separately.

Culture Is Shared   Culture exists only in relation to a specific social grouping; it is acquired and created by human beings only as members of society. Therefore, as groups constantly maintain some aspects of their identity while periodically modifying other aspects, individuals serve the dual function of being culture bearers as well as culture makers. This continual flux reflects what Berger refers to as "the cultural imperative of stability and the natural state of culture as unstable" (1967, p. 6). To put it another way, human beings are constantly in the process of becoming "*a part of*" and "*apart from*" a given cultural context (Adler, 1972). For example, a child is becoming a part of her home cultural environment as she learns the etiquette of speaking and ways to give or get information and to give or get attention appropriate to her ethnic group (Hymes, 1979). In school, however, she may grow apart from these patterns to some extent as she learns alternative forms of communication which characterize the classroom setting. It is through such social contact with members of her own and other cultural groups that her cultural identity develops.

While cultures define boundaries, these boundaries are usually quite porous. To use a saying which folksinger Pete Seeger attributes to his father, "plagiarism is basic to all culture." Throughout history, societies have borrowed a great deal from each other. This borrowing has been a principal source of the instability of culture, of the constant need for culture makers, and of the constant development of cultural patterns "apart from" the original ones.

Cultural Components Are Interrelated   When one characteristic of a culture changes, many other facets of the culture can be, and probably will be, affected in some way. Based on empirical observations of many societies, numerous anthropologists have used the concept of a functional "system," in one form or other, as an analytical tool for the study of cultural dynamics. Cancian, for example, describes an approach in which the units of a cultural system are assumed to be interrelated to maintain a steady state. As they are affected by internal and external stimuli, these units vary with respect to one another to produce stability. When one or more variables change beyond a certain limit without compensation by other variables, a shift occurs on the overall cultural pattern (1968, p. 31).

A classic example of one seemingly minor change radically altering an entire way of life is Sharp's analysis of the Yir Yoront in "Steel Axes for Stone Age Australians." The Yir Yoront originally had stone axes as tools. Much more than tools, however, these axes were made and owned by adult males, and their distribution defined all social relationships within the tribe as either subordinate or superordinate. They were integral to the mythology of the tribe and to the tribe's relationships with its trading neighbors. So when Christian missionaries began giving out more efficient steel axes, indiscriminately to men, women, and children, the resulting disequilibrium spread to every aspect of the Yir Yoront culture, foreshadowing, according to Sharp, its collapse and destruction (1952, pp. 69–90).

As another example, consider the introduction of compulsory formal schooling into remote Alaskan native villages. Athapaskan Indians of the Yukon traditionally followed a seminomadic way of life, moving from fishing camps to hunting camps as the seasons changed. In the 1930s, however, "compulsory education forced parents to keep their children in school and thus abandon their traditional seasonal rounds" (Simeone, 1982, p. 100). Thus with changes in the form of education also came changes in residential patterns, along with concomitant changes in subsistence patterns, the local economy, and patterns of social interaction, as a permanent community developed.

Culture Is Learned   In other words, culture is not carried in the genes. Consider a child who unknowingly touches a hot object. The immediate withdrawal of the hand is a physical reflex which does not have to be taught, but whether the unpleasant surprise elicits from the child a scream of "ay" or "ow" is a cultural artifact, something transmitted through social interaction. Because a newborn child comes equipped with virtually no cultural baggage, an essential characteristic of "being human" is the manner, consciously and unconsciously, in which we transmit cultural patterns to succeeding generations. The premise that culture is learned, not inherited, is so basic to all considerations of the concept that it has often been used as a definition of culture by itself.

Long before children enter the formal classroom, a rich mixture of culturally coded behavioral patterns have been learned through the enculturation process. Administration of justice, for example, does not follow one pattern which is innate to all humans. A pattern observed among some Hawaiian families is that when children are involved in argumentative behavior with siblings or friends, parents tend to discipline all involved rather than attempting to identify the guilty parties. Thus these children learn that it pays to take care of their concerns within their peer groups rather than sharing them with the adults (Gallimore, Boggs & Jordan, 1974). But the same children may also learn that in their classrooms, which operate out of a different cultural system, the teacher generally wants to know who is responsible for the unacceptable behavior. Such an approach may teach children to tell on each other and lessen the value they place on solidarity.

The more one considers culture, the more slippery the concept seems to become. The above generalizations provide some important grips, but they do not give one a comprehensive hold. Culture is shared and defines boundaries, but the exact same culture is not shared by all members of a social group, and the boundaries are highly permeable. Components of a culture seem to be interrelated as in a system, but this "system" does not always seem to behave according to clear, systematic rules. Culture is learned, but most of the teaching is unreflected on, and the content is somewhat modified as it is transmitted.

Finally, to make the subject even more evasive, there is the problem of inevitable bias. Because we are all culture bearers, when we study or simply observe the behavior of members of a cultural group, we can never dissociate ourselves completely from the topic of inquiry. Because we all view the world through our cultural lenses, objectivity is a limit which we can only hope to approach but will never reach. Cultural analysis requires the rare ability to become, to the greatest degree possible, a dispassionate observer of the human experience. As teachers, our goal is not to develop sophisticated cultural analyses of our students; however, as we work toward our specified learning objectives, we are making observations related to the cultural backgrounds of our students. It is therefore important to remember that our interpretations will always be somewhat colored by our own cultural and individual values.

Popular Views of Culture

While cultural anthropologists worry about objectivity and search for the universal significance of human evolution as it bears on contemporary life, nonanthropologists of the Western world, including educators, have often tended to view culture, not surprisingly, as the accumulation of the best knowledge, skills, and values found in the Western world. This "high civilization" view of culture conjures up the image of the sophisticated cognoscente scoffing at the unfortunate slob who "doesn't have any culture," implying that the person lacks knowledge of or appreciation for the literary and fine arts tradition of Western civilization. Curricula in the United States have implicitly and explicitly stressed the importance of Western ideals as the hallmark of culture. This view of culture (minus the snobbery) can, of course, be very justifiably taught as an appreciation of continuity with part of the heritage of the United States, and it is an important component of the liberal arts curriculum. But from the point of view of the education of language-minority students, stress on the social and aesthetic accomplishments of the Western or English-speaking world, at the expense of ignoring the poignant social, cultural, and linguistic realities which surround nonmainstream learners and their community, may have significant negative effects. Lack of acknowledgment of multiple cultural traditions can be related to high dropout rates, alienation, and low academic achievement (Ogbu, 1978).

Another common approach to culture—one that can be referred to as the "set-of-traits" point of view—is the tendency to view culture as a series of significant historical events and heroes, typical traditions, and culturally coded concepts or terms. Tongue in cheek, this has been called the "laundry list" approach, or the "facts, faces, and fiestas" approach. In Mexican-American culture, for example, the list of things to know would include such items as the Treaty of Guadalupe Hidalgo, Cinco de Mayo, Benito Juárez, Pancho Villa, Reies Tijerina, César Chávez, La Raza, *cholos, machismo,* Aztlán, *piñatas,* and *corridos.* The argument for this approach is that the better informed people are about a culture, the less culturally, racially, or linguistically prejudiced they will be. And there is some empirical evidence to support the argument (Lambert & Klineberg, 1967). However, this framework is limited and easily promotes the view that culture is highly static rather than a process of predictable and unpredictable modifications. There is also the danger that this type of cultural information, if not handled carefully, may lead to stereotyping, especially of already stigmatized minorities. One is inclined to assume falsely that everything on the cultural "list" is meaningful, and in the same way, to every member of the cultural group. This view of culture may also encourage one to feel a sense of distance from the everyday immediacy of cultural phenomena. The "bits" of culture become discrete abstractions, items that can be reduced to "right" or "wrong" on a multiple-choice test. As Saville-Troike puts it, "there are no 'canned' lists of culture traits which can be accepted out of hand" (1978, p. 17). Rather, it is important to observe the actual behaviors of students and parents in and outside of the classroom and to ask many questions. For example, instead of assuming that a given holiday or celebration is meaningful for *all* members of an ethnic group, the teacher may wish to ask the students and parents themselves, "What holidays or celebrations are most important to you? Why?" (Saville-Troike, 1978, p. 37). The responses to such inquiries may confirm what was already known, but they may also reveal new dimensions to a student's ethnic identity.

The set-of-traits approach obscures the reality of individuals as culture bearers and culture makers, who not only carry their culture but also may help to reconstruct their world if they so desire. This approach does not lend itself to the consideration of people's integration or assimilation into a new culture, nor does it portray culture as a configuration or system which is adapted to a particular context. Many generalized traits of Chicano culture could be cited, but Cuéllar (1980), for example, argues that to relate the Chicano subculture to educational policy requires an understanding of that subculture in the United States as it systematically relates to ecological, psychological, biological, socioeconomic, and historical circumstances.

Both the high civilization view of culture and the set-of-traits view have some pedagogical validity, but they are not in and of themselves sufficient to achieve an understanding of culture at large, or of culture in the multiethnic classroom. Both views deprive us of an awareness of culture as an integral aspect of our own lives—as the web we all weave, together and separately, day after day. Both views bypass a premise particularly essential to multicultural education: that no child (or teacher) is without culture. This premise is the critical source from which the role of culture vis-à-vis the classroom has to be built. An awareness of culture is not only the discovery of "others," but also the discovery of ourselves, of our own webs. The reaction of a group of students learning L_1 literacy in São Tomé, an island off the west coast of Africa, to a picture of their village—the first they had ever seen—illustrates this point:

> The class first looked at the picture in silence, then four of them got up as if by arrangement and walked over to the wall where the picture code of the village was hung. They looked attentively at the picture, then they went over to the window and looked at the world outside. They exchanged glances, their eyes wide as if in surprise, and, again looking at the picture, they said, "It's Monte Mario. That's what Monte Mario is like, and we didn't know it." (Freire, 1981, p. 30)

Biculturalism and Cultural Pluralism

In a society as complex and multiethnic as the United States, discovering what our cultural image is, and what it can become, is less than easy. A consideration of the concepts of biculturalism and cultural pluralism can help to unravel some of the issues which relate to the role of culture in bilingual and ESL classrooms.

Biculturalism   Much has been said and written about cultural pluralism because it is the cornerstone of public policy on bilingual education, but puzzlingly little thought has been given to biculturalism. For example, the extent to which learning a second language implies learning its culture is something that has not been carefully analyzed.

Biculturalism exists when a person has the volition and capacity to negotiate comfortably two sets of cultural assumptions, patterns, values, beliefs, and behaviors. Biculturalism in essence says that a person has come to terms with two worldviews—usually one which is learned from one's parents and an adopted one. Being bicultural, however, does not necessarily mean giving equal time to both cultures in terms of behavior. There may be many traits from one culture or both which are understood but not necessarily acted out, such as religious rituals, cosmological interpretations, or family traditions (Saville-Troike, 1978). The following statement by a Greek-American scholar provides a positive insight into the phenomenon of biculturalism in the United States:

> Living in two worlds, the one American, the other of the immigrant Greek, was not an emotional strain. It was a natural thing to do and made it possible to achieve early in my life a sense of identity, something which we are trying now to achieve with the cultural minority groups in our schools. . . .
>
> Phenomenologically, my work world and my social world are a seamless fabric of a continuing experience. This bicultural experience provides me with an active comparative and contrastive set of insights into American and immigrant cultures as continuing lived experiences. . . . I feel that the opportunity to experience cultural conflict and the cultural integrity earned through the resolution of that conflict are vital affective education. (Havighurst, 1978, pp. 15–16)

Anthropology, which has so much to say about culture, has very little to say about biculturalism. The term receives only a small paragraph, as a subheading under the term "acculturation," in the *International Encyclopedia of the Social Sciences* (Sills, 1968, p. 24). As an indication of its obscure standing as a social science term, it is compared to bilingualism rather than defined in its own terms.

Although the term "biculturalism" has not been used extensively in the field of anthropology, the related terms "acculturation" and "assimilation" have been used exhaustively to analyze culture contact. Acculturation is a process by which one cultural group takes on and incorporates one or more cultural traits of another group, resulting in new or blended cultural patterns. As Mexican youngsters, influenced by the media or more "up-to-date" peers, discard their *huaraches,* or laced leather boots, and start wearing jogging shoes, they are acculturating to one outward aspect of contemporary U.S. culture. While these children may adopt some U.S. clothing styles and musical tastes, such things as their language, kinesics, value systems, and social interaction styles remain Mexican. Acculturation can be seen as a means by which biculturalism can develop in certain circumstances, but it can also result in total assimilation. Assimilation is a process in which an individual or group completely takes on the traits of another culture, leaving behind the original cultural identity and being completely absorbed into the new cultural tradition. The absorption of many immigrant groups into mainstream U.S. cultural patterns and social structures has generally been described as a process of assimilation.

The inclination of many anthropologists in the past has been to focus on the imbalance of power when two cultural groups come into contact. Operating from such a perspective, a situation of "stable pluralism," which would allow biculturalism to occur, has been cast in the light of an anomaly, as if it were an abnormal or incomplete chemical reaction (Social Science Research Council, 1954, p. 982). This tendency is related to much early linguistic and psychological work which suggested that bilingualism is an undesirable trait. Diebold (1968) points out that in the past the general consensus was that bilingualism was detrimental to personality development since the knowledge of two languages was thought to imply two separate, culture-bound personality structures operating within the same individual.

When cultural change is viewed in terms of changes in ethnic identity, a different perspective emerges, one which lends itself more easily to the consideration of biculturalism. Ethnicity, as opposed to acculturation or assimilation, emphasizes the maintenance of identity by means of changes in cultural patterns. For example, based on a study of Japanese-Americans and Mexican-Americans, Clark, Kaufman, and Pierce (1976) suggest that culture contact in the United States generates "situational ethnicity." This involves for the individual a range of types of bicultural behavior that vary in their emphasis on traditional versus "American" models. In an investigation of the ethnic identity of Mesquakie Indians, Polgar (1960) found that the teenagers he studied regularly went through a process of biculturation. Through their reservation life and contact with the outside community (especially through the schools) they were said to have been simultaneously enculturated into contemporary American Indian life and mainstream American life. Based on research among Eskimo students in rural Alaska, Kleinfeld has also concluded that institutions such as schools play a highly significant role in the establishment of young people's cultural identities. She has noted that when the following two conditions are present in the life of the minority child, bicultural fusion is enhanced:

1. Significant reference groups in the majority culture (such as teachers, majority-group classmates, media) hold the minority culture in esteem and significant reference groups in the local minority culture (such as parents, peers, older youth who are trendsetters) hold the majority culture in esteem, and

2. Central socialization settings (home, school, religious groups, ethnic organizations) fuse elements from both cultures rather than separate them. (Kleinfeld, 1979, p. 137)

Kleinfeld's findings suggest that schools and communities which have a mutual respect for each other's values and which also exhibit openness and adaptability in their interaction with one another enhance children's ability to function effectively as both members of an ethnic group and participants in American society at large. What happens, then, when schools do not reflect the characteristics outlined by Kleinfeld? Based on observations of black American children, Valentine (1971) suggests that mainstream educational institutions may "block" the successful development of bicultural knowledge because the institutions themselves are operating out of a monocultural rather than bicultural model. But bicultural models, as Spolsky (1978b) points out, are not that easy to pin down for instructional purposes. He contends that generally educators have tended to view biculturalism in terms of modern versus traditional cultures. The "either-or" dichotomy between the modern and the traditional, according to Spolsky, needs to be replaced by an eclectic attitude which encourages a blend of the best features of both culture types. An effective bicultural education, therefore, would be one which accepts "appropriate features of the standard, unmarked civic culture, but without destroying the best features of traditional cultures" (Spolsky, 1978b, p. 24).

Cultural Pluralism   Cultural pluralism characterizes a society in which members of diverse cultural, social, racial, or religious groups are free to maintain their own identity and yet simultaneously share a larger common political organization, economic system, and social structure. It is almost unnecessary to mention that cultural pluralism is an extremely sensitive issue. Biculturalism can, conceivably, be seen as a matter of individual choice, but a positive or a negative stance on pluralism involves the way of life of all Americans, and it touches on the most basic structures of democratic society. With respect to schools in particular, the matter of pluralism raises the following pointed and complex questions:

1. Has the diversity of the constituencies exerting pressure on the public schools become so great as to render the notion that it serves a common goal an illusion?

2. How much cultural pluralism can a society accommodate? How much diversity in curricula, theory, and methods can the public school accommodate?

3. Can we distinguish between good and bad pluralism; between good and bad unity?

4. If some unifying principle is required for the public school to remain public in a fundamental sense, then for what principle can sufficient consensus be reasonably expected to make it possible? (Broudy, 1977, p. 1)

In answer to the second question—how much cultural pluralism can the schools accommodate?—some would say, "none." Epstein (1977b) and Glazer (1981), for example, argue that the business of the school is to promote implicitly the dominant mainstream culture as a means of advancing national character. Both Epstein and Glazer imply that schools should function precisely to homogenize American children, not to promote cultural pluralism by means of such instructional approaches as bilingual or multicultural education. The only two alternatives they see, apparently, are cultural homogeneity and destructive pluralism. But what about positive pluralism, as hinted at by Broudy's question, "Can we distinguish between good and bad pluralism?" (1977, p. 1). Havighurst defines "constructive pluralism" as pluralism that meets the following conditions:

a. Mutual appreciation and understanding of every subculture by the other ones

b. Freedom for each subculture to practice its culture and socialize its children

c. Sharing by each group in the economic and civic life of the society

d. Peaceful coexistence of diverse life styles, folkways, manners, language patterns, religious beliefs and practices, and family structures (Havighurst, 1978, p. 13)

The above interpretation of cultural pluralism is of course an ideal which has so far come quite short of its mark. With respect to public school policy, the controversy cannot be resolved to suit everyone's philosophical, ideological, pedagogical, or programmatic persuasion. Yet the fact remains that school systems across the country have to develop within the context of an ever-growing number of linguistic and ethnic minority students who are just becoming involved in the American experience. All one has to do is listen to what demographers are telling us. The sociocultural texture of American society is rapidly changing to include an increasing number of immigrants, especially from Latin America and Asia. The 1980 census, for example, reveals that as the U.S. fertility rate has decreased in the recent past, immigration has become a larger factor in population growth (President's Commission for a National Agenda for the Eighties, 1980, p. 17). The implications of such demographic shifts are reflected in the following statement:

> Adjusting to certain special immigrant needs—e.g., bilingual education in the schools—will assume even greater importance. Because discrimination has not been overcome, ethnic and racial minorities will continue to face special problems in finding employment and housing and in obtaining equal access to education. As the numbers of immigrants and minorities grow, it will be important—no matter what the economic circumstances of the coming decade—to take serious account of the problems facing these groups in formulating public policy. These groups will, in turn, be able to wield power in the political arena, fostering greater pluralism in America and, ideally, playing an important role in the coalition-building process. (President's Commission for a National Agenda for the Eighties, 1980, p. 17)

Conscious positive treatment of multiple cultures in the classroom can play an important role in fostering pluralism. And it can become an integral part of the schooling process without creating a danger to any postulated national character, as Epstein and Glazer suggest. National character, if it can be identified, is not something of a straitjacket—an all-encompassing yet vague force that causes particular types of behavior in particular groups. It has always been a developing and adjustable framework, very responsive to social and economic conditions. It would be very difficult to compare the "typical American citizen" of 1784 with the "typical American citizen" of 1984, if we could find them. In this sense, human interaction can be perceived as the continual and active construction and reconstruction of cultural patterns (Barth, 1967; Blumer, 1969; Geertz, 1973). This means that each person is in everyday life recreating, modifying, or interpreting his or her own cultural background.

How does this creative and flexible concept of culture help resolve the issue of unity versus diversity? It illustrates that cultural diversity does not necessarily equal total divergence of interests. Maintenance of any ethnic identity within the United States is not a result of adherence to rigid cultural laws but occurs within the context of adjustments to national social, economic, and cultural conditions. Language-minority children in a school which values their ethnic heritage would be highly unlikely, as a consequence of such schooling, to lock themselves into all the behaviors and values traditionally held by members of their ethnic group. While remaining secure in their ethnic identity, they would more likely alter some of the characteristics of that identity as they experiment with new behaviors that are effective in new social contexts.

As the growing number of children from non-English-language backgrounds receives greater opportunities for a linguistically and culturally sensitive education, there can be short-term and long-term social, cultural, and economic benefits for all Americans. A curriculum that allows *all* children (minority and nonminority) to become successful participants in the educational process can help mend social and economic tears in the national fabric. For a democratic, pluralistic, and complex society to function true to its underlying premises, its members need an awareness of their responsibilities as citizens, and they need skills to carry out these responsibilities. Learning to get along in a multicultural society should be an imperative of the schooling process, not a neglected option.

CONCEPTS RELATED TO CULTURE AND EDUCATION

The mission of the schools is most simply described as providing students with the explicitly necessary academic, social, and civic skills for negotiation with life in the dominant mainstream society. However, the purposes of the schools "encompass not only what is taught and learned, but also the organization, patterns, and process of education in their social and cultural settings" (Kimball, 1974, p. 25). To understand how cultural research and theory fit into the life of the classroom it helps to compare how educators and cultural anthropologists view their professions. In this regard, Kimball's assessment of their respective roles vis-à-vis schooling is appropriate:

> The sharpest differentiation between educator and anthropologist is likely to appear in the perspective, definition, and solution of educational problems. Teachers, school administrators, and other educational specialists are primarily trained for and engaged in activities subsumed under instruction. In contrast, the anthropologist, proceeding from the perspective of his disci-

pline, seeks to describe the social system and cultural behavior within the educational institution and to place it in the context of the community. (1974, p. 26)

Exploration of education for language-minority students with a map drawn from cultural analysis is important. Understanding concepts and research related to culture in multiethnic classrooms can help us to discover the "hidden curriculum"—that is, the implicit lessons taught and implicit messages sent among students, teachers, parents, and administrators.

When educators, politicians, or citizens notice that a particular segment of the school population is not profiting adequately from the educational system, the search for explanatory causes begins. Explanations, of course, are heavily colored by the assumptions on which they are based. For example, the procedure in the past was often to place recently arrived ethnic minority students in the lowest curriculum track, along with English-speaking children of the lowest achievement and ability levels. The apparent assumption was that lack of English-language skills equaled lack of academic potential (Moore, 1967). Then, rather than taking some of the blame for subsequent academic failure, the school system was apt to blame the victims for not taking advantage of its curricular options. One study found that in the past Hispanic children were more than twelve times as likely as white or black children to be candidates for educable mentally retarded programs based on IQ scores (Figueroa, 1980). Terms and concepts used in explanations tell a lot about the underlying assumptions. To evaluate explanations or descriptions of what happens to students of non-English-language background in school, and to observe and assess better what happens in one's own classroom with respect to the larger national setting, it is useful to examine the meanings and implications of concepts which play a role in how multiethnic educational issues are viewed. The concepts to be considered here are cultural deprivation, marked and unmarked cultures, ethnocentrism and cultural relativism, stereotypes, socioeconomic status as it relates to cultural background, cultural transmission and acquisition of ethnicity, and language variation.

Cultural Deprivation and Cultural Deficit

One of the various handles researchers and educators have used to explain why so many language-minority students achieve at lower levels than mainstream students is the concept of cultural deprivation, or cultural deficit. When unpacking this concept, one finds that what usually is implied is that the beliefs, values, and behaviors of minority children represent a view of life which borders on the pathological. In the United States the idea that some immigrant group's cultural traits are undesirable dates back at least to the second half of the nineteenth century, when the country experienced an influx of foreign-born workers. In an effort to eliminate the undesirable traits, many public schools with large numbers of immigrant students made Americanization classes an integral part of the curriculum. These classes included instruction in "dominant (WASP) cultural values, practices, beliefs, and traditions" (Franklin, 1983, p. 9).

In the 1960s as the federal government focused attention on efforts to improve the achievement of low-income and minority children, approaches based on concepts such as cultural deficit were used to analyze and explain the reasons for school failure. The basic premise was that the home sociocultural environment deprived the children of values and skills which they needed to succeed in school. Related to the civil rights movement, much of the research being done at this time focused on black Americans. Reflective of the pathological approach to the study of black Americans' educational and socioeconomic achievement was the Moynihan Report, issued in 1965 (Ryan, 1971, pp. 61–64). This report suggested that black cultural values produced an unstable, disorganized form of family life, and therefore that changes in education and employment opportunities would not help blacks advance unless the family was first strengthened and stabilized. Oscar Lewis' in-depth study of life among poverty-stricken urban Mexicans, which led to his concept of the "culture of poverty," also affected public policies and programs. Lewis speculated that a culture of poverty may perpetuate itself from generation to generation, with the implication that as children become enculturated into the supposedly problematic values and behaviors characteristic of their culture of poverty, they are unable to take advantage of greater educational and economic opportunities (Lewis, 1966; Ryan, 1971).

In the search for ways to improve educational opportunities for minority and low-income students, the idea of cultural deprivation provided a direction: change the child—not the teacher or the teaching methods or the political structure of school control. Although Lewis was very tentative in his conclusions regarding the culture of poverty and did not intend that the concept be applied in all low-income contexts, the cultural deprivation framework was an appealing one for educators looking for solutions. As a glaring example, an assistant superintendent of the Boston public schools stated that minority students' achievement had been thwarted by "parental lack of values" (Ryan, 1971, p. 32).

During this period, researchers and educators sometimes described "culturally deprived" children as present- rather than future-oriented, nonverbal rather than verbal, preferring immediate rather than delayed gratification, favoring concrete over abstract tasks, too dependent on the social environment for learning support, coming from fragmented families, being fatalistic, or lacking achievement motivation. And the list goes on: They were noncompetitive, didn't have proper role models in the immediate family, didn't have good study environments, had no reading materials in the home, and had insufficient early-childhood verbal stimulation. Heller (1968) and Madsen (1964), for example, gave accounts of such traits within the Chicano population.

Since the 1970s, however, many of the cultural deprivation categorizations have been dismissed as being inaccurate. As Saville-Troike points out in a review of literature on Mexican-American children, "Almost no generalizations about [them] can be substantiated by objective research" (1973, p. 32). As Ryan (1971) argues in his critique of cultural deprivation models, two of the traits ascribed to "culturally deprived" blacks were lack of interest in education and limited development of verbal skills, yet empirical research data fail to substantiate the validity of such traits. Valentine (1968), another early critic of the cultural deprivation model, concludes in a similar vein that "analysis in terms of 'the culture of poverty' may distract attention from crucial structural characteristics of the stratified social system as a whole" (p. 17). That is, any alleged "undesirable" traits need to be interpreted as products of economic and social stratification rather than as integral cultural characteristics of particular socioeconomically stigmatized subcultural groups.

Nonetheless, the idea that there is something wrong with minority cultural patterns continues to exist in many school settings. An analysis of teacher attitudes in a south-Texas, 75 percent Mexican-American community found that some teachers felt that Mexican culture encouraged low achievement, lack of industriousness, lack of discipline, and unwise use of money (Meadowcroft & Foley, 1978). The following notes from a 1978 staff development meeting at a predominantly Hispanic, low-income school in California also illustrate the survival of the cultural-deficit point of view:

> The principal describes to his teachers an open-structured, unregimented, very pleasant school which he has just evaluated. Involved in court-ordered integration, the school has a high proportion of white, English-speaking children of professional parents, with a sprinkling of Asians and Hispanics. The principal suggests to his staff that perhaps their own school is too concerned with straight lines and law-and-order issues. One teacher with 25 years of experience in the community becomes very upset and states, "Well, of course that school can afford to be unstructured, because those kids get a *lot* of structure at home. On the other hand, 'our kids' don't get any structure at home, so they have to have a lot of structure at school. *Our kids need structure*."

The concept of cultural deprivation is contradictory to the deep, complex, changing, and natural view of culture taken in this chapter. A person's intelligence is developed and operationalized relative to the home cultural system. Before it is claimed that a particular behavior is inappropriate because it mirrors unfamiliar patterns of action, the sociocultural and linguistic context must be understood. In his work among Eskimos, Athapaskans, and Aleuts, Collier discovered that "one of the casualties of acculturation, moving from one system of values to another, is that effective intelligence (the intelligence that worked in the original or home environment) can get left behind" (1973, p. 3). Thus accurate knowledge of how children function in their natural environments, often lacking among school personnel, is a prerequisite to judging fairly their academic worth. De Avila and Duncan (1979a), who have conducted cognitive development studies on bilingual students, argue that basic underlying cognitive skills are not tied to a particular sociocultural environment. Thus the challenge is not to change the child but to design the curriculum and pedagogy to tap the student's cognitive potential.

Because the concept of cultural deprivation violates basic principles of rational human adaptation to specific sociocultural contexts, it has come into disrepute among social scientists and educators. Today there is increasing awareness that all cultures have a built-in rationale for living. Such designs may be *different,* but they are not deprived. Children in bilingual and ESL classrooms, regardless of the prevailing cultural norms of the school, represent linguistic and cultural patterns which serve them well in their home environment.

Marked and Unmarked Languages and Cultures

The concept of cultural deprivation tends to place a negative value on ethnic or racial minority subcultures, and/or to confuse political, economic, and social issues with cultural ones. Focusing more on political and socioeconomic structures, the terms "marked and unmarked language," and by extension, "marked and unmarked culture," distinguish between the different degrees of status assigned to particular cultural groups, without assigning an absolute positive or negative value to them. The terms were coined by Fishman (1976), a linguist who has analyzed the education of language-minority students from a broad, international perspective. In the context of bilingual education, Fishman defines a marked language as one "which would most likely *not* be used *instructionally* were it not for bilingual education, that is to say, it is precisely bilingual education that has brought it into the classroom. Conversely, a language is *unmarked* in a bilingual education setting [if it] would most likely continue to be used instructionally, even in the absence of bilingual education" (1976, pp. 99–100). In other words, marked languages are the ones associated with less social status and political power. In the United States the unmarked language is standard English.

Expanding the concepts of marked and unmarked languages to the groups they most closely represent, unmarked culture in the United States tends to be associated with white, middle-class, Protestant, nonethnic, English-speaking groups. It is unmarked in the sense that it reflects a somewhat mythical generalization of the way the typical American is "supposed" to be. Marked culture, on the other hand, is associated with the stigmatized and sometimes subordinate status of socioeconomically or culturally defined minority groups. Most curricula in public schools in the United States tend to emphasize the unmarked cultural values, because formal education is the institution through which children are prepared for modern society. Using the concepts of marked and unmarked languages and cultures at an intuitive level, classroom teachers probably subconsciously place most of their students into one category or the other based on social, economic, racial, cultural, and linguistic criteria.

Spolsky (1978b), drawing on the work of Fishman (1976) and Lewis (1972), notes that throughout the world unmarked languages and cultures tend to be associated with such traits as internationalism, technological development, mass literacy, emphasis on civic citizenship over membership in a small community, a standard language, compilation of scientific knowledge, and academic literature and art. Marked languages and cultural groups tend to be more strongly associated with traditional structures, values, and institutions. While acknowledging that the posited traditional traits of a marked culture are difficult to unravel from socioeconomically related traits which may be independent of ethnicity, Spolsky suggests that one goal of bilingual education should be to enable language-minority students to experience unmarked civic life outside the boundaries of their marked culture without being alienated. For schools to allow this would imply their acceptance of the blending of characteristics of the unmarked and marked cultures. He describes such a conscious synthesis of marked and unmarked cultural patterns as follows:

> Rather than setting modern against traditional as thesis and antithesis, educators should be working toward a synthesis of postmodernism, an approach that attempts to recognize the best in each and permit the development of a series of new blends, different for each ethnic group, but common in recognizing the strengths and weaknesses of both modern and traditional cultures. (Spolsky, 1978b, p. 28)

Ethnocentrism and Cultural Relativity

Ethnocentrism can emerge in many different configurations within the multiethnic classroom. Ethnocentric reactions may occur on the part of the teacher toward the student, on the part of the student toward the teacher, between students, on the part of the parent toward the teacher, and so on. A negative ethnocentric reaction to another person's culturally based behaviors or values may range from unspoken feelings whose source one is not even aware of to explicit verbal responses. The sense of group identity attained by denigrating another group is demonstrated with the following story. After India gained its independence from Britain and there was a strong push to soften the rigid caste system, a group of idealistic students supposedly approached some members of the Harijan caste (the untouchables) and started to talk with them about the past injustices of the caste system. The students suggested to the Harijans that they should become politically involved and elect officials who would improve their lot. No sooner had the speaker finished his speech, when one of the outcast members said, "The only way the system can improve is to develop another group below us so that we can look down upon them."

In societies with myriad representations of cultures, such as the United States, the balance between cultural pride and negative ethnocentrism is delicate. Just how much ethnocentrism is innocuous cultural pride and how much is damaging to the social fabric? Consider the emotional high among thousands of Hispanics that a well-known Mexican pitcher generates when he wins a crucial game at Dodger Stadium. This may be a fairly harmless type of ethnocentrism, even a healthy cultural pride, but what happens to the self-concept of a language-minority child who absorbs so many negative evaluations of his cultural background that by the time he is 10 he prefers to hide his ethnicity as much as possible and avoids being seen with his parents? Or, conversely, what happens when, as Banks (1984) suggests, stigmatized minorities in the United States feel that one way to survive, at least psychologically, is to accentuate differences, preferably those differences which denigrate the unmarked culture? Bidney suggests that cultural pride itself need not be equated with ethnocentrism. He states that it is not "the mere fact of preference for one's own cultural values that constitutes ethnocentrism but, rather, the uncritical prejudice in favor of one's own culture and the distorted, biased criticism of alien cultures" (1968, p. 546).

Cultural relativism, as a guide to the evaluation of value systems, serves as an antidote to the damaging effects which conscious or unconscious ethnocentrism can have on the emotional and academic development of children. Cultural relativism, as described by Bidney, involves "tolerance based on skepticism of universal, objective standards of value as well as the idea of progress" (1968, p. 547). Cultural relativism as a philosophical doctrine which implies that there are no universal norms that are valued for all cultures raises many ethical problems. Is ritualized human sacrifice or the maintenance of large nuclear arsenals, for example, to be considered objectively acceptable on the basis of adherence to cultural relativism? As a *method,* however, for coming to understand a cultural system and for viewing cultural change, cultural relativism is basic to all cultural inquiry. It constitutes an attempt to interpret data from the viewpoint of the people being observed or studied, rather than applying the values of one's own cultural system to the subject (Bidney, 1968, p. 543). The novelist (and former anthropology student) Kurt Vonnegut, in an introduction to a children's book, proposes cultural relativism as a way of looking at how people may interpret their multiple worlds.

> . . . one thing I would really like to tell them [children] about is cultural relativity. I didn't learn until I was in college about all the other cultures, and I should have learned that in the first grade. A first grader should understand that his or her culture isn't a rational invention; that there are thousands of other cultures and they all work pretty well; that all cultures function on faith rather than on truth; that there are lots of alternatives to our own society. Cultural relativity is defensible and attractive. It's also a source of hope. It means we don't have to continue this way if we don't like it. (1974, p. 139)

Cultural relativity is, of course, easier to talk about than to practice in the classroom, especially when members of cultural groups subscribe to beliefs, values, or behaviors which run counter to those prescribed for traditional educational settings in the United States. For example, from a culturally relative point of view, standard and nonstandard versions of a language are of equal validity in terms of performing the function of communicating a message. Yet within the classroom it becomes very difficult for the teacher to accept the nonstandard dialect as a valid one and still believe he or she is providing adequate standard-language preparation for the students to attain social and economic gains. To consider another example, teacher-training institutions consider ability to use standard English as part of the requirements for becoming certified. An aspiring Alaskan teacher who wished to return to teach in her home village, however, expressed doubts to one of the authors as to whether teacher certification was worth the price of alienating herself from her home community by giving up her "bush" English.

All of us grow up with a basic core of set values; to have to reexamine them vis-à-vis other modes of behavior can be a disturbing task. The value of cultural relativity, nevertheless, comes with exposure to cultural variation, which can yield more tolerance for other ways of acting. From the relativistic point of view, the British do not drive on the *wrong* side of the road. They simply drive on the *other* side of the road.

To achieve the perspective of cultural relativism, understanding the *underlying premises* for behavior is as important as understanding the behavior itself. Culture is accumulated learning, and as such it involves a long history of people responding as needed to environmental conditions and problems. Consider another example from the Alaskan bush: An imported teacher from the "lower 48" was trying very hard to have her Athapaskan youngsters develop cuddly feelings for a pet rabbit that she had brought to the classroom. When the children responded in unexpected ways she became very puzzled and uneasy. After all, she had assumed that all children liked rabbits as pets. What she had ignored was that in the children's subsistence-oriented environment, a rabbit was more likely to be considered a source of food than something to be petted. From the children's point of view, it was the teacher's behavior that was "wrong."

Stereotypes

Although we have all been victims as well as users of stereotypes, they become particularly significant when talking about marked cultural groups. For instance, Latinos, or Hispanics, are often lumped into one group. Judging from the media, one might assume that they all like to shout *olé* or overthrow generals on a routine basis. Latinos, however, are not an easily identifiable group. Because of relative proximity to their homeland, most Latinos have been able to maintain a variety of linkages with their countries of origin, although which linkages they maintain and which customs they shed vary extensively. Latinos form a cultural, social, and historical mosaic. Mexicans eat tortillas, but Cubans do not. Most Hispanics are associated with Catholicism, but a growing number are Protestant. Some have become so acculturated that they speak little or no Spanish, while many have maintained a strong language loyalty. Most Latinos in the Southwest are second only to American Indians as our earliest residents, but many more are newcomers who have immigrated during this century. Many have strong ties with a rural tradition, while many more are firmly rooted within the urban context. Some families have chosen to preserve the custom of the *quinceañera*,* while

*A special observance of a girl's fifteenth birthday, usually involving a mass and a party or dance.

others have dropped it altogether. Even within one single Mexican-American barrio, one encounters many Mexican-Americans, not "the typical Mexican-American." Here is a description of El Hoyo, a Chicano neighborhood in Tucson, Arizona, by the author Mario Suárez:

> Perhaps El Hoyo, its inhabitants, and its essence can best be explained by telling a bit about a dish called *capirotada*. Its origin is uncertain. But, according to the time and the circumstance, it is made of old, new, or hard bread. It is softened with water and then cooked with peanuts, raisins, onions, cheese, and *panocha*. It is fired with sherry wine. Then it is served hot, cold, or just "on the weather" as they say in El Hoyo. The Sermeños like it one way, the Garcías like it another, and the Ortegas still another. While it might differ greatly from one home to another, nevertheless it is still *capirotada*. And so it is with El Hoyo's Chicanos. (Suárez, 1973, p. 102)

Sex roles are one type of cultural pattern which gives rise to stereotypical perceptions. All cultural groups have developed expectations, attitudes, and values associated with a person's gender, and mechanisms to maintain these expectations, such as the family, have been institutionalized. There are socialization patterns present in every culture which encourage certain behaviors along a perceived continuum from masculinity to femininity. Consequently, outsiders to a culture may expect masculine or feminine behavior of a group member to conform to stereotyped notions. If these notions appear to be in conflict with the predominant values expressed in the school, one may expect problems to arise. The real problem, however, may be that actual behavior patterns can change much faster than stereotypes do. Traditionally, little importance was placed on formal education for girls in Mexican society, for example, but today there is research that suggests that some Mexican-American girls place a higher value on education than their male counterparts (Cárdenas, 1970, p. 204).

Region of origin may account for some of the deviation a child shows from stereotyped patterns of behavior for a given cultural group. Just as in the United States there is a great variety of regional cultural patterns, there are also very striking regional differences within the countries of origin of most immigrant families. Among Cambodians established in the United States, for example, some may be offspring of Hmong tribesmen, who are from rural, nontechnological mountain villages, while others may be the children of white-collar apartment dwellers from Phnom Penh. Although all of them are Cambodians, the behavior and adjustment patterns exhibited by the two groups will be considerably different. The significance of place of origin also explains why one Mexican first grader in a school composed predominantly of recent immigrants doesn't "seem" like the other children and occasionally points out to her teacher and peers that her family is from the city of Ensenada, rather than from a small farm or *rancho*. She has taken upon herself the responsibility of making sure that the teacher doesn't stereotype her.

Because of the cultural damage stereotypes have inflicted on individuals and groups over time, educators are not "supposed" to have positive feelings toward them. Saville-Troike (1978) uses stereotypes as an example of what should *not* be done when analyzing cultures in the classroom. And yet, like some undesirable insects in nature, they do not seem to go away no matter how hard we try to eradicate them. Some educators argue that precisely because stereotyping is here to stay we should harness the concept in such a way that it undergoes critical analysis, carefully distinguishing for instance between personal traits and ethnic traits (Bem, 1970; Longstreet, 1978). For the teacher it becomes a process of balancing an awareness of general cultural or subcultural traits with an affirmation of the absolute uniqueness of every child, and of contrasting the cultural variations represented by students with the existing stereotypes. As a step toward teaching in the bilingual or ESL classroom, it is valuable to assess the diversity already existing within the school's cultural microcosm. In a multiethnic environment, the interplay between stereotyped behavior patterns and personal patterns is amazingly intricate for children as they adjust to their culturally varied settings—home versus television, school versus the street, first-generation adult values versus second-generation youth values, and so on. Seelye and Wasilewski suggest that multicultural environments provide a medium for much conscious and unconscious cultural experimentation on the part of children:

> The multicultural child begins life less able than the monocultural child to indulge in "thinking as usual" because he or she is the inheritor of a cultural pattern which provides alternative "recipes."
>
> As to the ability to deploy appropriate responses in the multicultural context, a child is always learning new responses to old stimuli, old responses to new stimuli, and totally new stimulus-response patterns. The child is always engaged in trying to figure out when to generalize a response across situations and when to contextualize responses, i.e., how to behave appropriately in different contexts. (1979, pp. 24–25)

The sociocultural background of the child in the bilingual or ESL classroom, therefore, may not emerge in clear-cut stereotyped patterns but in unexpected types of behavior. In understanding a student's behavior, it is helpful to strike a balance between a totally stereotypic perspective and a totally individualized perspective that does not take into account the powerful molding forces of culture.

Students and parents, of course, bring their own stereotypic views to the bilingual or ESL classroom. Some Chicano children may arrive in the kindergarten classroom with unconsciously formed expectations about *gabacho* (mainstream American) behavior based on parents' or older siblings' perceptions. A Korean immigrant parent may approach his first meeting with an American teacher with certain assumptions about the teacher's high degree of permissiveness. In understanding students' and parents' interethnic behavior in school situations, it is valuable for the teacher to remember that their actions are also colored by stereotypic expectations.

Socioeconomic Status and Cultural Background

Information related to socioeconomic status (SES) can account for some of the variations in cultural beliefs, values, and behaviors within an ethnic group. While in theory anthropologists and sociologists may have much to say on the subject, in practice it is very difficult to isolate clearly socioeconomic from cultural factors. Culture exists only within some social grouping of people, and every society is characterized by a set or various subsets of cultural patterns. In the United States, for example, certain differences in behavior attributed to culture could alternatively be analyzed from the point of view of social class. Educators have often noted that certain groups of students and parents have a tendency to avoid eye contact or to look down during interactions with teachers. This trait has been described as a culturally based behavior characteristic of Mexican-Americans, blacks, and Native Americans. However, such eye contact behavior can also be analyzed from the point of view of social class, reflecting the socioeconomically subordinate status of certain groups.

Another factor that is believed to reflect cultural values which affect achievement in American society is language. To communicate "I missed the bus," a Spanish speaker would likely say, *"El camión me dejó."* Literally this would be translated in English as "The bus left me." Peñalosa notes that such a language pattern has been used to suggest that speakers of Spanish tend toward irresponsibility and fatalism. He rejects this interpretation, stating that Mexican-Americans have an economic and political problem in the United States, not a language problem: "Analyses of Chicano linguistic and social behavior which proceed from culture analysis rather than class analysis are likely to be fallacious and only perpetuate stereotypes" (1980, p. 3).

The ability to perceive the relation between SES and cultural background variables is important in the context of bilingual and ESL instruction, because the terms "ethnic group," "minority," and "limited-English-proficient" are often associated with lower SES. They do not always go hand in hand, however. Using a typology which distinguishes between ethnic groups that have been relatively successful socioeconomically and those that are not benefiting fully from the social structures, Havighurst illustrates a variety of patterns which emerge through the interplay of ethnic identity, cultural models, and socioeconomic structures. Six groups are identified based on the way in which they fit into the U.S. socioeconomic structure:

A. Groups that are getting along fairly well, with present education and socioeconomic arrangements

   A1. Through religious and other cultural institutions (for example, Jews and Greeks)

   A2. Through family associations which assist individual families in socializing the children and through maintaining a good standard of living for members of the community (for example, Chinese, Hutterites, Amish, Black Muslims)

   A3. Upper-middle-class segments of racial-ethnic groups which have a large working-class component that is not so well off (for example, long-established Latinos of the Southwest, middle-class blacks, eastern and southern Europeans)

B. Groups which are not fairly served by existing economic and educational opportunities for minorities

   B1. Blacks (working class) in urban and rural areas

   B2. Latinos (working class) in urban and rural areas

   B3. Numerically small minority groups who are economically disadvantaged (for example, American Indians and Philippinos) (1978, pp. 14–18)

Havighurst reports that approximately one-fifth of the ethnic minorities served in the nation's school systems belong to group A, those who are getting along fairly well (1978, p. 16). Research in language-minority education, however, has largely ignored the role that SES plays in the education of language-minority students. Troike notes that of seven shortcomings found to invalidate most bilingual education "outcome" research, the principal shortcoming was a lack of control for SES (1978, p. 4). While an awareness of cultural differences which may affect academic achievement is certainly necessary, it would be inaccurate in examining the education of language-minority children to ignore socioeconomic areas of incompatibility, such as income level and negative societal perceptions of group characteristics (Cárdenas & Cárdenas, 1973).

Interestingly, SES affects not only the stereotypes developed regarding students' cultural backgrounds, but also the way language-minority education as a whole is viewed. For example, the degree of acceptance of the use of Spanish by Hispanic children in school has been related to the income level of those students. The U.S. Commission on Civil Rights in a 1972 study found that the no-Spanish rule "was more likely to be enforced when the proportion of Chicanos in the school was high and the socioeconomic status of the population was low" (Peñalosa, 1980, p.11). Bilingual education often has been associated with other "poverty programs," falling under the rubric of compensatory education. Some observers argue that the compensatory status ascribed to bilingual instruction has to some degree stigmatized it and therefore lessened its success (Fishman, 1976, p. 9). One bilingual teacher reflects on her feeling that bilingual education would not be so culturally threatening to its opponents if it were not associated with low-income groups.

> If I were telling people that I taught in a French/English program at an elite private school, I think it would be easy to rave about the virtues of bilingual education and get agreement from virtually everyone. But that is not quite the context of my school, which is about 95% minority and in one of the lowest income neighborhoods of the city. My students are too often perceived as problems rather than as promises, as members of the "culture of poverty" whose cultural values need to be changed. Because of this, I think many people lose sight of the asset that bilingualism can be to anyone and tend to focus on the fear that language-minority students, because of bilingual education, might not be properly socialized to fit into the mainstream United States sociocultural system.

Cultural Transmission and Acquisition of Ethnicity

A lifelong student of cultural transmission in Western and non-Western societies, Mead (1978) has concluded that, contrary to early notions of social scientists, the process by which new members learn the scope and detail of their own culture is not, and never has been, a smooth and painless one. The cultural adjustments taking place among language-minority families in the United States occur in a variety of ways and directions. The intrafamily means of cultural transmission are explored through Mead's paradigm, in which she looks at culture as mediated by parents and children in specific contexts. She refers to three kinds of cultural transmission processes: postfigurative, cofigurative, and prefigurative.

Postfigurative Transmission   This term refers to the process by which values, beliefs, and behaviors of a specific community are passed on to the upcoming generation with little alteration. Usually in such contexts the children do not question much the cultural patterns which they have received from familiar and respected ancestors. In the United States, the Amish and Hutterite subcultures most closely represent postfigurative processes. In such cases parental and communal values may be more powerful and more important than those of the school. Immigrants from traditional or rural societies may also have a background of strong postfigurative cultural transmission.

Cofigurative Transmission   Unlike postfigurative communities, in which the cultural mores are received only from respected forebears, in the cofigurative phase communities have multiple cultural role models—old ones and contemporary ones. Emergent cultural values may be attributed to the sharing between parents and children at a time when the traditional cultural patterns have lost the power of seduction over the young. Cofigurative communities may also be represented in immigrant groups which are partially disengaging from the past and beginning to relate in different ways with their children growing up in the United States. "But Mom, that's not the way you do it here," may be a beginning signal that culture change is occurring within the ethnic community.

Prefigurative Transmission   In this cultural transmission phase the children to a large extent create culture change. Immigrant parents in prefigurative situations vicariously experience much of American society and culture through their children. The reality that such children present to their parents has been secured from the formal school system and from many informal channels—peers, street culture, television, radio, magazines, newspapers, clubs, and organizations. Their offsprings' questioning and innovative ways may often bewilder nonnative parents. These children are also frequently the source of many answers for their parents' concerns. They serve as translators at the doctor's office, for example, or they write the school absence excuse for their younger siblings. Virtually everything new is filtered through the children, who frequently put aside old values as being obsolete. Frustration and stress sometimes begin to characterize many of the interactions between parents and children.

While varying degrees of prefigurative cultural transmission are ubiquitous within all groups in the United States, when the values of ancestral countries or cultures are cast against the backdrop of contemporary U.S. society, the issues become even more complex. Children, adolescents in particular, whose parents represent vividly different traditions (to which their offspring are not necessarily sympathetic) can be very unwilling to incorporate parents into the life of the schools. Students may even resent having their parents in school for fear that their peers may ridicule them. This potential embarrassment may be rooted in the perceived lack of congruity between the gradually vanishing world of their parents and their modern world in the United States. As Handlin puts it, referring to the acculturation process across generations, "the young wore their [U.S.] nativity like a badge that marked their superiority over their immigrant elders" (1951, pp. 253–254).

The acquisition of culture can be analyzed not only across generations, as Mead has done, but also as a developmental process within the child. Age is a factor in the way in which young people take on the cultural traits of their environment. Based on Piaget's work regarding the onset of abstract thinking skills, Longstreet suggests that up until the stage of formal operations, about age 11 or 12, ethnicity is acquired by children as if by osmosis, without much rational analysis.

> Children are not in full command of their intellectual powers when they are acquiring early cultural traits. It must be kept in mind that the onset of the human being's abstract thinking powers occurs somewhere between the ages of ten and twelve. Prior to this stage, children have only a limited capacity to judge ways of behaving that they are absorbing. The way they address an adult, how they say their sentences, even when they smile are shaped at "gut level" long before they know what they are doing. (1978, p. 19)

Longstreet postulates that ethnicity, which can be seen as a subset of culture, is that part of life which we all internalize prior to being able to give it much thought:

> Ethnicity is that portion of cultural development that occurs before the individual is in complete command of his or her abstract intellectual powers and that is formed primarily through the individual's early contacts with family, neighbors, friends, teachers, and others, as well as with his immediate environment of the home and neighborhood. (1978, p. 19)

From this point of view, much of the stuff from which our cultural backgrounds are derived was absorbed without critical analysis. Even after we are fully developed cognitively, therefore, we may still be captive to beliefs, values, and behaviors which have been unconsciously and uncritically internalized. For example, through visual, auditory, and kinesthetic "imprinting" as young children we have absorbed many subtle attitudes regarding variations in physical appearance, styles of verbal communication, and physical movement. We also absorb images of appropriate family roles.

In developing her approach, Longstreet draws a distinction between the culturally (not genetically) inherited ethnicity discussed above and scholastic ethnicity. However, she sees the process of acquiring scholastic ethnicity as similar to the acquisition of cultural ethnicity.

> Learning to be a student has many of the characteristics of learning to be a member of an ethnic group. A whole way of living is assimilated both from one's family life and from one's school life. The family way may not be at all like the scholastic way—or there may be many points of similarity and compatibility. (1978, p. 22)

Finally, Longstreet proposes a possible third ethnicity for children beyond the home ethnic heritage and the scholastic ethnicity. This is an American ethnicity which is transmitted primarily through the mass media. Therefore, the complexity of unpacking the cultural background of an elementary student increases as one admits the possibility of three distinct ethnicities which the student unknowingly carries. A language-minority child who has developed to Piaget's formal stage of thinking will absorb, modify, or react to scholastic ethnicity and American ethnicity more consciously than a younger child whose cognitive skills are not as well developed.

Language Variation and Home-School Mismatch

Languages function to enable humans to communicate messages to one another, but as an integral aspect of culture they also allow us to make other judgments beyond the basic message. "Mary doesn't live here anymore" and "Mary don't live here no more" both convey information as to Mary's current place of residence, but they also convey information about the sociocultural background of the speaker. Languages and their dialects symbolize and identify group memberships and are the principal means of mediating and manipulating social relations. They are a framework for the evaluation of others' social background, prestige, and personality as well as ethnicity (Saville-Troike, 1980).

In the United States, many of the children who qualify for bilingual or ESL instruction represent linguistic backgrounds that might be perceived by the college-educated teacher as "deficient." Such judgments are unconsciously woven in with judgments of the quality of the child's cultural background. Among children themselves, when a LEP child begins to communicate in English, her speech patterns may suggest to her fluent English-speaking peers that she lacks intelligence. Consider the following dialogue among three elementary-school students:

> Three middle-class teachers who work at a largely Hispanic elementary school have come in on a Saturday to catch up, in preparation for a state evaluation team. These teachers have brought their daughters with them, all of whom attend middle-class elementary schools. The two English-speaking, white girls and one very acculturated Mexican-American girl are working at a table cutting out decorations when a local mother comes into the classroom and carries on an extended conversation in Spanish with one of the teachers. After the mother leaves, this conversation arises among the children:
>
> Linda (Mexican-American): I know how to speak Spanish—my grandmother taught me. But I don't like to!
>
> Laurie: I know. There's a girl in my class who all she does is speak Spanish and she's so *dumb!* All she does is copy my work.
>
> Jennifer: People who speak Spanish aren't dumb. They just can't help it.

Culture is dynamic, and consequently, language along with culture is continuously changing. As subgroups within a larger group experience different types and degrees of sociocultural contact and historical circumstances, dialects or variations in the language emerge. The linguistic variation found among students in bilingual and ESL classrooms is an expression of the modifications that subcultural groups experience. To illustrate the extent of language variation which can exist in the school setting, a bilingual teacher has identified three varieties of English and three varieties of Spanish in her classroom. Each variety carries with it information about the cultural background of the speaker.

> Between the students and the teachers we speak a total of six socially coded dialects in our classroom. Instruction officially goes on in the standard forms of English and Spanish, but students use two other varieties of English— black English and Chicano English—and two other versions of Spanish— Chicano Spanish and a rural northern Mexican variety.

The child from a non-English-speaking background who has spent most or all of his life in an ethnic enclave may have quite a challenge in developing a standard form of either the home language or English. Much of the English heard in the street and among peers is nonstandard. English also tends to influence the home language, which may not have been a high status variety to begin with. A bilingual-education researcher describes his personal questioning of his language identity:

> With what language was I raised? What language do I speak in the Chicano community? Is it Spanish? Is it English? Is it even a language? Early in my elementary school days I learned that I was not speaking English; and later, in high school, when I was enrolled in what I thought would be an easy course, Spanish, I was told that I didn't speak Spanish! (Carrasco, 1981b, p. 191)

The natural occurrence of code-switching and language borrowing in all situations in which two languages come in contact, can be misinterpreted as confusion of the two languages. Nonlinguists sometimes refer to any blend of Spanish and English created in language borrowing as "Spanglish." Consider the word *grocería*. A Nicaraguan living in the Midwest may use this word to refer to a grocery store, when in fact *grosería* (spelled differently, but pronounced the same way) is an expletive. Although the person knows the "correct" Spanish word for grocery store, *mercado*, he or she is strongly influenced by the English environment. This person's daughters and sons, however, growing up hearing predominantly *grocería*, may have lost the original Spanish word *mercado*. Another example of what may happen when two languages come into contact is code-switching, discussed in chapter 3. For example, a bilingual Mexican-American child might say to another Mexican-American peer, "*Andale, pues,* I don't know," or "Gimme the ball, *que le voy a decir a la maestra.*"

Students who use nonstandard varieties of their first and second languages and make use of language borrowing and code-switching strategies have sometimes been labeled "alingual" or "semilingual" by school personnel. Although theoretical descriptions have discussed the term "semilingualism," it has never been proved to exist in experimental research conducted on the issue. Students' relative proficiency in each language is limited only by knowledge of the standard variety, or in the case of subtractive bilingualism, by loss of their first language in the process of acquiring the second one. The danger of a label like semilingualism is that it may go hand in hand with the label of culturally deprived, implying that the quality of the student's sociocultural background is unacceptable.

Some language behaviors labeled as reflections of semilingualism can be seen alternatively as natural adaptations to language-contact situations. Code-switching, for example, may be viewed as a reflection of the speaker's inadequacy to express herself completely in one language or the other. Research, however, suggests that code-switching among bilingual people follows common patterns and performs communicative functions. Jacobson describes this concurrent use of two languages as "far from being a random behavior of flipflopping of sorts, but a strategy used by bilinguals under certain circumstances and explainable on the basis of psycholinguistic and sociolinguistic criteria" (1979, p. 493). To the purist, word-borrowing and code-switching may seem a threat to the integrity of the standard language, but such language mixture is an aspect of natural language change and as such is part of the larger and inevitable process of culture change.

Focusing on language as it relates to the often lower academic achievement of minority students, Guthrie and Hall (1983) identify three successive frameworks for analysis which have emerged over the past 25 years: linguistic deficit, linguistic difference, and cultural difference. Although educators studying each of these have looked for some type of linguistic and/or cultural mismatch between the home and the school as an explanation for academic failure, the three frameworks differ very much in their implications. The linguistic deficit framework, developed in the 1960s and based largely on research on lower-class black English, suggested that the non-standard-English dialects were linguistically inferior to standard English and consequently handicapped students in their academic abilities. As sociolinguists actually began to analyze nonstandard varieties of English, however, they were deemed different from standard English but not deficient. The research conducted demonstrated that the phonology and syntax of nonstandard languages followed their own logical patterns and were governed by rules. Thus while a child's speech might be different from the standardized version, it is not deficient in terms of structure and sophistication of the language.

In the more recent past, cultural differences as they relate to language, rather than language differences per se, have come to be a focus of inquiry in the quest for a better understanding of the "home-school mismatch," and it is this approach that has significance for the education of limited-English-proficient language-minority youngsters as well as English-dominant youth. As Guthrie and Hall put it, "how minority children use language, rather than particular linguistic features of their speech, may have more to do with the miscommunication, misunderstanding, and educational difficulty they encounter" (1983, pp. 55–58). While for LEP students the gulf between home-language proficiency and English proficiency is the most obvious factor in miscommunication and difficulties in mastering content in English, the culturally based ways in which language is used also have an effect on success in school—for example, how requests are made, how turns are negotiated, how commands are given, and what kinds of questions are asked. Children from non-English-speaking backgrounds or from nonstandard-English-speaking backgrounds may be competent in styles of language usage which are not rewarded, not allowed, or not used in school, but unfamiliar with styles of language usage which are important to success in the classroom. As Cohen points out, cultural background can influence "whom students talk to, in what context, what they talk about, and which language or language variety they use." Therefore, it may be misleading "to use some majority-group framework for judging conversational skills and appropriate choice of language, when the minority culture would have another framework" (1983, p. 143).

Language variation, transmission of culture and acquisition of ethnicity, socioeconomic status, stereotyping, cultural relativism, ethnocentrism, marked and unmarked culture, and cultural deprivation are all concepts which can be considered in the process of observing, analyzing, or teaching within the multilingual school setting. As one reflects on what happens from day to day and how those events or patterns are interpreted by students, parents, teachers, and administrators, an awareness of how the above concepts can color any person's viewpoint or promote understanding will help to produce a more accurate sense of the school's explicit and hidden cultural agendas.

RESEARCH ON CULTURE AND EDUCATION

New empirical knowledge from cross-cultural studies is vast in some areas and incomplete in others, but usually controversial. The purpose here is to give a view of some of the research on culture and education which may have a direct impact on the instructional process and classroom management in bilingual and ESL settings. We concentrate on two areas: cognitive styles and cultural background, and social interaction. In each area we discuss some of the research that has been done.

Cognitive Styles and Cultural Background

As evidenced by the emergent literature (Baecher, 1976; Dasen, 1977; Davis & Klausmeier, 1970; De Avila, 1978; Ginsburg, 1978; Halverson, 1979; Kimball, 1974; Lancy, 1983; Ogbu, 1978; Ramírez & Castañeda, 1974; Seelye & Wasilewski, 1979; Witkin et al., 1972), there is much intellectual energy being devoted to the exploration of how people as individuals and as members of cultural groups function cognitively (i.e., how their thinking processes are shaped in contrasting and similar cultural contexts). As Ginsburg puts it:

The general strategy of cross-cultural research into cognitive development is to examine basic cognitive operations—memory, reasoning, language—in environmental and cultural contexts very different from our own, for example, cultures lacking in schooling, or cultures possessing a special form of written language. Simply stated, there are two basic aims underlying such a strategy: to see how other people differ from ourselves, and to see how we and they are the same. (Ginsburg, 1978, p. 28)

Cole and Scribner (1974), in their work on the relations between culture and thought, have found differences in cognitive style to be strongly correlated with differences in culture. One type of research on cognitive style has to do with field dependence (or field sensitivity) and field independence. Although the validity of the correlation between field sensitivity or field independence and cultural background has been questioned, the area reflects the type of research on cross-cultural cognition which has had an effect on instruction in multiethnic settings.

Based on Witkin's identification of two types of learning styles which arise from different child-rearing practices, Ramírez and Castañeda (1974) analyzed the relation between cultural background, field independence, and field sensitivity. In their work they found that Mexican-American students tended more toward field sensitivity, whereas mainstream American students tended more toward field independence. Their contrastive analysis of field-sensitive and field-independent characteristics yielded the following generalizations:

Field Sensitive	*Field Independent*
Perceives effect of the whole	Analyzes parts of the whole or arranges parts to make a whole
Concerned with social environment	Task-centered
Sensitive to support or doubt from others	More independent of external judgment
Personal client-therapist relationship preferred	Formal client-therapist relationship preferred
Works cooperatively with others; likes to assist	Prefers to work independently and for individual recognition
Verbal proficiency	Skilled in spatial areas such as math and science concepts

(Halverson, 1979, p. 62)

As researchers began to explore the relation between culture and cognitive style, there was a need to identify traits representing each style which could be observed and analyzed. Cognitive mapping strategies were developed for the compilation of data that could be translated into appropriate teaching strategies. Ramírez and Castañeda (1974), for example, developed field-sensitive/field-independent behavior observation instruments which could be used to determine a student's predominant cognitive style. The instruments were designed as diagnostic-prescriptive tools to be used by teachers as they observed student behavior, rather than as complex psychological tests. After preferred cognitive styles are identified, instructional strategies can be modified. For example, if a teacher were working with field-sensitive students, she might use a field-sensitive strategy such as a cooperative work pattern to teach field-independent–related concepts. While instruction in the United States has been traditionally associated with a field-independent style, Ramírez and Castañeda conclude that one of the goals of a culturally sensitive education should be to produce bicognitive individuals who can operate effectively in either mode.

Although Ramírez and Castañeda's findings have been challenged, they have had an impact on approaches to the education of language-minority children. Based largely on their work, Halverson, for instance, constructed a cultural learning–style chart designed as "a structure which would help educators identify cultural patterns relevant to learning styles and suggest classroom instructional strategies" (1979, p. 55). Based on a series of questions broken down into categories such as child-adult relations, child-child relations, and cognitive style, the teacher is to arrive at culturally related patterns of cognitive style which can be used to develop curricular strategies, classroom management techniques, and tentative hypotheses for addressing the cognitive styles of culturally diverse children. Trujillo and Zachman (1981) have proposed that tests should be given to students at the beginning of the year to identify their particular learning style. Also, they suggest that teachers' styles be assessed to identify areas of continuity and discontinuity with the styles of students.

Another approach to cognitive style which takes into account both cultural and personal traits is Hill's educational cognitive styles (ECS) model (1972). This rather complex model represents an attempt to identify how students perceive their environment and extract meaning from their observations. While the ECS model has twenty-nine factors to be observed, the three major categories are symbols and their meaning, cultural determinants, and modalities of inference. The category of symbols and their meaning includes such aspects as preferred senses for processing information, preferred mode for obtaining meaning (spoken or written symbols), and ability to communicate nonverbally as well as verbally. The cultural determinants category examines child-rearing and socialization practices, including factors such as attitudes toward authority, sex roles, the mother-child bond, and a preference for working in groups or individually. Modalities of inference refers to the variations in the way people reason. Such factors as how decisions are made, how problems are solved, and the use of inductive or deductive reasoning are assessed (Spiridakis, 1981). Hill did not design his ECS model with language-minority students specifically in mind, but Baecher (1976) has researched the use of the model for bilingual classrooms, incorporating both languages used in the classroom in the ECS mapping process. As such, the model has been used to identify the learning styles of elementary students in bilingual classrooms. Some of the questions to be considered in the development of such a cognitive profile are:

1. How does the bilingual* take note of his environment?

2. What symbols does the individual prefer to use in solving problems?

3. Is the bilingual student characteristically a "listener" or a "reader" for information?

4. To what extent is the individual capable of understanding concepts and comfortable in his native language?

5. In what way does the bilingual seek consensus with peers, make up his own mind, or rely on the judgments of the members of his or her family?

6. Does the bilingual child tend to reason in categories as does a mathematician; in contrasts, as does the artist; or in relationships, as does a social scientist? (Baecher, 1976, pp. 47, 50)

Baecher (1981) proposes that once a student's ECS has been assessed and the mode of understanding required for the successful completion of an educational objective determined, the degree of match between the two can be measured. For example, in analyzing the ECS of students in a Spanish-English bilingual class and comparing it with the mode of understanding needed to complete instructional objectives related to the reading of a Hispanic children's story, Baecher found a 42 percent match. Baecher proposes that by employing deliberate intervention strategies aimed at the areas of mismatch, the degree of match between the student's style and nature of the task can be augmented.

Reactions to cognitive styles research and to cognitive mapping have been varied, ranging from strong support (Baecher, 1981) to a great deal of skepticism (De Avila, 1978; Ogbu, 1978; Seelye & Wasilewski, 1979).

*The term "bilingual" as used by Baecher refers to "any individual who will benefit from some form of systematic and coherent bilingual instruction" (1981, p. 322) rather than to fluency in two languages.

Early in this chapter we noted that one of the controversial issues surrounding social science has to do with the specificity with which cultural phenomena can be examined. In the area of culture and the learning process, the social and behavioral sciences have sought to arrive at some sort of explanation for the variations and similarities in the learning process. As Spiridakis points out, however, "learning styles are still hypothetical constructs that have been defined differently by various researchers and are still in an embryonic stage" (1981, p. 308).

While some social scientists agree that microlevel (or classroom-level) research necessarily leaves out many macro variables (nationwide socioeconomic and political variables), they nonetheless maintain that this type of research has the potential of exposing specific factors which can be tested for a better understanding of the cognitive processes at work in multicultural learning contexts. On the other hand, Cohen (1980a) suggests that this type of research on cognitive styles merely highlights the inequities we already know exist in the system. Field sensitivity, for instance, has been associated with ethnic groups which historically have held a stigmatized position in U.S. society, and such a dichotomy of cognitive styles can potentially be associated with a "cultural-deprivation" attitude. As such, field sensitivity has been interpreted as representing such "negatively valued" traits as

1. Less proficient at problems requiring use of essential elements in a variety of contexts

2. A less well-articulated body concept

3. A less well-developed sense of identity

4. A tendency toward "global" defenses like repression and denial

5. Behavioral dependency (Seelye & Wasilewski, 1979, p. 16)

Therefore, before teachers can implement the research findings on cognitive style for diagnostic and prescriptive purposes, extreme caution must be used not to harm the child with an unfounded or untrue generalization. As has been suggested many times now, culture is truly complex, deep, and puzzling. As we survey lists of observable behaviors such as those developed for cognitive mapping, we need to keep in mind that there are usually uncharted waters surrounding those behaviors, and that we may not be in a position (by virtue of knowledge, training, or experience) to penetrate that reality.

Another approach to cognitive and home-school mismatch is based on schema theory. The term "schema" was used by Piaget (1966) in his work on the chronological development of the organization of knowledge among children. The term refers not only to the collection of information but also to the ways in which that information is organized or structured through the use of such relations as cause-effect, classification, and sequence. One premise of schema theory is that information—conveyed verbally, visually, or in written form—does not in and of itself provide meaning. The meaning is construed by the recipients of the message based on their previous background knowledge. These previously acquired knowledge structures which we carry with us and have acquired through our own experiences are called schemata. Schemata, based as they are on interaction with the environment, are partially determined by cultural background. Therefore, the relation between the child's schemata and classroom tasks has implications for the education of language-minority students. Carrell (1981) and Johnson (1981, 1982) have found in their research that if the content schemata of an assigned text is not part of the readers' cultural background, the text is more difficult to comprehend and to remember. Because language and culture are interrelated, Carrell and Eisterhold (1983) propose that when learners try to extract meaning from information presented in their second language, an awareness by the teacher of potential gaps between the learners' culturally based schemata and that presupposed by the text can serve as a guide toward instructional strategies to improve comprehension. An awareness of the relation between cultural background and schemata may also reveal that difficulty in mastering certain cognitive tasks may not necessarily be related to a difference in cognitive style but alternatively to different schemata. A Navajo child, for example, may successfully complete sequencing tasks if initially they are based on the care of sheep rather than on small pictures of a trip to an urban supermarket (U.S. Commission on Civil Rights, 1975).

Social Interaction

While research on cognitive style explores the configurations of thinking and learning processes, research associated with sociocultural interaction focuses on the nature of human relationships within the school setting. Our purpose is not to do an in-depth analysis of any study but to spotlight areas of research with potential for helping bilingual and ESL teachers understand the significance of the impact of social interaction on teaching and learning.

Undoubtedly, teachers as actors in the classroom more than any other persons have been objects of attention in both quantitative and qualitative research efforts. Carew and Lightfoot (1979), for example, summarize the large body of literature which addresses the subject of teacher as point guard in the teaching and learning process. While most of the studies they cite have not dealt exclusively with cultural themes, one can glean useful information from them regarding the sociocultural complexity which emerges in classrooms. Predictably, most of the research on teacher interaction suggests that the teaching and learning configurations of the classroom are quite varied and often difficult to measure. It is not surprising therefore that one conclusion arrived at with confidence is that there is no single best way to teach all students. Research does, however, suggest that content knowledge, enthusiasm, and flexibility are characteristics of most effective teachers.

One approach to the study of interaction in the classroom and its relation to the students' background involves ethnography. An ethnographic study of education approaches the school or classroom as a cultural microcosm; through long-term participant observation, the ethnographic researcher develops a broad description and interpretation of the cultural system as it is experienced by its members. The ethnography of the school can also be combined with an ethnographic portrait of the community from which the students come. Such ethnographic approaches which look at both the school and the community can offer a very different perspective on what happens to nonmainstream students in the public schools. Ogbu's (1974) ethnographic study of a lower-income black community and its neighborhood elementary school, for example, yielded very different explantions for the students' achievement levels that did studies which focused only on the school. One valuable aspect of community ethnography can be the compilation of life histories of community members. As Trueba (1979) argues, the collection of life histories of students' parents or grandparents has proved to be a useful means for educators to appreciate the motivations and worldviews of people from the learner's cultural background. The rich familial detail provided by life histories allows educators to see life from the point of view of the students' families, and as such it may allow the teacher to shift perspective from questioning what is "wrong" with nonmainstream families to questioning what is wrong with an educational system that does not effectively educate such students (1979, p. 155).

Educational researchers in recent years have become interested in a type of qualitative research called microethnography. Such an approach, as the name suggests, is more limited in scope than traditional ethnography. More specific delineations are made in microethnography to focus on specific classroom processes. Because ethnography takes into account the insider's or "native's" perspective in understanding behavior, the classroom teacher often becomes a collaborator in microethnographic research. Within a multilingual context, a microethnographer might be interested in determining "the role of communicative activities in determining how and what children learn in a bilingual setting" (Moll, 1981, p. 433). Another topic might be comparing an English and Spanish reading lesson for a group of students. Microethnography can provide insights into "how learning is mediated by adults in the classroom and how concrete activities of communication shape the way children cope cognitively with different learning tasks" (Moll, 1981, p. 442). Some of the aspects of social relations that can be observed are who listens to whom and how; cultural patterns for showing attention or interest; the topical relevance of children's talk with the teacher and peers; assessments which teachers make of students' capabilities based on the children's social performance; and the rhythm of classroom activities and speech as well as body motion (Erickson, 1981, pp. 27–28). As Gay points out, one of the basic assumptions of sociocultural research in multiethnic classrooms is that "student-teacher interactions constitute the core of the educative process" (1978, p. 46). Thus microethnographic research looks at the minute details of the thousands of interactions that occur in school each day.

Because school microethnographers concentrate on communication activities, they employ many sociolinguistic research methods and make extensive use of videotaping as a means of accurately recording verbal and nonverbal interaction. Four major areas of common concern in microethnographic research with language-minority education are (1) teaching styles and cultural congruence, (2) sociocultural roles of interaction, (3) children's social competence, and (4) language use for communication or miscommunication (Trueba & Wright, 1981, p. 39).

The work of Vygotsky (1978) has been influential in the development of the fields of ethnography and microethnography in educational settings, in the sense that it can be seen as a link between the psychological or cognitive framework and the social framework. Vygotsky postulates that children's cognitive structures are developed through the actions and speech of others (principally their caretakers) and are transmitted through social interaction. It follows, therefore, that culturally coded styles of speech and social interaction result in culturally related patterns of cognitive structure. To come to an understanding of students' cognitive structures, it is therefore important to develop a data base on the sociocultural interaction patterns surrounding the learner.

While the development and use of microethnographic techniques for educational research blossomed in the recent past, research focusing on social interaction in the classroom is not new. In the late 1950s, for example, Flanders designed a research method for interaction analysis which would quantify classroom verbal patterns. He developed a ten-category system that would enable the observer to code all talk that occurred in the classroom (Flanders, 1970). Given a particular research topic (e.g., "What type of student is a teacher most likely to praise?"), categories of verbal interaction could be chosen, their frequencies tallied through classroom observations, and subsequent quantitative analyses developed. Such data can yield interesting findings. For example, one study done in the early 1970s for the U.S. Commission on Civil Rights, based on observations of 494 classrooms in the Southwest, found that 21 percent more questions were directed to Anglos than to Chicanos, teachers praised or encouraged Anglos 35 percent more than they did Chicanos, and teachers accepted or used Anglo's ideas 40 percent more often (Jackson & Cosca, 1974).

While research like that of Flanders is useful in describing what happens in classrooms, it also brings to light other issues which probably cannot be captured in numbers. The comprehensive picture of social interaction may still remain elusive. For instance, paralinguistic and nonverbal phenomena as well as differences and similarities between home and school communication and organization styles cannot be easily harnessed for study.

Philips' study of students on the Warm Springs Indian Reservation represents an ethnographic, sociolinguistically based approach which focuses on the qualitative analysis of interaction within the classroom and community. In her research she studied the cultural differences in attention structure and regulation of talk between home and school. Among her principal findings were that Warm Springs Indian students "speak too softly, hesitate too long before speaking, and engage in too much visually received signaling *from the point of view of teacher expectations*" [italics added] (Philips, 1983, p. 129). Philips points out that the actor's position in the social structure influences how researchers and educators can perceive miscommunication. That is, because of the teacher's higher social status and authority, observers tend to conclude that it is the students who misunderstand, whereas logically it could just as well be said that it is the teacher who misunderstands. Based on her research, Philips suggests that even if teachers have good intentions, they and their students can miscommunicate nonverbally. She argues that because nonverbal behavior is extremely difficult to monitor consciously, ethnic discrimination by teachers may continue to occur even if deliberate efforts are made to eliminate it.

Another study of Native American education, conducted by Mohatt and Erickson (1981), focused on the instructor's communication style in an in-depth comparison of an Indian and a non-Indian teacher. Mohatt and Erickson observed such teacher behaviors as how directions were given and how student activities were monitored. They also studied the rhythm of the teachers' pause times between questions and answers. They found that the Indian and non-Indian teachers used different participation structures in the classroom. For example, the non-Indian teacher used more direct commands and singling out of students for individual responses or contributions. However, it is also interesting to note that as the school year progressed the nonnative teacher began to use more of the participation structures which were characteristic initially of the native instructor only. Mohatt and Erickson's study thus suggests two things for the teacher in the bilingual or ESL classroom. First, the ethnicity of the instructor can have an effect on the participation structure which evolves in the classroom and the degree to which that structure complements the students' own communication styles. Second, if teachers' ethnicity differs from that of students, it may be possible for teachers to adapt their style as they gain experience with classroom participants.

In another investigation of teaching styles, Morine-Dershimer (1983) studied the effect of teachers on the "communicative status" of students in multiethnic classrooms. Students with high communicative status were defined as those with a high frequency of classroom verbal participation and who were viewed by classmates as people one could learn from. In her exploratory research, Morine-Dershimer found that teachers could "create" varied distributions of communicative status within their classrooms, depending on the types of instructional strategies they employed. The types of students who attained high communicative status via a textbook-based teaching approach, for example, differed from the types of students who attained high status via an experience-based approach. Recalling the U.S. Civil Rights Commission finding that Anglo students tended to have higher levels of classroom participation than Mexican-Americans in the Southwest, one could extrapolate from Morine-Dershimer's exploratory work that a more equitable distribution of communicative status opportunities could be realized through the intentional use of varied types of instructional strategies.

The Kamehameha Education Research Institute has conducted a long-term series of studies on the matches among social interaction in the home, community, and classroom. Psychologists, cultural anthropologists, sociolinguists, and curriculum specialists have collaborated since the early 1970s in a broad spectrum of applied research studies on the academic achievement of Hawaiian-Americans, who have tended to have some of the lowest achievement levels of any group in the nation. In searching for cultural explanations for minority groups' tendency toward lower academic achievement, Kamehameha researchers have operated under the assumption that minorities are members of coherent cultural systems and that their difficulties are not the consequence of personal and/or social deficits and pathologies. Second, the classroom is held to be an interface of cultures in which the learning process is disrupted because teachers and pupils have incongruent expectations, motives, social behaviors, and language and cognitive patterns. (Gallimore, Boggs & Jordan, 1974, p. 261)

One area of mismatch between the home and school for Hawaiian-American youth, based on an ethnographic study of the community of 'Aina Pumehana, is the value placed on personal autonomy. The researchers found that in the home the children were socialized to value being contributors to the family's well-being rather than for independent living. In the classroom, however, personal accomplishment was valued for its own sake rather than as a contribution to the needs of others. Perhaps the negative academic results of such a mismatch could be compared to a game situation. If the players (students), based on previous experience, assume that the most points will be gained through behavior set A, while the designers and judges of the game (teachers) are assigning the most points to behavior set B, the degree of success of the players is minimized.

The metaphor of the game is somewhat reflective of the cognitive theory of culture, which holds that culture can be understood as a system of standards or rules that each person needs to know to act appropriately as a member of a particular group. Erickson points out that this cognitive theory of culture underlies many school-community ethnographies, which combine cognitive psychology, sociolinguistics, and anthropology. What this underlying theoretical framework boils down to in the classroom, as Erickson puts it, is, "What do teachers and children have to know in order to do what they are doing?" (1981, p. 29). That is, because classrooms are places in which standards of "good behavior" (whatever they may be) are heavily emphasized, and observance of these standards is rewarded while nonobservance is sanctioned in many different ways, the degree to which a student's cultural knowledge produces classroom-appropriate behavior will influence her or his success in the school's cultural microcosm.

Investigating under the framework of a cognitive theory of culture, LeCompte (1981) found five fairly uniform standards or "work norms" to be present in all four urban, multiethnic elementary classrooms she studied. The five standards which students were expected to follow were:

1. Conform to authority

2. Conform to a schedule and avoid wasting time

3. Equate academic achievement with personal worth

4. Keep busy

5. Maintain order (LeCompte, 1981, p. 179)

Thus all four teachers had adopted a similar "management core" of standards, probably not much different from those used in elementary classrooms throughout the United States. LeCompte found that both the Mexican-American and the mainstream American students had apparently internalized these work norms. Yet these classrooms were very different in the ways in which learning tasks were organized and carried out. The researcher found these differences to be attributed to what she termed a "discretionary core"; teachers varied a good deal in the degree of autonomy given students to organize their work and initiate topics for discussion, in the extent to which competition was stressed, and in the types of "rituals" used to maintain order. LeCompte acknowledges that nonmainstream children, depending on their ethnic background, may bring to the classroom standards which do not correspond to all of the management-core standards; she argues, however, that "barring radical changes in schools and society" (p. 195), this management core will not change significantly. Thus, it is within the discretionary core that teachers can reduce the tension between home and school rules of behavior, providing an atmosphere in which the students can participate more successfully in the classroom.

Individual studies such as the ones just discussed provide many valuable insights, but what is the larger pattern of findings emerging from the literature, and what are their applications for bilingual and ESL educators? Based on a review of fifteen microethnographic studies conducted in multiethnic settings (three of them bilingual classrooms) Trueba and Wright (1981) found that the usefulness of microethnographies fell into five general areas, demonstrating the following:

1. The importance of the context of interaction to an understanding of the dynamic nature of the teaching-learning process

2. The need for teachers to broaden the base from which they assess children's social competence, particularly that of racial and ethnolinguistic minority children

3. The close relationship between a teacher's assessment of a child and the nature of the educational program planned for him/her, and therefore the critical importance of an accurate assessment

4. The importance of structuring classroom interaction in ways that are culturally and linguistically congruent with children's previous experiences, as a

first and necessary step in learning to communicate appropriately in intraethnic and interethnic situations

5. The unique role of the underlying rules that govern the structuring of classroom organization and interaction, and the fact that a knowledge of those rules is required for full participation in the learning process in a given classroom (Trueba & Wright, 1981, p. 51)

While these five areas provide valuable guidance for the improvement of instruction, it would obviously be impossible for classroom teachers to be their own microethnographers of all the cultural detail involved in day-to-day interaction in the school and community. However, there are perhaps two "all-purpose" qualities which can enable teachers to adapt their actions to the cultural and sociolinguistic context. As Rodríguez (1980) found in an analysis of effective elementary teachers, the two most predominant characteristics which differentiated the "stars" from less effective teachers were (1) communication skills, involving the ability to interact effectively with children and parents, and (2) positive regard for children and parents, which included respect, high expectations, and a nonjudgmental, genuinely caring attitude. Although good communication skills and positive regard may serve as a strong base for culturally responsive education, of course things can still go wrong. Carrasco (1981a) reports on a case study of Lupita, a kingergarten student who was assessed by her very qualified and experienced bilingual teacher to be unprepared for promotion to first grade. Through viewing the researcher's videotapes of classroom interaction, the teacher gained an awareness of Lupita's competencies which she had not been able to discern before. That is, the videotapes showed Lupita in student-student interactions demonstrating social, verbal, and academic abilities (such as puzzle manipulations) which did not show up in her interaction with the teacher. Thus videotaping can be a valuable tool for the teacher as well as the researcher. Although videotaping classroom interaction is not often possible, there are alternative teacher-initiated observations which can yield useful data. For example, Carrasco suggests that teachers become in-the-field researchers by just periodically taking the time to look and listen in to a child's behavior.

At the other end of the continuum of research from small-scale informal teacher observation are large research projects conducted by interdisciplinary teams of anthropologists, sociolinguists, psychologists, and educators. Jointly, both types of research are powerful instruments for improvement in the instruction of language-minority students. Larger-scale research projects have the potential for generalization of findings and can therefore affect educational policy at the local and national levels.

The Kamehameha Education Research Institute, some of whose work has been previously mentioned, is an example of a large, coordinated research effort whose results ultimately have impact on instruction in the classroom. Institute members' work in the Kamehameha Early Education Program (KEEP), for example, demonstrates a three-stage process for improvement of instruction. First, KEEP researchers developed a knowledge base regarding Hawaiian children within the context of their natal culture and the school. They gathered information on such topics as home socialization, social motivation, language production, phonemics, sociolinguistics, cognitive strategies, and standard English acquisition. Second, researchers and teachers collaborated to apply this data base to the development and refinement of a proven effective program in the project's laboratory school. Finally, through in-service training and collaboration between consultants and teachers, the instructional program is being implemented in public schools that have a concentration of Hawaiian students (Tharp et al., in press). One of the project's videotapes, *Coming Home to School: Culturally Compatible Classroom Practices,* demonstrates how teachers, by getting a glimpse of native Hawaiian students' natural cultural environment at home, see these children demonstrating talents seldom revealed in the classroom. Teachers are then able to use the filmed information as a guide in selecting culturally and instructionally appropriate goals, objectives, and experiences.

While a culturally compatible curriculum is considered by the Kamehameha researchers to be a keystone for effective schooling without cultural marginality, identifying what is and is not essential in the match between the home and school is also important. Some important home cultural patterns identified through KEEP were positively applicable to the classroom. Language use patterns in the home, for example, were transferred to classroom reading instruction through emphasis on comprehension rather than phonics, and through an open, relaxed, "talk story" discussion approach in place of the "teacher-asks-a-question/one-student-answers/teacher-evaluates" format. Other home cultural patterns had a neutral effect on classroom performance. For instance, researchers found that the English of the classroom did not have to match the students' dialect of English for achievement to improve. Other home cultural patterns could not realistically be applied in the classroom; strategies were needed to help students shift to classroom patterns of interaction that were different from those of the home. One such case was the home tendency toward peer affiliation, which in the classroom had to be shifted somewhat toward attentiveness to the adult teacher (Jordan, 1977).

Another large-scale research study which focused on bilingual instruction practices is the Significant Bilingual Instructional Features study, funded by Part C research funds from Title VII. Part I of the study involved extensive data collection through observation at fifty-eight bilingual instructional settings throughout the United States, and Part II extended the data through an in-depth analysis of nine bilingual classrooms. Focus was on the organizational structure of each bilingual classroom, allocation of time, teacher variables, and student variables. Conditions for effective bilingual instruction were identified in the study, and the findings will be disseminated sometime during 1984–85 through the National Clearinghouse for Bilingual Education.

To recapitulate now, we have explored two areas of research on the connection between culture and the instructional process: cognitive style and social interaction. In reality they are not either/or categories but overlapping fields of inquiry which together provide a clearer picture of how children from diverse cultural backgrounds can learn better. After reviewing research on both cognitive style and social interaction, Cazden and Leggett (1981) make four recommendations for the achievement of "culturally responsive" education, which, based on the nature of culture and intelligence, is a fundamental aspect of optimal educational opportunities for limited-English-proficient students. First, they recommend that more attention be paid to the implementation of varied, multisensory modes of instruction, because children of diverse backgrounds differ in their sensory modality strengths. Second, additional research is needed in the area of field dependence and field independence before educational prescriptions can be made. Third, microethnographic monitoring of classroom participation should be part of the planning and evaluation process so that interaction patterns can be changed to "maximize children's engagement and thereby their learning" (p. 83). Along with this, ethnographic field research studies should be conducted to identify areas of incompatibility between the community and the school in interactional styles. Fourth, "all school systems should bring the invisible culture of the community into the school through parent participation, hiring and promotion of minority-group personnel, and inservice training for the school staff. . . . Case study descriptions of successful inservice programs should be accumulated and distributed widely" (Cazden & Leggett, 1981, p. 86).

As important as it is, cultural mismatch cannot realistically be considered the single independent variable in the education of LEP students, and hence culturally responsive education cannot realistically be considered the single solution for improved educational opportunities. There are also the paramount issues of language development and second-language acquisition. And, as discussed previously in the sections on socioeconomic status and cultural deprivation, it is difficult and yet important to distinguish cultural from economic, social, and political issues. In an effort to identify the details of cognitive style and social interaction, broader forces that are part of the society's structure may be overlooked. The effect which social status can have on academic achievement and second-language acquisition is demonstrated in the studies by Skutnabb-Kangas and Toukomaa (1976) of Finnish immigrants to Sweden and by Ilpola (1979) of Finnish immigrants to Australia. The results of these studies show that young Finnish children in the Australian schools did better in their new academic milieu than their Finnish counterparts in the Swedish schools. It is unlikely that the cultural mismatch was greater for Finnish students in Sweden than in Australia, and the researchers argue, based on their findings, that the differences in achievement were related to social status in the two societies. In Sweden Finns tend to have lower social status based on their position as a subordinate minority group, whereas Finns in Australia are more likely to be perceived as hard-working, nice people of higher social status.

In a slightly different vein, McDermott and Gospodinoff (1981) argue that culturally related differences in such things as gestural systems and interactional rhythms are not sufficient explanations for difficulties which some language-minority children experience in school. Rather, these phenomena are secondary to the political or power relations which are maintained between different groups of society. Dialect differences, interactional styles, and other communicative codes as such are not determinants of behavior but adaptations which people have made and will continue to make in their relations with others. McDermott and Gospodinoff argue that people do repair miscommunication when it is in their economic or political interest to do so, and conversely, that miscommunication is not repaired when it is in the interests of one or both groups to maintain differences. Thus the attempt to improve education for minority youth solely by inculcating teachers with more sensitivity to cultural communicative codes will not work because "in the course of talking or moving in one way rather than another, children and teachers are doing politics" (p. 215).

Whether or not one agrees that larger political and socioeconomic issues form the framework out of which analyses of language-minority education have to be drawn, culture is a vital part of the mosaic which depicts what happens in bilingual and ESL classrooms. Solá (1980) suggests that research on bilingualism and biculturalism has been an energizing force in the reorientation which he has perceived to be occurring in the social sciences in the past four decades. In this reorientation, according to Solá, "we are exchanging a culturally biased model of social communication for one that is unbiased" (p. 205). Reflective of the multiple ways in which culture has impact on the instructional process is the Council on Anthropology and Education's 1978 resolution on the role of culture in educational planning:

1. Culture is intimately related to language and the development of basic communication, computation, and social skills.

2. Culture is an important part of the dynamics of the teaching-learning process in all classrooms, both bilingual and monolingual.

3. Culture affects the organization of learning, pedagogical practices, evaluative procedures, and rules of schools, as well as instructional activities and curriculum.

4. Culture is more than the heritage of a people through dance, food, holidays, and history. Culture is more than a component of bilingual education programs. It is a dynamic, creative, and continuous process, which includes behaviors, values, and substances shared by people, that guides them in their struggle for survival and gives meaning to their lives. As a vital process it needs to be understood by more people in the United States, a multiple society which has many interacting cultural groups. (Saravia-Shore, 1979, p. 345)

Culture behaves in mysterious ways. Analyzing it is not easy, but we, as educators, are privileged to feel it and to see it work in the multiethnic classroom. Because so much of what happens in life is learned surreptitiously, the more aware teachers are of all the implicit and explicit messages brought from home and conveyed in the school setting, the more culturally sensitive they can be. In 1968 Jackson wrote in *Life in Classrooms* that schools have a hidden curriculum, and today we are still exploring all of the implications for children in bilingual and ESL settings. Children bring largely unstated and yet powerful beliefs, behaviors, and values to school with them, and in school they adapt to, learn from, or rebel against the largely unstated and yet powerful beliefs, behaviors, and values which schools manifest through the curriculum and teachers' interactions with students. For educators in multilingual settings the concept of culture remains "so near and yet so far." But the cultural tease must go on. We are all caught in culture's web.

RECOMMENDED READING

1. The winter, 1984, special theme issue of the *Educational Research Quarterly,* entitled "Culture, Language, and Education in Alaska, Canada, Hawaii, Guam, Puerto Rico, Australia, and New

Zealand," brings together ten articles on how educators and governments outside the continental United States deal with the schooling needs of their minority children. Minority status takes on a different meaning in the various geographical contexts. In Alaska, Hawaii, and Guam, for example, minority-language children are natives. In Puerto Rico, they are English-speaking migrants from the U.S. mainland. In Canada, they are French or Ukrainian speakers. In Australia, they are the aborigines, and in New Zealand, they are the Maoris. Guest edited by Carlos J. Ovando, this *ERQ* reaches out beyond the educational disciplines to include perspectives from such fields as law, anthropology, linguistics, and program development.

2. For an analysis of educational concepts, conflicts, and consequences surrounding pluralistic contexts, see also the winter, 1978 special theme issue of the *Educational Research Quarterly,* entitled "Cultural Pluralism: Educational Concepts, Conflicts, and Consequences," also guest edited by Carlos J. Ovando.

3. *Origins,* by Richard Leakey and Roger Lewin (1977), and *The Interpretation of Cultures*, by Clifford Geertz (1973), offer engaging anthropological perspectives on our past, present, and future.

4. For comprehensive documentation of the pluralistic nature of the American experience, consult the *Harvard Encyclopedia of American Ethnic Groups,* edited by Stephan Thernstrom, Ann Orlov, and Oscar Handlin (1980).

5. For hands-on suggestions regarding action research on ethnicity, see *Aspects of Ethnicity,* by Wilma S. Longstreet (1978).

6. Focusing on the interrelatedness of culture, language, and schooling, *A Guide to Culture in the Classroom* by Muriel Saville-Troike (1978) provides details for curriculum design and development. What she offers in the monograph is especially useful to the teacher from a nonminority background.

7. *Minority Education and Caste: The American System in Cross-Cultural Perspective* by John U. Ogbu (1978), an American-trained anthropologist of Nigerian ancestry, provides a thought-provoking explanation of how U.S. society is governed by castelike behaviors in its treatment of stigmatized minorities. Macro variables (e.g., economics and civic participation) and micro variables (e.g., classroom instruction and teacher-student re-

lations) are examined in relation to the touted egalitarian creed of American society.

8. Paulo Freire's *Pedagogy of the Oppressed* (1970) is a useful publication with a Third-World perspective on ways to problematize multicultural awareness.

9. Naturalistic (ethnographic) studies of U.S. schools are found in: George Spindler's (Ed.) *Doing the Ethnography of Schooling: Educational Anthropology in Action* (1982); *Growing Up American: Schooling and the Survival of Community* by Alan Peshkin (1978); *Case Studies in Bilingual Education,* edited by Bernard Spolsky and Robert L. Cooper (1978); *Ghetto School: Class Warfare in an Elementary School* by Gerald Levy (1970); *The Next Generation: An Ethnography of Education in an Urban Neighborhood* by John Ogbu (1974); and *Eskimo School on the Andreafsky: A Study of Effective Bicultural Education* by Judith S. Kleinfeld (1979).

10. Beliefs, values, and behaviors in the United States examined from a cross-cultural perspective are found in *American Cultural Patterns: A Cross-Cultural Perspective* by Edward C. Stewart (1972) and in *The Study of Literate Civilizations* by Francis L. K. Hsu (1969). Theoretical perspectives for analyzing values are provided in *An Introduction to Intercultural Communication* by John C. Condon and Fathi S. Yousef (1975); *The Silent Language* by Edward T. Hall (1959); and *Intercultural Communication* by Larry A. Samovar and Richard E. Porter (1972).

11. For a thorough and revealing synthesis of studies in classroom ethnography, see *Culture and the Bilingual Classroom,* edited by Henry T. Trueba, Grace Pung Guthrie, and Kathryn Hu-Pei Au (1981).

12. *The Invisible Culture: Communication in Classroom and Community on the Warm Springs Indian Reservation* by Susan U. Philips (1983), is a study of students on the reservation representing an ethnographic, sociolinguistically based approach which focuses on the qualitative analysis of the interaction within the classroom and community.

13. *Bilingual Education: Current Perspectives—Social Science,* published by The Center for Applied Linguistics (1977), has some excellent articles on the role of social science in bilingual schooling.

14. For the application of cultural themes to the instructional goals and objectives of the classroom, see also *Language and Culture in Conflict: Problem-Posing in the ESL Classroom* by Nina Wallerstein (1983), and *Multicultural Teaching: A Handbook of Activities, Information, and Resources* by Pamela L. Tiedt and Iris M. Tiedt (1979). A chapter which expands foreign-language educators' views of the integration of language and culture and provides many practical applications is "Doing the unthinkable in the second-language classroom: A process for the integration of language and culture," by Linda Crawford-Lange and Dale Lange (1984).

Chapter Five

SOCIAL STUDIES, MUSIC, AND ART

When you hear the term "social studies," what comes to mind? Teaching about countries, lakes, rivers, and capitals? Presidents, famous and infamous persons, wars, legislation? Exotic cultures, unfamiliar customs, rituals, foods? Boring? Maybe not to you, but it could be for your students

How do you teach social studies? What do you include? Why? Are lessons exciting and integrated into students' everyday lives? Do they have some meaning or purpose for students, aside from preparing for tests? Are students actively involved in the lessons, even in their creation? What can you as a bilingual or ESL social studies teacher do to bring intellectual excitement into the classroom for both English-speaking and language-minority students while also achieving the planned objectives of the school system?

A FRAMEWORK FOR SOCIAL STUDIES

Before discussing approaches to the teaching of social studies in bilingual or ESL classrooms, it is useful to examine briefly the rationale for social studies in the American educational system. Few educators would question the notion that an effective social studies curriculum promotes the development of effective social and cognitive skills, enabling citizens to deal with the complexity of modern times from a point of strength and in the best interests of humanity. Although they generally agree in principle with such a goal, educators tend to have conflicting views on the best ways and means to achieve it.

Lemlech (1984), for example, notes that Barr, Barth, and Shermis (1977) have identified three potentially conflicting social studies tradi-

153

tions: social studies taught as citizenship transmission, social studies taught as social science, and social studies taught as reflective inquiry (Lemlech, 1984, p. 153). In each tradition, the purpose of citizenship is supported through methods and content selection grounded in a philosophical point of view regarding what constitutes an ideal citizen.

For example, in the tradition of social studies as citizenship transmission, nurturing a good citizen means "inculcating right values as a framework for making decisions" (Lemlech, 1984, p. 153). Such a goal is achieved primarily through carefully planned instructional approaches and content selection reflective of vertical pedagogical authority. Content is transmitted through fairly structured procedures such as use of textbooks and lecturing.

The approach of teaching social studies as social science, on the other hand, suggests that effective citizenship comes about through a sophisticated knowledge of concepts, processes, and problems surrounding the social sciences. Accomplishing such a mission, therefore, involves discovering knowledge and confirming hunches through the various social science processes. What is taught represents "the structure, concepts, problems, and processes of both the separate and the integrated social science disciplines" (Lemlech, 1984, p. 153).

Unlike social studies taught as citizenship transmission and social studies taught as social science, social studies taught as reflective inquiry bases citizenship decision making on the reflective powers of the individual rather than on a particular set of values transmitted from the top down or a body of social science knowledge per se. In other words, appropriate values, beliefs, and attitudes are the consequence of careful reflection on issues and concerns surrounding the social order.

There are pedagogical implications for bilingual and ESL teachers which can be drawn from this triad of social studies traditions. Depending on the background of the students and the nature of the classroom, any of the three social studies frameworks may be partially or entirely appropriate. Bilingual, ESL, and monolingual teachers can profit from a large body of knowledge in social studies education. There are a variety of instructional approaches, readily accessible publications, and curricular materials in the general social studies field. At the same time, we have found a dearth of social studies resources and teacher-training guidelines specifically focused on bilingual and ESL settings.

Given the unique set of linguistic and sociocultural factors surrounding limited-English-proficient (LEP) students from both immigrant and indigenous communities, there are issues which need to be considered when designing and developing teaching and learning experiences for such students. For example, language-minority students often come to the classroom with rich and varied human experiences. In the hands of a resource-ful and able social studies teacher, such knowledge about human beings can be applied in the social studies context. In the process of experiencing life in a variety of geographical, social, cultural, educational, and lin-guistic environments, many of these students have become skilled in processing information, which enables them not only to share their lives with others but also to learn from others. Discovering how such students have processed information to facilitate their adaptation to new contexts can yield valuable knowledge regarding how people face and solve social problems. This particular issue fits in well with the approach to social studies as reflective inquiry.

Because language-minority students do not deserve pariah status in the schools, we purposely choose to emphasize that social studies as well as all content areas in a bilingual or ESL classroom are much more than remedial education. As educators, we want to challenge students not only with solid academic curricula but also with activities for creative, cooperative, reflective, and responsible citizenship. Thus our particular emphasis is on social studies taught as reflective inquiry, combined with the social science perspective. The suggestions we make in this chapter lean toward a problem-posing, risk-taking, and global approach to social studies curricula. In presenting such an approach, we explore four areas: bilingual and ESL classroom structures for social studies instruction, instructional approaches to cultural awareness, resources for social stud-ies, and the use of music and art as aspects of an interdisciplinary ap-proach to social studies.

BILINGUAL AND ESL CLASSROOM STRUCTURES

Differences in the program model, classroom design, grade level, lan-guage use, and heterogeneity of students in a class can all strongly in-fluence the structural setting for bilingual and ESL classes. Listed below are some of the classroom structural variations possible for teaching so-cial studies to language minority students, although these descriptions do not begin to exhaust all the possibilities.

Elementary-Level Bilingual Self-Contained Classrooms

Bilingual social studies lessons for younger children can be part of a transitional, maintenance, two-way, or immersion program. The method for teaching such a class can incorporate concurrent, alternate, or pre-view-review approaches for the use of two languages. Concurrent or preview-review approaches make use of both languages somewhere in the context of the lesson, while the alternate approach dictates that the social studies lesson be taught in only one of the two languages on a given day. (See chap. 3 for detailed explanations of these three approaches.)

In the elementary curriculum language arts development and mathematics usually receive the highest priorities. Some teachers then think of social studies and science as extras to be added only if there is time. When social studies and science lessons are taught, they can often be incorporated into the total curriculum. Some math and language arts objectives can be effectively taught through content-area activities in social studies and science. Generally, the elementary school curriculum can encourage the creation of multidisciplinary activities which can include a wide variety of stimuli, incorporating, for example, physical movement, visual stimuli, things to touch and make, music, and art. Social studies with natural, multisensory activities are much more motivating to students than standard textbooks and curricula designed for secondary and upper elementary levels which too often tend to emphasize discussion or pencil and paper tasks on abstract topics. The dual responsibility for teaching both language and content-area skills for every classroom activity complicates the tasks of a bilingual teacher, but a great deal of first- and second-language acquisition can occur naturally through children's strongly motivated involvement in classroom tasks which are not focused solely on language.

In a two-way bilingual class, there are many possibilities for effective social studies lessons which make use of the multicultural context. Because students are at all levels of skill development, teachers need to organize classes using a variety of total-class, small-group, two-person, and individual activities in varied learning centers around the room. Suggestions for curricular material for bilingual social studies lessons are provided in the sections of this chapter on instructional approaches to culture and geography and history.

Secondary-Level Bilingual Social Studies

Many secondary-level bilingual classes in the content areas are transitional, designed to get and keep recently arrived immigrant students at grade level while they are learning and acquiring English. For example, a seventh-or eighth-grade bilingual social studies class might develop skills in map analysis, measurement, following directions, use of the library, transportation systems, geographical terminology, analysis of current events, understanding the political system of the United States, or cross-country comparisons. A transitional bilingual class is usually taught in native language, with English vocabulary introduced from an equivalent social studies course for English speakers at that grade level. As students increase their proficiency in English, more content is taught in English.

A second type of secondary-level bilingual social studies class is designed for maintenance programs or programs for recently arrived immigrant students preparing to graduate from high school. This would be a course required by the school system but taught in a language other than English. For example, eleventh-grade U.S. history is a standard requirement for graduation in most schools. Several school systems have discovered that if they offer U.S. history taught in Vietnamese (for example) to Vietnamese students who have recently entered the United States, students may successfully master the content of the course and score at least as well or better than English-speaking students on a standardized test given in English at the end of the year, after they have had enough time to work on their proficiency in English in ESL classes. For those recently arrived students who are functioning at grade level in all subject areas, this is a very successful program strategy.

Maintenance bilingual classes serve a similar function. Students in a maintenance program receive half of their courses in English and half in their other language. If students are functioning at grade level, they will be equally successful on standardized achievement tests given in either English or the other language. The goal of maintenance classes is both content-area achievement in all subjects and bilingual-bicultural proficiency.

Secondary-level teachers may have many more school structures to combat than do elementary-level teachers, if they want to be innovative in any way. At this level, courses are usually more defined, sometimes with a fairly rigid set of objectives whose attainment is assessed with a standardized test. Many tests tend to measure lower-level, memorizable skills, and for some teachers it seems easier to emphasize the facts required for the tests than to organize activities which involve deeper, thought-provoking, problem-solving skills. One of the main messages of this book, however, is the importance of providing all students with both complete knowledge of a subject area and creative, complicated, problem-solving tasks. Every bilingual and ESL teacher should convey the expectation that every one of our students will be responsible citizens and consumers and creative managers of whatever life tasks they choose; as teachers, we provide some of the tools needed for them to be confident and responsible in those roles.

ESL Social Studies Classes

For at least a decade, ESL professionals have discussed the importance of teaching the content areas in ESL classes. ESL teachers who work in schools with no bilingual support staff have been encouraged to introduce social studies, science, and math concepts, symbols, and vocabulary through the second language at each student's level of English proficiency. In addition, ESL teachers frequently serve as tutors for their students to assist with coursework outside of the ESL class. To introduce concepts and skills in each subject area requires coordination with other classroom teachers. It takes an alert, sensitive teacher to manage a skillful balance between challenging students to think and expand their language skills and knowledge of social studies and providing class activities which are appropriate to or just a little beyond each student's level of language proficiency.

Another program model many school systems have implemented when there are not sufficient numbers of students of one language background for bilingual instruction to be feasible is to provide an ESL course for each content area. ESL social studies classes serve roughly the same function as transitional bilingual classes, but they are taught all in the second language and therefore content must be significantly simplified. Students are introduced to social studies concepts and vocabulary in English at their level of English proficiency. If some students are below grade level in skills needed for social studies lessons, they are introduced to activities which help them to master missing skills. Programs of this type have many different names, such as alternative English for speakers of other languages (ESOL), intensive English as a second language (ESL), or high-intensity language training (HILT). While these classes attempt to provide students with lessons at their level of English proficiency, an unresolved problem is that the special classes segregate limited-English-proficient students from native English-speaking students.

INSTRUCTIONAL APPROACHES TO CULTURAL AWARENESS

In chapter 4, we discussed the ways that culture manifests itself with respect to the education of linguistic minority students. We considered such issues as cultural relativity, cultural transmission, language variation, learning styles, and social interaction and explored how such issues affect the schooling of students of non-English-language backgrounds. In this section we examine ways to teach students about cultural patterns, cultural similarities, and cultural diversity from the perspective of social science instruction.

The subject of social studies includes such diverse fields as history, geography, economics, political science, anthropology, sociology, and psychology. Although in this section we approach culture as a component of the social studies curriculum, the points made in chapter 4 still apply—

that culture is learned, shared, and evolving, and that it has an elusive yet pervasive nature. This section focuses mainly on the teaching of anthropology and sociology.

Cultural patterns are reflected in the formal educational system, in ways ranging from how national standardized tests are designed down to the manner in which the individual teacher greets her students each morning. Yet educators generally have been reluctant to take seriously the issue of culture and to incorporate it consciously into the curriculum. There are several reasons for this. To begin with, most teachers have not been equipped with the necessary conceptual skills to become culture analyzers; it is not a significant part of the standard teacher training program. The depth, ambiguity, unpredictability, and sometimes even contradictory or oppressive nature of culture also make it very difficult to address. Teachers, parents, and administrators often prefer to avoid such culturally sensitive issues as racism, prejudice, stereotypes, desegregation, interracial mixing, social exclusion, ethnocentrism, or cross-cultural conflicts. With the increased pressure to return to basics in the curriculum, educators often question whether imbuing the teaching-learning process with culture- and language-related themes would in fact distract from the perceived business of the schools, i.e., to maintain the children at grade level and have them compete favorably with national norms in the principal content areas.

Given all these difficulties, it is understandable that teachers retreat to teaching a few distinctive features of other cultures (such as food bazaars, multicultural fairs, celebration of the lunar new year) to fulfill any obligation to include multicultural education in the curriculum. Most of the time, consequently, culture in the classroom is clothed in a costume of highly visible patterns and symbols of colorful or exotic societies. These observations are not meant to suggest that dealing with fairly obvious aspects of culture is wrong. In the primary grades especially there are limits to what one can do beyond the concrete level. But to explore the concept of culture in greater depth and complexity, it is crucial to include—and better yet, to begin with—the everyday culture of children and their community. The following sections explore a framework and provide specific suggestions for the construction of a student-based foundation in cultural awareness.

The Interdisciplinary Framework

When multicultural education as part of the social studies curriculum is based on an interdisciplinary framework, it holds great promise for program development and intellectual stimulation. The interdisciplinary approach is a well-established concept with a strong internal logic that ideally presents unlimited possibilities for bringing out myriad challenging cultural themes. In reality, however, the fact that multicultural education is a relative newcomer to the typical curriculum has frequently caused it to be added on to already existing schedules—squeezed in with art, music, and health—rather than incorporated organically into the instructional program.

Because multicultural education has usually been promoted as something new and innovative, it is easy to overlook its natural home as part of a subject that teachers have been teaching for years, social studies. What multicultural education really amounts to is an alternative, less ethnocentric lens with which to focus on an old subject—people and how they interact with one another and with nature. Banks (1984) provides a useful example of how culture can be taught across the various disciplines, starting from a foundation of social studies concepts. The approach is relatively easy to implement because it can be incorporated into existing subject-segmented curriculum structures. The curriculum can be injected with cultural content that teaches culture fairness and develops basic skills. For example, as Banks (1984) points out, teachers can take an area such as science, generally not associated with multicultural instruction, and formulate questions to be developed into lesson objectives:

How do humans vary physically?

How have various cultural groups explained scientific phenomena?

Which plants and animals are important to various groups?

How have scientific discoveries or inventions changed peoples' ways of life?

What experiments can be performed using objects, materials, or concepts that are important to a particular cultural group?

Remembering the dynamic nature of culture, with various facets influencing each other in multidirectional ways, interdisciplinary study is important to bring the real world back to the classroom. Two modern creators of cultural phenomena, Einstein and the Beatles, will serve to illustrate the interrelated nature of most sociocultural change. Modern society, through its emphasis on the value of scientific and technological progress, was able to nurture the work of Einstein; he had an appreciative audience. In turn, Einstein's work is gradually altering modern society's worldview—the way we look at the universe and our place in it. Turning to a more mundane example, the Beatles' music not only changed musical taste but also helped to change values and attitudes regarding government, drugs, "proper" middle-class lifestyles, and so on, in numerous subcultures. This impact was so powerful that in Argentina the music of the Beatles was banned temporarily because the government felt that the popularity of the group was subverting traditional Argentine culture.

The premise that the study of culture is interdisciplinary necessarily must underlie any comprehensive multicultural program. There are two principal goals to be obtained from such an emphasis. The first goal is to develop in the learner a first-hand awareness that culture is reflected in many different human activities, and consequently in many subject areas. The second goal, which necessarily builds on the first one, is to develop the skills to compare, contrast, and generalize information regarding culture from a variety of sources, for the final "metapurpose" of beginning to come to grips as humans with our culturally multiple and yet deeply unified images.

As implied above, incorporating various subject areas into lessons is really just a first step in learning to "see" things with an understanding of what culture is and how it works. It is when the student begins to compare facts and ideas and to integrate concepts, within and across cultures, that deeper cultural and personal understanding begins to develop. Without this awareness, even using an interdisciplinary framework, we may be back to the laundry list approach described in chapter 4; this approach loads the student with many facts and probably a few stereotypes but with little or no understanding of the dynamics or the closeness of culture.

Learning by observing and reflecting on how other cultures differ and are alike requires the careful development, refinement, and nurturance of both intuitive and analytic thinking skills. Bruner (1960) describes analytic and intuitive thinking as follows:

> Analytic thinking characteristically proceeds a step at a time. Steps are explicit and usually can be adequately reported by the thinker to another individual. Such thinking proceeds with relatively full awareness of the information and operations involved. It may involve careful and deductive reasoning, often using mathematics or logic and an explicit plan of attack. Or it may involve a step-by-step process of induction and experiment, utilizing principles of research design and statistical analysis.

> In contrast to analytic thinking, intuitive thinking characteristically does not advance in careful, well-defined steps. Indeed, it tends to involve maneuvers based seemingly on an implicit perception of the total problem. The thinker arrives at an answer, which may be right or wrong, with little if any awareness of the process by which he reached it. He rarely can provide an adequate account of how he obtained his answer, and he may be unaware of just what aspects of the problem situation he was responding to. Usually

intuitive thinking rests on familiarity with the domain of knowledge involved and with its structure, which makes it possible for the thinker to leap out, skipping steps and employing shortcuts in a manner that requires a later rechecking of conclusions by more analytic means, whether deductive or inductive. (Bruner, 1960, pp. 57–58)

Multicultural education provides a natural context for the encouragement of discovery skills as proposed by Bruner, skills which will strengthen children's critical thinking ability in all subject areas. As a theme in social studies, multicultural education provides learners with opportunities to develop cultural hunches; ask pointed questions; examine beliefs, values, and behaviors in other cultures; and integrate the data for personal and cultural meaning. The analytic and intuitive skills nurtured in cross-cultural study problems are transferable to other areas of the curriculum, such as mathematics and science, disciplines in which both intuitive and analytic reasoning are crucial.

Such thought-process-oriented activities, by their nature, cannot be carried out easily; they require careful thinking on the part of the teacher, plus caution. An illustration from an informal learning context demonstrates that the *casual* unplanned comparison of two groups of ethnically different children will not necessarily bring about positive results. In the early 1960s, one of the authors, then a naive sophomore in college, was serving as a day-camp counselor in the Midwest for a summer:

> During a hot and humid afternoon the group of black children with whom I was working took a long walk with me through a park preserve. After a while several of the children decided to plop themselves underneath a large oak tree. Eager to get back to camp, I told the children tongue in cheek that they should not be so lazy and that compared to an earlier group of Puerto Rican children they seemed sluggish. Immediately, one of the more perceptive campers snapped back, "I thought you were hired to work with us, and not to compare us with the Puerto Ricans." I apologized for my mistake and let them continue their much coveted *siesta*. Even when the intent is not to hurt, there is always the possibility of cross-cultural backfire.

MACOS   An examination of one particular program, *Man: A Course of Study* (Education Development Center, 1969), will illustrate how a critical-thinking comparative approach to pluralistic education can be implemented. MACOS touches on some highly sensitive and controversial cross-cultural values—for example, it treats cultural relativity through a discussion of senilicide among the Netsilik Eskimos; it deals with human evolution vis-à-vis the analysis of salmon, herring gull, chimpanzee, and baboon behavior; and it includes the study of mythological and religious beliefs, some quite similar to the Old Testament versions, but from a non-Judeo-Christian perspective. Consequently, it has generated profound controversy in many school districts in which it has been used. Notwithstanding such community ferment over some aspects of the program, many fine ideas, concepts, and curricular strategies, especially meaningful for cultural analysis, comparison, and participation, are introduced in the program. This type of curricular strategy is particularly appropriate for bilingual classrooms, in which multicultural analysis is a necessity. Of the three traditions for social studies education, MACOS falls into the category of social studies taught as reflective inquiry.

MACOS was designed by Bruner with the support of the National Science Foundation "to test the conjecture that young children can grapple with the mysteries of human nature in an intelligent way" (Dow, 1972, p. 22). To answer such a deep and provoking question as "What is human about human beings?", 10-year-olds are taken through a series of thought-provoking activities for 1 year. The curriculum consists of student booklets, simulation games and drama activities, anthropologists' field notes, and unnarrated films which allow the students to observe and draw their own conclusions. A host of universal themes is covered in the course: important events in a human lifetime; contrasts and continuities across human lifetimes, cooperation; biological dependency (child rearing); innate and learned behavior; the will to love and live; flexibility among humans; structure and behavior of human beings compared to animals; ecology and the elements in human survival; language and communication; nonverbal communication; power relationships among humans and animals; male and female roles; anthropological research by children; and traditional versus modern societies. In studying these varied themes, the children engage in personally meaningful activities which yield excitement about their own culture-bearing and culture-producing possibilities while at the same time learning about culture and how to generalize about cultural patterns and processes. As Dow points out,

> Materials of this kind are not designed to teach children a particular viewpoint about human behavior, but rather to heighten their awareness that human behavior, while complex, is understandable in some form. By employing certain approaches, such as the contrasting animal case studies, and by developing techniques of observation, children will hopefully arrive at new insights about themselves. Such understanding may even give them a modicum of increased power over their own lives. (1972, p. 72)

In relating this approach to cultural analysis to the lives of the students in a bilingual classroom, a teacher must deal with not only American mainstream culture and "foreign" culture but also the Americanized sub-cultures represented by the acculturated ethnic students in his or her class. The cultural patterns represented within the communities which feed the school are multiple. Because of this it is even more important for children to learn to look back and forth between cultures—comparing, integrating, and generalizing in the natural laboratory of their own community. This is very different from focusing on culture A, "mastering" its content, moving on to culture B, and so on. In relating and comparing traditional foreign cultures to life in the United States, Saville-Troike suggests three areas of inquiry:

a. What are the major stereotypes which you and others have about each cultural group? To what extent are these accepted by the group being typed?

b. To what extent and in what areas has the traditional culture of each minority group changed in contact with the dominant American culture? In what areas has it been maintained?

c. To what extent do individuals possess knowledge of or exhibit characteristics of traditional groups? (Saville-Troike, 1978, p. 19)

Teachers and Students as Cultural Researchers

Use of a comparative, integrative, critical-thinking approach can provide many opportunities to draw the student directly into the knowledge-production process, and under ideal circumstances mentors and learners can frequently be coproducers and co-consumers of cultural insights. It is only occasionally that we see classroom teachers and their students in such mutually supportive roles. In the first place, educational researchers and teacher-training institutions have historically perceived teachers as a fairly passive clientele who will pass on predetermined concepts and content to their students. Curriculum designers have felt, and somewhat realistically so, that teachers do not have the necessary training or time to carry out carefully designed and reliable research projects in the classroom. Teachers, in turn, have come to believe such a perception and thus seem reluctant to become, along with their students, their own anthropologists, sociologists, ethnographers, or sociolinguists. This is easy to understand, because "doing anthropology" takes years of training for anthropologists themselves. These facts notwithstanding, it is more meaningful for teachers and students to draw conclusions regarding cultural meaning from first-hand *observed* behavior. It is one thing for teachers to be told in a conference that a certain set of nonverbal communication gestures are commonly used by Korean students and quite a different and important step for teachers then to go back to the community or school and observe what local Korean children are actually doing.

In the following section we explore the characteristics of two approaches to research by students and teachers. One approach, based on Seelye (1974), although designed with the foreign-language teacher in mind, includes paradigms for activities appropriate to multicultural education in general. The second approach, Longstreet's "action research," is illustrative of procedures relevant to observation of subcultures actually represented in the classroom.

Simulated Cultural Exercises   Exemplary of a method in which students are passively fed cultural information, rather than encouraged to be researchers, is the traditional "high civilization" orientation typically used in secondary- and college-level foreign-language courses. The tendency has been to spotlight the elite, higher-class values of the cultures mirrored by the languages being studied. However, alternative approaches to the teaching of culture have been developed for the foreign-language classroom, approaches which involve learners in the acquisition of cultural awareness, rather than feeding them an exclusive diet of famous art, architecture, literature, and historical events. One such method, developed by Seelye (1974), contains ideas and activities that are transferable to many bilingual and ESL classroom settings. It is a more natural, complex, and varied interpretation of culture which requires participation on the part of the learner.

Because Seelye believes that the study of culture should be purposeful, deliberate, and operational, most of his suggestions are worded in such a way that the teacher and learner can examine beliefs, values, and behaviors cross-culturally, rather than in isolation. In an attempt to harness the broad concept of culture for instructional purposes, he identifies seven areas for cultural instruction: the sense, or function, of culturally conditioned behavior; interaction of language and social variables; conventional behavior in common situations; cultural connotations of words and phrases; evaluating statements about a society; researching another culture; and attitudes toward other cultures (Seelye, 1974, pp. 39–46). These cultural variables are clothed with what Seelye terms his own super cultural goal—that "all students will develop the cultural understandings, attitudes, and performance skills needed to function appropriately within a society of the target language and to communicate with the culture bearer" (1974, p. 39). The value of this framework for multicultural education in general is not to learn in depth how to act within a particular target culture, but to focus on "functioning" or acting as it varies across cultures. The student is learning about and experimenting with behaviors, not with lists of things and traits. Reading materials about a given culture which are personalized, warm, and empathetic will foster the development and internalization of positive attitudes. For example, if sixth graders in a classroom in the United States read a description of classroom life written by a 12-year-old living in Hong Kong, they will be able to develop their own observations about similarities and differences in patterns of classroom life.

Seelye (1974) suggests a series of cultural exercises which engage the student of culture in simulating an actual cultural event and grasping the behavioral expectations of such an event. These activities are minidramas, culture assimilators, culture capsules, and culture clusters.

Minidramas   The purpose of these presentations is to expose and sensitize students to the complexity of cross-cultural communication. Through these minidramas students role-play situations in both cultures and thus experience the psychosocial and linguistic aspects surrounding cultural misunderstandings. Each minidrama consists of three to five episodes, each one of them including a cultural "misfire." Eventual solutions and follow-up discussions are part of the process.

Culture Assimilators   These are episodes, about 3 minutes long, which describe a situation in which cross-cultural miscommunication has occurred. The student reads the brief cultural encounter and then intuits or reasons what went wrong between the two culture bearers. Usually the student is given four choices and is asked to select the most appropriate one.

Culture Capsules   A culture capsule focuses on one minimal difference between two cultures and explains the difference briefly in one or two paragraphs. When possible, photographs or other realia are included to help illustrate the difference.

Culture Clusters   Essentially a culture-integrating activity, culture clusters pull together at least three culture capsules and add a 30-minute in-class event which synthesizes the data presented in the capsules. A goal of this approach is to get all the students involved in a final presentation or skit.

Notwithstanding the limitations inherent in such simulated cultural learning experiences, Seelye's suggestions for engaging teachers and students in potentially useful and personalized cross-cultural experiences go far in providing a framework for vicarious culture learning, which can yield personal identification by the student with the target culture. Undoubtedly, there is some value in knowing and understanding the outstanding "high civilization" contributions which all cultures have made, but from the point of view of trying to motivate the learner to develop appropriate cross-cultural coping skills, Seelye's more diversified and personal view of culture should be a welcome instructional addition to the fields of pluralistic education and second-language instruction.

From the point of view of a bilingual educator, Seelye's suggestions raise some interesting and complex instructional dilemmas. Most bilingual school environments have a rather disproportionately large number of learners who are often stigmatized socially, culturally, economically, and educationally. Many such stigmatized children enter the schools with two strikes against them—they are poor, and their culture is not congruous with the ethos of the schools. They come to school speaking nonstandard versions of English—and often of their own tongue—and behaving in ways perceived as suspect by the school culture. The kind of cultural information which is comparatively easy to obtain for such popular cultures as German, Spanish, French, or Russian requires more personal initiative to develop for learners who represent beliefs, values, and behaviors which are part of the American fabric but seem contradictory to the dominant American experience. In the hands of teachers who make the necessary methodological, ideological, and cultural adjustments, however, Seelye's ideas could prove worthwhile in trying to bring life to sociocultural and linguistic realities surrounding children from the *barrios*, Chinatowns, and other ethnic enclaves.

Action Research   Action research, as proposed by Longstreet (1978), calls for teachers and students to become involved in the gathering and analysis of data on ethnically induced behavior. Ethnically induced behavior is defined as those aspects of a person's behavior patterns which develop without reasoning, or before the development of abstract thinking skills. This would include behavior patterns established roughly before the age of 10 or 12.

Recognizing that students and teachers are not professional social scientists, action research is to be anchored on "rational objectivity" rather than the "pure" scientific method. Observations of individuals and groups over a period of time and under varying contexts serve as the data from which hunches—or as Longstreet calls them, "tentative hypotheses"—are formulated and used for instruction and cultural understanding. This approach to the production of cultural knowledge, which acknowledges the futility of finding absolutely "right" answers, has the possibility of enabling students to become responsible culture analyzers.

Although it is impossible, as emphasized in chapter 4, to harness the concept of culture, we can approximate the meanings of specific behaviors and infer tentative conclusions from them once such behaviors have been observed in a repeated manner in analogous circumstances by various persons. As Longstreet argues, all teachers, simply as human beings, go on making all sorts of instructional and personal decisions based on stereotypes which have not been put under some sort of logical analysis. Since we cannot eliminate stereotypes from our view of the world, the next best thing is to study them.

There are many themes which lend themselves to cross-cultural research by teachers and students within the natural life of the school. Students can be given assignments to analyze their community or the lifestyles surrounding their families. There are possibilities for library research on the cultural history of the neighborhood. In large urban centers there is a great deal of internal ethnic migration within relatively short periods of time, and it is possible to find quite a rich mixture of ethnic influences in many neighborhoods. Students could either interview older members of their own families or seek out neighbors who have a repertoire of information regarding the development of the area. Students can also be asked to examine various aspects of contemporary life. For instance, children can be encouraged to interview persons from different cultural backgrounds and prepare reports or special activities to disseminate the information they have collected. Surveys could be done on how people spend their free time, how birthdays are celebrated, types of marriage ceremonies, and funeral practices. Nonformal learning can enter the classroom, such as a knowledge of herbal medicine, a scary ghost story that grandmother told, how to butcher a pig, or the words to a counting rhyme.

Data can be collected to cover a broad range of cultural issues. What are the behaviors that seem to reveal acculturation? Is there much evidence in the community of bilingualism and biculturalism? Do many families maintain contact either by mail or travel with the ancestral countries? Why, when, and how did immigration occur? Are persons from the country of origin still coming today, and are they still settling in the same locale? Are there local theatres which show movies in their languages? Is there much of a gap between the old and new generations? If so, how is this manifested? Is there any evidence that people cross cultural boundaries? If so, how is this done? Are there any special events during the year when the concept of culture takes on a great deal of symbolism? Do the modern teenagers of the group participate in such events?

Another example of action research is the examination of the relativity of intelligence as interpreted by various cultures (Collier, 1973). To say that intelligence is relative is to say that its manifestation is a phenomenon which is learned and expressed naturally within a given cultural system. In a Chamorro, Chicano, Crow, or Athapascan setting, there will be somewhat different ways of expressing intelligence. Any U.S. citizen who has traveled overseas could probably relate at least one experience of feeling awkward. Lessons designed with the understanding that intelligence is relative will likely reflect the intrinsic dignity and worth of all cultures.

While these sample topics are of a general nature, teachers and students can refine their own themes to such a level that the information can be interwoven into the natural life of the instructional process. Cameras, videotapes, old yearbooks, old records, family albums, newspaper clippings, interviews, observations, and journals are some of the means by which such data can be gathered. Besides constituting social studies research, much of the information can be incorporated into all subject areas. The action research schema also lends itself naturally to the nurturing of intuitive and analytic thinking as suggested earlier by Bruner. Rather than looking for absolute answers, one expects data subjectivity, data instability, and methodological uncertainty in all that is observed and reported. This type of consciously tentative cultural data can provide a powerful means of creating a personal meaning of culture, biculturalism, and pluralism for the teacher and student.

RESOURCES FOR SOCIAL STUDIES

Resources specifically designed for bilingual and ESL social studies classes are still relatively scarce. There are many adult education ESL textbooks designed for studying customs in the United States and preparing for U.S. citizenship, but few encourage a global or comparative cross-cultural perspective. A few more recent texts are beginning to appear which encourage reflective cross-cultural analysis, such as *Beyond Language: Intercultural Communication for English as a Second Language* (Levine & Adelman, 1982). Very few of these texts, however, are written for younger students. Tiedt and Tiedt (1979) is one of the best sources of materials for cross-cultural awareness for elementary-level social studies classes. This book includes references for readings for young children on many ethnic groups in the United States. Banks (1984) is also a thorough reference on ethnic groups for secondary-level social studies classes.

For materials prepared in the social studies field in general, the professional organization for teachers, the National Council for the Social Studies, is useful. In addition to the MACOS materials (Education Development Center, 1969) described earlier, there are other multicultural, interdisciplinary programs developed for grades K through 6, such as *Family of Man* (West, 1972), which includes units on an Israeli family living on a kibbutz, an Ashanti family, a Hopi Indian family, a Japanese family, a Russian family in Moscow, and a family living in early New England. These materials encourage reflective inquiry.

For bilingual classes, many school districts have developed their own social studies materials, drawing on resources from each individual community. Bilingual social studies lessons focused on cross-cultural awareness are especially specific to the individual language groups being served by each school. Thus there has been less national dissemination of materials developed. One source for curricular materials for K through 3 bilingual social studies lessons for Mexican-American students is provided in Almaraz (1979). These curricular guidelines were developed for the state of Texas. The Evaluation, Dissemination, and Assessment Centers (EDACs) have published some bilingual social studies materials for some of the major language groups in the United States.

Maps

The first gift all ESL and bilingual teachers can present to their students in the first week of class is an excellent, detailed map of the city or area in which they live. Almost all city governments produce a carefully drawn map which teachers can request free-of-charge for their students. This map can be considered one of their textbooks, to be treated and handled with care. Throughout the year a wide variety of activities can be carried out using the map, including those that develop language, culture, geography, history, and math skills. Just to give a few examples, students can:

1. Learn graph skills and use of symbols, through the key

2. Measure distances, which involves converting inches and centimeters to miles and kilometers

3. Learn how to give directions to get from one place to another

4. Become familiar with the total layout of their city or region, including industrial, social, environmental, and ecological boundaries

5. Develop knowledge of additional sources of enrichment available to students outside the school walls (e.g., museums, zoos, free movies, concerts, art shows)

6. Plot trips to special places

7. Share in social knowledge of the city or region

8. Develop maps of their local neighborhood, including geographic, historical, social, and cultural details

With the maps, teachers can encourage students to get around on their own and explore the richness of the environment that surrounds them.

In addition to local maps, detailed maps of the United States and all regions of the world are crucial for bilingual and ESL social studies classes. To reflect a more global perspective, maps of the world are more appropriate for a multinational class when the United States is not presented as the center of the world.

Periodicals and the Media

Another valuable resource for social studies classes is the local newspaper. Secondary social studies teachers for years have used newspapers, magazines, and TV news programs as resources for classes on current events. These continue to be excellent sources provided the language proficiency level of the students is fairly high. The local community frequently has at least one native-language newspaper which can add to the reading resources of a bilingual class. For students with beginning and intermediate levels of English-language proficiency, ESL teachers can find many good examples of simplified English in a local newspaper or journal to provide sources for understanding social and cultural phenomena. Advertisements, comic strips, the weather map, and editorial cartoons can be good sources for simplified English with "double loading" (language, culture, and social studies skills all combined into one lesson). Stores run by service organizations frequently have cheap copies of old journals which a class can use to cut out pictures or read articles on geographic, historical, cultural, and scientific topics being studied. Ethnically based TV and radio programs can serve as resources for class projects.

Resources in Consumer Education

Additional resources can be found in materials in the community which involve consumer awareness. ESL adult education teachers are most familiar with these techniques, but they are equally valuable for elementary- and secondary-level bilingual and ESL classes. Teachers can save old telephone books and develop lessons such as calling the police or fire department in case of emergency, choosing the numbers to call for social services, using the yellow pages, or learning simple telephone etiquette. Older students may want to get application forms from banks and other institutions to learn how to open a bank account, apply for a credit card, fill out a lease application, or file insurance claims or income tax forms. The list could go on. Many more recently developed ESL texts include some lessons focused on consumer education.

Resources for a Problem-Posing Curriculum

At the secondary level, bilingual social studies is generally designed for one of two purposes. In a maintenance bilingual program, students are expected to be fully proficient in both languages by the secondary level, and the course is used to focus on specialized knowledge in the subject area. Any language development which occurs in the course will be a beneficial side effect but not the chief focus. In a transitional bilingual class, on the other hand, the teacher hopes to impart some knowledge of social studies in the native language as well as social studies vocabulary and concepts in the second language. The teacher of a transitional class is thus concerned with the dual objectives of teaching both language and content.

When the focus is mainly on content, the multicultural context can be exploited to its fullest potential for challenging lessons. The curriculum of such a social studies class should include exposure to the nature of con- tradictory evidence, conflict resolution, problem posing, and problem solving, with teacher and students as risk takers. Social relations between people, regions, and nations can be examined in all their contexts to help students become responsible, thoughtful citizens. For example, students might study relations between the United States and their countries of origin; their own views of U.S. attitudes toward immigrants; the social and political system of the United States and how it functions; contradic- tions in U.S. value systems; politics in the country of origin and their current relation to that situation; or the process of assimilation and accul- turation to a new system of thought, behavior, and action.

Another type of risk-taking strategy centers around the study of stu- dents' personal value systems and a comparison of them with varying values of the surrounding communities and with overall societal values. Values clarification exercises are designed to explore students' percep- tions of their own value systems and those of others. A detailed bibliogra- phy on humanistic, personalized, values clarification exercises for the second-language classroom is available in Moskowitz (1978).

A wide variety of games focusing on nonverbal communication, cultural norms, and individual variation is available through materials on multicultural education, intercultural education, and cross-cultural training. One professional organization which publishes cross-cultural training materials is the Society for Intercultural Education, Training, and Research (SIETAR). Casse (1981) provides many exercises for teaching older learners about cross-cultural issues. Simulation games like Bafa-Bafa (or the elementary-level version, Rafa-Rafa) or Star Power provide students with powerful experiences in cross-cultural awareness. The East-West Center, located in Honolulu, Hawaii, also publishes a variety of very useful materials for teaching cross-cultural issues. The center is responsible for disseminating materials on Asian and Pacific-American concerns.

Electronic Media and Films

Even the most casual observer can tell you that the population of the United States—young and old—has been touched fundamentally by the mass media explosion. Consider for example the ubiquitous stereo headphones worn by joggers, walkers, bicyclists, and students; the proliferation of home video cassette recorders; cable television; inexpensive microcomputers families use to play electronic games, keep records, and do word processing.

What are bilingual and ESL teachers to make out of this electronic media explosion? Teachers should find out what access their students have to such media and try to link some classroom work with it. For example, the teacher may wish to ask her students who play such games, which ones are their favorites, and why. Depending on the answers, the teachers and students can explore themes such as conflict resolution theory and space exploration. From a more practical point of view, films and videotapes for instructional purposes can be quite useful in the hands of a creative and resourceful teacher.

Why get involved with films and videotapes when teachers tend to feel they are cumbersome, hard to get, and expensive to operate in a time of dwindling resources? Appropriate films and videotapes can provide the learner with a powerful sense of realism. They are the next best thing to being physically in the natural environment. Although it is a vicarious experience, learners have an excellent opportunity to surround themselves with visual imagery and powerful sociocultural themes which then can be translated into oral and literacy skills in the bilingual and ESL classroom. Because good films and videotapes can be quite alluring, they are excellent instruments through which students can see themselves and other societies. If human and material resources are available, students can become involved in filming or videotaping events or subjects which later can be shown in class for instructional purposes. In this way the learner and teacher become not only knowledge consumers but also knowledge producers—an important process in teaching and learning. The following questions are useful for considering films for social studies classes or other subject areas:

1. Does the film or videotape fit your specific lesson goals and objectives? What is the implicit and explicit message of the film or videotape? Are the content and level suited to the cultural, academic, and linguistic needs of the students?

2. Does the film or videotape facilitate not only observation but also participation, for example, through discussion or the carrying out of an assignment presented in the film or videotape? You can look for films or videotapes which examine any one or a combination of the following societal themes: environment, social stratification, politics, religion, ideology, utilization and availability of natural resources, economic systems, technology, demographics, enculturation and socialization of the young, and various forms of aesthetic expression in the society. Other related themes might be subsistence, kinship, conflict theory, development of material resources, daily routines, child-rearing practices, particular rights of different age and sex groups in society, traditional versus modern societies, and the distribution of status, power, and money in society. Old films can often be used to compare and contrast what is happening to the society. Vocabulary items, fashion styles, demographic factors, and ecological changes can serve to stimulate discussion and writing. For example, showing a film of any of our cities in the early part of the twentieth century and in the present can be quite revealing and stimulating for learners of varying academic, linguistic, and sociocultural backgrounds. Remember that a goal of social studies is to examine not only cultural universals but also our uniqueness, through abundant cultural detail.

3. Is there a written text which accompanies the film or videotape? If so, how does the text compare with the audiovisual treatment in terms of accuracy and historical fairness? Students can also compare and contrast what they see in a film to other written material appropriate to the film. They may also keep a journal of each film they see, recording their personal reactions; who produced, edited, and photographed the film; and other issues related to critical viewing techniques.

4. How much verbiage surrounds the film or videotape? How much commentary is really necessary? Would it be better to show the film or videotape without the running comments and let the viewers bring their experiences to the visual imagery? Because it is through such verbal loading in films and videotapes that much cross-cultural misinformation is transmitted, teachers must consider what verbal commentary to add to or delete from the film. You may want to start by showing the film or videotape without sound first and asking the children what they saw. You may be surprised at the range of responses you get. After the film has been discussed and some of the learners have had an opportunity to tell the class what the film is about, you may show the film with sound. Now the question is: What did you hear? Depending on the answer, you may want to spend some time discussing content, process, or vocabulary items. If you and the students are viewing a videotape which was produced by the class, the same procedures may be followed.

Social studies film viewing can not only develop the visual analysis skills of learners but also encourage students to examine cultural detail within their own and other societies. What takes place in a bilingual or ESL class has to fit the needs of each group. In any context, however, films can provide a powerful medium of instruction.

MUSIC

Music and art should be an integrated part of all subject areas; we separate these sections only to call the reader's attention to the importance of making music and art a part of many classroom experiences.

Good teachers are constantly searching for new ways to make the school world meaningful to their students without watering down the curriculum or presenting material clearly over students' heads. It is a tough job to create that appropriate balance in which students are clearly challenged but not overwhelmed in classes as heterogeneous as bilingual and ESL classes tend to be. One key to successful stimulation of students is to provide a wide variety of activities, not as entertainment, but as an integral, meaningful part of the curriculum. When students can see the purpose of each activity and its relation to the whole, and when they are included in the cooperative development of learning experiences, students will process and retain the information they have gathered at a deeper level.

To understand the process of imprinting learning on long-term memory (Stevick, 1976), it is helpful to recall a momentous learning experience in your life. What were the circumstances surrounding that event? What do you remember about the person (or people) you were with? Can you re-create a detailed visual image of the scene where that learning took place? Were there extrasensory stimuli? Was music associated with the event? Was there a fantastic visual image, such as art, photography, or a stunning outdoor or indoor scene? Were you physically involved in the experience? Did you touch someone or something? What smells do you remember? Did you taste something unusual or special?

Most likely that experience did not involve all senses at the same time, but you probably have retained a very sharp visual image of some aspects of the scene where that learning took place, and it probably involved more than just the senses we stimulate in the classroom when we focus so exclusively on pencil and paper tasks. Reading and writing skills are rightfully the most important skills we must teach in school, but they can be taught in a great variety of ways when integrated with other stimuli which reinforce and deepen the learning experience. Let's look at one area of additional stimulation which can be integrated quite effectively with daily activities and can add significantly to positive classroom climate: the use of music.

Including Music in Classroom Events

Whether you are a music enthusiast or just an occasional listener, you can collect enough simple recordings to learn with your students the power of a musical experience to stimulate the emotions, relax, or intensify the senses, thereby increasing the stimuli for retention of an experience. It is important to expose your students to a wide variety of musical experiences and to use those experiences in varied ways to reinforce skills learned in the classroom. Here are some possibilities:

1. Have music playing when students enter and leave the classroom (preferably *not* elevator music). The music sets the mood you want to establish that day. Repeating the same type of music each day for a week may subtly introduce students to a form of music they have not been exposed to before; for example, if the class is studying aspects of the Quechua and Aymara cultures, a tape of Andean Indian music of the Altiplano could be played as students enter and leave the room each day.

2. Different forms of music can be used to indicate changes in the classroom structure: break time, quiet time for reflection, creative composition, physical activities. You might persuade your school to use different types of music for signaling the change of classes instead of an unpleasant buzzer or bell.

3. Total-class or small-group activity can focus on specific songs or pieces of music which have significance for the particular skill(s) being taught. Social studies lends itself well to the introduction of songs which teach the social context, historical events, regional cultural differences, or dialectal variation.

4. Short taped radio spots and sequences can provide a variety of activities for the class to analyze.

5. Based on songs, jazz chants, commercials, or whatever variety of musical experiences the class shares, students can create their own poems, stories, lyrics, skits, and journals through the stimulation of their imagination.

6. The language laboratory can provide a variety of tapes of current music or music from the countries or regions being studied for additional listening comprehension exercises.

7. Occasional class trips to a community concert or musical event can reinforce class goals and provide a stimulus for additional learning.

Caveats

To avoid overuse of music, some words of caution are in order. The class needs to have an understanding of the purpose of each musical activity within the total scheme of skills to be mastered. It may take some time to establish a group process in which all students feel comfortable with a variety of activities, especially for those students who come from school systems in other countries in which traditional lecture methods are valued and knowledge is acquired chiefly through memorization. These students may view music purely as entertainment and therefore not appropriate in the classroom. To establish a classroom pattern in which music, games, psychomotor activities, use of multimedia, and varied patterns of individual and group work are accepted, students need to see clearly the gains that they have made from each activity. Music should not be introduced simply as a fun activity at the end of class on Friday afternoon but rather as a purposeful event, integrated into the total sequence of activities centered around a specific curricular unit. At the same time, music is fun and should be enjoyed for its wealth of emotional experience. An activity does not have to be approached with total seriousness for it to be worthwhile. It can include laughter, hilarity, and foot-stomping, finger-snapping fun.

A second caution involves the tendency of teachers to use a song as a show-and-tell cultural activity, emphasizing only the superficial, easily

visible aspects of a national culture. In keeping with the broader understanding of culture described in chapter 4, music should be taught in all its
forms so that students recognize the dynamic rather than static nature of
culture as represented in songs. This means, for example, that class activities involving U.S. music should include not only folk songs, children's
songs, and European classical music but also current rock, jazz, blues,
gospel, country and western, soul, bluegrass, and whatever forms of
music continue to be developed by groups of people. Most important of
all, students should discover the great variety of music produced by the
varied ethnic communities surrounding their school as a part of their
exploration of and increasing sensitivity to neighborhood social patterns.

The show-and-tell song tends to be one which is highly symbolic and
oversung. Young children may love these songs and appreciate singing
them (e.g., nursery rhymes, "Jingle Bells," "Old MacDonald Had a
Farm"). While they are quite appropriate for young children, teenagers
frequently give a teacher clues that they think the song is childish, or that
they hate being dragged through singing it again. In contrast, songs or
pieces of music which reveal new insights to students, stimulate students'
thinking, and naturally create many follow-up activities involving interpersonal sharing at a deep level are highly valuable learning events.

A third caution is not to use songs exclusively for teaching grammar
points, as emphasized in some ESL curricular materials. Every event in a
bilingual and ESL classroom involves learning language, but grammar or
pronunciation points when isolated out of context by the teacher tend to
lose their significance unless students themselves point out variations in
the grammar in a song they want to discuss. Songs are an excellent source
for discussion of dialectal variations and differences between spoken and
written varieties of language—for advanced students. We caution against
too much attention to minor grammatical details in songs, pointing out the
function of acquisition as opposed to conscious, formal learning, as
posited by Krashen (1981). If natural acquisition is the more important
process in second-language learning, activities which reinforce natural,
unconscious acquisition are to be encouraged in the classroom. Music
provides a very natural context for second-language acquisition to occur:
The socioaffective filter is lowered and motivation is generally fairly high.
Focus on tiny grammatical details may take away from the natural process established. On the other hand, students' interest and curiosity in
these details create a natural context for such discussions to take place
when they are not artificially imposed by the teacher.

A fourth caution concerns the choice of music to be examined in the
classroom. Generally, materials prepared especially for school tend to be
a bit contrived and too divorced from the reality of music as it is used in
the real world. Teenagers clearly prefer songs they hear on the radio over

any prepared for the classroom to teach specific points. With today's sophisticated recording equipment, students turn on to high-quality recordings done by professional groups. There is so much good, inexpensive material available that there is no reason for a teacher not to use live, actively sought-after, current music to teach language and good recordings of folk music to illustrate regional cultural differences.

Songs must also be chosen carefully for the level of proficiency and maturity of the students, so that they provide a slight challenge but are not overwhelming. Dialect and controversial topics must be used with care, but there is no reason to avoid controversy when students are exposed to it daily. A song might stimulate an excellent discussion on prejudice, drugs, or environmental issues, for example. Political controversy can be examined, provided the teacher has established firm rapport with the class and feels students can handle the discussion. In a Vietnamese-English bilingual class, for example, certain songs about South Vietnam might stir up emotional feelings; the teacher needs to decide how well the students can handle the activity. Nicaraguan students might want to study the songs of Carlos Mejía Godoy and the Sandinista movement. United States government immigration policies might be examined through the stimulus of a song such as "Deportee," by Pete Seeger and Arlo Guthrie. Depending on the age, proficiency, needs, and temperament of the students, the teacher may choose from a great variety of possibilities, but the choices need to be made carefully.

Learning Objectives for Musical Experiences

The following suggested activities form only a partial listing of the many ways to make effective use of music. Teachers may add their own ideas to this list. When planning musical experiences for their classes, teachers should try to include an integrated series of activities which achieves several of the following objectives, rather than focusing on only one or two. Each lesson should include multiple tasks which encompass a variety of levels of cognitive, affective, and psychomotor development.

I. Cognitive Objectives: Language Arts

    A. Listening comprehension

        1. Tapes in the language lab of current rock, bluegrass, folk, soul, country and western, or other music, with a full text of words of the songs available to students.

        2. Assignment: Students listen to a current hit tune they like on the radio and write down the words to teach the song to you and fellow students.

B. Speaking skills

1. Songs provide practice with sounds, rhythms, stress and intonation, sandhi-variation, and colloquial expressions of spoken language.

2. For learning English, see *Jazz Chants* (Graham, 1975). These can be short 2- to 3-minute activities introduced occasionally in class. After students catch on to the idea, they frequently like to write their own.

3. Sing a song chosen by the students. You know that you are on the right track when students initiate singing the songs or jazz chants you have introduced to them.

C. Introduction of new vocabulary in context

1. Use realia to reinforce the new words; the visual and tactile stimuli add another dimension to the total sensory experience for retention of language learned.

    a. A box of old clothes can be used to teach the jazz chant "Shoes and Socks," or you can make up a song, "I am wearing . . ."

    b. Sing "Old MacDonald" or "The Farmer in the Dell," using masks or puppets to represent the characters and animals. (Students can make the masks.)

2. Teach variations in dialect; historical differences in language development; slang; spoken versus written forms of language.

D. Reinforcement of grammatical structures

1. Use songs with questions and answers in a variety of tenses. Try "Billy Boy"—students can add more verses, incorporating humor and creativity, and practicing questions and answers.

2. Other examples of grammatical points are listed in Graham (1975) and Osman and McConochie (1979).

E. Communicative competence

1. Some songs call for creating dialogue back and forth between two or more people or the playful addition of verses which challenge the imagination of the singers. Some ex-

amples are *"La Bamba"*; children's songs such as "The Green Grass Grew All Around," *"Mata Rile,"* *"La Rana,"* and "The Old Lady Who Swallowed a Fly."

2. Students can create their own music or chants or write new words to familiar melodies.

II. Cognitive Objectives: Social Studies

A. Historical context of songs. In addition to materials in texts and historical information the teacher brings to the class, students can look up information on various songs in the library. One example of a text written for ESL students with brief summaries of the historical context of each of twenty-eight U.S. folk songs is *If You Feel Like Singing* (Osman & McConochie, 1979).

B. Geography. Different styles of music from one region to another demonstrate regional-geographic boundaries from which students can see the relations between natural environmental factors which help to define cultural and regional patterns.

C. Sociology and anthropology. Class discussion can focus on how music reflects values, lifestyle, and regional differences between groups. In a bilingual Spanish-English class, for example, students can study differences between various Hispanic American groups in the United States and the even broader spectrum of widely variant cultures represented by all those who speak Spanish throughout the world. (See, for example, Bensusan & Carlisle, 1978.)

III. Affective Objectives

Music can be invigorating, soothing, uplifting, fantasy stimulating, depressing, haunting. Whatever the type of music, it generally produces some kind of strong negative or positive emotional response. Some songs talk about feelings, self-worth, identity. They help students to struggle with their own emotional responses (e.g., "It's All Right to Cry" from the record *Free to Be You and Me*), or they help students resolve doubts about self-worth (e.g., "It's not that Easy Bein' Green," sung by Kermit the Frog on "Sesame Street"). Students in bilingual classes have many opportunities to affirm their cultural and ethnic identity through a variety of activities, one of which can be the sharing of music and the sense of pride in each region's unique contributions to the wealth of human variety.

IV. Psychomotor Objectives

There are many ways to incorporate physical movement into musical activities. Listeners who are just sitting rarely sit still; music encourages tapping fingers, bouncy feet, wiggly shoulders; the rhythms inspire movement. Children's songs almost always include active physical involvement directed by the teacher combined with spontaneous inventing by children. Folk dancing, square dancing, rock, disco, and all varieties of dance from each region of each country are full physical responses to music. Teaching folk dance involves a fair amount of time and may be considered an activity far removed from the essential school goals of content-area instruction. Teachers have to make difficult decisions about priorities, but dance may be a legitimate classroom activity.

Up to this point we have suggested musical activities that may be incorporated into language and social studies lessons. Creative math and science teachers might also find ways to incorporate music, art, and physical activities into the learning of skills. For example, if students become interested in the musical instruments used for a specific type of music, they can study the properties of the materials used to make the instruments and the physical principles involved in producing the sound; the project might culminate in the actual making of an instrument. Museums frequently have educational programs in which staff members work with students in designing projects which incorporate skills from several disciplines. Perhaps your school district has master teachers in specialized areas who can help you devise such a project, or there may be knowledgeable parents who would volunteer some time to work with the class.

Music in Extracurricular Activities

In addition to using music in the subject areas, for which activities should be carefully chosen for efficient, maximum use of time and relevance to the total curriculum, there are endless possibilities for music to be used in specialized music classes and extracurricular activities. Mutlicultural entertainment has become almost a trademark of many bilingual programs. The development of musical or folk dance groups can be very beneficial if students are genuinely involved in the decision making and are excited about participating. Parents and bilingual staff may work together in assisting students with celebrations of cultural events or creating festivals including music, food, and dance representing the varied traditions of linguistic and cultural groups within the student body. Many of the ideas for these events are developed spontaneously as students express desires to share special traditions. Some natural by-products of bilingual programs have been the development of an *estudiantina* (a band of serenading musicians, a custom originally from Spain and preserved in Latin America) and other musical groups; a celebration of the lunar new year; international clubs which sponsor varying events; soccer teams; and theatrical productions. The list could go on and on.

It is appropriate for bilingual staff to affirm students' desires to preserve pride in their heritage. The most important by-product of a successful bilingual school is the creation among students of a sense of self-worth and belonging, so that students feel that they have ownership in the institution and that the school will provide them with the tools they need to make it in the outside world. Here's where the rub comes: If the festivals and cultural events provide students with the positive feelings and tools for succeeding in school, they are well worth the effort; but if students and parents insist that students are not getting enough time on task to complete a well-rounded education comparable to all middle-class students in the United States, then bilingual staff should rethink their priorities. Festivals and folk dances and all the easily visible symbols of culture may become too much of a good thing. It is tricky to measure students' exposure to all aspects of learning, but it is very important to keep the balance.

Resources on Music

Watch for special concerts in your community. Some are major family events which you can encourage all your students to attend and can follow up on. One example is a popular Puerto Rican group, *Haciendo punto en otro son*, who sometimes tour the United States. As representative of the "new song" movement, they adapt traditional Latin American melodies, rhythms, and instruments using the latest advances in technology and sound.

Listen to the radio and TV, and tape programs that are part of the public domain to use in class. You can collect songs, commercials, and analyses of musical pieces. To ensure compliance with copyright laws, contact your local radio or TV station to determine which programs are copyrighted and write for permission to use a program if necessary. National Public Radio offers tapes of music for schools, and their catalogue is free.

One resource for Spanish-English bilingual programs is a complete 52-week radio series called *Raíces y ritmos: Our Heritage of Latin American Music* (Bensusan & Carlisle, 1978). This series on music presents extensive detail of regional variations within each Latin American country, Spain, Portugal, and the southwestern United States. Indian, Iberian, and black musical elements are explored separately and in combination, and many historical and contemporary trends are explored. The tapes or cassettes can be ordered from the Department of Modern Languages, Southwest Texas State University, San Marcos, TX 78668.

A new multilingual journal begun in 1980 and published by the University of Texas Press, *Latin American Music Review,* gives a lot of detailed information for older students who want to study Latin American music in depth.

In choosing between records and cassettes, consider that records produce higher-quality sound but cassettes are more practical for the classroom. One solution might be to buy records for your home collection and tape chosen selections for the classroom. Many current record albums include words to the songs. If you are a music enthusiast, you already have your own ideas of what to choose for your classroom. For teachers just beginning to explore the world of music, listen to the variety on radio and TV, including special programs for children. Radio stations usually specialize in one type of music and are frequently helpful to teachers who wish to get up-to-date information on current trends in music.

Most large record stores have an international collection, and there are specialized record stores in many ethnic communities which order records from other countries if they are not immediately available.

Occasionally, commercial movies are a good musical resource. Sometimes movies or videotapes produced by people in your local community are available. Local ethnic communities may have specialized theatres which show worthwhile movies. Preview each movie that you choose and make careful lesson plans for activities both before and after the showing so that students may get the greatest benefit from the experience.

Bilingual theatrical productions are increasing in recent years and can provide stimulating topics for oral and written activities for all students.

ART IN THE BILINGUAL AND ESL CLASSROOM

Etched deeply in our psyche is a powerful desire to affirm, to recognize, or to create beauty. For some of us our spiritual and mental selves have found a bond through the reflection of a full moon on the surface of a glasslike, tranquil, and secluded lake; a perfectly shaped rainbow hovering over a mountain range and valley; a stunning and prolonged sunset over a Pacific Ocean bay. For others, beauty has manifested itself in the form of the delicate and smooth texture of an infant's skin, an extraordinarily handsome face, a mother duck surrounded by her ducklings. As humans, we universally decorate ourselves or our artifacts. At some point in our lives most of us have found a strong urge to want to add something to ourselves—hats, ties, rouge, powder, eye shadow, after-shave lotion, permanents—in an attempt to improve on the way we naturally are. And when we are not decorating ourselves, we frequently identify objects which we like a great deal—a car, knife, book cover, flower pot, or canoe—and paint them, add curlicues, or in some other way personally identify them. People from all cultures make aesthetic statements using some kind of visual imagery, affirming or altering nature, or radically creating something entirely new.

Art, as a universal form of human expression, can become a powerful ally for the bilingual and ESL teacher. Artistic expression, whether in the form of drawing, painting, sculpture, pottery, crafts, puppetry, photography, printmaking, collage, weaving, or stitchery, evokes in us a wide range of emotional and cognitive responses, and therein lies its power for encouraging communication. As a vehicle for verbal and nonverbal communication in the bilingual and ESL classroom, artistic creativity has the potential of relaxing, personalizing, and cheering, as well as creating a natural environment for communication. Beyond helping to create a base for linguistic, cultural, cognitive, emotional, and psychomotor development, artistic endeavors complement and enrich a school curriculum which has tended to stress the mathematical and verbal aspects of the learning process.

Art allows the bilingual or ESL teacher to provide a socioculturally rich environment which encourages learners to acquire and learn language through story-telling. Art is a seductive way of peeking into a person's linkage of public and private self. By engaging the senses, the teacher and students are pushed and pulled toward each other's perspectives, and encouraged to exchange their views of the world. It is this type of environment which offers an additional seedbed for second-language acquisition and learning. Confirming this point of view, Geertz (1973, p. 82) writes, "in order to make up our minds we must know how we feel about things; and to know how we feel about things we need the public images of sentiment that only ritual, myth, and art can provide."

It is important, however, to understand the limits of creative expression. Art is necessarily grounded in values, beliefs, symbols, and behaviors which the person has experienced within the matrix of his world. When learners from diverse cultural backgrounds express themselves through a given form of art, the teacher has to understand that whatever he sees, hears, tastes, smells, or touches may have a multilayered reality which is only partially accessible to a person looking into the culture from the outside. The following are themes which lend themselves to the use of artistic imagination for emotional, sociocultural, and linguistic development within bilingual and ESL classrooms.

Building Acceptance of the Individual

By giving learners an opportunity to engage in truly personal expressive choices, teachers can avoid the homogenizing tendencies often exhibited in arts and crafts activities. Perhaps too often, children are given a subject—for example, a duck—followed by instructions, after which the students faithfully produce ducks which all look remarkably similar. While assembly-line crafts may under some circumstances be appropriate, children also need repeated opportunities to express themselves personally and to have that expression accepted. Students could, for instance, be given an assignment to prepare a photo essay on the local community, commenting on its ugliness and its beauty or on its human and material resources. The student might prepare several pictures showing aspects of her community which she particularly likes and other pictures revealing negative aspects. She could then make a presentation to the class regarding her perceptions of the pleasant and unpleasant aspects of community life, which may be very different from what the teacher or other students consider pleasant or unpleasant. Depending on what students do with such an assignment, it may be discovered that aesthetic expression is firmly grounded in specific values within specific cultural contexts and that in fact beauty and ugliness truly are in the eyes of the beholder.

Art Appreciation in Cross-Cultural Context

The powerful connection between aesthetic expression and culture is captured by McFee and Degge (1977, p. 291) in the following quotation:

> Most cohesive groups have some system of accounting for values and beliefs that relates the world as they experience it with the ordering system they develop to explain it. Languages and art are used to describe how the system works. Myths, folk tales, drawings, carvings, and paintings objectify a cultural group's concept of reality. Forces that are not explainable appear concrete and often are thought of as the force itself. Ceremonies, rituals, and artifacts explain weather, hunting and gathering successes, and crops growing or failing.

Having even a partial understanding of how we as cultural beings go about objectifying deeply rooted experiences which often border on the spiritual can be quite useful for the bilingual or ESL teacher in soothing cross-cultural misunderstandings. While this information is important in any educational setting, it takes on special meaning when teachers find themselves working in contexts in which traditional cultures and languages are undergoing severe stress from the forces of immigration, cultural contact, and modernization.

The establishment of cross-cultural understanding through exposure to the visual arts can be highly effective. It adds another personalizing dimension to cross-cultural studies as students explore and imitate the traditional and modern art forms of cultural groups within the classroom. As in any cross-cultural activity, however, care has to be taken to acknowledge the variety of personal styles found within the larger pattern of an ethnic style. Consider, for example, having to distinguish between art as a reflection of personal experiences and an art style as a product of ethnic forces. To what extent are the murals of East Los Angeles the personal artistic expressions of the individual Chicanos who painted them, and to what extent are they extensions of the ethnic experience as expressions of social protest?

Art and Language Learning

Many language lessons can be built around art. Because an art activity almost by definition has to involve concrete, visual demonstration, it lends itself well to language immersion. And because art is a form of emotional expression, it can be a naturally motivating context for second-language acquisition. Within an art lesson, vocabulary involving materials, verbs (fold, cut, squeeze, dry out), texture, shape, color, and feelings can be developed. For practice in writing the second language, students may be asked to keep a log of the process they went through in producing their art. If the art lesson was done in the second language, they already have been exposed to much of the vocabulary they will need. They can summarize the steps involved in their project and then describe the final product.

Chapter Six

MATHEMATICS
AND SCIENCE

I am an ESL teacher, and one of my students is Rui, a kindergarten boy. Rui arrived from Japan very recently, and consequently his English expressive skills are at this time limited to one- or two-word responses. Rui is the only limited-English-proficient (LEP) student in his classroom and I work with him for 45 minutes a day on a pullout basis. Although I am bilingual, I do not happen to speak Japanese, and among the activities which I use with Rui are mathematical manipulative-based ones.

Rui's classroom teacher often puts in "special requests," and one day when I came to get Rui, she asked me to teach him the terms "more" and "less." I used a variety of paired sets of real objects, and I had one of my puppets ask me which set had more or less. For each of the puppet's questions I modeled the target response by pointing to one of the sets and responding with the appropriate word, "more" or "less." Rui understood immediately and began taking his turn responding to the puppet's questions, exclaiming intermittently, "Easy, easy!" (He had learned this phrase from his kindergarten peers.) After a little practice with real objects, I tried the exercise with paired workbook pictures of sets, and he always responded correctly. Then, at a more symbolic level, I showed him paired numerals, again asking, "Which one is more/less?" He continued to respond correctly, minus some typical kindergarten confusion with 6s and 9s. It was clear that within the span of 10 minutes of instruction I had not taught him the concept of more and less; he showed that he already had that concept in his repertoire of cognitive skills. I had just taught him to associate the English words "more" and "less" with that concept.

Rui's teacher is concerned that he is not "keeping up" with the other students, and she often asks me for a quick progress report when I bring him back to the classroom. When I told her on this particular day that Rui could respond to more and less problems now, she threw up her arms in delight, went over to Rui, and exclaimed, "Boys and girls, boys and girls! Rui! Rui, tell all the boys and girls what more means!" Virtually every curious kindergarten eye was on Rui as he responded with frightened, uncomfortable silence. The teacher tried prompting. "More means..." But Rui was no more ready to explain with words in English what more *meant* than I was ready to explain long division in Japanese. The teacher looked over at me and smiled as she shook her head.

"He needs objects or numbers. He can show you," I explained.

"Oh, yes. Well. I see. Rui, that's all right, honey. I'm going to give you a big hug."

By this time Rui was almost in tears.

Rui's teacher means well, and when I talked to her later in the day she realized without my saying very much that she had gone about probing his skills in a less than ideal manner. Still, for Rui's sake, and for the sake of the other students' perceptions of Rui, I wish the incident had not happened.

From Rui's point of view, the "more-less" day was probably not one of the better ones in his kindergarten career. And there are many other experiences, in many other classrooms, for many other LEP students, which are less than optimal for the acquisition or demonstration of math and science skills. The point we wish to emphasize is that Rui had already mastered the concept of more and less and what he was being taught on that day was to associate the English words with the concept. This is an important distinction which, when overlooked, can lead to the underestimation of LEP children's ability.

What conditions can enhance the achievement of bilingual and LEP students in mathematics and science classrooms? To arrive at an answer to this question we discuss three topics: (1) the math and science achievement status of students in historical perspective, (2) the implications of cross-cultural cognitive development principles for math and science instruction, and (3) approaches for the appropriate use of languages and culture in math and science instruction.

Underlying this chapter is the assumption that the teacher's attitude is crucial to the student's development of mathematical and scientific skills. When teachers have a clear understanding of the functions of mathematics and science in postmodern society, when they know how to separate language from concept development, when they make the math and science curricula responsive to the local cultures, and when they themselves are enthusiastic and curious about the patterned phenomena of numbers, matter, and nature, better learning can take place.

ACHIEVEMENT STATUS OF STUDENTS IN MATH AND SCIENCE

For the past 19 years, Scholastic Aptitude Test (SAT) scores have been sliding downward, although in 1982 there was a slight increase in scores over the previous year. During this time mathematics scores dropped much more than verbal scores (Toch, 1982, p. 1). The sense of urgency associated with such a decline has been regularly documented by the national media, the College Entrance Examination Board (1977), the National Science Foundation (1980), and math and science teachers in informal accounts. Because our world is powerfully controlled by science and technology, flabby test scores understandably generate concern within society.

The overall record of declining math scores cannot be attributed to any one factor. In looking for easy answers, however, some have associated minority students with the decline in SAT scores. The argument is that there are many more poor and language-minority children in school who are taking college entrance examinations today and that they tend to weigh down the average scores of the general population. The following factors, in various combinations, have also been cited as responsible for the declining test scores: scientist- and mathematician-designed rather than teacher-designed curricula; poorly motivated students; lack of discipline in the schools; too much television and overindulgent parents; student math anxiety; inadequately trained math and science teachers; textbooks which are too difficult for the majority of the students; and cultural and linguistic factors which inhibit cognitive development in these areas. The difficulty of finding simple answers is illustrated by Maeroff (1982, pp. 1–2):

> Those who like neat, easy answers were most disappointed that the College Board speculated on factors ranging from the breakup of the traditional family, to the turbulence stirred up by the Vietnam War, to the kinds of courses students take in high school.

The pattern of declining test scores has corresponded with a period of much change in the design of math and science curricula. It was the launching of Sputnik in 1957 by the Russians that touched off federal concern for new ideas in math and science education. The National Science Foundation was established and in 1958 Congress passed the National Defense Education Act. Stimulated vigorously by the cold-war pressures, educators in the 1960s moved to alter radically the nature of math and science curricula. Influenced by a cadre of brilliant mathematicians and scientists, the new curricula in these disciplines were aimed to get learners away from rote memorization of facts and formulas and toward an understanding of the source, meaning, and logic of mathematical and scientific principles and methods. The new curricula, with their emphasis on guided inquiry and the development of scientific mind sets, sought to affirm the inherent intellectual strength and natural curiosity which nearly all young learners have for science. As Bruner, a leading proponent and formulator of the inquiry-based curricula, put it, "any subject can be taught effectively in some intellectually honest form to any child at any stage of development" (1960, p. 33).

What were some of the results of these educational innovations? Seeking to assess the impact which the "new math" and inquiry-based science of the 1960s had on the growth of mathematical and scientific knowledge, the National Assessment of Educational Progress in Science authorized a survey. Among the findings was the following:

> All age groups experienced statistically significant declines in physical science achievement during the first test interval—1969–70 to 1972–73. There were no significant changes during the second test interval—1972–73 to 1976–77. (National Science Foundation, 1980, p. 71)

The weak or inconclusive impact of the new math and science programs, coupled with parent and teacher dissatisfaction and a general back-to-basics mood, has produced in the past decade a gradual shift back to more traditional teaching methods. But it is most likely only a brief pause. Current issues involving the international balance of technological and industrial expertise, the rapid incorporation of microchip circuitry into every aspect of our lives, and the search for new and more efficient means of producing and using resources as the world's population grows all are factors that guarantee future reassessment and modification of the methods of mathematics and science education.

While math and science mastery levels as a whole may be unsatisfactory, it has been evident that generally the average scores of most socioculturally and linguistically different racial and ethnic groups scrape the bottom of the achievement barrel in these subjects (Anick, Carpenter & Smith, 1981; Biemeller, 1982; Coleman, 1966; Mell, 1982; National Science Foundation, 1980).

For example, the nationwide longitudinal study entitled "High School and Beyond," conducted by the U.S. Department of Education, shows that average test scores of Hispanics, American Indians, and blacks are lower than those of whites in math and science. Asian-Pacific Americans' average scores are slightly but not significantly higher than whites' in math and slightly but not significantly lower in science. (See Table 6-1.)

TABLE 6-1   Comparative Test Scores of High School Seniors

Racial/ethnic group	12th grade average test scores	
	Mathematics	Science
American Indians	10.3	8.7
Asian-Pacific Americans	18.8	10.8
Blacks	8.2	6.4
Hispanics	9.1	7.5
Whites	17.6	11.3

SOURCE: Peng, Owings, and Fetters, 1984, p. 6.

Although these figures reveal overall deficiencies in the quality of education offered to blacks, Hispanics, and American Indians, they also hide the complexities of the issue. For the sake of generalization the categories compare racial groupings with ethnic groupings: white, for example, is a racial categorization, while Hispanic is essentially a cultural categorization. Also lost is the extensive cultural, sociological, and socioeconomic heterogeneity within each group, as well as the effect of language proficiency and length of residence in the United States. Tsang (1982) points out that the image of Asian-Americans as the model minority is reflective of research done largely in the 1960s which focused principally on Chinese- and Japanese-American samples. The present Asian-American population, however, is a much larger and more diverse one. The increasing numbers reflect such factors as changes in immigration laws and economic conditions and the political turmoil of Southeast Asia.

Educators often predict informally that ethnically diverse or limited-English-proficient students will have fewer problems with mathematics than language arts because "math is a universal language." (Maybe they haven't talked to a teacher who has tried to teach word problems in English to a LEP student.) However, when we look at the average scores of groups whose members are likely to be in bilingual or ESL programs—Asian-Pacific Americans, American Indians, Mexican Americans, and Puerto Ricans—we find that this differential is not always seen. The 1981 SAT scores, for example, show that, with the exception of Asian-Pacific Americans, such ethnic minority students' averages trail whites' scores by about as many points on the math section of the test as they do on the verbal section. (See Table 6-2.)

When it comes to explaining why so many ethnic minorities are not doing well in math and science, socioeconomic class, culture, language, length of residence in the United States, and quality of instruction are

TABLE 6-2   Points Below (−) or Above (+) White Group's Scores on 1981 SAT

	Verbal	Math
Asian-Pacific Americans	− 45	+ 30
American Indians	− 51	− 58
Mexican-Americans	− 69	− 68
Puerto Ricans	− 81	− 87

SOURCE: Biemeller, 1982, p. 14.

among the factors cited. In the case of the SAT, lower scores do correlate with lower family income levels and lower levels of parent education, blurring the determination of what combination of socioeconomic status, language-minority status, and unequal educational opportunity produces the measured lower achievement levels. The effects of cultural background, English-language proficiency, and length of residence in the United States have been relatively unexplored. One recent study of Asian-Americans which considered the relative weight of school experience factors versus racial-ethnic and family background factors found that, particularly in the area of math, school experiences were as important as family background in determining the amount of student learning. In other words, as the authors state, "students can excel if they are given or guided to proper school experiences" (Peng, Owings & Fetters, 1984, p. 17).

In an overview of issues related to the math achievement of language-minority students, Cocking and Chipman (1983) note that among the important variables to be considered are socioeconomic status, teacher competency, opportunity for learning, parental factors, and assessment procedures. For example, they suggest that teachers of language-minority students may be more likely to have less training and skill in math pedagogy and that instructional time allotted to math may be partially crowded out by a heavy emphasis on language arts for language-minority students. In the case of assessment procedures, it may be that the actual competence of the students is being undermeasured because the style or format of the instrument fails to tap their actual concepts and skills.

On the other hand, if the gap really does exist, despite test error, where does it begin? Ginsburg (1981) found that differences among young children in mastery of basic math concepts were not related significantly to social class or racial background. In other words, preschool children from the varied backgrounds he studied had very similar levels of understanding of basic number concepts. For school-age children of some language-minority groups, however, there is evidence that as they advance through the grades their average scores lag farther and farther behind the averages for majority students. For example, for Hispanics and Native Americans at ages 9, 13, and 17, the math achievement gap increases at each age level (Cocking & Chipman, 1983, p. 17).

COGNITION AND CROSS-CULTURAL RESEARCH

Despite the pendulum swings in curriculum design, teachers are charged with working with the program used in our schools on a day-to-day basis. While we cannot be expected to sit home each night and totally redesign the next day's math and science lessons for our multiethnic classes, these content areas lend themselves to imaginative and linguistically appropriate curriculum doctoring. We need to know how to go about identifying our students' math and science needs and learning potential and how best to address them. Math and science can pose a challenge even to the typical English-dominant, upper-socioeconomic-status, college-preparatory student, so it is a challenge to provide optimal achievement opportunities for students who speak limited English, or who speak non-standard English, or who seem culturally different, and who often bear the additional stigma of being poor. How do we know which approaches are best suited in these circumstances to the development of memory, reasoning, and language—cognitive skills which are important in ordering, classifying, and systematizing science and math information?

To answer the question posed we need an understanding of how learners under various cultural and environmental conditions come to grips with knowledge about their worlds. Knowing "how people perceive the environment, how they classify it, how they think about it" (Cole & Scribner, 1974, p. 5) is extremely relevant to bilingual and ESL classrooms. There is important information on these subjects available from developmental psychology, especially as it is applied in cross-cultural research. In the areas of math and science, to what extent do culturally diverse students approach learning in different ways, and to what extent in the same ways? In asking such a question we do not intend to suggest a "straitjacket" cultural determinism position. However, such cross-cultural research enables us to examine the conditions under which particular approaches to math and science learning are successful. It is also a useful way to refine hypotheses about how people respond to diverse environmental conditions.

The Cognitive Deficit Framework

With the development in the 1960s of such federally funded programs as Headstart, Title I, Title VII, and Migrant Education, researchers began to probe the interplay of race, ethnicity, class, and language with intellectual development. As discussed in chapter 4, there were competing points of view regarding the causes of the generally lower achievement levels of minority students, but psychologists holding on to the "cognitive-deficit" view tended to prevail. While the research which developed into the cognitive-deficit school of thought was not generally labeled as cross-cultural research, it has important implications for the effect of culture on the thinking processes. In essence many researchers believed that a combination of cultural and environmental factors contributed to the posited cognitive deficit so commonly found in lower-class or minority students. These students were perceived as bearers of subcultures which transmitted less than optimal skills for success in the classroom (Ausubel, 1964; Deutsch, 1965; Herrnstein, 1971; Jensen, 1969; Prehm, 1966; Ross, 1914). While the results of the educational innovations associated with this point of view are often disputed, there is considerable agreement that the philosophical and programmatic underpinnings of many of these programs were not affirming the natural culture of the learners and subtly implied the superiority of mainstream white culture.

Although the cognitive-deficit framework points to the home culture as in need of alteration, educational researchers of other viewpoints argue that the problem of schooling for all children, but especially those from socioculturally and linguistically different backgrounds, rests as much, if not more, on the school's ability to respond to the culture of the students. The following statement by Ginsburg focuses on poor students but also is applicable to language minorities:

> While it is easy for the psychologist and educator to speculate on intellectual deficiencies to explain poor children's school failure, it is harder to take seriously the possibility that defects in the system of schooling itself contribute heavily to current educational problems. To improve poor children's education, we need to examine the functioning of the school as closely as we investigate the poor child's intellect. (Ginsburg, 1978, p. 43)

Developmental Universals and Cross-Cultural Research

In the contemporary period Piaget (1929, 1954) stands out for having originated a theory of intellectual development which is based on a series of four distinct and predictable stages of thought, or logicomathematical thought structures. Children progress through these stages—sensorimotor, preoperational, concrete operational, and formal operational—by a process of equilibrium, in which they reconcile discrepancies between their current forms of understanding and new physical experiences that contradict those forms of understanding.

Although Piaget's theory has important implications for all aspects of pedagogy, its focus on logicomathematical structures makes it particularly relevant to a discussion of math and science learning for language-minority students. One of the early implications of Piaget's work was that the stages would be universal across varied cultural contexts, and Piagetian scholars have produced a variety of cross-cultural research evidence which seems to confirm this (Dasen, 1977). Expanding Piaget's notion of universal intellectual development, Ginsburg found through his research in the Ivory Coast that all children, regardless of any formal preschool experience and regardless of tribal affiliations, have been given through their biology and culture a "good mathematical 'head start'" (Ginsburg, 1978, p. 43). He found, for example, that all the children in his sample could solve the majority of "more" problems. "The results also showed that in judgments of *more*, African children use the same methods of solution as do American children" (Ginsburg, 1978, p. 37). In essence, before even entering a classroom, all children possess an intuitive notion of more, and this notion is not based on counting per se, which is a cultural artifact. Thus when a teacher claims that a kindergarten child does not demonstrate understanding of more, it may well be that the child does not understand the language of instruction, the context, or the format, but not the concept.

The position that Piaget's stages are cross-culturally valid is rooted in the idea of the common biological origin and physical environment which humans share. As Cole and Scribner (1974, p. 28) put it:

> The characteristics of these structures and their order of appearance are considered to be universal. They are the outcomes of adaptive processes between human organisms, whose biological heritage is the same the world over, and environments, whose fundamental physical properties (coordinates of space and time, behavior of objects under gravitational forces and the like) are identical.

The role of culture then, in the Piagetian school, is generally cast as one which may perhaps affect the rate of movement from one stage to the next. As Cole and Scribner (1974, p. 29) go on to point out:

> More recently, Piaget has opened up the possibility that the "final" stage of development—that of formal, propositional thinking, which in Western cul-

tures becomes elaborated during the age period of twelve to fifteen years—
might not appear at all in more restricted and less general form, among
cultures and individuals whose experience is limited to one or few technical
or specialized occupational activities.

The issue of the development of formal operations among adolescents,
however, might also be seen as a product not of Western versus non-
Western cultures, but of the presence or lack of formal postelementary
schooling, which places great emphasis on formal operations.

The effect of culture and other social experience on Piaget's stages of
intellectual development is a complex and unresolved issue. However,
continued research suggests that perhaps the stages are not as universal
as earlier thought. Considering the work of Dasen and Heron (1981),
Lancy (1983) points out that "although Piaget's theory would extend the
period of biologically motivated development into adolescence, cross-
cultural research undertaken by his colleagues shows that only the earliest attainments associated with the sensorimotor stage (0 to 2 years old)
are universal" (1983, p. 196). More specifically with regard to number
conservation, Saxe and Posner (1983) note that there is research evidence
pointing to the universality of the development of that concept through
the concrete operational stage (7–11 years), but that children show variation across cultures in their performance on various tasks within the
stage. Because the primary focus of Piagetian studies is on logical operations and the equilibrium process rather than on experimental or cultural
structures, Saxe and Posner suggest that such studies are unable to "ex-
plicate the manner in which cultural factors contribute to the development
process" (1983, p. 300) in such an area as numerical thought.

The idea that thought processes are universal seems to run counter to
the commonly held notion that people from different cultural or language
backgrounds think differently. A typical example is that of color words.
The way in which the spectrum of colors is divided for naming, and the
number of colors specifically identified, varies across cultural and linguistic groups. Still, underlying all of the different categorizing systems are
the same cognitive skills of classifying and application. Even the
frameworks that formal scientists build for the interpretation of facts are
shaped by their sociocultural environment with its particular value system
(Kuhn, 1970). The work of Vygotsky (1962) is useful in approaching math
and science learning from this point of view. Saxe and Posner (1983) have
compared the Piagetian and Vygotskiian approaches to understanding the
development of mathematical thinking from a cross-cultural perspective
and point out that while the Piagetian approach focuses on logical opera-

tions, the Vygotskiian approach focuses more on the cultural context of how problems are solved.

The basis of Vygotsky's approach is that there are two types of learning: (1) the learning of "spontaneous concepts," which the child engages in independently and which entails specific solutions to particular problems, and (2) the learning of "scientific concepts," which is carried out through interaction with formal and informal adult teachers and which entails generalized knowledge structures that can be applied in a variety of contexts and comprise part of the group's cultural value system. The interaction between these two types of learning is the mechanism for the development of the intellect within a particular culture. The scientific concepts learned through interaction with mature members of the group gradually begin to direct children's approaches to their own spontaneous problem solving; although they become more independent in their ability to solve problems, the style of cognitive functioning which they use is more or less a replica of that of their cultural group. Whereas from the Piagetian perspective children are seen to interact with the physical world directly, from the Vygotskiian perspective cognition is a mediated activity in which children interact with representations of the world, including such culturally rooted systems as language and numeration. Researchers basing their work on Vygotsky hypothesize that culturally different groups will exhibit different approaches to the solution of math problems. Looking at numeration systems in particular, Saxe and Posner point out that "in general, the research consistent with Vygotsky's approach has provided documentation concerning the way numerical skills are interwoven with particular numerational systems and culturally organized practices" (1983, p. 306). Hatano (1982, cited in Saxe, 1983), in a review of studies, found cultural influences in the math achievement of Japanese students. For instance, extensive abacus training provided calculation skills which were transferable to pencil-and-paper computations; number words are regular and reflect place value (for example, the Japanese equivalent for eleven is "ten-one," for twelve is "ten-two," and for twenty-one is "two-tens-one"), which facilitates the comprehension of multiple-digit operations; and the language provides a regular rhyming system for the memorization of multiplication facts.

Saxe and Posner conclude that because of the different emphases of the Piagetian and Vygotskiian approaches, a combination of the two holds the greatest promise for an understanding of the development of mathematical thought from a cross-cultural perspective. In some ways the dichotomy between the two is akin to the issue of nature versus nurture. As Lancy asks, "At what point does genetic evolution stop and cultural evolution take over in managing the development of cognition?" (1983, p. 196). Saxe and Posner propose that the "formation of mathematical concepts is a developmental process simultaneously rooted in the constructive activities of the individual and in social life," and that the research objective is to establish how these two factors are interwoven (1983, p. 315).

Just as cultural variables may alter the way in which cognitive processes are expressed, some researchers suggest that the development of dual language skills may work interdependently with the development of cognitive skills. Saxe (1983) cites studies which indicate that bilingual children have a greater awareness of the "arbitrary property of number words" (p. 23). Kessler and Quinn (1980) cite many studies from a variety of sociocultural contexts which indicate that bilinguals may have an advantage over monolinguals using some measures of cognitive flexibility, creativity, and divergent thinking. In their own research, they compared the ability of monolingual and bilingual sixth graders to formulate hypotheses for science problems. They found that the bilinguals scored significantly higher than the monolinguals in hypothesis quality. Basic to Piaget's theory of intellectual development is that the child's observation of discrepant events produces conflict within his or her existing thought system, which in turn results in intellectual development through assimilation and accommodation. (A discrepant event, for example, would be the observation that a crayon which sank in a tub of tap water floated in a tub of salt water.) Kessler and Quinn suggest that bilingual children, through their experience of learning two languages, have experienced more conceptual conflict than monolinguals, and that this conflict activates the equilibration processes of assimilation and accommodation for cognitive development. There is not, however, an extensive research database to support the existence of a positive relation between bilingualism and hypothesis-generating abilities or between bilingualism and any other logicomathematical operations. The effects of bilingualism on Piagetian equilibration processes, as well as any resultant relation between such processes and content mastery in math and science, are largely unexplored.

Inferences for Teaching

Although there are many unanswered questions, both Piaget's concept of universal developmental stages and Vygotsky's concept of mediation between the child's independent knowledge base and the adult's culturally influenced knowledge structure have important implications for teaching method. None of the observations which follow are formulas for new math and science curricula; they are ideas to keep in mind when working with existing textbooks and developing lessons.

Natural Competencies   Because all children, regardless of cultural and environmental conditions, come to know aspects of the physical and mathematical world in a rational and predictable fashion, bilingual and ESL teachers who start by affirming and searching for these natural, non-school-based competencies are going to be better able to encourage the development of new skills. Going back to the concept of "more," a pretest that comes with the commercial school program, with its culture-based format, may indicate that a child has not mastered the notion when in fact she has. Basing instruction on the pretest results without delving any deeper may result in valuable instructional time unnecessarily spent on the concept and in the teacher's underestimation of the child's ability. The point here is that while early cognitive developmental stages may be universal, the way in which they are manifested may be somewhat specific to a given cultural matrix. Knowing this we are more apt to question the nature of the math and science lesson formats as they relate to the experience of the child rather than questioning exclusively the child's capability.

Children's natural competencies in math and science generally do not go beyond the Piagetian developmental stages predicted for their age groups. Research in science education, however, indicates that science lessons frequently are presented in formats which *are* beyond the logical thinking stage of the students, resulting often in failure to master targeted concepts (De Luca, 1976) For young children at the preoperational and concrete stages, for example, manipulation of objects enhances the logical thinking process. Macbeth (1974) found that the extent to which pupils manipulated materials was positively associated with the acquisition of elementary science skills. Knowing this, use of materials which students can touch, push, pull, smell, taste, cut up, heat, cool, weigh, and measure takes on even greater importance in a classroom in which more than one language is represented, because such activities facilitate context-embedded communication. An awareness of the relation between cognitive developmental stages and math and science delivery modes makes for good teaching regardless of class composition, but it takes on greater significance when the class has a diverse ethnic composition. A child who has not completely mastered the English language is going to be more likely to master a math or science lesson presented in English if he is dealing only with a partial language barrier and not with a language barrier combined with a cognitive barrier. A limited-English-proficient child who is thinking at a concrete level in his native language is going to have a better chance at comprehending a science lesson presented in his second language if it is presented at the concrete rather than formal operational level.

Use of Home Context   The materials or subjects used in psychological assessment have been shown to play a role in the reliability of results across groups. In discussing the validity of many findings of social-class or ethnic-group differences in cognitive development, Cole and Means reported

> The problem of nonequivalent task materials has also affected inferences about social-class and ethnic-group differences in cognitive development. Simmons (1979) found an effect of what he calls the *cultural salience* of test materials on the sophistication of children's classification strategies. Culturally salient pictures are those showing objects, people, or activities that are both familiar and highly valued within a particular subcultural group. (Cole & Means, 1981, pp. 48–49)

Simmons took a previous research finding that lower-class children made less use than middle-class children of descriptive and category groupings in classifying pictures and replicated the study, this time using pictures that were culturally salient to each group. He concluded that the previously reported differences in scores were related to the types of materials rather than differences in conceptualization processes (Cole & Means, 1981, pp. 49–51).

In addition to an awareness of culturally salient topics, a knowledge of the application of math and science skills to the home context will also enhance instruction. Certain concepts may be almost self-evident to a child based on their application to home experiences, while others may require more reinforcement in school due to a lack of related exposure at home. Although underlying cognitive processes and potential may be essentially the same across cultures, specific skills vary according to the activities practiced within varying environments. Kpelle tribesmen, for instance, were better than Yale undergraduates at estimating the number of objects in a pile (Gay & Cole, 1967). From the point of view of the Kpelle, the Yale student could be considered culturally deprived based on the ability to estimate. For the purpose of formal education, cultural deprivation is really difference: difference between what the home environment emphasizes and what the school environment emphasizes. Ginsburg, in comparing two tribes in Africa, found that one group promoted the development of the mathematical concepts of more and less through extensive commercial activities, while the other group, because of its lesser amount of commercial activity, was less likely to provide opportunities for children to practice the concept. In a formal school lesson on more and less, a child from the former tribe might appear to have more ability than a child from the second tribe, while in fact their innate ability levels could be the same but their experience unequal.

To take another example, a student who has observed his parents slaughter goats or pigs would benefit from teacher guidance in applying his study of internal organs (as perhaps a part of the sixth-grade health curriculum) to that process. A child who is familiar with some herbal remedies would have an advantage over a student who knows only about commercially produced pills in drawing a relationship between human needs and the properties of plants. Taking some time to find out from students something of their home responsibilities and experiences is time well spent in relating the formal math or science curriculum to varied cultural backgrounds.

Language, Scientific Worldview, and Second-Language Competencies   Sapir and Whorf have long been associated with the hypothesis that language determines an individual's worldview. And with respect to science and math we still have to at least consider Whorf's statement that "we dissect nature along lines laid down by our native languages" (Whorf, 1956, p. 213). Is our interpretation of observed phenomena directly influenced by the lexicon and syntax of our mother tongue? It is true that the word or grammatical structure used in a language to describe a scientific or mathematical concept may not have an equivalent in another language. For example, there is no word for "line" in some Native American languages (Lovett, 1980, p. 15). Does this mean that a Native American child for whom English is a second language will have more trouble than an English-dominant Native American child in learning to identify a line? Some research does in fact indicate that "people more readily discriminate between things they have different names for" (Berelson & Steiner, 1964, p. 190).

Although there is some variation in the way languages categorize or describe scientific and mathematical concepts, languages do not form impermeable walls closing off cross-cultural transmission of scientific or mathematical content. In many cases a loan word will give a label to a concept that can be mastered in any language. Algebra was developed in an Arabic cultural context, and the English word "algebra" is of Arabic origin. However, there is no evidence that non-Arabs consistently have more difficulty than Arabs in mastering algebra. Again, we have to go back to the empirical universality of certain basic cognitive processes. Such universality applies to much of language itself.

> . . . languages are composed of organized sequences such as sentences; all have rules for generating acceptable sentences; all have expandable lexicons. These assertions combine to form a point of view that deemphasizes cognitive differences among different linguistic (cultural) groups. (Cole & Scribner, 1974, p. 27)

Crucial to this discussion is the expandability of all languages. Because languages have always borrowed extensively from each other for vocabulary to express new objects, ideas, or processes, language by itself is not a boundary preventing the acquisition of nonnative concepts.

In dealing with math and science pedagogy, however, the choice between the cognitive-universal and the language-determination points of view is not an absolute one. The aspect of our mind that processes observations into language is still to a large extent a black box—unknown territory to researchers. Despite underlying human commonalities, language is undeniably a sophisticated and subtle filter of human experience. Time, in the short term (time to respond to questions) and in the long term (time to reach proficiency), is an important factor in math and science instruction in the multilanguage classroom. In short-term analysis, one researcher found that the amount of time teachers waited for student responses to their questions affected discussion of ideas and the amount of inquiry exercised. Longer waiting times stimulated use of the inquiry mode and higher levels of thought (Rowe, 1974). Rowe's research was done assuming a monolingual English context, but the importance of waiting time takes on even more importance when the classroom includes students who must process their verbal response into a language whose full extent they have not mastered.

In the long term, the time it takes to reach proficiency in a second language affects the ability to master science and math concepts in that language. Cummins distinguishes two types of language proficiency: context-embedded (face-to-face) communicative proficiency (BICS) and context-reduced (academic) communicative proficiency (CALP).

> Context-embedded face-to-face communicative proficiency refers to the students' ability to achieve their communicative goals in situations where the linguistic message is embedded within "a flow of meaningful context" (Donaldson, 1978), i.e., supported by a wide range of situational and paralinguistic cues. Context-reduced communicative proficiency, on the other hand, refers to the ability to handle the communicative demands of situations where the range of extralinguistic supports is very much reduced (e.g., reading a difficult text, writing an essay). Clearly, context-embedded communication is more typical of the everyday world outside the classroom, whereas many of the linguistic demands of the classroom reflect communication which is closer to the context-reduced end of the continuum. (Cummins, 1981a, p. 34)

As discussed in chapter 3, Cummins' research suggests that it takes only about 2 years for a student to reach an age-appropriate level of context-embedded proficiency in a second language, but 5 to 7 years to reach an age-appropriate level of context-reduced proficiency (1981a, p. 35). It is easy to be deceived by a student's apparent facility in everyday informal communication and assume that there is no language difficulty in the math or science classroom. However, as Cummins points out,

> To extrapolate from the considerable English proficiency which language-minority students display in context-embedded face-to-face communication to their ability to handle the context-reduced communicative demands of an all-English classroom or an English psychological test risks creating academic deficits in students. (1981a, p. 35)

There are two implications here for delivery modes of science and math content. First, the math and science achievement of non-English-background speakers can be enhanced by instruction in the native language continuing for several years after they have mastered basic English-language skills, because students are still more adept at processing abstract cognitive operations through their home language. Second, if sufficient instruction or tutoring cannot be provided in the home language due to the lack of human or material resources or to the presence of multiple languages within one classroom, activities designed to use concrete, visual, and context-embedded learning formats will increase the ability of the language-minority student to master required skills and concepts.

Because math and science principles lend themselves to demonstrations and hands-on experiences, context-embedded communication activities can readily serve as a link to the mastery of concepts presented in a context-reduced form. The use of context-embedded pedagogy can result in both the acquisition of content-area objectives and an increase in proficiency in context-reduced communication. For example, if algebra problems involving such terms as "twice as long as," "half as wide as," or "ten times as many as" are presented in a context-embedded format, the LEP student will learn not only how to solve the problems but also English terms which can subsequently be applied in context-reduced paper-and-pencil assignments. Metaphors can be of value in "context embedding" a lesson which might otherwise be too context-reduced. Metaphors provide a bridge between the familiar and the unfamiliar or the available and the unavailable. Most schools do not have a surgical ward for the first-hand observation of a heart in action, but a bicycle pump can be brought to school. Initially, students can feel the bursts of air coming out of it and transfer that first-hand experience to the concept of the rhythmic bursts of blood coming out of the heart. As the lesson is refined, areas of similarity and dissimilarity between the pump and the heart can be explored. It is also difficult to bring a live baleen whale into the classroom (along with a large supply of sea water), but the feeding function of the baleen can be demonstrated using a sieve-baleen metaphor or a Cuban coffee filter–baleen metaphor.

LANGUAGE AND CULTURE IN MATHEMATICS AND SCIENCE CLASSROOMS

A teacher may have in her science or math class a mix of non-English speakers; bilingual students; English, monolingual majority students; and English, monolingual racial or ethnic minority students. How can she go about meeting the language-development and cultural-awareness needs of all of these students while at the same time providing all of them with the math and science knowledge appropriate for their grade levels? There are no immediate, absolute, or universal answers.

As reflections of logical processes and verified facts, math and science have universal currency. But as instruments of cultural content they also carry with them all the richness and limitations associated with such systems. Consider, for example, the functional and symbolic meanings surrounding the numbers "three" and "thirteen" in the Western tradition. Besides its counting function, the number three shapes Western stories, which generally have a predictable three-part format—beginning, middle, and end. Even Christian theology, with its affirmation of the Holy Trinity, is an example of a numerical concept associated with a cultural meaning. The number thirteen is so laden with superstition that some airline companies and architectural firms delete it from their plane seats and multiple-story buildings. Such numbers, however, may not have the same symbolic, magical, or organizational importance in other cultures. Athapascans, for instance, tend to divide stories into four rather than three logically integrated subparts, an approach which perplexes the Western mind. Thus the incorporation of scientific and mathematical concepts into everyday life is tightly interwoven with interpretations of reality. Every person engaged in the teaching of math and science to ethnically diverse populations does not have to become a sophisticated expert on every detail surrounding the cultural variation in application of math and science concepts; however, we need to know that as culture bearers we naturally bring the perspective of our own cultural background to the lesson arena. It is only after becoming aware of this that we are in a legitimate position to begin the construction of a math or science program for the multiethnic classroom.

Wherever there is culture, there is language; in planning for math and science instruction in an ethnically heterogeneous classroom, neither one can be ignored. But should the twin areas of cultural awareness and second-language development become intentional aspects of the math and science curricula, and if so, how? Because of the primacy of language as a vehicle for cognitive communication, let us start by examining ways in which languages can be used in the math or science classroom.

Use of Language

In any math or science program, the first thing that has to be done is the assessment of the students' knowledge. With LEP students an adequate diagnosis requires that the teacher speak the LEP learner's language or that he or she have the help of a speaker of the learner's home language. Through this initial screening teachers can determine whether the students know in their primary language the skills and concepts appropriate to their grade level. Regarding skills and knowledge which students demonstrate through their home language, the teacher may wish to focus on the acquisition of vocabulary and grammatical structures to transfer the abilities to English. However, for objectives which limited-English-proficient students have not mastered in their home language, instruction in that language will more likely ensure successful learning. In other words, content instruction is most effective if done in the home language; it will take time for the skills to be demonstrated in the second language. Research in the mathematics achievement of the student population as a whole generally shows a significant positive relation between math achievement and verbal ability. Although the question of how these two areas influence each other is largely unanswered, Cocking and Chipman (1983) note that some researchers posit a dependence of math achievement on proficient language skills. The so-called universal mathematical language is communicated, or mediated, in the classroom through the oral and written language of instruction and thus proficiency in the language of instruction can reasonably be expected to have an effect on acquisition of concepts and skills. In Begle's review of the literature (1975, cited in Cocking & Chipman, 1983) he concludes that math computational and reasoning skills of Hispanic students are enhanced through bilingual instruction.

While the choice of instructional language depends on the assessment of student competencies in the home language, it also can depend on the extent to which the most effective acquisition of skills and concepts is stressed, and to what extent the development of English-language skills during math or science instructional time is stressed. The use of language can run on a continuum from 100 percent instruction in the home language to 100 percent instruction in English; in the former the emphasis is on efficiency of acquisition of knowledge for LEP students. Between the two extremes there are many mixes of language, methods, and groupings. Choosing, in a zero-sum format, between content mastery in the home language and second-language development is artificial, but for the purpose of clarifying the many uses of language in the math and science content areas, we divide the discussion into these two categories.

Content Mastery in Two Languages   If the instructor decides to omit any intentional ESL objectives from the lessons and to concentrate on initial mastery of concepts and skills through the home language, there are at least three language-delivery approaches which she can employ in the multilingual classroom—concurrent, alternate, and preview-review. These have been described in chapter 3 but are considered here as they relate to instruction in the content areas of math and science.

The concurrent approach, switching back and forth in one lesson between two languages, is in disrepute with linguists as a means of second-language acquisition, because such an approach does not control for fifty-fifty balance of the two languages, does not provide students with a clear distinction between the two languages, and may not motivate students to learn the second language because the first-language explanations are so immediately available. The facts of life, however, are that the concurrent method is alive and well in many bilingual classrooms. Teachers who have a full command of two languages or who have a bilingual team partner or paraprofessional, find it tempting to use both to guarantee that all students, English-dominant and LEP, understand the lessons. Good concurrent teaching is a skill. It requires giving equivalent rather than literal translations as well as avoiding inappropriate repetitions of material. It requires careful decisions about switches to the other language, based on knowledge of students' proficiency levels in each language and appropriate instructional strategies of code-switching. It also requires that the teachers or paraprofessionals have a sound knowledge of science and math terminology in both languages.

The rationale for the skilled use of the concurrent approach in math and science is to make sure that the information contained in the lesson is automatically comprehensible to all students. The concurrent method might be appropriate for a math or science demonstration in which the understanding of each step requires a clear understanding of the previous step. It would also be useful in situations in which students are asked to generate hypotheses about the cause of a given phenomenon. Because the teacher wishes to encourage contributions in whichever language the child speaks best, he can accept ideas in whichever language they come and have students restate those ideas in the other language so that every child, regardless of language background, comprehends all of the hypotheses generated.

The alternate-language approach, in contrast to the concurrent approach, clearly structures a separation between the two languages. But for students of limited proficiency in one of the languages of instruction, the language chosen for content-area instruction can involve a complex decision. In early stages, students should receive math and science lessons in their first language, but as they develop increasing proficiency in a second language, they may be introduced to an increasing amount of science and math instruction in their second language. Once students have reached full proficiency in both languages in a bilingual maintenance program, all models of the alternate-language approach are efficient methods of instruction. In subject-area alternation, for example, one year of a program might include math in Vietnamese, science in English, social studies in Vietnamese, and language arts in each language, and the following year each subject area would be taught in the other language. For a half-day alternate bilingual program, all lessons conducted in the morning might be in English, and those in the afternoon in Arabic on one day; on the following day, Arabic would be the language for morning lessons and English the language in the afternoon.

With the alternate approach to bilingual teaching, exact repetition of lessons in each language is clearly eliminated. A spiraling curriculum, in which students at each grade level are introduced to increasingly complex levels of material presented in previous grades, can be adapted very easily to the alternate approach to bilingual instruction.

In the preview-review approach, the teacher introduces a math or science lesson in one language and presents the body of the lesson in the second language. In the preview session, the teacher gives an overview of the concept and accompanying science and math terminology to be presented in the lesson, so that they will be understood when they appear in the main body of the lesson. Part of the preview, for instance, in Korean, of an elementary science lesson to be presented in English on measurement of temperatures might include an explanation of such English words to be used in the main body of the lesson as "increase" and "decrease." After the main body of the lesson is completed, the lesson may be reviewed in one of two ways. The students may be divided by language dominance, with reinforcement activities conducted in each group's dominant language, or the lesson may be reviewed and expanded with all the students together, using the concurrent approach to elicit what was learned from the presentation. As with the concurrent and alternate-language approaches, the success of this approach rests to a great extent on the linguistic sophistication of the teacher and the care with which the lesson is designed. Again, the point of this approach is that the LEP students as well as the English-dominant students understand what is going on in the math and science classroom.

Although two languages are used in the preview-review method, the main body of the lesson is presented in only one language. For students of limited proficiency in one of the languages, therefore, this approach may lend itself best to lessons which have many visual or physical cues. For example, if a combination math and marine biology lesson involves the measurement on the playground of the average length of the blue whale, the activity itself will provide many cues even though the student does not understand the language in which the activity is being conducted. On the other hand, if a lesson is highly context-reduced, a student who does not speak the language of the main presentation may become lost despite the introduction in her native language.

Second-Language Development   While the above approaches concentrate on the mastery of objectives regardless of the language used, second-language instruction coordinated carefully with the math and science curricula can do much to enrich and contextualize second-language development. Math and science topics possess great motivating powers for engaging the LEP student in the forms of the English language, and in an enrichment program they are a promising means of second-language development for the English-dominant student. Children are great admirers of natural and human-made math and science phenomena. They are fascinated by a snake in a cage in the book corner or by a new row of computers in the media center. Therefore, the teacher who is able to mix second-language-development activities with math and science content will be providing highly motivating lessons. Students like to smell, touch, see, hear, taste, connect, disconnect, heat, cool, and quantify things. They like to know why certain things work the way they do and others work differently. And because math and science deal with quantifiable and material subjects, it is possible to frame some learning in such a way that students develop second-language skills in tandem with the development of cognitive skills in these subject areas. Because much of the content of math and science lends itself to physical representation, it is possible for ESL teachers to use many manipulatives, demonstrations, and experiments to involve students not only in the discovery or reinforcement of new subject knowledge but also in the practice of newly acquired vocabulary and grammar. This type of language instruction fits well with the linguistic premise that learners acquire a second language more quickly when they are interested in what they are learning and when they are allowed a sufficient level of context-embedded manipulation of the language.

If some math or science lessons are going to contain ESL objectives, how much attention should be given to language correctness at the same time that a math or science concept is being elaborated? Some research suggests that focusing on the communicative functions of English as opposed to its form gives better results in second-language learning. If a child says, "the heart pump blood" instead of "the heart pumps blood," he has adequately communicated the scientific fact despite the grammatical error. While it is understandable that teachers are concerned about correcting the language errors of their students, there is evidence that only 4 to 12 percent of such errors in children are due to first-language interference and that the rest are temporary and developmental in nature. Furthermore, error correction does not seem to cure the mistakes (Dulay, Burt & Krashen, 1982), and maintenance of a positive language-learning environment can be impeded by a teacher who becomes too impatient with his students' errors and flags them down on the spot.

Perhaps the most important thing to keep in mind in developing a math or science lesson that includes second-language acquisition is the need to identify a few specific objectives. As the lesson proceeds in the second language, students are exposed to a very large lexicon and a considerable array of grammatical structures. As they respond to the lesson, however, their opportunities for verbal expression should focus on (but not be absolutely limited to) certain vocabulary sets or sentence structures. Simply presenting the lesson in English, as if everyone had mastered the language, might under some circumstances provide practice in listening skills for the advanced student. But such a lesson would not necessarily result in growth in second-language expressive skills. Following are some brief examples of second-language objectives which may be integrated into math or science activities.

In a Canadian program in which students received all of their mathematics instruction within the context of second-language instruction, Cantieni and Tremblay reported considerable success through the use of "school materials in which properties can be immediately observed and manipulated" (1979, p. 248). Attribute blocks were used extensively. (Attribute blocks are sets of geometric figures possessing several specific attributes—size, thickness, color, and shape, for example. There is a large thick blue circle, a small thick blue circle, a large thin blue circle, a small thin blue circle, a large thick red circle, a small thick red circle, and so on, with blocks to represent many possible combinations of attributes.) While manipulating these objects, the second-language learner may be working on the objective of adjective placement in English: "the red triangle," not "the triangle red," or "the big red triangle," not "the red big triangle." If students are classifying the blocks into a six-compartment grid based on two attributes (e.g., color—red, yellow, or blue, and size— big and little), the following question and answer exchange could take place:

> Where does it go? (holding up a block)
>
> It goes here/there. (taking the block and placing it in the grid)

Or, at a slightly more advanced second-language level:

> Where does this big red block go?
>
> It goes in the third box in the first row.
>
> Where does this little blue block go?
>
> It goes in the first box in the second row.

As Cantieni and Tremblay point out in the description of their program, use of materials such as attribute blocks provides an "immediate concrete situation in which vocabulary can be learned and questions and answers formulated" (1979, p. 249). Cuisenaire rods are another device which frees the learner mentally and allows her to make the linguistic connection between manipulation of a math concept and use of a second language. Practice with *is* and *are* and with comparisons (as ___ as), for example, could be combined with the exploration of mathematical equality and the commutative property:

> One orange rod is as long as ten white rods.
>
> Ten white rods are as long as one orange rod.

The sentence structures learned through the manipulation of attribute blocks and Cuisenaire rods can be applied to everyday situations outside the context of the math classroom.

While Cantieni and Tremblay describe an entire math program incorporated into second-language instruction, in most cases the teacher will probably wish to combine math or science with second-language learning only as far as language and content objectives overlap. If beginning LEP students need to work on simple positive and negative statements and are also building a vocabulary of plants and animals, and if at the same time classifying skills are being taught in science, an ESL lesson can provide practice with the following sentence patterns as the students sort picture cards:

The turtle is not a plant.

The pine tree is a plant.

English terms of comparison (longer than, shorter than, taller than, wider than, thinner than, more than, less than) can be incorporated with practice in measurement, or with the introduction of the mathematical symbols for more than (>) and less than (<). In the upper elementary grades, as LEP students become literate in English, they may gain practice by composing math word problems. Development of grocery store vocabulary can be combined with practice in the use of two operations (e.g., multiplication and addition) in the solution of problems.

Masumi bought five cans of soup, three boxes of frozen pizza, and two cartons of soda. The soup cost 43 cents a can; the pizzas cost $3.79 each; and the soda cost $1.89 a carton. How much did the groceries cost?

The above are only examples of ways in which second-language instruction can be combined with math or science content, and the authors are not advocating that an entire math or science program be built around second-language learning objectives. Because most bilingual programs have, by definition, a formal block of ESL instructional time, use of math and science lessons to promote second-language learning constitutes neither a full math and science program nor a full ESL program. Lessons that integrate the content areas with second-language learning, however, are extremely enriching learning experiences because they provide much practice for the application of the second language to real-life activities.

There is an unwieldy number of factors to consider in determining language usage within the math or science context: the skill and knowledge level of students in their home language, the LEP students' degree of proficiency in English, the context-reduced versus context-embedded nature of the various math and science lessons, the ethnic proportions in the classroom, the organization of the school's bilingual program, and the availability of appropriate human and material resources. There are three basic guidelines, nevertheless, that are particularly important to remember:

1. New math and science skills, facts, or concepts are most effectively learned in the student's native language.

2. When second-language instruction is incorporated into a math or science lesson, identification of specific language objectives to match the targeted math or science objectives will provide more opportunities for students to practice particular vocabulary sets or sentence structures.

3. The more context-embedded the presentation is (for example, observation of a thermometer's response to hot and cold), the more likely LEP students can master the content even if presented in English. The more context-reduced a lesson is (for example, explaining the meaning of gravity), the more important it becomes to provide instruction in the native language.

Human and Material Resources   It would be nice if every time a language-minority student enrolled in a school, she automatically came equipped with an appropriately trained bilingual teacher, just in case the school did not happen to have one. And it would be nice if every teacher had at her disposal a computer terminal connected to a central data bank which would automatically provide her with a math or science lesson in whatever objective she indicated and in whatever language she needed. But things are not so. Working with students who represent varying degrees of proficiency in English, varying degrees of sophistication in math and science, and varying schooling backgrounds introduces a high level of complexity into the teaching process, and the lack of bilingual personnel and materials naturally limits the choices available in planning for first and second language usage. To meet the content-area needs of language-minority students, a variety of alternatives for human resources can be explored: use of bilingual paraprofessionals trained to work with students in math and science; in-service training for monolingual staff in math and science terminology and symbols in languages other than English; integration of local bilingual professors of math and science into the life of the school; and use of bilingual cross-age and peer tutors. Brown describes a secondary-level program in which an English monolingual teacher, by capitalizing on the language mixture in his classroom, can optimize learning opportunities:

> The teacher can, for example, group students into four teams of two Spanish-dominant (or other language) and two English-dominant (monolingual) students per lab table. Teams can then be supplied with bilingual instructions for activities which demand relatively little reading but maximize reasoning and manipulation of materials and equipment. (Brown, 1979, p. 232)

Brown's suggestion that "teams can be supplied with bilingual instructions," however, introduces the other problem: material resources. Like most other subjects, math and science lessons are controlled to a large extent by the available textbooks, workbooks, and supplementary materials. Until fairly recently, the quality and quantity of bilingual materials produced for math and science classrooms were minimal. And when such materials appeared, they were often imported from outside the United States, which meant that the realities represented in the texts sometimes conflicted with American procedures, or they were alien to young language-minority students who had lived most or all of their lives in the United States and were not familiar with the format for math and science in their countries of origin. (For example, ten thousand and thirty-eight hundredths is written as 10.000,38 in some countries rather than 10,000.38.) Faced with the problem of cultural disparity, some publishers from South America began in the 1970s to produce Spanish curricular materials custom-made for the Spanish-speaking population in the United States. Many major U.S. publishers are also expanding their selection of math and science texts and supplementary material in Spanish.

Illustrative of the emerging efforts of smaller organizations to produce professional bilingual materials for the science class is the Spanish/English publication *Wet and Wild: A Bilingual Supplementary Marine Education Curriculum Guide for Teachers, Grades K-6* (Murphy, 1982). The guide includes units on the physical ocean, the biological ocean, marine ecology, the economic sea, ocean management, and research. Each unit includes background information for the teacher, about twenty-five interdisciplinary lesson plans, and a list of reference books and films. Another set of science materials for the multiethnic classroom is the multimedia program *Children, Families, and the Sea* (1982). It is a set of books, read-along cassettes, and sound filmstrips about five culturally distinct families from five different coastal environments. The environments studied are in Maine, British Columbia, Japan, Trinidad/Tobago, and Baja California.

While major publishing companies can be readily consulted for the availability of textbook series and supplementary materials for the principal language groups, exploration can yield useful material on a smaller and more adaptable scale. A publication dealing with math resources is *Resources for Teaching Mathematics in Bilingual Classrooms* (Lovett & Snyder, 1979), available through the ERIC Clearinghouse for Science, Mathematics, and Environmental Education. The small monograph includes issues surrounding the teaching of mathematics in bilingual settings, bibliographic data, sources of bilingual materials for mathematics, and selected Spanish/English mathematical terms and expressions. ERIC has also produced another publication, *Language Factors in Learning Mathematics* (Aiken, 1972). Teachers interested in doing a bit of investigating on their own may also find *Arithmetic Teacher, The Mathematics Teacher,* and the *Journal for Research in Mathematics Education* helpful. Occasionally these journals have articles that are relevant for teaching math in the bilingual context. There are many journals which occasionally publish articles on teaching science to students of diverse backgrounds, such as the *Journal of Research in Science Teaching, Science Education, Science and Children, Science Teacher,* and *School Science and Mathematics.*

The *TESOL Quarterly* and *NABE Journal* also include articles which may be of interest to math and science teachers working with limited-English-proficient students. The Evaluation, Dissemination, and Assessment Centers (EDACs) funded by Title VII have published a variety of sets of materials for math and science bilingual and ESL classrooms. In addition, today many large school districts have some bilingual-multicultural science and math bibliographies and materials which have been developed to meet their needs.

As important as conceptually sound materials are, they become deadwood unless the teacher is resourceful and imaginative in integrating them into the bloodstream of the curriculum and in relating them to the students' experiences. While teachers do not always have a great range of choice in the language and style of commercially available math and science materials, they are in a position to supplement or enrich such adopted texts with teacher- and student-produced topics and materials tailored for the backgrounds represented in their classroom.

An Interdisciplinary Framework

It might be argued that mathematics and science are culture-free, that they contain an enormous amount of challenging information to be mastered, and that there is no time or use for the incorporation of cultural themes into such objective disciplines. On the other hand, scientific research indicates that a portion of our mind is made to integrate separated concepts and knowledge into unified wholes. The mind is impatient with disjointed configurations; it likes gestalt.

Although intellectually we may affirm the concept of academic interdependence, in general our schools are still structured in such a way that their parts have been atomized and made legitimate from within rather than across disciplines. One gets the feeling that the followers of each discipline believe that they have a monopoly over its content and process.

This is so even in such closely related subjects as mathematics and science. Although it is true that pinpointing and drawing out the connections among subjects requires nonconventional approaches, the inherently interdependent infrastructure is always there. As Thomas puts it, in *The Lives of a Cell,* "the circuitry seems to be there, even if the current is not always on" (1975, p. 15). Because most young learners tend to have a good deal of curiosity about the physical and biological world around them, mathematical and scientific concepts can be drawn from what such learners observe, analyze, and experience in their natural, culture-laden environments. Similarly, much of what is taught and learned in math and science classrooms can be applied to social studies, language arts, music, health, physical education, and art.

Designing a math or science framework which takes into account the impact of culture entails at least the following two competencies on the part of the teacher: (1) sophistication in math and science content, and (2) some knowledge of and a high degree of empathy with and intellectual curiosity about the cultural, linguistic, and economic circumstances surrounding the varied student backgrounds. Although the first competency ostensibly can be obtained in college, it can be argued that teachers of language-minority students need to be especially well-versed in elementary math and science, or, at the secondary level, in their particular subject area—physics, chemistry, biology, computer science, or math. To be able to explain concepts when language is also an issue requires intellectual flexibility, creativity, and a keen understanding of the subject matter. Such quality preparation allows teachers to deviate from or go beyond the "cookbook" approach which may be provided in the teachers' manual and to develop lessons based on their own expertise. The second competency, sociocultural and linguistic sensitivity, can be obtained by virtue of ancestry, residency, travel, formal study of the language and culture of the target populations, or any combination thereof. When we become engaged in first-hand experiences in cross-cultural and cross-social communication, we are likely to be touched by the powerful forces which affect who we are, how we behave, and what we consider of importance in life. The following list of teacher education concerns, developed by Cocking and Chipman (1983), is useful in addressing the competencies needed by math and science teachers of language minority students:

1. When teaching mathematics to bilingual students in a bilingual atmosphere, teachers should have (*a*) an adequate command of the technical math vocabulary in the language involved; (*b*) a sound preparation in the mathematical concepts of the elementary school curriculum; (*c*) techniques for minimizing the effects of the language and cultural variables

with the purpose of maximizing mathematical thinking and mathematical processes.

2. More emphasis on mathematics is needed in the preservice training programs for prospective elementary school teachers in order to increase their effectiveness in teaching mathematics.

3. Preservice mathematics education programs for teachers should (a) encourage prospective teachers to utilize homemade teaching materials; (b) facilitate first-hand experience in problem solving and applications of mathematical concepts in a variety of different situations; and (c) enable prospective teachers to develop math labs and math interest centers.

4. Courses integrating mathematics content, information about the learning characteristics of children, and mathematics teaching methods are needed.

5. Bilingual mathematics specialists should be used at the K-6 level to impart mathematics instruction in the vernacular language of the students. (Cocking & Chipman, 1983, p. 44)

Even with the appropriate personal and professional background, however, adapting math and science to the values and interests of the bilingual and ESL classroom can still be a delicate and somewhat unpredictable undertaking. It is not just a matter of randomly mixing themes and disciplines, but rather of understanding the rationale behind them and understanding how they fit the populations which they are intended to serve. Given the key role of mathematics and science in maintaining the social organization of modern society and in providing resources for the world's growing population, these subjects have the power to chip away forcefully at traditional cultural values and patterns. The tension between tradition and innovation is particularly well illuminated in situations involving immigrants or indigenous persons from colonized backgrounds. This was brought home to one of the authors quite forcefully through a play presented by a theater group of Greenlandic Eskimos. This theatre group used the name *Tukak* (meaning harpoon in the Innuit language) as their symbol of the simultaneous search for progress and attachment to the past. Reflecting on the harpoon metaphor, many Eskimos today are interested in nurturing their ethnic identities vis-à-vis whatever benefits science and technology may bring to their circumpolar regions of the world (for example, snowmobiles, air transportation, modern medicines, motorboats, and heating systems).

Because few programs are designed from a multicultural perspective, modifying math and science disciplines in such a way that the learner comes to see their relations to cultural phenomena requires on the part of the teacher creativity, dedication, and the ability to seek out appropriate programs. Most teachers do not have total freedom in the selection of math and science textbooks, and if used unimaginatively these books tend to control lesson formats. Scope-and-sequences developed by local school districts may carefully spell out sets of math and science competencies for each grade level, kindergarten through twelfth, and few if any explicit relations may be drawn between these objectives and the objectives of other disciplines. The bilingual or ESL teacher has some curricular constraints, but there is still much opportunity to integrate sociocultural themes into the standard program on an ongoing basis or to conduct periodic enrichment activities following a lesson or unit.

In drawing relations between mathematics or science and cultural traditions, it is important to consider all students, majority and minority, English-dominant and LEP. Presenting a unit of the Mayan numerical system in such a way that it appears to be especially for the Mexican-American and Guatemalan students, for example, may actually engender negative attitudes. When a subject from a particular ethnic group's cultural background is incorporated into a lesson one cannot assume that all the children from that group will warm up to it. Despite the importance of corn in Mexican culture, a Chicano student living in Anchorage, Alaska, may have no more feeling for the development of a corn seed into a corn plant than a fourth-generation Swede living in Los Angeles has for the chemical processes involved in the preparation of *lutefisk*. Indigenous minority-group and immigrant children continually assess, consciously and unconsciously, the pros and cons of affiliation with their home culture, and if the cons outweigh the pros they might not want to look at Mayan gods or Hopi motifs on the margins of their math worksheets. For these students, symbols become important in positive and negative ways. Perhaps the students who are least likely to react negatively to the inclusion of traditional history, beliefs, artifacts, tools, foods, and games are the recent immigrants. Because many of them are just beginning the process of acculturation, they are still inclined to relate positively to symbols representing their countries of origin. But again one has to be sensitive to the likelihood that some parents want their children to assimilate as quickly as possible and to discard ancestral traditions.

It is not our intent to negate the value of including topics from outside mainstream U.S. or Western tradition but to alert the teacher to the possibility that there may be extensive attitudinal variation among LEP and English-dominant minority students. Depending on how the nonmainstream learners are perceived by the larger society, they may or may not wish to affirm traditional cultural symbols. However, if topics or examples are presented in such a way that it is clear that they have a bearing on actual math or science content, and if they are presented as lessons to be absorbed by all students regardless of linguistic background, they can have academically sound and culturally enlightening results. For example, study of the solar equinoxes and solstices can be related to the astronomical observations of the Mayans, Incans, and Anasazi. The fact that their astronomical achievements now serve as a basis for a newly created field called archeostronomy serves as evidence of the significance of their accomplishments. In such a unit of study all the students are exposed to information which reinforces astronomical concepts and at the same time affirms the background of students who may be speculating about who their ancestors were and what they did.

The inclusion of multicultural examples in the curriculum can serve well as a means of practice of application of target math or science objectives. Rather than being an added nuisance which "softens" the curriculum, they can be designed to help students internalize new concepts. Science texts draw on many examples to illustrate concepts. The piano may be used to demonstrate the vibrations of strings and sound production. As Yao (1979) points out, however, many musical instruments from other cultures can also be used to demonstrate the physics of sound production. She describes a model conceived by the Science Curriculum Improvement Study in which students relate topics such as sound or the basic tools of physics (lever, inclined plane, and so on) to a variety of musical instruments or real tools of varied cultural origin.

> [The] learning cycle first introduces the knowledge of content to children through their direct exploration of diverse physical materials to discover their properties, how they work, and why they work in certain ways. After exploration, scientific terms and concepts are introduced to children to help them describe and explain their observations. Finally, further activities are furnished to lead children to discover the applications of these newly learned concepts that form the scientific basis underlying the operations of various cultural artifacts or tools. (Yao, 1979, p. 72)

Such application of scientific or mathematical principles should not be limited, of course, to traditional cultural artifacts or to the students' culture as it existed in the country of origin. (Again, consider the culture change that a Mexican-American in Anchorage, Alaska, or a Vietnamese-American in Detroit experiences.) The study of energy can be related to the oil well just behind the student's backyard fence, or principles of physics can be applied to the antics of a "low-rider" car.

While not suitable to every geographical area of the United States, an exciting approach for weaving culture into mathematics and science is linking the schools with museums of science and history. The Ontario

Science Centre in Toronto is one example of a museum which provides an excellent resource for interdisciplinary and context-embedded learning. Tirrell describes the growing movement toward "living" museums:

> Thousands of elementary and secondary school students participate in educational programs provided by museums in the United States. These students may be involved in tours of exhibits and laboratories, discussions and media presentations, "hands on" exercises with artifacts, simulated excavations, actual field excavations, and laboratory work. The educational material associated with these programs may include readings, films, loan kits of artifacts, educational guides, and units of study coordinated with existing curricula. (1981, p. 1)

Archeology is particularly representative of the natural union between culture and math and science. Students learn "how people, separate from themselves in time, technology, and worldview, shaped and were shaped by the environment" (Tirrell, 1981, p. 1), but at the same time they may learn about such things as measurement, coordinates, statistics, radioactivity, and the effect of climate on plant communities.

Teaching that applies mathematics and science concepts to cultural phenomena or that uses examples drawn from disparate cultural backgrounds to illustrate math or science objectives is intellectually stimulating for both the teacher and the students. But as most experienced teachers would confirm, it is impossible to obtain all the resources and field trips which we would like or to maintain excitement and intellectual vibrancy at all times throughout the 180 days or so that we have students in our schools. However, we can glean from the interdisciplinary framework vital ideas and instructional approaches for periodic integration into the bloodstream of the more everyday happenings of life in multiethnic math and science classrooms, enriching our students' lives and our own. The curricular possibilities for improvement and enrichment of science and mathematics instruction are truly exciting and are limited only by our imaginations.

Chapter Seven

ASSESSMENT

At a recent conference, a group of distinguished educational researchers and linguists were exchanging ideas and sharing results of their research in an informal seminar. A director of a Title VII program who was in the audience addressed a question to everyone in the room: "I promised my school board members and all my staff that I was coming to this conference to find out from the *experts* the best test to use for oral English proficiency, so I would like each of you to discuss the test that you would use as the entry-exit criterion for a bilingual program."

There was absolute silence in the room. After a long wait, the Title VII director worriedly added, "I'm really serious. This is a pressing issue our school district has to resolve in the very near future, and I know if there is anyone who can answer this question, you are the ones who know the most about testing. Please help me!" After a continuing silence, one researcher finally offered the suggestion that, for an exit criterion, it would be very important to test literacy skills as well as oral skills and added that no one has "the magical" test. Even though many tests have been developed, some with excellent reliability and validity, they all still leave a lot to be desired. No one in the room disagreed.

Attempting to understand all the issues in the assessment of language-minority students is challenging, complicated, and sometimes very confusing. School personnel frequently have to make quick decisions in response to legal mandates or administrative pressures, without the benefit of a testing expert or the time or financial resources to carry out a carefully planned testing component of a school program. Teachers complain bitterly that many tests mandated by the school system seem to be inappropriate because they include items with cultural bias or vocabulary to which the students have not yet been exposed, test skills with which the students have not yet had experience, do not measure what they say they measure (lack of content validity), are normed on white middle-class children, do not reflect the cognitive styles of the children, or involve a culturally inappropriate testing situation, and so on.

All of the above may be legitimate or not-so-legitimate complaints, depending on the circumstances and purposes for which a test is being used. One problem often encountered in bilingual education is that so many bilingual staff members consider most testing inherently suspect that the negative feelings and despair make it very difficult for a testing expert to tackle the issues. Yet schools continue to use testing to make life decisions for us—reading and math tests, achievement tests, minimum competency tests to graduate from high school, Scholastic Achievement Tests to enter a university, tests that decide who gets into what professions (Owen, 1983). To survive in this test-conscious society, we need to learn how to give bilingual bicultural students well-constructed, appropriate tests, and we need to teach our students the skills needed so that the tests can measure the students' ability with maximum accuracy.

This chapter does not attempt to give you "everything you always wanted to know about assessment but were afraid to ask." All bilingual and ESL teachers are encouraged to take at least one course on educational tests and measurements. It is very important to have a general background in educational assessment to understand some of the complex issues involved in assessment of language-minority students. This chapter assumes a basic knowledge of testing and is designed to introduce school personnel to some of the specific issues involved in the assessment of language-minority students. For those who wish to delve further into the topic, there are many good references mentioned in this chapter. The chapter is divided into four sections: (1) an overview of the purposes of assessment in bilingual and ESL programs, (2) a discussion of some of the thorny issues in the assessment of language-minority students, (3) a brief review of some currently available assessment instruments, and (4) suggestions for test construction by teachers.

PURPOSES OF ASSESSMENT IN BILINGUAL AND ESL PROGRAMS

Throughout this chapter, we use the term "test" to refer to an objective, standardized measure of a sample of behavior or skill development, and the term "assessment" to imply a broader approach to testing, which could include multiple measures and observation of students. Assessment is used for many different purposes in bilingual and ESL settings, including placement (language dominance, proficiency in first and second languages), diagnosis (of first- and second-language acquisition, subject-area achievement, cognitive style), exit from a program (more achievement testing), and evaluation of a program (with possible use of norm-referenced tests and attitude scales). All of these uses of testing have been influenced by the federal government guidelines provided in the *Lau Remedies,* so we shall start our discussion with a review of these guidelines.

Testing Implications of Lau Remedies

The identification and assessment procedure for limited-English-proficient (LEP) students recommended by the federal government is based on the protection of rights provided by Title VI of the Civil Rights Act, in which

> No person in the United States shall, on the ground of race, color, or national origin, be excluded from participation in, be denied the benefits of, or be subjected to discrimination under any program or activity receiving federal financial assistance. (Public Law 88-352, Section 601, July 2, 1964)

The first memorandum regarding national origin minority groups with limited English-language skills was issued by the Office for Civil Rights on May 25, 1970. For compliance with Title VI of the Civil Rights Act, it recommends the following:

1. Where inability to speak and understand the English language excludes national origin–minority group children from effective participation in the educational program offered by a school district, the district must take affirmative steps to rectify the language deficiency in order to open its instructional program to these students.

2. School districts must not assign national origin–minority group students to classes for the mentally retarded on the basis of criteria which essentially measure or evaluate English language skills; nor may school districts deny national origin–minority group children access to college preparatory courses on a basis directly related to the failure of the school system to inculcate English language skills.

3. Any ability grouping or tracking system employed by the school system to deal with the special language skill needs of national origin–minority group children must be designed to meet such language skill needs as soon as possible and must not operate as an educational dead-end or permanent track.

4. School districts have the responsibility to adequately notify national origin–minority group parents of school activities which are called to the attention of other parents. Such notice in order to be adequate may have to be provided in a language other than English. (U.S. Office for Civil Rights, 1970)

In addition to this 1970 memorandum, the *Lau Remedies*—set forth in a memorandum from the Office for Civil Rights in 1975—are still in effect as of 1984. These guidelines issued by the federal government state the recommended procedures for local school districts to be in compliance with the U.S. Supreme Court decision of *Lau v. Nichols* (1974). Language assessment is one of the key components of the *Lau Remedies*.

1. *Identification.* The first step in the *Lau Remedies* is to identify the target population: all students with a primary language other than English who are (*a*) limited- or non-English-speaking and/or (*b*) achieving below grade level. Identification can be carried out by means of a home-language questionnaire, parent interview (K-8), or student interview (9-12).

2. *Language assessment.* The second step is classification of the identified students into five language categories:

   A. Monolingual speaker of the language other than English (speaks the language other than English exclusively).

   B. Predominantly speaks the language other than English (speaks mostly the language other than English, but speaks some English).

   C. Bilingual (speaks both the language other than English and English with equal ease).

   D. Predominantly speaks English (speaks mostly English, but speaks some of the language other than English).

   E. Monolingual speaker of English (speaks English exclusively).
   (U.S. Office for Civil Rights, 1975)

Those students who are classified as belonging to categories C, D, and E are entitled to special services in schools only if they are achieving below grade level. This determination is done through proficiency testing in both English and the first language, combined with school achievement scores.

3. *Diagnostic-prescriptive process.* After the students are placed in a special program, the third step involves regular ongoing diag-

nostic-prescriptive evaluation in all subject areas, just as in any school program.

4. *Exit criteria*. For decisions regarding when it is appropriate for students to leave the special program, "a district must provide predictive data which show that such students are ready to make the transition into English and will educationally succeed in content areas and the educational program in which he or she is to be placed" (U.S. Office for Civil Rights, 1975). Most school districts have chosen to determine exit suitability through assessment of students' English-language proficiency, although another interpretation could be that it would be more appropriate to give achievement tests in all subject areas.

A number of problems have arisen from use of the *Lau Remedies*. The document was conceived and written in response to the legal mandate, without a solid theoretical or empirical research base on which to build the categories and definitions. Thus while the *Lau Remedies* have provided general guidelines to meet immediate practical needs of school systems, they do not provide the assessment expert with operational definitions for actually carrying out the required task (De Avila & Duncan, 1979b, p. 443). The Lau Centers (National Origin Desegregation Assistance Centers) were established by the Office for Civil Rights (OCR) to aid school systems in complying with the standards of the law. During the Reagan administration, OCR has not carried out vigorous enforcement of the requirements, but school systems are still required to identify students of limited English proficiency and provide some kind of special services for them.

The 1980 proposed changes in the *Lau Remedies* were an attempt by the federal government to address some of the problems which had arisen in implementation. The changes, however, were so specific that there was a furor of opposition to the proposed regulations from both opponents of bilingual education and bilingual educators. As a result, the federal government, which had by then changed hands from Carter to Reagan, chose to withdraw the proposed regulations, continue the existing 1975 *Lau Remedies*, and leave decisions on the specifics of assessment and program design to individual school districts. At the time, the media completely misrepresented the decision, with headlines such as "Bilingual Education Scrapped," but Secretary Bell made it clear that even though the 1980 proposed OCR regulations were being dropped, federal support for special programs for limited-English-proficient students would continue:

I am announcing today the withdrawal of the proposed bilingual education policies set forth by this Department as national policy on August 5, 1980.

I take this action for many reasons. The policies are harsh, inflexible, burdensome, unworkable and incredibly costly. The rules are fiercely opposed by many, supported by few. . . .

We will protect the rights of children who do not speak English well but we will do so by permitting school districts to use any way that has proven to be successful. . . .

I am committed to civil rights and to all the responsibilities that go with the job in this Department. No school administrator should read anything to the contrary in this action today, and no school administrator should misread this action as an invitation to discriminate against children who face language barriers. The responsibility of schools to provide equal educational opportunity for all children is recognized and will be honored by this Department. (Bell, 1981)

Another difficulty with the continuation of the 1975 *Lau Remedies* is their emphasis on proficiency in oral skills alone as a basis for entry, which leads many school districts to use the same assessment instrument for exit. The five language categories listed previously refer only to speaking skills. On the other hand, federal funds available from Title VII (the Bilingual Education Act) are designed to include all four language skills. When Title VII was reauthorized in 1978, the terms "non-English-speaking/limited-English-speaking" (NES/LES) were changed in the bill to "limited English *proficient*" to reflect concern for the importance of teaching and testing for proficiency in reading and writing in English as well as oral skills.

When one examines carefully Cummins' (1979a) distinction between basic interpersonal communicative skills (BICS) and cognitive-academic language proficiency (CALP) (see chap. 3), the distinction between oral and written skills becomes even more important. Most limited-English-proficient students attain mastery of BICS in English, which includes oral skills in face-to-face interaction with native speakers and functional use of the language, in 2 years. In contrast, CALP, which includes context-reduced, academic tasks in abstract thought and formal written language, takes an average of approximately 5 to 7 years for language-minority students to master in a second language. Furthermore, many of the skills in CALP transfer from first to second language; therefore, the most important issue for children's successful achievement in school is a solid academic base, whether it be taught in first or second language. Cummins' theory and research imply that measurement of language proficiency for meeting exit criteria should not be based on oral skills alone. Rather, program decisions should be based on a comprehensive assessment of first and second language proficiency and achievement in all school subjects. While the existing *Lau Remedies* may lead school systems to assess oral skills only for exit from a special program, Title VII guidelines encourage all programs to go beyond this and to test for full English proficiency in oral and written skills.

Placement Testing

Following identification of all students in a school district whose primary language is not English, the next step in assessment is placement testing to determine who should be in what type of program. If there are enough students of one language background to make bilingual teaching feasible, bilingual education is a serious program option. In some states it is mandated; in others it is encouraged but not required (see chap. 2). In an ESL-only program, language dominance testing is not necessary, but for a bilingual program both language dominance and language proficiency are assessed for placement.

Language Dominance and Proficiency Assessment   The question of which language is dominant when a student enters a program is really a question of language proficiency. The appropriate method of assessment of language dominance is therefore a test of proficiency in the first language compared with a similar test of proficiency in the second language. Although this sounds simple, language-dominance testing gets more complicated in actual practice.

First, there are school districts which use their identification survey alone as a measure of language dominance. Using surname, ethnicity, or parents' language dominance as an indicator of ability in first and second languages is highly questionable (Woodford, 1982, p. 104). Other definitions of language dominance which have serious limits when used as the only measure are the language in which a speaker feels most comfortable, the language first learned, or the language used at home. A questionnaire or interview to determine some or all of the above variables is not sufficient to measure language dominance.

Unfortunately, to take seriously accurate measurement of full proficiency in first and second languages, one may end up with more variables to be assessed than practically feasible. Ideally, the following variables should be assessed:

1. First dimension: linguistic components

    a. Phonology (pronunciation)

    b. Morphology and syntax (grammar)

   c. Semantics (meaning)

   d. Lexicon (vocabulary)

   e. Discourse (organization of formal thought patterns in speech and writing)

   f. Paralinguistics (for example, volume, pitch, pauses)

   g. Nonverbal behavior (for example, gestures, touching, eye contact, time, space)

2. Second dimension: sociolinguistic components

   a. Style (for example, intimate, casual, formal)

   b. Function (use of language in appropriate context)

   c. Domain (use of language at home, school, in the community, or other places)

   d. Variety (use of dialects for appropriate community interaction)

3. Third dimension: language skills

   a. Listening comprehension

   b. Speaking

   c. Reading

   d. Writing

   e. Metalinguistic skills (knowledge *about* the language)

This outline is an expanded version of two figures from Hernández-Chávez, Burt, and Dulay (1978) and Zirkel (1979). It can be thought of as a three-dimensional figure, in which each dimension intersects with the other two dimensions, for a total of $7 \times 4 \times 5$, or 140, components which should be assessed for a complete picture of one student's proficiency in each language. It is virtually impossible to assess all these components of one student's competence and performance in first and second languages in a placement test. It *is* possible through regular assessment throughout a school year or microethnographic observation and recording to collect such a detailed analysis for each student, but it is extremely time-consuming and costly. Let us be practical.

Options are available for language dominance and proficiency testing which fall somewhere in the middle of the spectrum between unacceptable questionnaire data and acceptable but impractical complete assessment. These are indirect indices of bilingualism, in which the student is asked to do tasks that involve integrating several linguistic skills. From performance on those tasks, a student's relative level of overall proficiency can be inferred. Although most teachers are not satisfied with a single measure, it can serve placement purposes and can be followed by more extensive diagnostic assessment as the student continues in the program. Types of indirect measures are free production tests (in which a picture or topic is presented and the student is asked to talk or write about it), word association tests, and cloze tests (Hernández-Chávez, Burt & Dulay, 1978). Another type of placement test which can be given involves the direct measurement of language proficiency through eliciting natural communication, such as the Bilingual Syntax Measure (Burt, Dulay & Hernández-Chávez, 1975).

First-Language Proficiency   There are few valid and reliable instruments available for assessment of first-language proficiency other than English. It is definitely not an acceptable practice to translate tests available in English directly into other languages. This violates the statistical support for a test (for example, item analysis and all statistical procedures for establishing validity and reliability must be reestablished for the translation), and a straight translation will be culturally and linguistically irrelevant (Erickson & Omark, 1981, p. 6). Some references with reviews of instruments available in languages other than English are listed in the section entitled Assessment Instruments in this chapter.

Language Aptitude Testing   Some school systems use aptitude testing as part of the placement process. Subject-area aptitude tests in English do not serve any useful purpose for limited-English-proficient students, since LEP students are not yet proficient enough in English for the test to measure what it is intended to measure. Language aptitude tests are equally troublesome. Foreign-language aptitude tests are designed to measure phonetic coding ability, grammatical sensitivity, and inductive ability to guess grammatical and semantic rules in an artificial language created for the test (Carroll, 1973). All of these abilities correlate positively with conscious, formal learning of language but not with acquisition. Therefore, a language aptitude test might predict a student's successful school achievement in formal classroom instruction. Another student, however, might do very poorly on the test but could be an excellent acquirer of English. Since, according to Krashen (1981, pp. 19–39), language acquisition is more important than formal language learning, a language aptitude test would seem to have little meaning for placement purposes in a bilingual or ESL program.

The theoretical basis for decreasing the use of language aptitude tests is discussed in more detail in this chapter in the section entitled Issues in Assessment of Language-Minority Students. Discrete-point, integrative, and pragmatic tests of language are discussed in conjunction with a definition of communicative competence and its importance for testing. Aptitude tests tend to measure grammatical abilities only but not full communicative competence.

Diagnostic-Prescriptive Process

Throughout a school program, ongoing assessment is used to measure students' mastery of the objectives of the curriculum. This may include teacher-made tests, tests available in the curricular materials, teacher observation, skills checklists, homework assignments, standardized criterion-referenced tests, and other appropriate data. While teachers are frequently very critical of standardized tests, the tests and grading systems which teachers develop for their own day-to-day assessment are subject to many pitfalls, such as overly subjective scoring; construction of test items which are not valid or reliable; or the measurement of easy, trivial tasks and avoidance of problem solving and other more complex tasks. The process of constructing valid and reliable tests is time-consuming but nevertheless worthwhile. Some suggestions for development of skills in test construction are given in the section of this chapter entitled Teacher-Constructed Tests.

Teacher-Made and Textbook Tests   A common strategy of teachers who know little about test construction is to use unit or chapter tests provided in the textbook and accompanying materials chosen for a subject area. The advantage to this strategy is that the department or school has consistency in the objectives being tested across teachers, and this frees teachers from time spent on test construction. However, there are serious problems with this approach for bilingual and ESL classes, as this type of testing locks the program into teaching for the objectives of the particular set of materials chosen. Teachers usually find themselves teaching to the test rather than the needs of the students. When a homogeneous group of students starts at a given base with a specific body of material to be mastered, and the tests provided actually measure the objectives set by the teachers, then unit tests provided by the materials may be appropriate. However, this ideal situation is rarely present in a school setting, and the tests provided by the materials are frequently poorly constructed. Most bilingual and ESL classes are heterogeneous, with students demonstrating greatly varied levels of proficiency in the material being mastered, and teachers have to individualize their teaching to meet those varied needs by pulling lessons from many different materials and by developing their own lessons. Tests also have to be varied greatly as teachers discover skills their students have not yet mastered. It is therefore very important for bilingual and ESL teachers to have training in test construction and to understand issues in assessment, so that they can construct their own tests and critically analyze other tests.

Standardized Tests   The same problems are even more apparent with use of standardized tests for diagnostic purposes with students of limited English proficiency. Each school district generally uses at least one standardized test at the beginning and end of the year to measure students' attainment of the overall grade-level objectives in specific subject areas— for example, the testing of reading and math skills for primary-school children. The tests used may be norm-referenced or criterion-referenced, but criterion-referenced tests are used more often for diagnosis, as they focus on specific objectives to be mastered according to previously stated criteria and keep all items at roughly the same level of difficulty. A criterion-referenced test does not create differences between students but simply measures each student's mastery of each objective in the curriculum. In contrast, norm-referenced tests have both easy and difficult items to create a wider spread of score differentiation among students. Norm-referenced tests should not be used at all with students of limited English proficiency, because they have been normed on native speakers of English, and comparing LEP students to English-proficient students is not valid. The test will consistently underestimate the abilities of LEP students.

For diagnostic purposes, criterion-referenced testing in a student's native language is most appropriate, if a test can be found which measures the objectives of the curriculum. However, most tests developed in other countries are not appropriate for students in this country because of dialectal, vocabulary, or curricular differences. Most school systems, unable to find the appropriate test, resort to testing exclusively in English. There are many appropriate, valid, and reliable standardized tests developed for native speakers of English which can be used with students of limited English proficiency *after* the students have approached reasonable mastery of the English language. Until that time, whether it is intended to measure math, science, or social studies skills, the test will actually be a test of English proficiency and little else. It is inappropriate to make program decisions on the basis of such tests because they track students below their actual ability.

One strategy that some school systems have taken is to exempt all limited-English-proficient students from norm-referenced and criterion-referenced tests for their first 1 or 2 years of study in the United States. Another possibility is to let students take the tests for the sake of practicing test-taking skills but not to count the scores until bilingual or ESL staff have determined that the students have achieved sufficient English proficiency for the test to be an accurate measure of their skills. While students are building skills to prepare for taking standardized tests, a strategy for ongoing diagnosis is the task analytic approach, as used by special educators. Task analysis breaks down target behavior into its component skills. Each subskill is seen as a building block for the target behavior. The student's performance is continually and progressively measured as an integral part of the teaching process.

Cognitive Style   Another area sometimes assessed is cognitive style. As discussed in detail in chapter 4, the field-independent–field-sensitive (or field-dependent) dichotomy has been analyzed a great deal by researchers who study language-minority students, because a large number of such students have been found to be field-sensitive when first tested. Valencia (1981, p. 63) provides a summary of some characteristics of the two styles of learning:

> Field-independent persons tend to differentiate stimuli found within a perceptual field; . . . prefer tasks requiring factional information and problems based on analytical processes; . . . and prefer individual and independent type activities in the learning process, with the teacher serving as a resource person rather than a model.

> Field-dependent or field-sensitive persons tend to see complex perceptual fields as a whole; . . . tend to give greater attention to persons and things in their social surroundings; . . . appear to be more socially perceptive and responsive to external directions; . . . and tend to prefer lessons prefaced with supportive assurances from the teacher, problem solving strategies modeled by the teacher, and a humanized instructional setting.

Many language-minority students who are proficient in both English and another language have been found to be bicognitive, taking advantage of both styles of learning. The most common test used to measure field independence–field dependence (sensitivity) is the Embedded Figures Test or the Children's Embedded Figures Test (Witkin, 1967).

While field independence–field dependence has received a lot of attention in studies of language-minority students, it is just one of many dimensions of cognitive style. For example, there are analyzers and synthesizers, convergent and divergent thinkers, impulsives and reflectives, levelers and sharpeners, scanners and focusers, visual and auditory learners, and so on. Being aware of differences in cognitive style can help teachers to appreciate the strengths of each student and to build on those strengths.

Exit Criteria

For students to be mainstreamed (taken out of their special program), some decision must be made regarding the criteria they must meet to join classes receiving the standard curriculum. A common practice in the past was to use the same assessment instrument used for placement and to test only oral skills in English. However, it is clear that oral proficiency in English does not necessarily correlate with successful school achievement. Reading and writing abilities in English are more closely related to the cognitive-academic decontextualized language used for school tasks. Therefore, if exit assessment must be carried out, the minimum necessary is to test full English proficiency in both oral and written skills.

Many researchers and assessment experts have pointed out that the implications of the *Lau v. Nichols* decision go well beyond the testing of English proficiency to determining what will predict successful achievement in school. Those students who can be identified as in need of a special program include not only limited-English-proficient students but also those with another language background who are proficient in English but are underachievers in school. To assess students' ability to succeed in mainstream classes, overall academic achievement must be considered. Tests at exit level should test the skills these students are expected to have mastered in each subject area at the appropriate grade level, just as for any other student. Rudolph Troike (1981, pp. 4–5) summarizes as follows:

> The difficulty we find ourselves in with regard to language assessment is that our original rationale for bilingual education is coming back to haunt us. Having successfully argued for bilingual education as a means to overcome the language barrier, we not surprisingly see English proficiency defined as the sole criterion for program entry and exit, even though we now realize that this may be a third- or fourth-order factor or even completely misleading. . . . I believe we may be making a mistake in attempting to assess language at all. The purpose of bilingual education should be *educational*, not just the development of English proficiency. Consequently, *language assessment may very well be an inappropriate basis for educational decision making for limited-English-proficient students.*

Since the demands for language assessment are there, mandated by law and court decisions, what can we do? . . . We need to work to convince legislators, administrators, and others that *academic achievement,* rather than English proficiency, should be the basis for exiting from a bilingual program. Better than that, we should seek to remove the compensatory label from bilingual education and work to institutionalize it as a permanent program option which is available to all students and in which requirements for program exit would not exist.

Program Evaluation

Assessment is also used in bilingual and ESL programs for the purpose of program evaluation. Evaluation of bilingual and ESL programs should be taken very seriously, as many federal, state, and local educational decisions are based on results of evaluations, whether or not the data are appropriate or the study is methodologically well conducted. Teachers can cooperate and actively participate in the evaluation process, as described by Cohen (1980a).

It is not the purpose of this section to discuss specific aspects of program evaluation for evaluators, but simply to provide an overview of assessment in evaluation for teachers. Cohen, Bruck, and Rodríguez-Brown (1979) provide some analysis of issues in bilingual program evaluation. Cohen's (1975b) evaluation of a bilingual program is considered an example of well-designed, in-depth program evaluation.

Norm-Referenced Tests   In bilingual or ESL program evaluation, test instruments may be used to measure language skills, content-subject mastery, and affective consequences of a program. Tests used for diagnosis may be a part of the evaluation, or an evaluator may use additional instruments as approved by the school system. If norm-referenced instruments are chosen, care must be taken that the norm group is appropriately chosen for comparison with the program students according to the goals desired. Most widely used norm-referenced tests have norm group information for various social-class and ethnic groups but not for students of limited English proficiency. Until students are proficient in English, a norm-referenced test in English will simply test their English skills; it will not be a valid test of their subject-matter knowledge.

If a norm-referenced test is to be used with bilingual students who have reached a sufficient level of proficiency in English to be tested in comparison with a norm group of native speakers of English, great caution should be taken with use of regional or ethnic norms, which are now provided by most test publishers.

Another major response of the testing industry to criticism has been to establish or to propose establishment of regional and ethnic norms. Such a practice leads to lower expectations for minorities, which in turn may lower children's aspirations to succeed. Furthermore, ethnic norms do not take into consideration the complex reasons *why* minority children on the average score lower than Anglo-American children on IQ tests. Ethnic norms are potentially dangerous from the social perspective because they provide a basis for invidious comparisons between racial groups. The tendency is to assume that lower scores are indicative of lower potential, thereby contributing to the self-fulfilling prophecy of lower expectations for minority children and reinforcing the genetic-inferiority argument advanced by Arthur Jensen and others. (De Avila & Havassy, 1978, p. 381)

At the appropriate time, a norm-referenced standardized test may be a valid measure of bilingual students' academic achievement, even when comparing such students to a norm group consisting primarily of middle-class mainstream American students. The most impressive evaluations of bilingual programs are those which have demonstrated that students have achieved scores above the national averages in English academic skills and subject matter as measured by standardized norm-referenced tests after 4 to 5 years of bilingual instruction. (See Troike, 1978, for a review of some of these effectiveness studies.)

Decisions about the norm-group comparison and appropriate tests should be made carefully. Woodford (1982, p. 105) recommends the following as minimal questions to be asked when making decisions about use of standardized tests:

Is the content sampled in the test representative of the classroom content of the program? What are the characteristics of the reference population (the children in the norming sample)? Does the test require a skill that the children have not developed? (For example, must they be able to read in the home language to answer questions when they might not have been taught to read yet?) Is the variety of the home language used on the test familiar to the children? Will the information to be gotten from the test be useful?

Attitudinal Assessment Although affective consequences are not assessed in many evaluations, this can be a very important aspect of bilingual and ESL programs. For example, attitudes of the students toward the program itself may be measured. Attitudes toward the language being taught and toward speakers of the language have been shown to correlate with proficiency in the language (Gardner & Lambert, 1972). Other attitudes can be measured, such as changes in values or, in an integrated program, changes in students' perceptions of each other. There are many instruments for measurement of attitudinal variables, such as sociograms, the Semantic Differential technique, the Matched Guise, the Cultural Attitude Scales, and so on. These and other instruments for measurement of attitudes in bilingual and ESL programs are reviewed in Gardner and Lambert (1972), Zirkel and Greene (1976), and Oller (1979). Oller's review provides an extensive discussion of the limitations and possibilities of these instruments.

Naturalistic Evaluation   Teachers may be asked to participate or to be observed in naturalistic evaluation. This process provides an evaluator with more descriptive information for better design of the study. Naturalistic evaluation is now popularly called "ethnographic" observation, but anthropologists argue that the term *ethnography* has been misused in educational evaluation. The anthropological approach to ethnography involves all-consuming long-term study in which a trained anthropologist is immersed in the setting for observation and analysis. Naturalistic observation is used in bilingual and ESL program evaluation because there are so many hundreds of variations in program design and background characteristics of students. It is virtually impossible to design a methodologically appropriate study without initial and occasionally continuing observation of classrooms and all other aspects of the program (Cohen, Bruck & Rodríguez-Brown, 1979). Techniques of data collection which can be employed in naturalistic assessment include classroom observation and videotaping, interviews, questionnaires, and analysis of school records.

Longitudinal Studies   Teachers should be aware that the most helpful kind of program evaluation is longitudinal, in which similar measures are used from year to year to determine students' progress over several years. A well-designed longitudinal study can provide valuable information about the process of language acquisition and successful program characteristics, in addition to aiding the refinement of assessment techniques and instruments. Especially valuable are data from students who have remained in a program for a number of years—a program in which there has not been a lot of attrition. Norm-referenced and criterion-referenced tests, along with many other measures, can provide a wealth of information for program decisions and for researchers in education and linguistics.

Much useful knowledge about bilingual education and language acquisition has been generated from the longitudinal studies in Canada and in the Culver City, California, immersion bilingual programs. For a summary of the Canadian research over the last 10 years, see Swain and

Lapkin (1981). For a summary of some of the Culver City research, see Cohen (1976) and California State Department of Education (1984).

ISSUES IN ASSESSMENT OF LANGUAGE-MINORITY STUDENTS

Issues that need to be resolved regarding the assessment of language-minority students include language assessment, bilingualism and intelligence, assessment for bilingual special education, and cultural bias in tests.

Language Assessment

Assumptions and theories about the assessment of language have undergone radical change during the last 10 years. This change is important for language teachers to understand, for it strongly influences the type of tests chosen for language assessment purposes.

Informal Assessment   The earliest type of language assessment was carried out by classroom teachers informally through subjective judgments based mainly on experience with previous students. This type of informal assessment is not concerned with statistical validity or reliability nor with linguistic theories of language. Many educators still accept this informal, less carefully planned assessment for classroom purposes, although assessment experts would not condone the practice (Genesee, 1982, p. 31).

Discrete-Point Tests   Based on theories from structural linguistics and behavioral psychology, discrete-point testing became popular in language assessment during the 1960s. Best represented by Robert Lado's *Language Testing* (1961), discrete-point tests attempt to focus on one specific element of a language and one skill for each item tested. For example, one might choose one phonemic contrast (such as ship /i/ and sheep /iy/) and test a student's listening comprehension of the phonemic distinction in this minimal pair. Or a discrete point in the morphology, syntax, or vocabulary of the language could be chosen and tested in one skill area (e.g., listening, speaking, reading, or writing). Most discrete-point items are multiple-choice questions which are easily scored, can be administered to groups, and can be tested for validity and reliability. Thus when discrete-point tests became popular, they were widely hailed as a big improvement in psychometric measurement of language. Most standardized language tests available today, such as those put out by the Educational Testing

Service (for example, the TOEFL: Test of English as a Foreign Language), contain a large number of discrete-point items.

The major problem with discrete-point tests is that they are not based on the most current theories of language, which have arisen from Chomsky's initial critique of the structuralists and succeeding linguists' critiques and refining of Chomsky's views. Most contemporary linguists now support more recent theories of language, which look at language as a creative, complex, interactive phenomenon not appropriately measured by examining only the small, isolated parts. Sociolinguists first started the critique of discrete-point tests, pointing out that these tests fail to measure the communicative aspects of language. Since then, many others have joined the bandwagon, calling for the teaching and testing of communicative competence.

Communicative Competence   During the 1970s and early 1980s, many linguists and foreign-language educators have struggled with theoretical definitions of communicative competence (for example, Brière, 1972, 1979b; Canale & Swain, 1980; Savignon, 1972, 1982; Slaughter & Bennett, 1981). No consensus has yet been reached, which makes it difficult for testers to know what they are supposed to be testing for.

In spite of the lack of consensus, we believe that communicative competence involves some combination of knowledge *about* a language (grammatical competence) and knowledge of how to use that language in a real-life context (sociolinguistic competence). Sociolinguistic competence might include knowledge of sociocultural rules or appropriateness of use of language varieties, domains, repertoires, skills, roles, statuses, attitudes, settings, topics, channels, registers, styles, and so on (Brière, 1979; Troike, 1982). Grammatical competence includes knowledge of rules of phonology, morphology, syntax, semantics, and the lexicon. Paralinguistics and nonverbal behavior are also components of communicative competence. In addition, Swain and Canale would add strategic competence, which includes

> verbal and nonverbal communication strategies that may be called into action at times when the flow of speech might otherwise be impeded due to performance variables or to insufficient competence. (1982, p. 49)

Canale (1981) also adds a fourth area, discourse competence, which includes

> mastery of how to combine meanings and forms to achieve a unified text in different modes (e.g., telephone inquiry, argumentative essay, and recipe) by using (*a*) cohesion devices to relate utterance forms (e.g., pronouns and

transition words) and (*b*) coherence rules to organize meanings (e.g., repetition, progression, consistency, and relevance of ideas). (Cummins, 1981b, p. 7)

What does all of this discussion have to do with bilingual and ESL education? These seem to be theoretical arguments prompted especially by foreign-language educators who have been frustrated with methods (audiolingual) and assessment approaches (discrete-point) generated by theories in structural linguistics. These arguments are useful to examine because we are finally coming closer and closer to a full definition of communicative competence, and tests are being developed which focus on communicative aspects of language proficiency. As these tests become available, we should not lose sight of the overall skills we wish to measure in tests for language-minority students.

First, we must keep in mind that we want students not only to internalize knowledge about the new language but also to know how to use the known rules in communicative acts, or in *performance*. If a test measures only receptive skills (listening and reading), it is not testing a student's productive skills (speaking and writing) and therefore may not be considered a measure of all aspects of that student's proficiency in the language tested. A testing program for bilingual and ESL students should include measurement of communicative competence *and* performance (Brière, 1979b; Swain & Canale, 1982).

Second, our definition of communicative competence includes grammatical knowledge. However, in their eagerness to move away from the older, more traditional ways of teaching language, which focused almost exclusively on grammar, some linguists and educators have overemphasized the importance of teaching functional use of the language. These authors would define communicative competence as mainly sociolinguistic knowledge of the language, or that needed for real-world survival. Let us not lose sight of the importance of keeping a balance between the teaching and testing of both grammatical and sociolinguistic competence and performance of the language.

Again, Cummins' (1979a) distinction between BICS and CALP is helpful here. If we are teaching an adult education ESL class and the main goal is survival skills, we want to teach and test mostly basic interpersonal communicative skills. But if we are teaching students in K-12 and the overall goal is students' academic achievement, we want to teach and test students in all skills needed for cognitive-academic language proficiency, as well as BICS with beginning classes. BICS and CALP are thus both incorporated in our broader definition of communicative competence.

Tests of Communicative Competence: Integrative and Pragmatic Tests   In contrast to discrete-point tests, integrative tests attempt to measure a student's ability to integrate many of the small pieces of a language together at the same time. The term "integrative test" was first proposed by Carroll (1961). Oller (1979) prefers the term "pragmatic test," referring to the branch of linguistics called pragmatics, which examines language in context. Thus a pragmatic test would include tasks that involve an integration of skills and are as close to natural language use as possible. Examples of language tests which are both integrative and pragmatic are dictation, oral or written cloze, oral production, paraphrase recognition, question answering, oral interview, and composition or essay writing (Oller, 1979, pp. 45–49).

Three of these types—dictation, cloze, and question answering—can be easy to score, can be examined for validity and reliability, and can be administered to groups. The other types of integrative or pragmatic tests may be less practical for group administration but very important and useful tools for day-to-day diagnosis. Composition and essay writing are more difficult to score objectively, but are nevertheless very important to assign for development of writing skills. When time and personnel are available to administer a test on a one-to-one basis, all of these types of tests might be used effectively for placement, diagnosis, exit, or evaluation purposes, as long as the criteria of natural language use and integration of language skills are met in the test items or tasks.

It is not at all easy to construct a good test, but integrative, pragmatic tests are important to develop if the goal of the program is full competence and performance in all aspects of functional language use for all students. Pragmatic tests also usually involve higher level processing of information, challenging students to think, problem-solve, and be more creative in language use, rather than to memorize rules as encouraged by the discrete-point approach to testing. There are appropriate times for discrete-point testing, however, interspersed with integrative, pragmatic testing. Discrete-point tests may be used when lower-level skills are being first introduced, or for practice in preparation for a standardized discrete-point test required by the school system. Keep in mind that discrete-point language tests still dominate in the commercial testing market.

Observation   Another method of language assessment which is the most time-consuming of all but the most rewarding in rich detail is observation of a student in a structured or natural setting such as school, home, or community. Linguists, sociolinguists, and psycholinguists collect speech and writing samples in natural settings to unlock the mysteries of language; the technique can be equally effective in helping teachers to understand their students' use of languages, if a teacher has time to focus on each individual student at various times during the year. Nonjudgmental observation can help a teacher to understand better each student's use of first and second languages and language varieties in varying contexts, the role of code-switching, nonverbal communication, and many other aspects of language use which may not surface in formalized teacher-student interaction in the classroom. An excellent reference with detailed explanation for carrying out observational assessment is Omark (1981).

Bilingualism, Intelligence, and IQ Tests

Bilingualism and Intelligence   The varying definitions of bilingualism, described in detail in chapter 3, have caused confusion in the realm of intelligence testing when investigators have attempted to choose "bilingual" subjects for studies. Many studies have compared bilingual with monolingual students on standard intelligence tests, and until the early 1960s, with a few notable exceptions, most of these studies concluded that bilinguals had some kind of deficiency or disadvantage supposedly as a result of their bilingualism. The so-called negative cognitive effect is now thought to have been an artifact of poorly designed studies. For example, some studies had no control for subjects' relative language proficiency in L_1 and L_2, because of lack of an established definition of what constitutes bilingualism; in other studies inappropriate instruments were used or middle-class monolinguals were compared with lower-class bilinguals. In a reversal of most previous studies, Peal and Lambert (1962, p. 6) were surprised with the findings that their bilingual subjects scored better than monolinguals on various measures of intelligence:

> The picture that emerges of the French/English bilingual in Montreal is that of a youngster whose wider experiences in two cultures have given him advantages which a monolingual does not enjoy. Intellectually his experience with two language systems seems to have left him with a mental flexibility, a superiority in concept formation, and a more diversified set of mental abilities. . . . In contrast, the monolingual appears to have a more unitary structure of intelligence which he must use for all types of intellectual tasks.

Since the publication of this well-designed study, many other studies have found that bilinguals with sufficient proficiency in L_1 and L_2 have cognitive advantages over monolinguals on measures of cognitive flexibility, linguistic and metalinguistic abilities, concept formation, divergent thinking skills, creativity, and diversity (De Avila & Duncan, 1979a; Díaz, 1983; Duncan & De Avila, 1979; Iiams, 1976).

For example, De Avila and Duncan (1979a, 1980) have conducted continuing studies on bilingualism and cognitive functioning, controlling for relative linguistic proficiency and socioeconomic status. They have found that proficient bilinguals significantly outperform monolinguals on Piagetian intellectual tasks and in cognitive-perceptual processing.

> The nature of these differences or advantages can be described in terms of superior development of egocentricity or ability to restructure or reorganize intellectually a three-dimensional display; in the relative ability to separate out part of an organized field from the field as a whole; and in level of development of articulation of body concept. (De Avila & Duncan, 1980, p. 129)

These authors contend that bilinguals seem to have a head start over monolinguals in metacognition and metalinguistic awareness, or awareness of one's own cognitive and linguistic processes.

IQ Tests   IQ tests are just one of many types of tests which can be used to examine a student's cognitive abilities and potential. We know that IQ tests are predictors of academic potential because of high positive correlations of IQ scores with academic achievement tests. But "extreme caution is necessary in assessing the intelligence of students from backgrounds other than the dominant cultural group because of the possibility of cultural or linguistic bias" (Cummins, 1982, p. 1). Cultural bias, which will be discussed in the next section, is particularly a problem on IQ tests because so many items are designed to meet socialization norms of the culturally dominant group.

> The use of the IQ test has been defended on the basis of its ability to "predict" achievement scores. Numerous authors have criticized this argument as being circular, since the content of both achievement and IQ tests is virtually indistinguishable. In this way the IQ test fails to distinguish background learning experiences (repertoire) from the child's ability to encode or transform information (capacity) within his or her repertoire. Because of this limitation and numerous others, many researchers have turned to less culturally specific assessment approaches. (De Avila & Duncan, 1980, p. 111)

Linguistic bias is present when IQ tests are administered by school psychologists in English to students who are not yet proficient in English. Cummins (1982) criticizes school personnel who assume a child is proficient in English because the child has ability in communicative skills (or BICS) and then blame the student's low score on an IQ test on deficiencies in the student or in his or her background. IQ tests normed on the culturally dominant group should not be administered to limited-English-proficient students in English until they have had a sufficient number of years to attain cognitive-academic language proficiency—which might be as many as 5 to 7 years.

If IQ tests must be administered for special needs assessment, they should be given in the student's first language by a bilingual specialist. Furthermore, it is very important to have multiple measures, obtained through several different types of appropriately chosen tests, especially when the assessment may lead to placement in a program with a very specialized curriculum, such as special education. Until recent years, it has been a sad but fairly common practice to misassign many minority students to classes for the mentally retarded (Bernal & Tucker, 1981). A dramatic reversal of this practice came with the court case *Diana v. California* (1970), in which the plaintiffs were migrant, Spanish-speaking children who had been tested with an instrument to measure intelligence in English and placed in classes for the educable mentally retarded. The settlement ordered the retesting of all such children in California, using both English and the students' primary language; proposed that an intelligence test appropriate for Mexican-American children in California be developed and normed on Mexican-Americans; and provided for the use of nonverbal tests of intelligence to diagnose mental retardation. Since this court case, use of nonverbal measures of IQ has become standard practice in California. Hispanics' performance on nonverbal IQ measures is virtually equal to that of white, English-speaking children, even with large social-class differences (Figueroa, 1980, pp. 148–149). This court case and other similar cases had an impact on the development in 1975 of Public Law 94-142, the Education of All Handicapped Children Act, which includes provisions for nondiscriminatory testing and an appropriate education for each child. P.L. 94-142 will be discussed shortly.

Threshold Hypothesis   An important corollary to the studies on bilingualism and intelligence is Cummins' (1976) hypothesis that there may be threshold levels of linguistic proficiency in L_1 and L_2 that bilinguals must reach to receive the benefits of the cognitive advantages associated with bilingualism. Clearly, the studies to date have demonstrated cognitive advantages of bilinguals with high proficiency in both L_1 and L_2. Partial bilinguals (those with nativelike proficiency in one language but partial proficiency in the second) tend to perform similarly to monolinguals on tests, with neither positive nor negative cognitive effects. Limited-English-proficient students who have low scores on tests of proficiency in both L_1 and L_2 may experience negative cognitive effects or low academic achievement in school.

A large majority of the "negative" studies were carried out with language minority children whose L₁ was gradually being replaced by a more dominant and prestigious L₂. Under these conditions, these children developed relatively low levels of academic proficiency in both languages. In contrast, the majority of studies that have reported cognitive advantages associated with bilingualism have involved students whose L₁ proficiency has continued to develop while L₂ is being acquired. Consequently, these students have been characterized by relatively high levels of proficiency in both languages. (Cummins, 1981b, p. 38)

Some Swedish researchers have used the term "semilingualism" to refer to the phenomenon in which some students score low on proficiency tests in both languages (Hansegård, 1968; Skutnabb-Kangas & Toukomaa, 1976); however, most other linguists have avoided use of this term because of its pejorative connotation. The label tends to lower teachers' expectations of these students. A very limited amount of research has been carried out on this subgroup of limited-English-proficient students, most of whom speak a language variety which is not considered standard, even though it may be a cognitively valid, fully developed system which may combine some aspects of the two languages (Dulay & Burt, 1980). If there are sufficient numbers of students who speak a language variety, it may be an appropriate programmatic decision to help students learn bidialectally by providing a bridge from the community dialect to one standard language (either Spanish or English, for example). Some researchers have recommended that these are the students most in need of instruction in CALP in first language (Cummins, 1981a; Skutnabb-Kangas & Toukomaa, 1976).

Assessment for Bilingual Special Education

Since the passing of the federal Public Law 94-142, the Education of All Handicapped Children Act of 1975, significant changes have taken place in procedures for the assessment of language-minority children with special needs. The law states that "tests and evaluation procedures will be selected and administered so as not to be racially or culturally discriminatory" and that they must be "administered in the child's native language" (Public Law 94-142, 1975, Section 612). The law paved the way for encouraging the development and use of new assessment instruments which are less discriminatory. IQ has ceased to be the predominant construct for special education assessment, while measurement of adaptive behavior and assessment of linguistic abilities have come to be equally important (Figueroa, 1980).

The process of assessment for special education is a complicated one for each student referred. During the screening process, team members are selected for the assessment who have the appropriate cultural and linguistic background. These team members decide the purpose of testing, select the instruments to be used, and administer those instruments. The data obtained in the multiple assessments are then interpreted by the team; decisions are made whether other data are needed; placement decisions are made; and if special placement is recommended, an individualized educational program is designed for the student.

Ironically, because of court cases such as *Diana v. California* (1970), which brought to educators' attention the overrepresentation of language-minority children in classes for the mentally retarded, and because of the special provisions of P.L. 94-142, which requires assessment procedures that are not racially, culturally, or linguistically discriminatory, there is now an *under*representation of language-minority students in special education. One reason for this problem is the critical shortage of trained bilingual special education personnel to conduct appropriate assessments and provide an instructional setting which is culturally and linguistically appropriate for the child (Ortiz & Yates, 1983).

At the same time, great strides have been taken in initial attempts to develop appropriate assessment instruments for students of non-English-language background who have been referred for special, individual assessment. One of the first attempts to create a more comprehensive and culturally fair instrument is the System of Multicultural Pluralistic Assessment, or SOMPA (Mercer, 1979). The SOMPA provides a set of medical, social, and pluralistic tests which gives an extensive profile of the student. It was developed and normed on large, equal numbers of Hispanic, black, and white children. The SOMPA has been criticized for lacking measures of language proficiency and for a variety of other measurement problems, but as a first attempt to meet special assessment needs of minority students, it has served an important function.

The Kaufman Assessment Battery for Children, or K-ABC (Kaufman & Kaufman, 1983) is a recent and promising addition to available measures of intelligence and achievement. Normed on white, black, Hispanic, Asian, Native American, and exceptional children, ages 2½ to 12½, the K-ABC also has a Spanish version. The measurement of intellectual processing is done with a minimal amount of verbal involvement.

Other instruments with Spanish versions which are used extensively are the Brigance Inventory of Early Development (Brigance, 1978), the Brigance Inventory of Essential Skills (Brigance, 1981), and the Woodcock-Johnson Psycho-Educational Battery (Woodcock & Johnson, 1977). The Brigance instruments are task analytic in approach—target behaviors are broken down into their component skills and each subskill is measured. The Woodcock-Johnson battery of tests integrates tests of cognitive ability, learning aptitude, scholastic achievement, and interest level.

In addition to new and adapted assessment instruments which are being developed for language-minority students, the field of bilingual special education continues to grow and contribute to our understanding of assessment in general. Bilingual special educators speak of the importance of ecological assessment, which addresses the whole child and his or her interaction with the social environment. Sources on assessment in bilingual special education are appearing in increasing numbers. Two recommended readings are Baca and Cervantes (1984) and Plata (1982).

Cultural Bias

A lot has been written about cultural bias in assessment instruments. Given the integral, interwoven relationship between language and culture, it is virtually inevitable that any test which uses language as a means of assessment will have accompanying cultural content. Sometimes that cultural content is appropriate for the students being tested and other times it is not. Through eagerness to correct inappropriate uses of tests, some members of ethnic minority groups have moved to condemn all testing procedures and tests as being culturally biased toward white middle-class Americans. The arguments surrounding cultural bias are sometimes emotional and subjective and sometimes based on empirical research, but they are important to consider in decisions about appropriate tests for language-minority students.

Item Content   The most comon type of bias identified through subjective judgment involves an individual item on a test which represents one cultural frame of reference when a broader point of view would call for a different answer. For example, an item such as "Bananas are (*a*) black, (*b*) yellow, (*c*) red, (*d*) green," is clearly an invalid item to anyone who has traveled south of the United States and knows that all the above answers are correct depending on the type of banana one is talking about. Jensen (1974) identifies this type of bias as "culture-loaded"—the item content is subjectively judged according to its relative familiarity to a given culture. These types of items on tests are especially inappropriate for placement, intelligence, and aptitude tests for language-minority students, as they are invalid representations of the students' abilities. Countless examples of biased item content could be given from older intelligence tests, but many current standardized instruments are attempting to eliminate these types of items from the tests.

In an effort to counteract traditional cultural bias toward middle-class, white, English-dominant students, some tests have been developed which are culturally specific or loaded, such as a test of skills in beadwork in which Native American children compared favorably to white, English-dominant children (Klineberg, 1935), or the Black Intelligence Test of Cultural Homogeneity (Williams, 1972), on which whites do poorly. These tests were developed mainly to sensitize test makers to obvious cultural differences which can be written into tests and make the test more valid for one group than another.

Illustrations   Sex and/or racial bias might be considered present if there is an imbalance in ethnic minorities or sexes represented in the illustrations for the test. Sometimes tests have been criticized for representing non-whites in stereotyped roles or for not casting nonwhites and females in professional or intellectual roles (Zoref & Williams, 1980).

Socialization   Item content may also be inappropriate if an item measures the child's family value system and the referent is that of the white, English-dominant middle class. For example, an old Binet item, "What is the thing for you to do if a playmate hits without meaning to do it?" distinguishes between deliberate and accidental injury, which is a value distinction many people do not make. These types of questions have little to do with a student's ability to process, manipulate, and/or code information. Instead, they measure the student's socialization to a particular ethical system (De Avila & Havassy, 1978). Many of these blatant value judgments have been removed from current standardized assessment instruments.

Language of Instructions   Even directions for a test can be a form of linguistic bias for language-minority children as well as for young children. Kennedy (1972) describes developmental stages in first-language acquisition which should be understood for writing test instructions at an appropriate level of difficulty. Similar developmental stages for second-language learners make it equally crucial for test instructions to be more simplified than they usually are. For example, test instructions for young children and second-language learners should avoid the passive, the conditional, and deletions, and should be in short sentences. Thus a common form of test instructions, "Do not turn this page until told to do so," would be better understood by more children in the form: "Turn this page when I tell you to do it."

The Testing Situation   Other forms of linguistic or cultural bias can center around the examiner and the testing situation itself. An examiner of the same cultural and linguistic background can make the student feel more comfortable in the testing situation. The testing situation is frequently a very awkward and uncomfortable one for any student. The more natural and linguistically and culturally appropriate for the student the testing situation is made, the more reliable a measure of the student's true abilities the test will be.

Empirical Research   Some researchers have attempted to prove the existence or nonexistence of cultural bias through examination of internal criteria such as item difficulty levels and predictive validity (for example, Jensen, 1974, 1980; Sandoval, 1979). Although these studies do not clearly indicate item bias, other researchers have pointed to various methodological problems with the studies. Summaries indicate that we cannot yet state empirically whether cultural bias heavily influences score differentiation on tests (Kumar & Treadwell, 1982). Until more is known, we can make only subjective judgments of what is and what is not cultural bias; the concept of cultural bias has not yet been empirically proved.

Valiant efforts to create culturally *free* tests (for example, Cattell, 1940; Davis & Eels, 1953; Porteus, 1937) are now considered futile. Instead, efforts have gone toward creating culturally *fair* instruments. Most educators agree that there will always be cultural content in any test that makes use of language (Sax, 1980, p. 377). Even nonverbal tests may have cultural loading. For limited-English-proficient students, many items on tests designed for native speakers of English are both linguistically and culturally inappropriate. However, as these students increase their acquisition of English and its accompanying cultural component, tests for native speakers become increasingly valid measures of the skills the broader society expects these students to have mastered to be participants in that society. When students become fully proficient in both languages (the time frame for which is usually significantly underestimated by school personnel), tests which measure the skills that must be mastered are culturally and linguistically appropriate.

For language-minority groups with a history of discrimination against them, cultural bias on tests is a more difficult problem to deal with. Nonidentification with the testing situation, the goals of the tester, or the test content "may have subtle effects on immediate performance and long-term demoralizing effects on academic and work aspirations" (Kumar & Treadwell, 1982, p. 51). Cultural bias on tests for these groups is more subtle but more devastating. For an extensive review on the topic of cultural fairness in testing of minorities in the United States, see Kumar and Treadwell (1982).

ASSESSMENT INSTRUMENTS

In bilingual and ESL education, we can no longer complain that we have no assessment instruments appropriate for our students. Many, many instruments are being developed, refined, and tested. At the same time, one cannot point to any one instrument as the solution to all problems. Each test has been criticized, refined, and criticized some more. There will never be a perfect assessment instrument for language-minority students because this is a population of students with incredibly diverse needs. To respond to those needs, we must be open to many different methods of assessing our students' strengths and to use of multiple measures on varied assessment instruments.

The following review of available assessment instruments cannot be complete, for that would take the space of several books. Instead, this section provides a sampling of some tests of oral language proficiency which are available for use with language-minority students and a guide to some references which provide more comprehensive reviews of many other types of instruments.

Tests of Oral Language Proficiency

Discrete-Point Language Tests   Keeping in mind the very serious limits of discrete-point tests discussed earlier in the section on language assessment, we mention a few in this review because of their prominence in the commercial testing market. These tests tap a student's metalinguistic knowledge *about* the language, but they do not test a student's communicative competence and performance in the language. The tests mentioned here are reviewed in a reference on communication assessment of bilingual-bicultural students (Erickson & Omark, 1981) which reviews a number of language tests used with language-minority students.

One example of a discrete-point test is the James Language Dominance Test (James, 1975), which was developed and normed on kindergarten and first-grade Mexican-American children for testing oral skills in Spanish and English. It is essentially a vocabulary test, calling mostly for one-word (noun) responses to questions about pictures. It is easy to administer and score, as are most discrete-point tests, and it attempts to compensate for dialectal variations. However, it has been criticized for its lack of reliability and validity and the limited number of skills tested.

The Dos Amigos Verbal Language Scales (Critchlow, 1974) was developed to test oral skills in Spanish and English for Mexican-American children, aged 5 to 13. Again, ease of administration is a plus, but no reliability and validity studies have been reported. It was normed on a very large sample of Mexican-American children in Texas. Other discrete-point tests reviewed in detail by Erickson and Omark (1981) are the Short Test of Linguistic Skills (Fredrickson & Wick, 1976), which was designed and normed by the Chicago school system to assess language proficiency and dominance of students of 7 to 15 years of age; the Boehm Test of Basic Concepts (Boehm, 1971), which assesses picture recognition vocabulary in Spanish and English for children in K-2; and the Test of Auditory Comprehension of Language (Carrow, 1973), developed in Spanish and English for Mexican-American children of 3 to 7 years of age. The Short Test of Linguistic Skills has parallel tests in English, Arabic, Chinese, Greek, Italian, Japanese, Korean, Pilipino, Polish, Spanish, and Vietnamese. All of these tests have been criticized for not reporting studies on their reliability or validity.

In making decisions about the kind of test you wish to use for your students, it is fairly easy to identify a discrete-point test by its emphasis in each test item on the minute parts of language; for example, a sound, a grammar point, a vocabulary item. Most reviews of test instruments do not bother to discuss the distinctions among discrete-point, integrative, and pragmatic tests. There is good reason to understand the differences as you set your program goals and choose appropriate tests, as the following example shows. This example discusses one misuse of comparisons of results from discrete-point and integrative or pragmatic tests (which measure global aspects of language) through the following comparison of English speakers learning Spanish or French in immersion programs with Spanish speakers learning English:

> Our reports on these children [in the Culver City, California, immersion program] have emphasized the positive and impressive acquisition of the second language in global terms, measures which closely parallel those for the St. Lambert [Canada] project. Global measures show that they are able to function extremely well in their second language. But such measures do not and cannot reveal problems with particular grammar structures nor do they reveal the degree of variation in performance among children within the program.

On the other hand, studies of children in East Los Angeles tend to stress the language problems of Spanish-speaking children who receive their education in English. Their problems with subject-verb agreement (*he sing* for *he sings*), possessive markers, etc. are "well known," and there is concern that remediation programs be used in order to help them "become proficient in English" or to allow them to "achieve in reading skills." In this case, global measures have not been used and the truly impressive language acquisition of the children has been overlooked. Since discrete testing is done, the morphology problems of these second language learners have been stressed. (Hatch, 1977, p. 75)

Combined Discrete-Point and Pragmatic Language Tests   There is a special group of tests that make use of natural language (a characteristic of pragmatic tests), but which use a discrete-point approach to scoring or combine some discrete-point questions with more pragmatic or integrative tasks. One of these is the Bilingual Syntax Measure (Burt, Dulay & Hernández-Chávez, 1975). This test was designed to measure language dominance and proficiency in English, Spanish, Italian, Tagalog, and other languages (being developed) for oral skills of children in K-2. It is especially praised for its colorful, entertaining illustrations and natural format, which spark the interest of young children and elicit natural language but criticized for discrete-point scoring. There have been some validity and reliability studies done on the Bilingual Syntax Measure, but they are not yet complete. The test has been normed on Mexican-Americans, Cuban-Americans, Puerto Ricans, Italian-Americans, and Philippinos, and will be normed on other language groups. A limitation for some is that it does not accept dialectal variations but tabulates scores based only on standard varieties of the languages tested.

The Basic Inventory of Natural Language (Herbert, 1977) is designed to measure language dominance and proficiency in any language for students of any age, although it seems most appropriate for K-6. Norms are provided for Spanish, English, Portuguese, and Italian. This test is praised for its natural language elicited through talk tiles, sequence stories, and story starters and for helping students to feel more comfortable with the testing situation. However, it is criticized for its scoring system, which emphasizes discrete points and scores according to a grammatical index of complexity which is not consistent with findings in second-language-acquisition research. Once again, there are no studies reported of the validity or reliability of this test.

The Language Assessment Scales (Duncan & De Avila, 1977) measure oral skills in English and Spanish of students in grades K-6+. Tasks are more varied than on most tests, with measures of pronunciation, vocabulary, sentence comprehension, and oral production (paraphrasing) included. This test combines discrete points and integrative tasks and, like the Bilingual Syntax Measure, has received a number of positive reviews. The test was standardized with Spanish speakers of Mexican-American, Cuban-American, Puerto Rican, and Latin American ethnicity. Test administration and scoring is considered very manageable.

Because these three tests have been used extensively in California and Texas, two large studies of intertest correlations were carried out to compare the three (Ulibarri, Spencer & Rivas, 1981; Wald, 1982). Both studies found that comparability was poor, with each test identifying a different set of criteria for language proficiency. Each test placed the same limited-English-proficient students in different "Lau" categories. The California study found that with a change in classification strategies, or equivalency tables, comparability can be established for the Bilingual Syntax Measure and the Language Assessment Scales.

Pragmatic and Integrative Language Tests   The Foreign Service Institute Oral Interview (see Educational Testing Service, 1970, for manual) has been in use by the federal government for over 20 years as a means of judging the second-language proficiency of government workers preparing to serve overseas. Two interviewers (a native speaker and a certified tester) conduct a natural conversation in the language being tested in a 15- to 30-minute period, skillfully directing the conversation to elicit responses which will test the examinee's ability in functional use of the language. The test has an extremely high interrater reliability (correlation between trained interviewers). Validity and reliability have been established, and the test has gotten high praise from reviewers in comparison to most other tests. The test is described and reviewed at length by Jones and Spolsky (1975), Oller (1979), and Erickson and Omark (1981). Administrative time and scoring procedures are considered lengthy but worth the effort. In its present form, it is appropriate for testing adults only, but it could easily be adapted to test children.

The Ilyin Oral Interview (Ilyin, 1976) is also designed for adults but has been used successfully with students in grades 4 through 12 and for placement testing in ESL programs. The rating scale gives credit for understanding a question or task, responding appropriately, and using correct structure in the response. This instrument is fairly easy to administer and score.

Other integrative instruments mentioned by Erickson and Omark (1981) are the Savignon Communicative Competence Tests (Savignon, 1972), which test oral proficiency in French, and two instruments described by Bond, Epstein, Matz, and Cazden (1977), the Productive Language Assessment Tasks and the Mutual Problem-Solving Tasks. The latter two test children's linguistic and communicative competence through story-telling and writing and through description of a task such as mother and daughter baking cookies together.

References on Tests Almost all of the tests we have reviewed so far measure oral skills principally. For placement testing and the assessment of very young children's language skills, oral language assessment is sufficient, but for exit assessment, tests which include reading and writing are important for measures of full proficiency. In other words, this review is just a bare beginning of an overview of all the types of tests that might be used with language-minority students. In addition to assessment of language dominance and proficiency in both oral and written skills, there are achievement tests in all the subject areas, attitudinal tests, and cognitive-style tests. In previous sections we have mentioned a few instruments used for assessing attitudes and cognitive style and for individual assessment in special education. The following references provide additional information on assessment instruments developed for language-minority students.

An analysis of problems with oral English proficiency testing is provided by Dieterich and Freeman (1979). In analyzing thirty-eight assessment instruments, the examiners found many problems with test validity, such as (1) requiring literacy for tasks on a test that purports to measure oral skills only; (2) not defining grammatical structures from simple to complex according to more recent studies in second-language acquisition; (3) using too limited a task to measure overall proficiency, such as reducing the test to vocabulary knowledge, mimicry, or passive comprehension; or (4) designing linguistically artificial test tasks, such as expecting complete sentences (natural oral language uses many abbreviated answers), giving overly complicated instructions, or testing knowledge *about* the language rather than functional use of the language.

Another analysis of oral language tests is by Silverman, Noa, and Russell (1976), published by the Northwest Regional Educational Laboratory. This review, along with the detailed reviews of Dieterich and Freeman (1979) and Erickson and Omark (1981), can help a school system in choosing an oral proficiency assessment instrument, but they also are very discouraging in illuminating how much more work needs to be done on all the tests which have been developed.

Another review of assessment instruments is provided by the Center for Bilingual Education, Northwest Regional Educational Laboratory (1978), with descriptions of 342 oral and written tests (mostly Spanish-English) for bilingual and ESL programs. Pletcher, Locks, Reynolds, and

Sisson (1978) have also published a comprehensive review of tests for native speakers of Chinese, French, Italian, Navajo, Portuguese, Spanish, and Tagalog. The reviews in both of these books include descriptive and technical information and brief cultural and linguistic information for each test, but an analysis of each assessment instrument is not provided. The review by Pletcher et al. (1978) includes tests on language proficiency, achievement in various subject areas, attitudes, learning styles, and scholastic aptitude.

A few instruments for use with language-minority students are reviewed in detail by Cohen, Bruck, and Rodríguez-Brown (1979) and Seidner (1982, 1983). Other language tests are examined in detail in Oller and Perkins (1978). Occasional detailed reviews of individual instruments can be found in the *NABE Journal,* such as a review by Gray and Potter (1981) of the Student Placement System developed by the Southwest Regional Laboratory for Educational Research and Development. This comprehensive system of assessment for entry and exit for bilingual programs is complicated to administer (with a five-volume, 1600-page manual) and has not received the support of many linguists as an adequate representation of current linguistic theory. Again, we have come a long way in the development of appropriate assessment instruments for language-minority students, but we still have a long way to go.

Two annotated bibliographies are available on testing bilingual children, one of selected references gathered by the staff of the National Clearinghouse for Bilingual Education (Kirsch, 1981) and one from the Center for Applied Linguistics (Lange & Clifford, 1980). The latter is a compilation of every source in the Educational Resources Information Center (ERIC) system on testing in foreign languages, ESL, and bilingual education, from 1966 to 1979. Two important general references for test analysis are the *Eighth Mental Measurements Yearbook* (Buros, 1978) and *Tests in Print III* (Mitchell, 1983).

TEACHER-CONSTRUCTED TESTS

In addition to the assessment instruments chosen by a school system for placement, diagnosis, exit, and evaluation, teachers must also develop their own tests for daily or weekly diagnosis. Development of an appropriate test is much more complicated than one might assume. The first step for teacher preparation is to take a course on educational tests and measurements to learn some of the basic principles in test construction. A textbook for this type of course which teachers can use as a general reference on testing is by Sax (1980). Two other references which focus on language test construction are Oller (1979) and Cohen (1980b). This overview cannot begin to cover adequately all the important points a teacher needs to know to develop useful and appropriate tests, but we use some examples from language assessment to summarize a few.

Measures in Language Assessment

Objectives "Teachers need a sharply defined idea of what they want to accomplish" (Sax, 1980, p. 53). The first step in diagnostic evaluation for teachers is to focus on the specific growth they want their students to make in cognitive, affective, and psychomotor domains. After defining what is to be measured, the task of constructing appropriate measurement tools becomes clearer. It is easier to measure the lower levels of Bloom's (1956) taxonomy of the cognitive domain (knowledge and comprehension), but it is very important that students also be tested for the more complex, higher levels (application, analysis, synthesis, and evaluation). Too many examinations test only rote knowledge, at the lowest level. If our overall goal is to help our bilingual-bicultural students to become creative thinkers and problem solvers, we should construct tests that measure all levels of cognitive growth.

True-False and Matching Tests True-false tests are probably the least useful for measuring language learning. True-false items tend to emphasize rote memorization and divide the world of knowledge into "black and white," whereas most absolute judgments have exceptions to them. Language is especially irreducible to true-false distinctions. Another disadvantage is that students guessing the answers have a 50 percent chance of getting them right. True-false items are easy to construct and score, but they rarely measure higher levels of cognitive development. Matching tests are useful for developing skills of association, but once again most tend to measure trivial information. Matching does reduce the effects of guessing, however, in comparison to true-false tests (Sax, 1980, pp. 91–122).

Multiple-Choice Tests These tests have many advantages: for example, they can measure simple to complex knowledge; scoring is objective; the effects of guessing are reduced in comparison to true-false; and item analyses can be carried out to test for validity. Multiple-choice tests are most popular in standardized testing because reliability and validity can be established, and they are relatively easy to administer to large groups. For teachers, however, good multiple-choice tests are very difficult to construct and may give the least useful information for measuring students' growth in language acquisition. In language assessment, a multiple-choice test (as well as true-false and matching) can measure only receptive skills (listening and reading) of a language. While good multiple-choice items can be written to test all the skills along the continuum from discrete-point to integrative, most teachers tend to write discrete-point items and test the simpler levels of Bloom's taxonomy.

To construct a good multiple-choice test, one needs to pretest the items; run an item analysis to check for ambiguity, miskeying, potential for guessing, item discrimination, item difficulty, and item improvement; assess the validity of the finished product; test the students; and go through the same process again. Oller (1979, pp. 231–259) believes that multiple-choice tests are so time-consuming for teachers to prepare properly that they are not worth the advantages of ease of administration and scoring. He also feels that they are counterproductive to effective language instruction, for they are deliberately conceived to confuse students with subtle "best" answers and they rarely focus on natural language and measurement of communicative competence.

Dictation   Surprisingly, one old language-testing technique from the grammar-translation method has come back into acceptability. Oller (1979, pp. 262–302) discusses in detail variations in the use of dictation, which he classifies as pragmatic, because if done correctly, it meets the criterion of naturalness. Dictation requires that the student understand spoken discourse and be able to produce it in written form, thus integrating many language skills and using natural language. For construct validity, the errors generated by dictation correspond closely to the errors learners make in language use in real life. Once a scoring system is set up carefully, scoring can be relatively easy and objective.

Oral Production Tests   These are also pragmatic and integrative. Oral production tests can include structured and unstructured interviews, oral cloze procedures, story retelling, picture(s) and questions, or an article and questions. These tasks are very important to assess in language acquisition, but they require increasingly subjective methods of scoring.

Cloze Procedure   Another integrative and pragmatic task which can test spoken and written skills is the cloze test. A lengthy discussion of varieties of the cloze technique and methods of scoring is available in Oller (1979, pp. 340–380) and Cohen (1980b, pp. 90–110). Most cloze tests delete every fifth, sixth, or seventh word in an oral or written passage. On a written cloze, the student is instructed to fill in the blanks. Exact-word scoring will lower all scores; students generally feel the test is fairer if contextually acceptable word scoring is used. Both types of scoring produce similar groupings. It helps students if a few sentences or a paragraph with no deletions is included at the beginning of the passage, before the section with words deleted. Cloze scores correlate positively with scores on standardized reading comprehension tests and on many types of placement tests. Cloze tests are very easy to construct and can be relatively easy to score.

Writing Tasks   Essays and compositions require the most of a student and are therefore very important to assign. However, they are the most difficult to score objectively. Important prerequisites for the written task to be a pragmatic one are that the student have something to say (usually something of personal value) and someone to say it to. Otherwise, it will not validly assess the student's writing ability.

These examples do not cover every type of language test a teacher could construct. They merely suggest a range of possibilities. For many examples of a variety of items to test listening, speaking, reading, and writing skills, see Cohen (1979b).

The following statement developed by the professional organization Teachers of English to Speakers of Other Languages (TESOL, 1979) summarizes many of the important points made in this chapter.

TESOL STATEMENT ON STATEWIDE PROGRAMS
OF COMPETENCY TESTING

More than 60% of the states of the United States have mandated programs of competency testing in the basic skills during the last few years, and several more are about to do so. Because the insights gained from recent movements of competency-based program design and of individualized instruction have made us increasingly aware of the complex nature of this kind of measurement, we would like to bring to your attention the following considerations to bear in mind when planning a testing program.

A. The professional organizations and academic departments specializing in the teaching of English to speakers of other languages provide expertise and should be consulted when decisions are made concerning competency testing of students whose home language or dialect is other than standard English.

B. Parents of the groups being tested and the students themselves need to be consulted. Questions about relevance and appropriateness of topics, the language to be tested, and the purposes of the tests all need student and parent input.

C. The development of effective measurement instruments is time consuming and costly, but we warn against any cost saving shortcuts that might be considered.

    1. Translating existing tests from one language to another does not result in a reliable instrument.

    2. Tests developed for or normed on native speakers of a language are not valid or reliable indicators of the language knowledge or skills of a person who is not a native speaker of that language.

    3. Tests of proficiency in the modern foreign languages designed for English-speaking students in the United States are scaled inappropriately to measure the talents and knowledge of students who are native speakers of those languages.

D. No single instrument can adequately measure students' competency in the basic skills. We urge, therefore, that a variety of opportunities be given to students to demonstrate what they know, and that decisions regarding competency never be made on the basis of a single test.

E. Sound objectives and precise goals are essential to any effective testing program. Therefore, the starting point must be to reach agreement on the meaning of "basic" in "basic skills." (For example, specialists in the area of reading know that different reading skills are "basic" to different purposes. What is the purpose of the reading test in your state? To assure success in an academic career? To assure success in a vocation? To document that a student can read directions? a manual? a novel? an application form?)

F. Knowledge of language must be separated from knowledge of subject matter. A test of one should not be used to measure competency in the other. It is particularly important that as a student is acquiring a second language or dialect and is concurrently adding to this knowledge in subject matter areas the testing of the latter be conducted in the *first* language. Further, it is of utmost importance that students who are acquiring knowledge of the language and the content areas simultaneously receive the benefit of considerable instruction in both areas before being tested in either.

G. Because students whose home language is other than standard English may enter a curriculum late in its progression, it is imperative that alternative measures be provided for the testing of late-arriving students.

H. We support a program of assessment which periodically measures the progress of each student, a program of assessment which helps ensure educational success for all students by providing a measurement of what the school needs to do to help the student, e.g., offer remediation or programs of career guidance. We oppose an assessment program to weed out students, to end their academic advancement.

Assessment is one of the most important but misunderstood areas of education. Yet accurate and appropriate assessment is the key to useful diagnosis and prescriptive teaching for the academic success of language-minority students. Even though the issues appear complex at first glance, bilingual and ESL teachers must both understand the concepts behind assessment and apply linguistic and cultural sensitivity to the assessment process. Then assessment will not be used inappropriately to label, sort, or track students. Teachers *can* make a difference.

Chapter Eight

SCHOOL AND COMMUNITY

In 1968 the large, predominantly Mexican-American community of East Los Angeles was startled when hundreds of Chicano high school students refused to attend classes for several weeks until their demands, which centered around sociocultural and academic issues, were met by school officials. The magnitude of such solidarity and the timing and symbolic importance engaged the attention not only of parents, teachers, students, school principals, board members, and civic leaders, but also of the media.

The incident which provoked the walkouts was the cancellation by a vice principal of a play at Wilson High School. Initially the protest centered around the rights of students to stage whatever play they wanted. But later the protest expanded to other high schools and was injected with ideology, particularly the issue of equal educational opportunity for Chicano students, who believed they did not have a fair shot at upward mobility in American society.

The protesting students, along with some sympathetic teachers and community activists, ultimately pressured the Los Angeles Unified School Board to respond to their demands by addressing the sociocultural and academic needs felt by the Chicano community. The issues included developing relevant curricula, serving more Mexican food in the cafeterias, stopping corporal punishment, using more bilingual materials, hiring and promoting more Chicano teachers and administrators, counseling Chicano students away from vocational tracks and into more college preparatory courses, providing in-service training for teachers and administrators on the nature of the Chicano community, writing more proposals for bilingual programs, and hiring only Mexican-American administrators for Mexican-American schools. Except for the last demand, which Julian Nava, then president of the board, considered racism in reverse, all of the concerns were gradually and in varying degrees acted on.

Some observers of the walkouts questioned the positive impact which such civil disturbances had on the long-term educational gains of the Chicano community in Los Angeles, but the vigorous involvement of segments of the student population alerted Chicano parents to the pressing reality that neighborhood schools were not fulfilling the needs of their children. Consequently, parents and community activists in East Los Angeles became directly involved in community action programs aimed at redressing existing academic, linguistic, cultural, economic, and political problems. As proof of such broad-based community participation, parents in the San Fernando Valley and Pacoima also became involved in similar concerns. And 2 years later in East Los Angeles, teachers and Chicano parents interacted to address a broad range of problem areas—Pygmalion in the classroom (or the self-fulfilling prophecy of low expectations), class size, overcrowding and year-round schools, ignorance of bilingual methods of instruction, lack of bilingual materials, poor teacher preparation and attitudes, student discipline, school safety, and substandard community housing. Parents were now pressing for a sustained partnership with the schools as coworkers and coplanners. Since the nature of the curriculum and the school environment would inevitably determine the educational futures of their children, parents believed it important to become involved in the life of the schools.

All of these episodes confirm Hechinger's contention that "American educators have always courted danger and defeat when they ignored the impact of major cultural and social currents" (Hechinger, 1977, p. 1). A major social current today is the growth of ethnic- and language-minority groups. Such groups, which constitute the principal clients for bilingual education today, have tended to exist on the periphery of the decision-making process associated with the modern sector of American society. But given that the articulated egalitarian principles of the United States stress the importance of participation by all citizens in the total life of the society, the central thesis of this chapter is that one effective way to attract historically excluded sectors of the society into the mainstream of decision-making processes is through linking the life of the school with that of the ethnic community. Through such engagement with the schools, parents can achieve a strong sense of ownership in the education of their children. Understanding the function of the community—both as a geographical place and as a bonding force—is particularly important for segments of society which socialize and enculturate their children in manners which are often misunderstood, unappreciated, ignored, or disliked by the power-wielding segments of society. While in a narrow context the bilingual community can be defined as the parents of bilingual children attending a particular school, in the broadest sense Brisk defines a bilingual community as "a group of people interested in the development and improvement of the education of bilingual children" (1979, p. 3). In this sense the community can consist of a coalition of parents and family, neighbors, informal groups, professionals, and formal organizations.

There are several interrelated themes which will help us to understand the function of ethnic communities as, in partnership with the schools, they orbit the next generation of recent immigrants, indigenous minorities, and mainstream Americans into a changing world. These themes are (1) the development and types of ethnic communities, (2) legal cases and community organization, (3) community profiles, and (4) community involvement in language-minority education.

DEVELOPMENT AND TYPES OF ETHNIC COMMUNITIES

In working to create the dream of the United States, founding statesmen pinned high hopes on the communities and schools to serve as efficacious instruments of national unity. Yet the process of unification has always tugged at the national fabric as dreams and ideals have had to confront reality. Therefore, to keep the nation from falling apart, the early leaders designed and tried to implement a national agenda that would be capable of handling the complex issues surrounding the embryonic nation. As Hechinger argues:

> The facts of history are quite clear; they cannot be rewritten or revised. Those facts show clearly that the founding fathers viewed the United States as a country with a unified history, with unified traditions, and with a common language. For proof you need only to read Benjamin Franklin and his virtual phobia of foreign-language enclaves. The history of nation-building is clear in any view of the American past. The concept of the melting pot was very much part of the American tradition, and it was accepted virtually by all. The reason why the melting pot is in disrepute today, and rightly so, is not because the concept was not a good one but because it was used dishonestly. Some people were excluded from the unified country. The melting pot's main failure was that it did not include all persons from all groups at all times. (1978, p. 130)

What the early leaders in fact had in mind by a "country with a unified history, with unified traditions, and with a common language" was a United States ruled by English institutions, language, and cultural patterns. Therefore, early in the nation's history, the stage was set for tensions associated with the culture, religion, and languages of the non-English-speaking and non-Protestant groups arriving in the United States in large numbers.

Chronology of the Status of Ethnic Communities

The sociocultural drama hinted at by Hechinger is illustrated for the last 150 years by Havighurst (1978) in the following overlapping chronology of events.

Defensive Pluralism: 1830–1910   This was a period in American history when many non-English and non-Protestant ethnic groups defended their religious preferences against pressure to conform to English religious patterns. This was done, for example, by forming their own schools and by establishing their own communities in frontier areas.

Defensive Pluralism, Phase II: 1840–1914   In search of better economic opportunities, large numbers of immigrants from Europe and China formed ethnic enclaves in industrial centers close to where they worked. Like earlier immigrants, they wanted to be free to practice their religion, culture, and languages. And so they struggled to keep ethnic loyalty while participating in the civic, educational, and political life of the larger society. Among the immigrants represented were Poles, Hungarians, Italians, Greeks, Croatians, Chinese, and Russian Jews. Interested in nurturing their languages and cultures as well as seeking economic improvement, northern Europeans also settled during this period in the North Central and Great Plains regions.

The Melting Pot: Circa 1900   The melting pot concept held that out of the great diversity of immigrants with their multiple races, languages, cultures, religions, ideologies, political views, skills, and talents would emerge an individual who, after being immersed in the American experience through the schools and society, would be an American representing the best of all worlds. As noted earlier by Hechinger, the concept was not totally honest in the process of selecting *who* should be melted. For example, within its historical context the validity of such a concept was questioned vigorously by some social scientists of the time who believed that eastern and southern European immigrants were of inferior genetic stock.

Laissez-Faire Pluralism: 1920–1970   Convinced that environmental factors such as child-rearing practices were responsible for key personal and mental characteristics, social scientists began to affirm that it was acceptable for ethnic groups to socialize and enculturate their children in such a way that their own beliefs, values, behaviors, and symbols were nurtured while concurrently participating in the civic, economic, and educational life of the larger society. Unity in diversity became a leading article of faith.

Constructive Pluralism: 1970–present   Unlike laissez-faire pluralism, this movement promotes the heterogeneous texture of American society. One now finds multicultural education, bilingual education, and ethnic studies in the public schools. Many people consider cultural and linguistic differences to be a source of pride. The nation has to a large extent accepted the reality and persistence of ethnicity as a fact in American life and seems less fearful about the possible polarization or tribalization of society.

Characteristics of Immigrant and Indigenous Ethnic Communities

Another important step in understanding the nature of contemporary ethnic communities in the United States is to place them in their appropriate geographic and generational contexts. While there are myriad configurations of ethnic communities which can be explored, here we focus on ethnic communities of two types: those composed primarily of immigrant or foreign-born parents, and those consisting of indigenous minorities who have been in the United States for several generations. While in many cases both groups live within the same neighborhood, it is useful to consider their characteristics separately.

Immigrant Communities   Ethnic communities composed primarily of foreign-born parents represent a diverse configuration of backgrounds, talents, needs, and aspirations. The United States is a nation of immigrants who have uprooted their families and left homes, friends, relatives, customs, food, and language. To do this, family decision makers must have reflected carefully on the pros and cons of such a geographic shift and concluded that the overall benefits surrounding the move outweighed the powerful wish to stay home. As noted earlier in this chapter, there are strong economic, political, professional, ideological, religious, or educational forces which push immigrants from their home country and pull them toward another nation.

A point to keep in mind when examining the attitudes immigrants have toward this country is that many of them feel a strong sense of optimism in their lives. The United States, after all, has been advertised as a place in which resourcefulness, intelligence, and perseverance are rewarded. But equally important to remember is the fact that along with the original voluntary immigrants may be involuntary ones—children, spouses, relatives, or other dependents who joined the migration without a strong say in the matter and who as a result may have mixed feelings about the move. Besides the matter of initial choice there are other important factors which fundamentally affect the way immigrants feel about the host country, such as age, sex, marital status, economic condition, educational experience, occupation, language, health, size of family, extent of personal ties, and the political and economic situation of the home country. This feeling, of course, is intimately linked to the perceived and real economic and psychological support given to them by American-born persons.

As teachers, we are interested in knowing how this information relates to the classroom. In the first place, many of these families have children who attend our schools shortly after arrival and who most likely experience some form of cultural, social, or linguistic trauma in the process. Experience tells us that the outcome of this acculturation or assimilation phase is closely linked to the age, sex, and previous schooling of the learner, as well as to the attitudes and philosophy of the parents. Generally, we can say that younger children experience less difficulty learning English and make a smoother cultural transition (really more like an evolution). But perhaps they will not do as well academically as older siblings who may have had more formal schooling in the home country. A significant correlation seems to exist between the academic performance in the United States and the age and literacy skills of the learner before immigrating. (See chap. 4 for research related to this topic.) Adolescent immigrants experience other problems, however. This is not surprising given that even under the best of circumstances teenagers often face challenging developmental stress.

Another point to keep in mind is that ethnic parents vary a great deal in the importance they place on speed of their children's assimilation or acculturation to American society. Some parents want to allow their children time to come to grips with the variety of new linguistic and cultural experiences and are not in a hurry to push their children to become Americanized. Others, on the other hand, feel tremendous pressure to push their children to adopt American cultural patterns by learning everything which is needed to fit snugly in the dominant society—for example, learning standard English, dressing the part of middle-class Americans, behaving in ways congruent with middle-class values, and anglicizing their children's names. Some parents feel nostalgia about their ancestral lands while others wish to forget their past. Some parents are accepting of religious changes or marriage outside the ethnic boundaries, while others feel quite strongly about keeping their ethnic identity partially insulated from mainstream American lifestyles. Some families wish to construct a division between their private and public ethnic lives. They may wish the school to focus on a monolingual, monocultural English curriculum and take care of home-language education and culture at home or in private weekend classes.

In addition to the mode and speed of cultural transmission found in ethnic communities, also to be considered are the range of perceptions that ethnic parents may have of the school itself as an institution. Because generalizations about any community are virtually impossible to make, the following comments are intended merely to provide a frame of reference regarding the possible range of perceptions which may exist. We may start by noting that what foreign-born parents expect from the American experience for themselves and for their children to a large extent is determined by the nature of their educational and economic experience in their ancestral countries. In most cases, therefore, their notions about the American school experience may be highly speculative. They do not have a first-hand experience with schooling in the United States, or they may have highly colored perceptions from the information their children bring home. Their awareness of how schools function in the United States is often limited, and they may have inaccurate perceptions about what social, cultural, and academic skills it takes to succeed socioeconomically.

There are a variety of attitudes toward school that may limit the extent to which parents feel at ease playing active roles. Some community members may feel very grateful to have been given the opportunity to come to the United States and therefore may feel that it is not appropriate for them to complain or critique American educational institutions. To many immigrants these institutions may seem superior to what they had in their native countries. Because in many other countries community involvement in school planning is not significant, many parents believe the right thing is to place all the responsibility for educating their children on school leaders. Such parents might not consider it appropriate to go beyond seeing that their children's homework is completed, requiring that their children behave well in school, or attending an open house. Foreign-born parents are not necessarily disinterested in the education of their children, but because of experiences rooted in the past they often tend to be tentative about taking too much ownership of the formal schooling process. What this may mean from the educator's point of view is that their children are frequently left on their own to make sense out of and to adjust to American schools. Older students may somewhat independently have to make choices regarding general graduation or vocational and academic programs—choices which may have an impact on career opportunities later in life.

Indigenous Minorities   *"Ni chicha ni limonada"* is a popular saying in Latin America which roughly translates to English as "neither fish nor fowl." In a vivid way such a saying captures the cultural dilemma surrounding many indigenous minorities in this country such as Native Americans, Native Alaskans, Chicanos, Puerto Ricans, and second- and third-generation Asian-Americans. Their situation may be considered a dilemma because, living more often than not outside the resource-rich center of the American experience, choosing between sociocultural alternatives offers them many unresolved propositions.

Indigenous minorities have roots in the United States and elsewhere, and being accepted in either the original or the new cultural milieu has often been quite tricky. There is a tendency in the United States for mainstream whites to perceive indigenous minorities as being non-American, even if they have been here for generations. It is not uncommon, for example, for a mainstream white person who is familiar with the Southwest to place Chicanos south of the Río Grande. On the other hand, natives of the ancestral culture can immediately identify their emigrant counterparts as being American. Such a dilemma is illustrated by the statement of a Japanese-American regarding her trips to Japan: "I feel American when I'm in Japan, but when I'm in the United States I feel Japanese." United States–born persons of Mexican ancestry frequently tell of being ostracized by native Mexicans for trying to straddle two cultures and two languages, supposedly without mastering either one fully. The somewhat derogatory term *pocho*—what a Mexican calls a Mexican-American—reflects the ethnocentric view of Mexican nationals toward Mexican-Americans. It is difficult for them to view Mexican-American culture as a long-term, rational adaptation to a specific linguistic and cultural context in the United States.

The economic profile which emerges for indigenous minority groups confirms their predominantly pariah status. For example, in an index of economic success in the United States, with a mean of 100, Mexican-Americans recently scored twenty-four points below the mean, and Native Americans forty points below the mean (Sowell, 1981, p. 5). While the reasons for such economic marginality are too varied and unresolved to discuss here, the clustering below the mean suggests a certain amount of social, cultural, economic, political, or educational inequality.

Stability versus Mobility   Related to the distinction between immigrant and indigenous groups, Lewis (1978) has developed a community typology based on degree of stability versus mobility or migration. He finds the comparison of communities to be facilitated by considering the following range of types: (1) relatively stable communities, (2) mobile populations, (3) populations experiencing permanent migration, and (4) communities experiencing involuntary migration. Relatively stable communities may be products of extreme geographic isolation, the "enclavic restrictiveness" of dominant political policies (for example, the Basques or American Indians), self-imposed boundaries (for example, the Amish), or segregated urban residential and business patterns. Mobile populations are those which move back and forth across boundaries, usually for economic reasons. An example of permanent migration is the dispersion of some American ethnic groups as their members move from urban centers to the suburbs, while involuntary migration is represented by refugees forced to leave their country of origin.

LEGAL CASES AND COMMUNITY ORGANIZATION

As seen in Havighurst's four stages—defensive pluralism, the melting pot, laissez-faire pluralism, and constructive pluralism—the theme of ethnic diversity and how to deal with it starts early in American history. Even when free public schooling was made available to all children after the middle of the nineteenth century, such groups as blacks and Native Americans were excluded from participating in policy decisions affecting the schooling of their children (Tyack, 1981). These decisions sometimes clashed with values and beliefs held in high esteem by such groups but which often ran counter to the expectations of dominant American society.

Faced with great religious, cultural, linguistic, and educational obstacles, some groups opted to create their own school systems (for example, Catholics and blacks), while others chose to use the legal system to seek changes in the public schools. The following sample of legal cases illustrates the nature of the relationship between ethnic communities and public schools.

Legal Cases

Brown v. Board of Education of Topeka (1954)   Leaning on the Fourteenth Amendment, which prohibits state-imposed separation of the races in public schools, the Supreme Court ruled that the "segregation of children in public schools solely on the basis of race, even though the physical facilities and other tangible factors may be equal, deprives the children of the minority group equal educational opportunity" (Hooker, 1978, p. 84). Institutions were gradually responding to the sociocultural and political forces which were dramatically different from those of the past. From now on ethnic communities would resort to a greater degree to the court system to buttress their demands, expecting at least a sensitivity to the blighted hopes and slighted rights of parents and children who wanted a fair shot at economic prosperity through equitable participation in the schools. The nation's leaders had decided that the arbitrary separation of people solely on the basis of race was not only wrong but potentially damaging to the unity of the American experience.

Tobeluk v. Lind (1976)   It was the practice in Alaska for rural high school students to leave their villages to attend high schools away from home. Parents brought a civil class-action suit against the state on behalf of their secondary-school-aged children, arguing that it was discriminatory for these students to be required by law to leave their homes. In the settlement the governor of Alaska signed a consent decree stating that it was the right of every child to attend school in his or her local community and that educational facilities had to be provided for villages with school-aged children. This was a major victory for the integrity and development of community life in rural Alaska.

Lau v. Nichols (1974)   As noted in chapter 2, there have been at least eleven court cases from 1971 to 1981 involving ethnic communities and the issues of education, language, culture, and racial isolation. In those 10 years, historically stigmatized ethnic communities have with varying degrees of real and symbolic success used the U.S. court system as an instrument of social reform. But the *Lau v. Nichols* decision—a ruling that the communicative competence of LEP children had to be considered in designing and implementing the curriculum to protect the civil rights of the learners—remains the most significant victory for parents who want their children to retain their primary language and culture while adapting to American linguistic, academic, and cultural norms. Although the decision does not address curricular or methodological issues, it does compel schools to attend to the academic, cultural, and linguistic needs of children of limited English proficiency.

Serna v. Portales Municipal Schools (New Mexico, 1974) and Aspira of New York v. Board of Education of the City of New York (1974)   Both of these settlements grew out of the communities' dissatisfaction with the educational programs provided to Hispanic students, and both resulted in court orders which rejected the school officials' programs in favor of implementation of the plaintiffs' proposed programs and remedies.

Ríos v. Read (Patchogue-Medford, Long Island, 1977) and Cintrón v. Brentwood Union Free School District Board of Education (New York, 1978)   Both of these cases challenged the quality of already implemented bilingual education programs, again pitting community expectations against school policy. In *Ríos v. Read* the school district was sued to make public its students' achievement records to determine whether the bilingual programs were effective. The plaintiffs won their case; the court found that the establishment of a bilingual program per se was not in compliance with the *Lau v. Nichols* decision if the program's quality was questionable. In *Cintrón v. Brentwood* the school district had reduced its staff due to declining enrollment; because most of the bilingual staff had been recently hired and had little seniority, this resulted in the dismissal of more than two-thirds of the bilingual staff. The dismissed teachers were to be replaced in the bilingual program by teachers who were not trained in bilingual and ESL techniques. Based on *Lau v. Nichols* and the *Ríos v. Read* "quality" ruling, parents filed suit and the court ordered the district to rehire the qualified bilingual teachers (Teitelbaum & Hiller, 1977b).

Despite these favorable rulings, careful scrutiny unmasks unresolved issues involving the interplay of linguistic, economic, political, demographic, regional, and educational factors which continue to contribute to the problems facing many communities. Still it is through such legal evolution that educators and community members can begin to understand and wrestle with the current relationship between the schools and peripheral ethnic groups. For one thing, many ethnic communities seem to have come of age politically and appear more willing to flex their legal muscle. As a middle-aged Chicana community activist colorfully put it, "School leaders can't 'mau mau' [fool] the parents like they used to." Despite periodic setbacks, such parental predisposition to use the legal system will continue to shape the public school policy slowly as parents push for quality education for their children and for themselves.

Beginning with the Brown decision in 1954, we have seen a gradual shift on the part of the federal government toward protecting the civil rights of minorities along racial lines. Twenty years later in *Lau v. Nichols* the Supreme Court affirmed the need to protect the civil rights of LEP children. While currently some observers of the American experience sense that the country may be experiencing "compassion fatigue"— exhaustion from all of the civil rights and human welfare campaigns of the fifties, sixties, and seventies—ethnic groups have gained a momentum for potential power far greater than that available to them in the past. As

Gamboa points out, the development of equitable language-minority programs received its greatest impetus from the courts rather than from research, and now "at the same time that the public at large is putting pressure on government (including the courts) to get out, the minority community continues to rely on the courts to retain jurisdiction so that school authorities remain accountable" (1980, p. 236).

Community Organization Efforts

As important as court cases have been in the establishment of equitable language-minority education programs, community organization for negotiation with school districts outside the courtroom is an alternative approach which has been used successfully by groups throughout the country. We discuss four such case studies here, all of them casting bilingual education programs within the larger context of the communities out of which they grew.

Benavides (1979) traces the development of bilingual education in a small city in Michigan with a minority Hispanic population. He found that parents initially were dissatisfied with the elementary school curriculum and particularly with the staff but felt powerless to do anything about it. A community social agency with interested mainstream American "brokers" organized a meeting of Mexican-American leaders and state officials which resulted in the formation of a parent advisory council. An important role of the community activists was to demonstrate to the school board, which was not aware of the total number of Hispanics and LEP students in the system, that a problem *existed* in terms of equitable education. Once the need was established, a program was implemented based on what community leaders had requested. However, in Benavides' opinion the ending was not entirely happy. He observed that perhaps to a harmful degree the program was based on community demands rather than educational needs according to the professional judgment of persons knowledgeable in bilingual education. Arguing that the quality of school-community relations directly affects the quality of education which children receive, Benavides concluded that communities need to learn how to work with and not against the school system, and school officials need to realize that ethnic parents, like any parents, want success for their children.

Guskin (1981) studied the implementation of bilingual education programs in Milwaukee, Wisconsin. These programs grew out of the civil rights movement of the sixties, becoming not only a means of instruction for LEP students but also a symbol of recognition and respect for the

Hispanic community. Because Hispanics in Milwaukee wield little political power, the community's strategy was a mixture of confrontation and cooperation. Crucial to the success of their movement was a cadre of parent advocates (trained by community organizers), a mainstream American administrator who was knowledgeable about bilingual education and served as a "broker" between the community and the school district, a few supportive school board members, and the fact that money was available from the state to support 70 percent of the expenses. However, once the programs were begun the battle was not over. Court-ordered school desegregation plans threatened to disperse Hispanic students throughout the city in such a way that bilingual classrooms could not be organized. It was, according to Guskin, through community activism that the court agreed to consider the impact of desegregation on bilingual schools and to save them from being dismantled.

As seen in the preceding examples, activism for bilingual education brings with it challenges and mixed success for the communities. However, it is also a source of community development, as seen in the following two instances. Waserstein (1975) documented the development of bilingual education through community effort in Wilmington, Delaware, and found that as an important spin-off the process served as a natural training ground for leadership skills within the ethnic community. The movement was started through the efforts of the bilingual community in the broadest sense—a mixture of Hispanic and non-Hispanic laypersons and professionals. This core of interested people developed parent support through extensive personal contact and through already established institutions such as the church, school, and local community center. The community meetings served as a forum for the development of community organization strategies and leadership skills. The community chose to negotiate with the school district rather than sue, the approach which Waserstein feels was the more effective of the two. Once again, part of the problem was that the school officials were unaware of the growing numbers of Hispanic students and the academic inequities they were facing. At the beginning of the negotiations the involved community members were perceived as outsiders by the school district negotiators, but toward the end they were seen as the local experts on bilingual education and their opinions carried considerable weight in deciding district bilingual policies. As a result of their efforts, the community not only achieved the implementation of bilingual programs but also gained valuable skills for organizing themselves over future local issues.

One of the authors, Collier (1980), in her study of the development of bilingual education over 9 years in Washington, D.C., found a similar pattern of community involvement. Here, too, efforts to implement programs for second-language learning and home-language instruction began with the community in the large sense of the word—community leaders, priests, and local bureaucrats. As the movement evolved, however, it facilitated the establishment of grass-roots Hispanic community identity and made the community more visible as a political reality in the schools and larger community. As the bilingual program was implemented, the community members became more politically active and more experienced in the strategies of bringing about change. This development of civic participation and leadership skills was additionally enhanced by the schools themselves through the efforts of the school-community coordinators; the hiring of bilingual teachers and aides who lived in and participated actively in the community; and parent participation in the community advisory councils and Saturday workshops on language arts, math, and ESL. Collier found that the bilingual administrators played an important role in raising community consciousness, so that the community itself took on new characteristics in the process of working with school staff for the improvement of educational opportunities for their language-minority children.

COMMUNITY PROFILES

The evolution of pluralism in the United States, the types of ethnic communities, and litigation and community organization efforts provide an overview of the role of the community in the education of language-minority students; however, there is also a wealth of linguistic and social detail to be considered which affects the planning and outcome of schooling efforts. Based on the analysis of a variety of studies of bilingual education programs, Jacobson suggests that the success of the effort "depends to a large extent upon the social, cultural, and attitudinal conditions prevailing in the immediate neighborhood of the school hosting such a program" (1979, p. 483). And yet there is often a lack of knowledge about these important details of community life when programs are being planned, implemented, or evaluated. Saravia-Shore (cited in Cohen, 1979a), for example, found in a survey of New York City bilingual programs that in only 31 percent had parents been asked their opinion on the use of the non-English language as a medium of instruction. Guzmán (1978) concluded in his study of a bilingual program in Oregon that unexamined community attitudes affected the outcome of the project. There was a value conflict in the community between supporters of pluralism and supporters of assimilation, and because the issue was not directly addressed in the design and implementation stages, it became a hidden factor in the ineffectiveness of the resulting program.

Language Use in the Community

Because the approach to language is what most differentiates bilingual from nonbilingual education, it is perhaps ironic that "much implementation of bilingual education programs has occurred without comprehensive sociolinguistic analyses of the target student populations, and their respective school-community environments" (Aguirre, 1980, p. 47). To understand the significance of the languages used at school, there is a need for knowledge regarding the languages used in the community and how they are used. Such knowledge, which could be compiled through ethnographic research, would enable planners to make their educational programs more sensitive to the community environment (Mehan, 1981). For example, if educators are cognizant of the varieties of languages or dialects used in the community as well as the level of proficiency in the various codes, they are better able to select appropriate materials or anticipate language difficulties that come up because of the materials which are available. Information on community language use may also be of value in the evaluation of programs. For example, as Cohen (1983) points out, if one of the goals of a program is native-language maintenance, then long-term research on patterns of language use in the community can help to determine if that goal is being met.

Language use, language variation, language attitudes, and language change are all topics which might be considered in developing a linguistic profile of a community. Among the areas that could be assessed are when and how each language is used in the community and what demand there is for each language, the level of proficiency of parents and teachers in both languages, and the degree of support for the proposed or actual proportions of time allotted to each language in the schools (Aguirre, 1980, p. 48). The degree of support for the goals of the bilingual program for each language also could be assessed.

While all of these factors could be assessed within a static time frame, a diachronic look at language use in the community will also reveal pertinent information. For example, over a period of time a community may maintain the use of a particular language in predictable contexts, or the community may experience a shift in language use such that one language is replaced by another language. Drawing on the work of Gaarder (1971) and Weinreich (1953), Cohen lists a series of factors which will affect language maintenance or language shift within a community:

1. Size and homogeneity of the bilingual group

2. Access to renewal from hinterland

3. Reinforcement by in-migration and immigration

4. Relative proficiency in both languages

5. Modes of use (reading, writing, listening, speaking)

6. Specialized use by domain and interlocutor

7. Status of the bilingual groups

8. Attitudes toward each language

9. Function of each language in social-advance
   (Cohen, 1975a, p. 210)

This list reveals something of the complexity of patterns of language use within a bilingual community and also demonstrates the power of social forces and demography in language choice. The majority of factors listed by Cohen reflect sociological or demographic conditions. Thus researchers talk not only about linguistic analyses of the community, but also about sociolinguistic analyses. In sampling some of the research and thought on community description, we consider not only issues of language use and proficiency but also broader social effects in the community of language-education programs for language-minority students.

"Diglossia," a term coined by Ferguson (1959), refers to a situation in which two languages or varieties of languages are both used within the same community but in separate circumstances or contexts. For example, one language might be used for everyday occasions and the other for more formal occasions. Barker (1975) describes a pattern of diglossia among Mexican-Americans in Tucson in the 1940s as follows: the local variety of Spanish was generally used in intimate and informal contexts; English was used in formal contexts, even when both persons spoke the local variety of Spanish, because they had not learned the formal, standard Spanish which they felt appropriate to the occasion; and finally, English was used in Mexican–mainstream-American relationships. Along with diglossia another language pattern often found in bilingual communities is code-switching, in which two languages are intermingled in discourse. Although the desirability of code-switching and its role in language development is debated by educators, some researchers argue that there is a function and logic to its use in natural discourse.

Jacobson, arguing that interactional norms found in the community can be brought into the classroom to meet educational objectives, cites as one example the use of code-switching in Laredo, Texas. Based on an understanding of the distribution and logic of code-switching in the community, a training program was implemented for Laredo teachers to develop skills in functional intersentential code-switching in which Spanish and English received approximately equal time. This carefully designed code-switching was to be used in all areas of the curriculum except the language arts, in which Spanish and English were separated. Jacobson argues that "the balanced distribution of the two languages in teaching any one of the school subjects other than language arts, suggests to the learner that switching between languages is for him a way to cope with the bicultural-bilingual setting in which he functions" (1979, p. 490). By selectively using in the school a language pattern found in the community, a closer match between home and school could be achieved. For additional discussion of code-switching, see chapters 3 and 4.

As previously mentioned, one of the uses of community studies is to see if the stated goals of a particular education program are being met. Cohen (1975b) compared students in a bilingual-education program with those not in such a program within a community in the Southwest to see how the bilingual-program experience affected language use outside the classroom. The bilingual program was designed as a language-maintenance program, and Cohen found that students who were in the program used more Spanish with their parents and in the community than students who were not in the program. It was interesting to note, however, that in lunch and recess periods at school, the bilingual-program students were more likely to use English with their peers. Cohen speculates that because the bilingual-program students used Spanish in the classroom, they did not have as great an "escape valve" need for Spanish as a means of expression at lunch and recess. In his detailed sociolinguistic study of this southwestern community, Cohen also found that the language attitudes of the parents were affected by their children's participation in a bilingual program. In comparing parents of bilingual-program children with parents of non-bilingual-program children, he found the bilingual-program parents to be more supportive of the need for learning Spanish as well as English, more likely to see Spanish as being useful for getting a job, and more likely to see positive effects of Spanish-language use on English-language development.

In another community study, Aguirre (1980) reports on a situation in which the language goals of the teachers and parents were not congruent. Conducting a survey of a small rural Colorado community, he found several areas in which the predominantly Mexican-American teachers and the Mexican-American parents differed. The community's general language-use preference was Spanish, while the teachers' (although Mexican-American) was English. Similarly, the parents preferred their children to use Spanish among friends and family, while the teachers preferred the use of English. And while the parents indicated a preference for a language-maintenance program, the teachers indicated a preference for a partial or transitional model. Aguirre attributed the conflicts which arose between the school and community regarding the program to these consistently differing attitudes and concluded that the lack of match had damaged the effectiveness of the bilingual program.

Social Relationship between School and Community

A surface effect of a language-education program on a community may be simply to promote non-English-language maintenance or to promote a shift to greater and greater use of English in the community. There usually is, however, more at stake than how much a particular language is used and when. Spolsky (1977) suggests that the basic, underlying motivation for the establishment of a bilingual program is usually not a linguistic one. Rather, there are social, economic, political, psychological, or cultural factors which trigger the desire for something other than monolingual instruction. Conversely, it follows that when a particular language-education program is not locally initiated, reaction to it by the community will not be based solely on linguistic factors, but more likely on socioeconomic, political, psychological, and cultural factors. Lamenting the tendency of educational planners to focus on rather specific pedagogical issues, Kjolseth states that

> The relevant issue today is not simply monolingual vs. bilingual education, but more essentially what *social* goals will serve the needs of the *majority* of ethnic group members and what *integrated set* of program design features will effectively realize them. Currently most programs are patchwork affairs, each searching for some distinctive gimmick and focusing its rhetoric and design toward the individual pupil in isolation from his family, peers, neighborhood, and community. (Kjolseth, 1972, pp. 109–110)

A revealing example of the sociological effects of a bilingual-education program on a community is that of the Otavalo Indians of highland Ecuador, as analyzed by Carpenter (1983). The Ecuadorian government implemented bilingual programs in Spanish and Quichua, a variant of the Quechua language family, with the stated goal of facilitating the sociocultural and economic integration of the Quichua-speaking minorities, but the program design was based on the erroneous assumption of homogeneity among the Otavalo Indians. In reality, there are two rather distinct social classes among the Otavaleños, and their reactions to the bilingual programs were quite different. This in turn affected the potential for success of the programs. Otavaleños derive their livelihood largely from subsistence agriculture and traditional weaving, for which there is a substantial tourist market. The weaving is sold principally in a famous regional artisan market which is held every Saturday. The (relatively speaking) wealthy Otavaleños who market the Otavalo crafts are generally urban Protestants who are bilingual in Spanish and Quichua and alternate between traditional and modern dress depending on the situation. The poor Otavalo Indians are generally rural, Catholic, subsistence farmers and are more likely to be monolingual Quichua speakers. Carpenter reports that the wealthy, urban Otavalo Indians, concerned over some of their youths' loss of Quichua, have warmly accepted bilingual education as a means of maintaining their ethnic identity. The maintenance of this identity is crucial to their economic success as Otavalo Indians in the artisan market. On the other hand, the rural Otavaleños see the transitional bilingual program—in which reading is first introduced in Quichua—as an attempt to keep them from attaining fluency in Spanish and thus to bar them from socioeconomic advancement. As one rural, anti-bilingual-education Quichua informant put it, "almost nothing is written in Quichua, so why on earth would anyone want to learn to read and write that language? Anything to be read is in Spanish, and anything worth writing about will also be in that language" (Carpenter, 1983, p. 104). Carpenter's conclusion is that for a bilingual-education program to be successful, program designers cannot assume homogeneity within any particular ethnic group and must be prepared to "incorporate the concerns of the target population in their design" (p. 106).

In a similar vein, Kjolseth speculates on the "diachronic effects of the maintenance-assimilation [bilingual] program on the local community dominance configuration" (1972, p. 113). He first differentiates between *local* ethnic language varieties and *world* ethnic language varieties; within the ethnic community, there is usually a minority elite group whose members are more likely to be fluent in the world or standard variety of the ethnic language. The school's bilingual program also most likely uses the world variety of the minority language. Kjolseth then suggests that a maintenance program may have at least two unexpected consequences. First, because most community members are not proficient in the world variety promoted in the school, the local variety of the ethnic language will be gradually supplanted by a greater use of English to avoid the problem of trying to communicate in the world or standard variety of the minority language. Second, because the minority elite group tends to be more proficient in the world variety than the non-elite group, they will gain more power within the local community as the school promotes the world variety while explicitly or implicitly rejecting the local variety.

Finally, in exploring the relationships between ethnic-language education and the sociology of the community, there is the interesting and little-known phenomenon of the many private, ethnic-community-sponsored, mother-tongue schools in the United States. Fishman (1980a) has identified approximately 5000 such schools in the United States and estimates that there may be another 1000 "out there." In investigating the nature of these private schools, he finds that they reveal information pertinent to the public schooling of language-minority children. Again, the function of these schools is not strictly linguistic. Instead, these schools, through their use of the ethnic language, serve as "loci of community viability, creativity, and identity" (p. 10). They reflect a pursuit of biculturalism which the community has found to be functional and meaningful, a type of biculturalism which is not conceived as an affirmation of foreigners but rather as a part of the "indigenization of ethnicity as an American way of life" (p. 11). However, these schools generally serve English-dominant second-, third-, and fourth-generation ethnic people, who have already become socioeconomically integrated into American society, and, in a situation similar in some respects to that of the wealthy urban Otavaleños, the benefits of pursuing ethnic-language instruction outweigh any potential costs.

Taking a closer look at biliteracy in French, Hebrew, Chinese, Armenian, and Greek schools in New York City, Fishman (1980b) found that, despite differences in writing systems and dialect among the students and teachers, biliteracy is not seen as being difficult or problematic, as it often is in the public schools. Rather, it is seen as something which is normal and achieved as a matter of course. One factor is that there is a separate function for literacy in each language; there is a *reason* for learning to read and write in each language, and children are immersed in two "cultures of reading." Impressed by the apparent success of these schools, Fishman asks,

> If ethnic communities in New York City—surrounded as they are by the world of English—can manage to organize schools that effectively teach predominantly English-speaking children reading and writing in the particularistic languages of their respective ethnocultural traditions, why cannot most of our public schools in New York City organize themselves to effectively teach English reading and writing to non-English mother tongue children or adults? (1980b, p. 60)

Although Fishman admits that he is raising more questions than he is answering and that there are many factors to be considered, he postulates that, "given societies where reading really makes a difference in what counts and what works for its members, most of their children will learn how to read rather well and rather early" (1980a, p. 59). In other words, all of the methodological furor over how to approach black English or dialectal differences in Spanish in the classroom may not be as crucial to promoting literacy as a consideration of the "culture of reading" in the immediate and wider communities, as well as the ways in which the social rewards for literacy are distributed. Fishman concludes that without favorable input from families and neighborhoods into schools and without the appropriate societal opportunities and rewards, language-education experimentation which focuses on methodology within classrooms per se may not make a big difference.

Informal Community Description and Reflection

The goal of understanding every detail of school and community relations is highly unrealistic: few bilingual or ESL programs come equipped with full-time community sociolinguists and ethnographers. Yet it is on the accumulation of such linguistic, social, and cultural detail that a realistic understanding of the community is based. While formal research in community sociolinguistics can suggest patterns on which to base observations, administrators and teachers who want to develop a sound knowledge base will have to rely largely on themselves for the acquisition of a detailed community perspective.

One step toward achieving that goal is to examine the personal and cultural histories that children carry with them from the community when they enroll in school. Learners don't come to school in the form of a tabula rasa. In fact, by the time children enroll in school they have had myriad and complex experiences—learning to read a few things on their own, learning to understand the linguistic and cultural demands placed on them, adopting values and bypassing others, expressing self-confidence and insecurity, coming to grips with life by being able to communicate their needs and interests, being snuggled by their parents, and being left alone in the schools. Such learners come to school already equipped with a wide array of communicative skills, verbal and nonverbal, which enables them to negotiate with life with varying degrees of success.

There are many important social and cultural expressions, hidden and glaring ones, which may be hints or screaming statements about how parents and schools perceive each other's roles in the lives of the children. It is unrealistic to expect every teacher, regardless of social science skills, sophistication, and attitudes, to become intimately involved in the observation of numerous everyday interactions between parents and educators, parents and students, and students and teachers. We do believe, however, that we can do a better job than we have done in the past in developing a realistic knowledge base about the community patterns surrounding us. Sound curriculum planning emerges from such a platform.

Basic is a sense of language use in the community, even if it is based on informal observation and questioning. Awareness of the roles of the various languages in the community may symbolically or realistically nurture ties between the school and the surrounding neighborhood. Beyond having a sense of who uses what language when, it is also important to examine our attitudes regarding the speech patterns of community members. Because the languages of ethnic communities often are not standard ones, there is the strong possibility of cross-cultural misfire. And because language, as a tool for communication and socially ascribed phenomena, to a considerable degree influences the nature of school experiences and attitudes, we can readily see why language plays an important role—subtle or obvious—in school and community relations.

There is a tendency in all of us to be tentative in affirming any linguistic reality which is alien to our own current norms. In fact, teachers from a lower socioeconomic background who once spoke nonstandard English may tend to be quite hard on children who do not speak standard English. In the interest of affirming the cultural and linguistic backgrounds of such children and thus of their community we all need to be reminded that languages fit, like warm mittens on a cold and windy day, quite snugly in the lives of the persons who speak them. Teachers may question how children will learn a standard language if they are not guided toward it, and we are certainly not against the use of standard English. After all, we are told in countless ways that we need it to survive and move within the resource-rich center of American society. But we also need to build on the cultural and linguistic configuration that is already programmed into the child, to give the child more options without taking away those which the community has given him.

Broader traits to consider in getting to know the community are the distribution and proportions of immigrant as opposed to indigenous minority-group members. How isolated from, or integrated with, the mainstream community is the language-minority community? To what degree does it represent a stable or a mobile population? What is happening to community members in terms of maintenance of ethnicity and acculturation or assimilation? Do the children show interest in their home language and culture by practicing appropriate behavior for such contexts? Or are the children mainly interested in learning English? Is it noticeable through any shift in dress or behavior that children or parents are opting to disengage from their primary cultural and linguistic traditions? If so, what is influencing them? From a more political point of view, information on demography; associational patterns; patterns of local influence and power; and attitudes toward such factors as ethnicity, language, and schooling would also be of value.

Knowledge about the relationships between parents and their children will also reveal useful information. What are parents' aspirations for their children, and how do they communicate those aspirations? When you see the children with their parents, do they seem at ease with each other? Do the children enjoy having their parents visit the school? When there are conflicts, how are they usually handled between the school and the parents? When the children are doing well in school, how is this success shared with the parents?

It is also rewarding to probe into the types of social, physical, recreational, and academic activities which children are interested in doing at home. What do they do in their free time with their peers? With their parents and other family members? Be on the lookout for special talent in the children, their parents, and others in their communities. Musicians, artists, weavers, artisans, dramatists, photographers, writers, poets, athletes, dancers, and story tellers can all be linked to the life of the school.

A lot of information can be gained over time through experience and interaction with the community, provided one is prepared to notice the relevant details and build them into a sense of the structure of community life. However, in some cases a more systematic approach to information-gathering may be warranted. For example, Ochoa (1979) proposes that a first step in any plan to promote community involvement in bilingual education should be a community research phase. To make the task less formidable, the work could be divided into subject areas, with each person on the informal research team assigned to a particular topic. (With his proposed model for such a research phase, Ochoa includes a good list of suggested sources from which to get the desired information.)

Throughout this book we have underscored the importance of building curriculum and instructional methods from the natural base of the child. There is no better way to make the learners and their communities feel accepted than to affirm their sociocultural reality. Once this reality has been affirmed we can add new experiences which will enrich, expand, and produce positive development in the lives of learners. Because community and school relations take on personal meaning when we experience them in real settings rather than as mere concepts, this section ends with some reflections on the interplay between a school with a large bilingual program and the surrounding community. The following profile by an elementary-school teacher hints at the sociocultural diversity that permeates environments which to the casual observer may seem highly homogeneous. While it is only a limited picture of one community, we hope that the following perceptions by a teacher of her work environment will stimulate others to become observers of and reflectors on the community detail enveloping them as they work in bilingual settings.

A TEACHER'S REFLECTIONS ON THE COMMUNITY

The area served by my school is the most economically depressed of the city. Less than a third of the adults have completed high school. The average annual family income is well below the national median, and nearly a third of the students receive Aid for Dependent Children. Nearly all of the students receive free or reduced-price breakfasts and lunches at school. According to the California Assessment Program Background Factor Summary, normed for all schools in California, the area's socioeconomic indicator is at the first percentile, the parent education index is at the fourth percentile, and the number of children on Aid for Dependent Children is at the seventy-eighth percentile.

The community lacks full development of many basic urban services. Until recently there were several unpaved streets, and most alleys are still unpaved. There are few health services available in the immediate community; there are only a few small neighborhood stores; and bus stops are as much as ½ mile from many of the homes. Numerous homes are well maintained and have pleasing gardens, but much of the housing is substandard, consisting of one-, two-, and three-room frame rental units.

The community is at least 80 percent Hispanic and about 10 percent black. That, of course, adds up to at least 90 percent minority group. It would be safe to say that the dominant language in the community is Spanish. Many of the business establishments are named after places in Mexico; there is a Spanish-language theater; and billboards commonly appear in Spanish.

There is a strong network of family and church relationships. Most children have grandparents, aunts, uncles, cousins, or godparents who live close by. Many families frequently make return trips to family in rural Mexico. The local Catholic church serves many families and operates a K-6 parochial school in which many upwardly mobile families enroll their children. The Catholic Youth Organization also maintains a community center across the street from the school. This center provides many youth and senior citizen activities. Much social interaction occurs within the homes, in front of the homes, on the sidewalks, and in the streets.

Seen from the inside, however, the community is not homogeneous. There are devout Catholic Hispanics and devout Protestant Hispanics. There are Hispanics who get along well with blacks and those who have strong racial prejudices. There are rural Mexicans who still wear cowboy hats and boots and slaughter goats, pigs, and chickens in their backyards. And there are Chicanos who buy their children's clothes at Sears, take vacations in campers, and barely speak Spanish. There are parents who take their children to the library and there are parents who can't sign their own name. There are teenagers who keep the neighborhood walls decorated, use drugs, and vandalize the school. And there are teenagers who belong to religious organizations or attend college.

Most parents in the community place great importance on the role of schooling for their children. They want them to do well. What they don't realize is the extent to which schools such as the one in their community have traditionally failed to keep students competitive with the national norms. Neither do most parents realize the extent to which schools such as theirs are singled out by policymakers as problems which can be given assorted labels and attacked with money for special remedial programs. For example, of the 1200 students at school this year, 91 percent are Hispanic and 5 percent are black, making it a minority, segregated school. This qualifies it for special court-ordered funding which is supposed to alleviate the adverse effects of racial isolation. Also, first graders score each year at the first percentile in the California Assessment Program's test of entry level skills. This, along with the economic status of the community, entitles the school to federal Title I funding.

Despite the gap between the aspirations of parents for their children and the highly politicized and institutionalized intricacies of the public school system, bilingual education has enabled parents to become more closely involved in the elementary schooling process. Because the language barrier has been removed, they can talk to most of the teachers, participate in meetings, understand programs, and help children with their homework. Most of the educational aides at the school are members of the community. The Hispanic-dominated PTA and the school decision-making committees have provided opportunities for Hispanic community leaders to emerge and to develop their leadership skills. Most parents are supportive of bilingual education, in varying degrees, although the program is not the result of a grass-roots community movement. Some parents favor a maintenance bilingual program, and some favor a transitional bilingual program. A few are against bilingual education altogether. And many aren't quite sure what is happening but want to trust the school and sign just about anything they're asked to sign.

The "standard" English and "standard" Spanish which we use at school are imports from outside the community, and we the teachers are imports too. Nearly all the teachers, myself included, come into the barrio to teach and then retreat to our own enclaves by 4:30 every afternoon. Despite extensive use of Spanish and recognition of Mexican and Chicano cultural traditions, we still comprise an alien and often puzzling institution. The teachers at school vary in their degree of support for bilingual education, especially with respect to maintenance of the home language. Some seem to be holding their noses as they warily implement the bare requirements, and this message must get through to the students. By second grade many LEP students have already figured out that English speakers seem to have more status among peers and more verbal interactions with teachers. By sixth grade former LEP students frequently claim to know little or no Spanish. And in some instances former Spanish speakers really have lost their Spanish fluency.

In the eyes of the outside world, the community where I work seems to have developed into one large, negative stereotype. I remember the principal telling me about an incident involving a large mural at the school entrance which some local teen-aged boys were painting under the auspices of a local artist. Most of the boys involved wore the uniform of the *cholo* [young people who often join gangs]. The principal was proud of the project and wanted the area newspaper to cover it. However, he told me he was repeatedly unsuccessful in getting a reporter out until he finally called and hinted that the mural had something to do with gangs. That got the story printed.

Despite the many negative traits of the community from an outsider's point of view, from the child's point of view it is home, and the neighborhood houses, stores, playgrounds, gardens, parks, vacant lots, railroad tracks, repair shops, junkyards, and industries carry many emotional connotations. Although teachers may think in terms of the undesirable nature of the community, the children have found a great deal of joy and warmth there. Without romanticizing poverty, it is important to remember that an outsider's perception of the community is different from the insider's. This struck me clearly one day when a group of first graders in my class had completed a writing assignment—several sentences about positive and negative aspects of the community. We were studying the local community as a social studies unit and had just returned from a long neighborhood walk. After some group discussion I modeled a mixture of sentences, both positive and negative, based on my comments and theirs. Biased by my own awareness of the less-than-optimal socioeconomic and environmental realities of the community, I expected from the students a lot of sentences reflecting negative traits; to my surprise, every child came up with a product that began along the lines of "(name of community) is pretty." I had also been surprised, when we first began the community unit, to see how quickly the students learned to read and spell the rather long name of the community. Another incident which made me think about the community from the child's-eye view was the following:

> Arturo: Teacher. Teacher! They cut a boy all up, on his face, last night. From here to here (pointing).
> Angela: They were *cholos*.
> Nakia: *Cholos* are bad.
> Me: Well, some *cholos* do some bad things. But some do good things too.
> Alejo: Teacher, some *cholos* live in my house. *They're* good.

Being "sensitive" to the community involves more than celebrating holidays read about in a book or trying an ethnic recipe. It involves beginning to see the community the way the parents and children do—as an ethnographer would.

COMMUNITY INVOLVEMENT

Formal schooling is perceived by individual members of ethnic communities as an important instrument for upward mobility. As institutionalized instruments of state and federal governments, schools have clearly articulated sociocultural, political, ideological, technical, and academic goals which guide what they want the citizenry to learn. How do such national goals complement or contradict those of ethnic communities—communities which often nurture in their children natural linkages with ancestral traditions while concurrently expecting them to become affiliated with the social and economic American "good life"? What do schools want? And parents? And students? Are the rules of the game understood by all participants? How do parents know whether token parental participation is anything more than a smoke screen to hide serious academic problems in the school? How do administrators know whether parents involved in community action are sincere advocates of school reform or "troublemakers" trying to get some visibility? Where, when, and how do parents attempt conflict resolution?

Comparing the business of the school with that of the ethnic community entails an examination of the explicit and implicit assumptions surrounding their missions. As transmitters of consensual values, educators often see their mission to homogenize students cognitively and socioculturally. They transmit cultural objectives appropriate to the functioning of a large, anonymous, technological society. Such a process is carried out through school socialization—a process by which children learn to respond correctly to the demands and requirements placed on them by other society members—and through enculturation, "the process of learning a culture in all its uniqueness and particularity" (Mead, 1963, p. 187). Meanwhile, socialization and enculturation go on intensively in the home, and with quite a head start. Usually, school administrators and teachers who work with stigmatized ethnic groups learn fairly quickly that the ongoing perceptions which they and the children's parents have about each other are often wired to conflicting socioeconomic and linguistic-cultural factors. Therefore, educators and parents cannot always assume a common basis of understanding. Such perceptions, moreover, are often reflections of issues that contain shades of gray rather than black and white only. To complicate matters, ethnic children—as culture makers—often have their own notions, apart from those of the school or parent, of what is and is not important in their lives.

Schools generally want parents to be cooperative, to buttress the school's norms and those of American society, to exhibit a positive attitude toward the school and trust its teachers, to help children with their homework, to ensure that their children attend school regularly and on time, to instill a drive for academic achievement in their children, to participate in school social functions, to attend parent conferences, and not to be overly anxious about school policy matters. Administrators generally do not like parents to get intimately involved in the governance of the school. They may well feel very satisfied if most parents—like some nominally religious persons who attend church during Easter and Christmas—come to school sparingly but faithfully on the appropriate symbolic occasions.

School administrators and teachers could argue that it is not that they don't want parents to get involved but that the parents either don't want to, don't have the time or energy, or feel that school-related policy issues should be the business of school professionals. Ethnic parents, in turn, could argue that schools notoriously make then feel unwanted when it comes to matters related to governing the school. Naturally they don't want to be involved where they don't feel appreciated. Ethnic parents often sense or see that they are being treated as nonequals in matters of school policy.

Parents wonder: How well are my children doing in school? Are they being prepared for jobs or college? Are the teachers properly equipped to do their job? Is the curriculum pro-learner? What is the bilingual or ESL program doing for my child? Are children safe in school? Do teachers and administrators care? These and many other issues quite often serve as the fragile platform on which the relationship between school and community is built.

Embedded in questions such as the ones above is the desire of humans to perpetuate themselves culturally. Translated into formal education, this becomes the "communal function" of schooling (Peshkin, 1982, pp. 64–65). Thus the nature of the bond between the school and community hinges on how the issue of cultural perpetuation is resolved by both sides. In modern times the resolution of such concerns has become more complicated by the complexity and heterogeneity of society. In such a world, the implicit and explicit values of the community vis-à-vis the school become blurred despite the possibly good intentions of the school to serve the will of the parents (Peshkin, 1982). The situation becomes more interesting when it involves the education of culturally diverse language-minority children. Because of the key function parents play in the success and continuity of bilingual or ESL schooling, the issue of their involvement calls for a greater understanding of the forces at play. As Fishman notes, "the area of parental involvement in bilingual education is far too crucial to the direction and success of such education to remain as little explored as it is at the moment" (1977, p. 45).

Ironically, one of the things we have learned regarding parental involvement in bilingual education is that one of the costs of court-mandated bilingual education may be a *lack* of community involvement. Community involvement can be a slow, grass-roots organizing process, and the rush to meet court deadlines can preclude or bypass such activities. Because court mandates have emerged as a result of deficiencies in the schooling process, their primary intent has been remedial in nature. Well-conceived and strongly supported community action programs, on the other hand, can take bilingual education beyond remedial goals into the realm of sociocultural authenticity and control of the schooling process (Brisk, 1979). Some bilingual education programs conceived and controlled by Native Americans provide a case in point. The Navajo Rough Rock Demonstration School, for example, is the first school system in modern times operated by an Indian community. Using voting power to elect an Indian-controlled school board, parents in many Native American locales have been able to take control of the educational system or particular educational programs. When they are a minority, parents have been able to establish a separate Indian school district (Wabaunsee, 1977). Another successful method has been for the community to contract with the Bureau of Indian Affairs (BIA) to educate their children with money the bureau would have used. The BIA then turns over the facilities to the contractor—the community. Rather than a result of litigation, bilingual education in these instances is the by-product of the rise of Indian-controlled schools. According to Wabaunsee, "as tribes have established and strengthened their sovereignty, the use of Indian languages in school systems has become a major political issue in Indian communities" (1977, p. 66).

Legislation for Community Participation

Despite the rather distinct history of community participation in Native American bilingual education, much of the impetus for formal parent involvement in most other contexts has been derived from federal and state legislation. Under the Johnson administration the Elementary and Secondary Education Act of 1965 (ESEA) was born, with the specific goal of redressing social and economic handicaps of low-income Americans through improved educational opportunity. With an initial authorization of over $1 billion, Title I of ESEA appeared to provide some realistic optimism for low-income communities. As Davies put it, "it appeared that for the first time communities and their schools should have enough money to make a difference for those children who had not succeeded in the past" (1981, p. 149). Beyond the money itself, it was through Title I and the federal Headstart program that the concept of structured guidelines stipulating parent involvement began.

Many low-income groups, including Native Americans, Asian-Americans, Puerto Ricans, black Americans, Mexican-Americans, and other Hispanics, welcomed such federal intervention, with its concomitant educational innovations and opportunities for parent participation. However, while the intent was to help low-income communities break away from poverty through education, and while some achievement gains may be attributed to federal intervention (Thomas, 1980), ESEA programs also helped to create a "disadvantaged" ethnic community in the eyes of laypersons, teachers, administrators, college professors, and policymakers—a term which still lingers when we speak of indigenous or immigrant groups who are overly represented in the lower layers of the economic system of this country. It could be argued that the ethnic community continued, through the federal dollar, to exist in a state of structural dependency despite small to moderate academic gains in such programs and despite supposed opportunities for parent involvement in planning and implementation.

The Bilingual Education Act of 1968, an offspring of ESEA, also included provisions for parent involvement in the planning, implementation, and evaluation of Title VII programs. Becoming even more specific, the Bilingual Education Act of 1974 mandated such participation by parents. State bilingual education programs today also generally specify mechanisms for community involvement in programs implemented at the local level. As a result, bilingual programs throughout the nation include some type of parent advisory council.

Parent Advisory Councils   Just as community efforts to establish bilingual education programs have resulted in opportunities for participants to develop their organizing and leadership skills, parent advisory councils can serve as valuable training grounds and springboards for greater participation in the politics of education. Some parents who work on ESEA-derived or state-derived advisory councils have become well known in the larger community's educational circle and in some cases have become members of local school boards.

More often than not, however, parent advisory councils seem to have fallen short of their goals. For example, research findings for Title VII indicate that "with few exceptions, Community Advisory Committees were not deeply involved in governance" (as reflected in decisions regarding program content, project budget, and project personnel), and that "most did not advise or otherwise contribute to decisions" (System Development Corporation, 1981). The researchers also found that the rare instances in which parents were involved in policy formulation provided a cogent statement about the ideology of the project director. In such cases the director from the beginning wanted an articulate, strong, and caring cadre of parents and he or she wanted them to participate in a meaningful way. In most other cases parents played perfunctory roles such as signing forms or being supportive on social occasions when it was symbolically important to be seen with the project director and staff.

Cruz (1979b) found a similar situation in his nationwide survey of parent advisory council members. Members ranked as their primary functions such activities as interpreting the program to the community and serving as a public relations body for the program, rather than having an effect on the nature of the program itself. Cruz also found that there was no functioning monitoring system to provide feedback as to whether a council was performing its role effectively. Rodríguez (1979) analyzed fifteen councils in Texas and classified their roles into five types on a power continuum: placation (the least powerful level of participation), sanctions, information, checks and balances, and change agent (the most powerful level of participation). Of the fifteen councils, four were found to be operating at the placation level, five at the sanctions level, and six at the information level. Thus, although federal law prescribed functions which, according to Rodríguez, would be categorized at the checks and balances level, all the councils were performing at lower levels. Important contributions listed by members whose advisory councils tended to operate at the placation and sanctions levels were such things as judging contests, making decorations, turning negative parent feelings into positive ones, and assisting in the classroom. In other words, according to Rodríguez, the main focus at these levels was to improve or change parent behavior rather than allow parents to play a role in improving or changing the program. At the information level, which begins to approach checks and balances, the school administration did accept insights from the parents and act on those insights, and concomitantly the parents felt important in disseminating to the community information about the bilingual program.

García (1979, p. 237) identifies four reasons why community groups such as advisory councils usually have failed to ensure the adequacy of their programs through a checks and balances or change-agent level of participation:

1. The community is not in a bargaining position with the school district. It lacks power sources such as pertinent information, appropriate training, legal help, media exposure, and technical advice from teachers and professors.

2. Community organizations usually respond to crisis situations, the so-called band-aid approach to problem solving.

3. They have not had data (such as achievement test scores) on which to base decisions. As García puts it, community organizations need a system for collecting and maintaining data "which parents can understand and control."

4. Community groups have failed to plan with an eye to the "big picture," so that they can be prepared for issues as they emerge and be aware of the school's power hierarchy and their own rights.

Shifting the focus from the community participants to the school personnel, there is another important view as to why parent advisory councils do not always perform at an optimal level. The adage of parents' "lack of interest" may in reality be a reflection of the administrators' "lack of interest" in parent participation. What Mizell (1979) says referring to Title I (now entitled Chapter I) is applicable to bilingual and ESL programs: "Unless Title I officials make a conscientious effort to understand what parents need to be effective parent advisory council members and respond to those needs, the parents may perceive the school officials as not being interested in them, and they may respond to their responsibilities as parent advisory council members in kind" (p. 82). In other words, if members sense that their participation really doesn't matter to the administration, they will feel that membership is not worth their time and effort. Among the "self-serving reasons" an administrator may consciously or unconsciously have for the existence of an advisory council are their provision of free labor, rubber-stamping, and shock absorption—all roles designed to preserve the status quo rather than produce change (Ochoa, 1979).

It is not easy for parent advisory councils to operate at the checks and balances or change-agent level, because it is at these levels that conflicts must be resolved. In just one parent advisory council meeting, for example, a participating teacher reported to one of the authors that the parents disagreed with the administrator and staff on three issues: (1) the parents wanted a greater emphasis on Spanish grammar than did the principal and teachers; (2) the parents preferred to use a limited fund for a math coordinator while the principal and teachers preferred having a music/orchestra teacher; and (3) the parents wanted letter grades (A-F) while the principal and teachers preferred *at-, above-,* or *below-grade-level* marks along with effort grades of *outstanding, satisfactory,* or *not satisfactory*. The school personnel "won" on all three points. Despite the difficulties in obtaining successful higher-level participation, there is evidence that such participation can play a role in the effectiveness of programs. Based on visits to bilingual education programs across the country, contributors to *A Better Chance to Learn* (U.S. Commission on Civil Rights, 1975) observed that the degree to which the home-school gap was closed depended greatly on the extent to which the community was involved in the design and implementation of the program.

Improvement of the role of parent advisory councils depends on a variety of factors. Cruz (1979b) believes that a prerequisite for the effectiveness of such councils is a clear and specific definition of the group's roles and functions. Once these functions are defined it follows that the body's performance can be evaluated. In a similar fashion Mizell (1979) suggests that advisory council members be provided with a job description which outlines their roles and responsibilities. Furthermore, they should receive training in federal guidelines and jargon as well as committee and school procedures; they should have opportunities to learn about instructional programs through first-hand observation; they should be made aware of possibilities for leadership development; their efforts should result in specific, tangible products; and their membership should be publicly recognized through various media. As important as the other issues—if not more so—is the fact that school officials need training in how to work with parents on a more equal footing. Thus, the success of a parent advisory council depends on both the community members and the school officials.

An example of a formal effort to develop effective advisory councils is the Chicago Latino Institute's Parent Leadership Training Program, as described by Cerda and Schensul (1979). In a 3-year period the program supported the organization, training, and development of dozens of advisory councils in the Chicago area. It provided for teacher in-service training in community relations, helped in the election of thirty-four parents to district and city advisory positions, influenced city and state legislation, disseminated information to hundreds of parents, and resulted in the public schools' institutionalization of the parent training program.

Parents as Mutual Partners

Contributors to *A Better Chance to Learn* (U.S. Commission on Civil Rights, 1975) describe a Chinese bilingual-bicultural program in which the community provides workshops for the school staff in Chinese kite-making, puppetry, music, and dance. They tell about Navajo parents at Rock Point sharing traditional stories in school and teaching weaving, silversmithing, and leather crafts. As attractive as such activities sound, however, the authors point out that such participation does not reach its full potential if parents do not share in the school's decision-making process. Thus, while we survey in this section the broader aspects of community involvement in language-minority education, it should be viewed within the perspective of the importance of community participation in decision making, as discussed in the section on parent advisory councils.

There are numerous roles for parents and other community members to assume: learner, teacher, decision maker, adviser, community representative, being the "eyes and ears" for informing the school of the needs of the community. As learners, parents can gain knowledge in such areas as bilingual education, individualized instruction, team teaching, use of paraprofessionals, and first- and second-language acquisition. As decision makers, they can take the initiative if the school is not providing the skills that they expect for their children. They can work as volunteers in the classroom, foster an open-door policy at school, or take an active role in maintaining home-school communication (Sancho, 1979).

Of course, reality can get in the way of the potential for such wide-ranging involvement. Not long ago one of the writers asked a high school principal to comment on his school's relations with ethnic groups in the community. The administrator pointed out first of all that a good principal is skillful in selecting community members to work with him and for him—persons who can help put out the frequent fires in school and community relations. Then he went on to point out that his main problems have been with indigenous Chicano parents who, according to him, tend to be more assertive, single-issue-oriented, and ill-informed than immigrant parents, and frequently a thorn in his side. He described recent immigrant parents, on the other hand, as cooperative and easy to work with. This anecdote points out the critical issues of stereotyped perceptions and asymmetry in power relationships. Intentionally or not, school personnel tend to treat indigenous parents differently from immigrant parents, and lower-income parents differently from middle-income parents.

Lareau and Benson (1984), in a comparative study of two schools, found that the middle-class school had established a much stronger partnership with the parents than had the working-class school. The difference however, was not related to the amount of parental interest in the education of their children. According to Lareau and Benson, it was related to sociocultural differences in family life and the ways in which the schools responded to these differences. What resulted was a pattern of interdependence between home and school life at the middle-class school and a pattern of almost total separation of family life from the process of schooling at the lower-class school. Among the identified sociocultural factors which produced the different home-school relationships were social network patterns and child socialization networks. Among families in the lower-class school, for example, kinship played a more important role in social networks than contact with fellow parents through the school network. The middle-class families, however, being more socially and geographically mobile, tended to be more isolated from their relatives and consequently depended more on other parents in their neighborhood for their social relationships. Through frequent contact with fellow parents, parents with children at the same middle-class school had much more information about what actually happens in the classroom as well as about funding, school policy, and staffing procedures. It follows then, as Ochoa points out, that "if parents are provided with information about the education of their children, they are more likely to participate in the school program" (1979, p. 74).

An example of different child socialization practices is the type of activities the children participate in after school. The lower-class children were more likely to be involved in informal, often family-related, activities, while the middle-class children were more likely to be involved in such formal activities as Brownies, organized athletics, or piano lessons. These formal activities, in turn, strengthened the parental social network and won the approval of teachers, who judged the activities to be educational and enriching. The ultimate result is that even though parents at both schools had an equal level of interest in their children's education, teachers tended to develop higher expectations for the middle-class children because it *appeared* to them that the middle-class parents were more interested. Lareau and Benson conclude that, because of socioeconomically based sociocultural differences, a well-intentioned effort to increase parent partnerships with the school could change, in lower-income schools, into a teacher-principal attitude of cultural deficiency toward families in the community. To counteract this possibility, they argue, teachers should be prepared to take some initiative in fostering a climate of mutual interdependence, and they must be willing to explore a variety of partnership alternatives based on varied sociocultural patterns.

Although Lareau and Benson's study was conducted outside the context of bilingual or ESL education, the issues of sociocultural differences and the importance of teacher attitudes in the establishment of home-school interdependence are very relevant to the education of language-minority children. In interviews conducted with bilingual and ESL staff in a Massachusetts community, Ringawa (1980) found that many teachers perceived the primary functions of parent involvement to be improving such things as school attendance, discipline, and parent attitudes toward the teachers and school. Seeing these as *principal* reasons for parent involvement may reflect a one-sided attitude in which parents and their children are seen as objects which need to be changed to fit the school rather than as individuals with interests, aspirations, expectations, resources, and skills which can contribute to the improvement of the school. As Ringawa puts it, teachers seemed to be willing to work with parents within the confines of the school—on their own terms, so to speak—but were somewhat reluctant to go out into the community and see the home-school partnership from that perspective.

While it is important for teachers and school administrators to avail themselves of opportunities to learn about parents, the community, and the school's relationship to the community, very positive use can also be made of opportunities for parents and other interested community members to learn about bilingual education, second-language acquisition, and methods for working with their children that will benefit them academically. One first step might be an assessment of parents' "entry level" knowledge and opinions regarding bilingual education. To get such information would require an "informal, natural environment in which honest comments would emerge" (Cohen, 1983, p. 147). According to Cohen, if parents are to make a real difference in the planning, operation, and evaluation of their child's bilingual program, they need information which will enable them to do more than just endorse bilingual education as an abstraction. There is evidence that many parents have limited information about the programs in which their children are enrolled. Manna (1975, cited in Cohen, 1979), for example, found that among a group of Hispanic parents surveyed in Los Angeles, 16 percent said they understood what bilingual education was about, 32 percent said they knew only a little about it, and 52 percent said they knew little or nothing. A survey of parents of bilingual-program students in East Austin also found that the majority were unfamiliar with the objectives of bilingual education (Santelices, 1981). Despite plans on paper to inform the community about bilingual education, it is unrealistic to assume that the community will absorb basic or detailed information without face-to-face interaction and closer ties between the school and the community, in which information is disseminated through first-hand observation and established social networks.

A common approach to the concept of parents as partners is to provide them with workshops or classes on ways to develop children's skills at home and reinforce what is learned at school. Many federal- and state-funded school improvement programs have provided for such parent workshops. Often parents are paid a small stipend for participating, and babysitting is provided to ease parental involvement. The focus is often on early childhood education, and parents learn about such things as reading-readiness skills, how to reinforce basic math concepts, oral language development, the role of self-concept, and the use of games for skills development.

One interesting approach to early childhood bilingual education that maintains very close ties to the home—and one which goes beyond a series of parent workshops—is that of the Cuahtemoc Home-Centered Bilingual Preschool of Redwood City, California. The Cuahtemoc program designers distinguished between bilingual *education*, which can occur anywhere, and bilingual *schooling*, which happens within the confines of a formal classroom; they also based their program on the data that suggest that 50 percent of the intelligence that one has at the age of 17 is developed in the first 4 years of life. Considering the broad definition of bilingual education and the rapid growth of intelligence in early childhood, a program was developed in which 3- to 5-year-olds met with a bilingual teacher in groups of six in parents' homes, a week in each home. Each group of six included four Spanish-dominant children and two English-dominant children, and the goal was to have children who were not only very well prepared for first grade but also ready to learn in two languages (Andersson, 1975).

Another example of home education coordinated with formal schooling is the Del Pueblo Community School Project of Denver, Colorado. Noting that the most common reason given for parent involvement is that it improves academic achievement, Cervantes, Baca, and Torres (1979) argue that a crucial focus of parent involvement should be in activities which relate directly to academic tasks. The authors argue that the "resource" role often prescribed for parent involvement limits them to such activities as the "making of tortillas and guitar playing" (p. 74). The specific objective of the Del Pueblo project was to enhance parents' and childrens' reading attitudes and reading-related behavior through a series of ten instructional sessions. Activities for communication skill building and reading to children were modeled for parents, and the parents had opportunities to practice the activities in class as well as at home. At the end of the sessions both parents and children in the treatment group had significantly higher scores on a reading attitude inventory than did the control group. Thus Cervantes, Baca, and Torres conclude that modeling is an effective method for training parents in skills for working with their children at home.

As valuable as some parent education programs may be in certain contexts, there is also a danger in their misuse. As already noted in the discussion on sociocultural differences which can affect the degree of home-school interdependence, such differences may be misconstrued as deficiencies. Once again the theme can emerge that the burden is on the parent and child to change to fit the school. In a perhaps well-intentioned attempt to strengthen the role of the parent as a partner, the degree of mutuality—inherent to the concept of partnership—instead may be diminished.

It can be soundly argued that specific kinds of parent behavior have an effect on academic achievement. Among the home environment factors that Martínez (1981) found to predict higher achievement of students in bilingual-education programs in northern New Mexico were verbal interaction, time spent reading with the child, and parental aspirations for their children. Such findings would suggest the desirability of intervention in parenting practices. On the other hand, schools which convey to students and parents an attitude of sociocultural denigration are also schools which are most likely failing to tap or develop the experiences, skills, and abilities of their clients. Therefore, forays into "parent education" will most likely have positive effects on the partnership only if they are conceived and developed as mutual parent-professional dialogues.

The visual image of parent education might be of a circle of chairs, rather than rows of desks with a teacher in front. Flores and Hendricks (1984) report on a series of discussions for Hispanic parents in Fairbanks, Alaska, on child development and the role of the parent in academic development. As rapport grew, the sessions became opportunities to share mutual concerns, worries, successes, or problems. In many areas the parents concurred with the "professional" advice presented in a series of filmstrips. One professional prescription with which the parents tended to disagree was that young children should be encouraged to establish social relationships apart from their family's own network. In the workshop environment the parents felt free to disagree, and the objective of the discussion coordinators—who were bilingual teachers—was not necessarily to change anybody's mind. However, both the teachers and the parents as a result became aware of and more sensitive to this cultural difference.

Models and Suggestions for Community Involvement

Trying to get staff and community opinion on how to spend funds for program development, the principal of a language-minority elementary school called a staff meeting to create a marketplace of ideas. Facing the staff and one parent who was the home-school coordinator, the principal stood ready to write on the board, brainstorming style, all suggestions. According to one of the teachers present at the meeting, when the parent offered an idea the principal acknowledged it verbally but failed to write it down as he had for all the teachers' ideas. No one seemed to notice, and the parent said nothing else for the rest of the meeting.

If it were not for the uneasy balance characteristic of school-community relations, the above incident could be dismissed as a minor detail unworthy of attention. Given the reality, however, that even under the best of circumstances purposeful and sustained parental engagement with the schools is not easy, such episodes take on special meaning regardless of the motive. It is the cumulative effect of details like this that can make relationships go awry. Parents find it difficult to work in school environments in which they are outranked professionally, not treated as peers, and frequently viewed by school personnel as necessary evils because of federal and state regulations (Cruz, 1979a). When warm, caring, and supportive interactive processes exist there is a good chance for parents and schools to develop a positive symbiotic relationship (Comer, 1980; Ogbu, 1974). The improvement of school-community relations, however, requires more than just goodwill. It requires careful analysis of the details in both worlds—details such as the failure to write a parent's suggestion on the board. This section surveys some models, maps, and suggestions for community involvement in the education of language-minority children.

Brisk (1979) describes stages involved in community planning for bilingual education programs. First, however, she identifies two areas in which problems generally arise in any effort to organize the community. First is the establishment of communication networks, which becomes particularly crucial when the community involved is not linked geographically. Second is the establishment of good working relationships among groups. For example, lay participants often distrust professionals, and consequently the best strategy for professionals is often to serve in an advisory capacity. Bilingual teachers may be of greatest value in allying themselves with the community rather than getting "caught in the middle" between the community and school administrators.

With provisions made for communication and the establishment of effective working relationships, the first stage in the actual planning of a program is a survey of the language-minority school children for such information as ages, grades, school attendance patterns, promotion histories, and language skills. If such surveys are done by the community, they serve to increase community awareness of the issues it faces and also as a preliminary step to greater organization. After a survey is completed, the next stage is goal setting, which may be done by a coordinating committee with the result disseminated to the community for evaluation. (At this point, Brisk points out that it is handy to have a media person on the coordinating committee.) Through this process the goals will be based on the philosophy of the community (for example, maintenance versus transition), the needs of the children, and relevant legislative constraints.

Once the goals are disseminated, evaluated, and modified, the third stage is to deal with technical issues. Here again, Brisk proposes that it is the community that should be doing the research on language types, curricular materials, testing instruments, and personnel qualifications. In addressing technical issues, a survey of other programs and an inventory of the school's own human resources will provide important information. Finally, after a program is established through this process, community monitoring will be more effective because of the close involvement of the community in the initial process and the school-community trust which has been established. The stages outlined as they are by Brisk suggest a long-term planning effort, but as she points out, well-known successful programs such as Coral Way in Florida, Rough Rock in Arizona, and Oyster School in Washington, D.C., were all preceded by a lengthy planning effort on the part of the community. While many more programs were started from scratch in the 1960s and 1970s than are being initiated today, the 1980s is a period of revision and evaluation of programs, and Brisk's stages could be seen in a cyclic manner—first resurveying needs, second reformulating goals, and finally addressing new technical issues.

In the process of monitoring and improving programs, myriad decisions have to be made, and management strategies which have proved successful in other contexts can sometimes be modified for use in the school context. Ochoa (1979) provides a variety of suggestions for effective community participation in school policy. One helpful hint for community members as they survey the complexity of an established school program is to identify one problem or weakness which can realistically be ameliorated—such an issue as racial conflict, coordinating community resources, improving materials for LEP students, or improving school achievement. By focusing in on and tackling one tangible concern at a time, the community is more likely to produce actual changes. The steps involved in implementing changes can be modeled after the sequence used by the Institute for Cultural Pluralism as it provided training for community bilingual steering committees:

1. Formulate the issue.

2. Set objectives for dealing with the issue.

3. Determine all the environmental criteria which impact on the issue.

4. Analyze resources and constraints.

5. Develop alternatives to resolve the issue.

6. Evaluate the alternatives.

7. Arrive at a consensus as to which alternative to follow.

8. Determine the compatibility of the alternative with other relevant guidelines.

9. Designate responsibilities and time line dates.

10. Implement the chosen plan.
    (Ochoa, 1979, p. 62)

Curriculum development is an area that often is handed over to professionals because it is felt that community members do not have the expertise to direct such an enterprise. However, there are established strategies which can be applied. Ochoa cites Leonard's Community Input Process for Curriculum Development, which teaches community participants a twelve-step curriculum-development method. Using this process, the members of the curriculum-development group know what questions to ask and are able to use the professional curriculum developer as a resource technician. As a result community participants become decision makers regarding the content of their children's education.

Padres de Babel, Inc., is an example of parent involvement in a program through training that focuses not only on parents but also on administrators and also provides opportunities for the participants to practice the ideas and strategies they have developed. A San Francisco Bay area project, Padres de Babel has two goals. One goal is to provide parents with the knowledge that they need to defend the rights of their family and to participate in educational activities which will enhance their children's achievement. Parents participate in discussions in such areas as leadership and the law, reinforcement of the primary language, and careers for bilingual persons. The other goal is to educate school principals of LEP students regarding cultural, linguistic, and pedagogical issues which affect the quality of service provided to language-minority children. An important aspect of the model, the aspect which takes it beyond discussion to action, is that participants develop a plan or specific goal for their school and make a commitment to implement activities designed to attain that goal (El proyecto Padres de Babel, 1980).

While most community efforts focus on a specific school or school district, the National Puerto Rican Task Force on Educational Policy is an example of an organizing group that reached out to the nationwide Puerto Rican community and expanded its concern for bilingualism beyond the formal classroom. Using a document that was widely circulated among educators, social scientists, lawyers, community groups, and community activists, the immediate goal of the task force was to implement a "mechanism for coordinated grass-roots discussion of the language options before us" (Bonilla, 1979, p. 210). After 2 years of discussion, a consensus on the goal of bilingualism was reached, but more significantly, a policy was formulated which "must project action in extra-school contexts and institutions in ways that are responsive to the richness of language events" (p. 209). In other words, the task force determined the need for bilingualism to be reflected not only in the classroom but also in such areas as professional and organizational life, in poetry, and in the theatre. The task force's conclusion echoes Fishman's contention, after observing private ethnic community–sponsored mother-tongue schools, that formal bilingual schooling most likely can be successful if it is part of a larger community in which bilingualism has an important integrative or instrumental function and is held in esteem (1980b). It might also be added that business can play an important role in such expanded community support for bilingual or ESL education. As Timpane (1984) notes, there are several factors which are currently directing the business community toward greater involvement in the improvement of education than had been the case in the 1960s or 1970s. Among these factors are the greater need for employees with complex skills and the ability to continually learn new skills, the need for more effective world competition, and the need for workers who understand people in all their diversity. Thus such business programs as adopt-a-school and direct grants to schools for improvement projects can potentially become partners with the schools in the expansion of bilingual or ESL education beyond the walls of the classroom.

In reviewing the role of the community in bilingual and ESL education, it becomes apparent that the scope of potential involvement is quite broad. A sample of the activities of a Title VII school-community coordinator in Washington, D.C., reflects the wide range of concerns (Collier, 1980, p. 193):

1. Survey schools for LEP students.

2. Facilitate the provision of social services and provide follow-up.

3. Visit schools for the placement of new students, transfers, and follow-up.

4. Visit homes.

5. Establish links with other community agencies.

6. Organize cultural and social programs for students.

7. Coordinate with adult education programs.

8. Coordinate workshops for staff, students, and community members.

The Mississippi Choctaw bilingual program is an example of a program in which the community is involved in all three roles that can characterize community participation: making decisions, providing resources, and developing parents' skills. First, the program grew out of the community's awareness of a need. As described by York (1979), the situation involved children who were diglossic; they could use Choctaw informally with family and friends but were unable to carry on discourse in Choctaw in formal situations such as public meetings. Realizing that this diglossia was harmful to community interaction, the community applied for and received a Title VII grant so that twelve Choctaw teachers could be certified and children's Choctaw as well as English skills could be developed. Parents were involved in decision making for the program through the advisory board and in the development of instructional materials. The results of a survey which indicated that most parents favored using both Choctaw and English in the school were published in the local paper. As resource persons, community members demonstrated crafts, music, and dance; told stories; and organized special events and activities. As learners the parents were involved in a variety of activities. They participated in literacy programs and learned the school orthography for Choctaw. They learned about the school curriculum and had opportunities to clarify conflicting values and goals. Some community members participated in a writers' workshop so that they could create Choctaw literature based on their experiences (York, 1979).

Such success stories do not just happen. They require careful planning, a supportive administration, informed and empathetic staff, collaborative parents and students, and a willingness of all concerned to work hard, experience joys and sorrow, and relax with partial answers to complex questions. Decisions affecting school governance and the status of professional educators versus laypersons are tough ones to make. They take a great deal of understanding and compassion regarding the conflicting issues surrounding all concerned. As earlier confirmed, details can make a difference. Ochoa (1979) provides a valuable list of suggested activities for parent involvement, interest, and support which begins to get at the specifics of home-school interdependence. Also of use may be Warden's (1979) list entitled "Critical Questions on Citizen Participation":

1. What is the purpose(s) of the citizen participation effort and who determines such purposes?

2. Who is to be involved and what strategies or tactics are to be employed?

3. What are the limitations, if any, placed on such participation efforts?

4. What are the personal benefits to be derived by the participants themselves and the community in general?

5. What are the implied criteria of "successful participation" and who determines such criteria?

6. What resources are available to support such efforts?

7. How will the relative functions of both lay and professionals be addressed?

8. If participation is to be linked to an agency or organization, where is it to be located in the organizational structure?

9. To what extent will the participants have access to decision makers?

10. What local conditions or factors need to be considered relative to the participation efforts?

The "community school" concept is perhaps the ultimate in home-school interdependence. As defined by Warden,

> The community school transforms the traditional role of the neighborhood school into that of a total community center. It provides a wide range of educational, social, recreational, cultural, and community problem-solving opportunities without restriction as to the people to be served, facilities to be utilized, or time of day. (1979, p. 11)

The concept may be traced to Dewey's educational philosophy, and the immediate history of the community school is traced to a movement in Flint, Michigan, in the 1930s to open the school playground for after-school recreation. Today there are over 5000 community schools operating under a much broader definition. Still, this number represents only about 6.5 percent of schools in the United States (Smith & Wiprud, 1983).

Although it is an essentially untapped resource, the community school holds great promise for increased interdependence between schools with bilingual or ESL programs and the communities they serve. Roberto Clemente High School in Chicago is one example of a school with a comprehensive bilingual program designed in conjunction with a community school concept. Smith and Wiprud (1983) report on a growing awareness of the value of community education in fulfilling the needs of immigrants and refugees. Effective community school programs for such populations have been established, for example, in Boston, Massachusetts, and Chula Vista, California. They have also been implemented in Minnesota, New Jersey, Florida, and Texas. Coordinated into the life of the local public schools, these programs—among other things—provide language, employment, and acculturation assistance and help to ease community tensions and heighten cultural awareness. Smith and Wiprud note that such programs can have a positive impact on the development of cultural pluralism within communities.

The power of the home-school partnership concept is evidenced by its ability to span the political spectrum. The so-called radical Saul Alinsky was an outspoken community organizer whose ideas spawned a variety of grass-roots problem-oriented organizations. In a quotation which can be applied to the education of language-minority children, Alinsky stated,

> To give people help, while denying them a significant part in the action, contributes nothing to the development of the individual. In the deepest sense it is not giving but taking—taking their dignity. Denial of the opportunity for participation is the denial of human dignity and democracy. It will not work. (1971, p. 123)

Within the more conventional context of contemporary school reform, in which a conservative, back-to-basics tendency can be discerned, the refrain for home-school cooperation can also be heard. As Seeley argues, although the current reform movement is focusing primarily on changes to be made within the school, expanded and improved home-school "partnership can be the secret weapon that will enable us to win the war on ignorance" (1984, p. 388).

To put it simply, parents and communities want the best for their children, and they pin great hopes on the school to enable their children to succeed in life. They may not always have the time, energy, self-confidence, or institutional understanding to demonstrate that concern in ways that the school will recognize, but language-minority parents, as any parents, do want a match between the quality of the schools and their own child's reality. When promises are not kept, frustration, anger, alienation, confrontation, cynicism, or withdrawal from the schools may occur.

School matters to these parents, and they do notice when academic scores plummet to the lower percentiles or are not up where they should be; when their schools lack the aesthetic characteristics of schools in mainstream-American neighborhoods; when teachers lose the sense that their work can really make a difference in the lives of their students; when some of their schools resemble maximum security prisons rather than gardens of the mind; when they as parents don't feel welcome in the schools; when their children sit in overcrowded classrooms; when they and their children are perceived as sociocultural pariahs rather than human beings functioning quite rationally within their specific contexts; when their children do not get into college because they have not been prepared to do so; when their children's education lacks enrichment on the grounds that such children need remedial work in reading, writing, and mathematics—not art, poetry, music, drama, social studies, calculus, and foreign languages; when their children are told that to get a good education they will have to be driven across town to areas in which affluent parents and children live; when their schools pay lip service to linguistic and cultural issues but in reality practice benign neglect.

The communication of expectations between parents and educators is seldom a one-way street, although most school communication is through rather formal channels and most parental communication through rather informal channels. Educators, parents, and students all impact and change each other in predictable and unpredictable ways. Social change, something that touches the lives of all of us in penetrating and unsettling ways, always involves "changers" and "changees." This means that parents, educators, and students all have to be recognized for what they are—caring and hating, intelligent and confused, idealistically inclined and pragmatic, assertive and nonassertive, punctual and nonpunctual, manipulated and semiautonomous, part culturally governed and part individualistic human beings who are constantly testing the waters to determine what to do next. And the dichotomies continue. The success and strength of home-school relationships in bilingual communities will depend on the locally appropriate balance regarding the following issues: (1) teachers' and administrators' needs to learn about community language use, resources, strengths, values, and desires versus parents' needs to learn about school procedures, pedagogy, and home reinforcement of academic development; and (2) the power of parents to determine the form and content of the school program based on community needs and values versus the power of the school to prescribe form and content based on professional expertise.

Earlier in this chapter we quoted Hechinger as saying that "American educators always courted danger and defeat when they ignored the impact of major cultural and social currents" (1977, p. 1). This means that if we want to have engaging and supporting working relationships with each other as parents, students, teachers, and administrators, we have to be in tune with each other's sometimes strident, sometimes soft, sometimes calm, sometimes anxious voices. (Yes, even in silence.) Ethnic parents, like all parents, will appreciate and help work toward community and school efforts which value their contributions, yield positive academic results, and encourage positive interpersonal and intercultural relationships.

RECOMMENDED READING

Andrew D. Cohen's *A Sociolinguistic Approach to Bilingual Education* (1975b) is a carefully designed and thorough evaluative study of a bilingual community, its residents, and the functions of both English and Spanish in their lives. This study provides an excellent example of a detailed analysis of language use and attitudes in the community.

Virginia P. Collier's doctoral dissertation, "A Sociological Case Study of Bilingual Education and Its Effects on the Schools and the Community" (1980), chronicles the complex evolution from 1970 to 1980 of the Washington, D.C., Bilingual Program and its impact on both the community and the schools. It presents an analysis of decisions and negotiations involving administrators, federal representatives, bilingual and monolingual teachers, counselors, students, and parents. The study suggests that the bilingual program served as a powerful unifying force in the life of the D.C. Hispanic community.

Ethnoperspectives in Bilingual Education Research, Volume I: Bilingual Education and Public Policy in the United States, edited by Raymond V. Padilla (1979), has one section which deals exclusively with the involvement of the community in bilingual education. The six articles cover such topics as language policy formulation, a case study of a bilingual community, community involvement and fiscal accountability, insights from sociolinguistic research, and citizen participation in ESEA Title VII programs.

Two publications by the National Clearinghouse for Bilingual Education—*Information packet: Parent and Community Involvement in Bilingual Education* (n.d.) and *Working with the Bilingual Community* (1979)—provide useful information and resources dealing with bilingual education and community involvement. The first publication includes a legislative summary, funding sources, relevant journal article reprints, a bibliography, and references on materials, organizations, associations, and institutions. The second volume consists of five valuable and diverse pieces focusing on crucial aspects of community participation in bilingual education.

Although not a publication directly focused on bilingual or ESL education, John W. Warden's *Citizen Participation* (1979) is a succinct and useful overview of such community involvement modes as Alinsky organizations, citizen advisory committees, community audio and video access, community development corporations, community resource-information centers, community schools, neighborhood associations, and parent involvement councils. It also provides a summary of quotations from researchers, theorists, and practitioners on community involvement.

REFERENCES

Adler, P. S. (1972). Beyond cultural identity: Reflections on cultural and multicultural man. In L. Samovar & R. Porter (Eds.), *Intercultural communication: A reader* (pp. 362–380). Belmont, CA: Wadsworth.

Aguirre, A., Jr. (1980). The sociolinguistic survey in bilingual education: A case study of a bilingual community. In R. V. Padilla (Ed.), *Ethnoperspectives in bilingual education research, Vol. 2: Theory in bilingual education* (pp. 47–61). Ypsilanti, MI: Eastern Michigan University.

Aiken, L. R. (1972). *Language factors in learning mathematics*. Columbus, OH: ERIC Information Analysis Center for Science, Mathematics, and Environmental Education. (ERIC Document Reproduction Service No. ED 068 340).

Alinsky, S. D. (1971). *Rules for radicals*. New York: Random House.

Almaraz, F. D. (1979). Social studies: A curricular cornerstone in bilingual education. In H. T. Trueba & C. Barnett-Mizrahi (Eds.), *Bilingual multicultural education and the professional* (pp. 300–318). Rowley, MA: Newbury House.

Andersson, T. (1975). Extending bilingual education into the home. *Foreign Language Annals, 8*(4), 302–305.

Andersson, T. (1981). *A guide to family reading in two languages: The preschool years*. Rosslyn, VA: National Clearinghouse for Bilingual Education.

Andersson, T., & Boyer, M. (Eds.). (1970). *Bilingual schooling in the United States* (1st ed., Vols. 1–2). Washington, DC: Government Printing Office.

Andersson, T., & Boyer, M. (Eds.). (1978). *Bilingual schooling in the United States* (2nd ed.). Austin, TX: National Educational Laboratory Publishers.

Anick, C. M., Carpenter, T. P., & Smith, C. (1981). Minorities and mathematics: Report from the National Assessment of Educational Progress. *The Mathematics Teacher, 74*, 560–566.

Arvizu v. Waco Independent School District, 373 F. Supp. 1264 (W.D. Tex. 1973), *aff'd in part, rev'd in part, and remanded*, 495 F.2d 499 (5th Cir. 1974).

311

Asher, J. J. (1977). *Learning another language through actions: The complete teacher's guide*. Los Gatos, CA: Sky Oaks Productions.

Ashton, B. (1979). A practical reading course for the slow learner in high school. In H. T. Trueba & C. Barnett-Mizrahi (Eds.), *Bilingual multicultural education and the professional* (pp. 289–294). Rowley, MA: Newbury House.

Ashton-Warner, S. (1963). *Teacher*. New York: Simon & Schuster.

Aspira of New York v. Board of Education of the City of New York, 72 Civ. 4002 (S.D.N.Y., consent decree, August 29, 1974), 394 F. Supp. 1161 (S.D.N.Y. 1975), 423 F. Supp. 647 (S.D.N.Y. 1976).

Associated Press. (1978, August 25). Crisis in Quebec cited as Hayakawa opposes U.S. bilingual program. *Philadelphia Inquirier*, p. 12A.

Ausubel, D. P. (1964). How reversible are the cognitive and motivational effects of cultural deprivation? Implications for teaching the culturally deprived child. *Urban Education, 1*, 16–38.

Baca, L. M., & Cervantes, H. T. (1984). *The bilingual special education interface*. St. Louis: Times Mirror/Mosby.

Baecher, R. E. (1976). Bilingual children and educational cognitive style analysis. In A. Simões, Jr. (Ed.), *The bilingual child* (pp. 41–61). New York: Academic Press.

Baecher, R. E. (1981). Matching the cognitive styles of bilingual students. In R. V. Padilla (Ed.), *Ethnoperspectives in bilingual education research, Vol. 3: Bilingual education technology* (pp. 321–348). Ypsilanti, MI: Eastern Michigan University.

Bancroft, W. J. (1978). The Lozanov method and its American adaptations. *Modern Language Journal, 62*, 167–174.

Banks, J. A. (1984). *Teaching strategies for ethnic studies* (3rd ed.). Boston: Allyn & Bacon.

Barker, G. C. (1975). Social functions of language in a Mexican-American community. In E. Hernández-Chávez, A. D. Cohen, & A. F. Beltramo (Eds.), *El lenguaje de los chicanos* (pp. 183–201). Arlington, VA: Center for Applied Linguistics.

Barkin, F., Brandt, E. A., & Ornstein-Galicia, J. (Eds.). (1982). *Bilingualism and language contact: Spanish, English, and Native American languages*. New York: Teachers College Press.

Barr, R. D., Barth, J. L., & Shermis, S. S. (1977). Defining the social studies. *National Council Social Studies Bulletin, #51*.

Barth, F. (1967). On the study of social change. *American Anthropologist, 69*, 661–669.

Begle, E. G. (1975). *Test factors, instructional programs, and sociocultural economic factors related to mathematics achievement of Chicano students: A review of the literature.* Palo Alto, CA: Stanford Mathematics Education Group, Stanford University.

Bell, T. H. (1981, February 2). *Press release: Statement by Terrel H. Bell, Secretary of Education.* Washington, DC: U.S. Department of Education.

Bell, T. H. (1982). *The condition of bilingual education in the nation, 1982.* Rosslyn, VA: National Clearinghouse for Bilingual Education.

Bem, D. (1970). *Beliefs, attitudes, and human affairs.* Belmont, CA: Brook/Cole Publishing.

Benavides, A. H. (1979). A midwestern bilingual community and its schools: An analysis of mutual images and interactions. In R. V. Padilla (Ed.), *Ethnoperspectives in bilingual education research, Vol. 1: Bilingual education and public policy in the United States* (pp. 212–228). Ypsilanti, MI: Eastern Michigan University.

Bensusan, G., & Carlisle, C. (1978). *Raíces y ritmos: Our heritage of Latin American music.* Flagstaff, AZ: Northern Arizona University.

Berelson, B., & Steiner, G. A. (1964). *Human behavior: An inventory of scientific findings.* New York: Harcourt, Brace & World.

Berger, P. (1967). *The sacred canopy.* New York: Doubleday.

Bernal, E. M., & Tucker, J. A. (1981, February). *A manual for screening and assessing students of limited English proficiency.* Paper presented at the Council for Exceptional Children Conference: The Exceptional Bilingual Child, New Orleans.

Biascoechea, P. (1980, March 18). *The transition team for Bilingual Education and Minority Languages Affairs.* Address delivered to the Forum on Bilingual Education, Washington, DC.

Bidney, D. (1968). Cultural relativism. In D. L. Sills (Ed.), *International Encyclopedia of the Social Sciences* (Vol. 3, pp. 543–547). New York: Macmillan.

Biemiller, L. (1982). White students score highest on SAT exams. *Chronicle of Higher Education, 25*(7), 1, 14.

Birdwhistell, R. (1970). *Kinesics and context: Essays on body motion communication.* Philadelphia: University of Pennsylvania.

Blair, R. W. (Ed.). (1982). *Innovative approaches to language teaching.* Rowley, MA: Newbury House.

Blatchford, C. H. (Ed.). (1982). *Directory of teacher preparation programs in TESOL and bilingual education: 1981–1984.* Washington, DC: Teachers of English to Speakers of Other Languages.

Bloom, B. S. (Ed.). (1956). *Taxonomy of educational objectives: The classification of educational goals, Handbook I: Cognitive domain.* New York: Longmans, Green & Company.

Bloomfield, L. (1933). *Language.* New York: Holt.

Blumer, H. (1969). *Symbolic interactionism.* Englewood Cliffs, NJ: Prentice-Hall.

Boehm, A. E. (1971). *The Boehm Test of Basic Concepts.* New York: Psychological Corporation.

Bond, J. T., Epstein, A. S., Matz, R. D., & Cazden, C. B. (1977). Methods for assessing the language production of the young child. *Anthropology Education Quarterly, 8,* 84–86.

Bonilla, F. (1979). Toward a language policy for Puerto Ricans in the United States: An agenda for a community in movement. In R. V. Padilla (Ed.), *Ethnoperspectives in bilingual education research, Vol. 1: Bilingual education and public policy in the United States* (pp. 205–211). Ypsilanti, MI: Eastern Michigan University.

Bradley v. Milliken, 402 F. Supp. 1096 (E.D. Mich. 1975).

Brière, E. J. (1972). Are we really measuring proficiency with our foreign language tests? In B. Spolsky (Ed.), *The language education of minority children* (pp. 182–192). Rowley, MA: Newbury House.

Brière, E. J. (Ed.). (1979a). *Language development in a bilingual setting.* Los Angeles: National Evaluation, Dissemination, and Assessment Center, California State University, Los Angeles.

Brière, E. J. (1979b). Testing communicative language proficiency. In R. Silverstein (Ed.), *Occasional papers on linguistics, No. 6: Proceedings of the Third International Conference on Frontiers in Language Proficiency and Dominance Testing.* Carbondale, IL: Southern Illinois University.

Brigance, A. (1978). *Brigance Inventory of Early Development.* North Billerica, MA: Curriculum Associates.

Brigance, A. (1981). *Brigance Inventory of Essential Skills.* North Billerica, MA: Curriculum Associates.

Brisk, M. E. (1979). The role of the bilingual community in mandated bilingual education. In *Working with the bilingual community* (pp. 1–13). Rosslyn, VA: National Clearinghouse for Bilingual Education.

Brisk, M. E., & Wurzel, J. (1979). An integrated bilingual curriculum model. *NABE Journal, 3*(2), 39–51.

Broudy, S. (1977). Educational unity in a pluralistic society: An abstract. *Viewpoints, 53*(6), 1–3.

Brown, R. (1973). *A first language: The early stages.* Cambridge, MA: Harvard University Press.

Brown, R. K. (1979). Science teaching in the bilingual classroom. In H. T. Trueba & C. Barnett-Mizrahi (Eds.), *Bilingual multicultural education and the professional* (pp. 228–236). Rowley, MA: Newbury House.

Brown v. Board of Education of Topeka, 347 U.S. 483 (1954).

Brumfit, C. (1982). Methodological solutions to the problems of communicative teaching. In M. Hines & W. Rutherford (Eds.), *On TESOL '81* (pp. 71–77). Washington, DC: Teachers of English to Speakers of Other Languages.

Bruner, J. (1960). *The process of education.* Cambridge, MA: Harvard University Press.

Buros, O. K. (Ed.). (1978). *Eighth Mental Measurements Yearbook.* Highland Park, NJ: Gryphon Press.

Burt, M. K., Dulay, H. C., & Hernández-Chávez, E. (1975). *Bilingual Syntax Measure.* New York: Harcourt Brace Jovanovich.

California State Department of Education. (1981). *Schooling and language-minority students: A theoretical framework.* Los Angeles: Evaluation, Dissemination, and Assessment Center, California State University, Los Angeles.

California State Department of Education. (1984). *Studies on immersion education: A collection for U. S. educators.* Sacramento, CA: Author.

Canale, M. (1981). From communicative competence to communicative language pedagogy. In J. Richard & R. Schmidt (Eds.), *Language and communication.* New York: Longman.

Canale, M., & Swain, M. (1980). Theoretical bases of communictive approaches to second language teaching and testing. *Applied Linguistics, 1,* 1–47.

Cancian, F. (1968). Varieties of functional analysis. In D. Sills (Ed.), *International Encyclopedia of the Social Sciences* (Vol. 6, pp. 29–43). New York: Macmillan.

Cantieni, G., & Tremblay, R. (1979). The use of concrete mathematical situations in learning a second language: A dual learning concept. In H. T. Trueba & C. Barnett-Mizrahi (Eds.), *Bilingual multicultural education and the professional* (pp. 246–255). Rowley, MA: Newbury House.

Cárdenas, B., & Cárdenas, J. (1973). Chicano—Bright-eyed, bilingual, brown, and beautiful. *Today's Education, 62(2),* 49–51.

Cárdenas, R. (1970). Three critical factors that inhibit acculturation of Mexican Americans (Doctoral dissertation, University of California, Berkeley). *Dissertation Abstracts International, 32,* 661A–662A. (University Microfilms No. 71-20, 780).

Carew, J. V., & Lightfoot, S. L. (1979). *Beyond bias: Perspectives on classrooms.* Cambridge, MA: Harvard University Press.

Carpenter, L. K. (1983). Social stratification and implications for bilingual education: An Ecuadorian example. In A. W. Miracle, Jr. (Ed.), *Bilingualism: Social issues and policy implications* (pp. 96–106). Athens, GA: University of Georgia Press.

Carrasco, R. L. (1981a). Expanded awareness of student performance: A case study in applied ethnographic monitoring in a bilingual classroom. In H. T. Trueba, G. P. Guthrie, & K. H. Au (Eds.), *Culture and the bilingual classroom* (pp. 153–177). Rowley, MA: Newbury House.

Carrasco, R. L. (1981b). Review of *Chicano sociolinguistics: A brief introduction,* by F. Peñalosa. *Harvard Educational Review, 51,* 191–193.

Carrell, P. L. (1981). Culture-specific schemata in L2 comprehension. In R. Orem & J. Haskell (Eds.), *Selected papers from the ninth Illinois TESOL/BE annual convention* (pp. 123–132). Chicago: Illinois Teachers of English to Speakers of Other Languages/Bilingual Education.

Carrell, P. L., & Eisterhold, J. C. (1983). Schema theory and ESL reading pedagogy. *TESOL Quarterly, 17,* 553–573.

Carroll, J. B. (1961). Fundamental considerations in testing for English proficiency of foreign students. In *Testing the English proficiency of foreign students.* Washington, DC: Center for Applied Linguistics.

Carroll, J. B. (1973). Implications of aptitude test research and psycholinguistic theory for foreign language teaching. *Linguistics, 112,* 5–13.

Carrow, E. (1973). *Test of Auditory Comprehension of Language.* Austin, TX: Learning Concepts.

Casse, P. (1981). *Training for the cross-cultural mind* (2nd ed.). Washington, DC: Society for Intercultural Education, Training, and Research.

Castañeda v. Pickard, 648 F.2d 989 (5th Cir. 1981).

Cattell, R. B. (1940). A culture-free intelligence test, Part I. *Journal of Educational Psychology, 31,* 161–179.

Cazden, C. B., John, V. P., & Hymes, D. (Eds.). (1972). *Functions of language in the classroom.* New York: Teachers College Press.

Cazden, C. B., & Leggett, E. L. (1981). Culturally responsive education: Recommendations for achieving Lau Remedies II. In H. T. Trueba, G. P. Guthrie, & K. H. Au (Eds.), *Culture and the bilingual classroom* (pp. 69–86). Rowley, MA: Newbury House.

Celce-Murcía, M., & McIntosh, L. (Eds.). (1979). *Teaching English as a second or foreign language.* Rowley, MA: Newbury House.

Center for Applied Linguistics. (1977). *Bilingual education: Current perspectives, Vol. 1: Social Science.* Arlington, VA: Author.

Center for Bilingual Education, Northwest Regional Educational Laboratory. (1978). *Assessment instruments in bilingual education: A descriptive catalog of 342 oral and written tests.* Los Angeles: National Evaluation, Dissemination, and Assessment Center, California State University, Los Angeles.

Cerda, M. B., & Schensul, J. J. (1979). The Chicago Parent Leadership Training Program. In *Working with the bilingual community* (pp. 15–27). Rosslyn, VA: National Clearinghouse for Bilingual Education.

Cervantes, H. T., Baca, L. M., & Torres, D. S. (1979). Community involvement in bilingual education: The bilingual educator as parent trainer. *NABE Journal, 3*(2), 73–82.

Children, families, and the sea. (1982). Glendale, CA: Cypress Publishing.

Chu, H. S. (1981). *Testing instruments for reading skills: English and Korean (Grades 1–3).* Fairfax, VA: Bilingual Education Program, George Mason University.

Cintrón v. Brentwood Union Free School District Board of Education, 455 F. Supp. 57 (E.D.N.Y. 1978).

Clark, H. H., & Clark, E. V. (1977). *Psychology and language: An introduction to psycholinguistics.* New York: Harcourt Brace Jovanovich.

Clark, M., Kaufman, S., & Pierce, R. C. (1976). Explorations of acculturation: Toward a model of ethnic identity. *Human Organization, 35,* 231–238.

Clark, R. C., Moran, P. R., & Burrows, A. A. (1981). *The ESL miscellany: A cultural and linguistic inventory of American English.* Brattleboro, VT: Pro Lingua Associates.

Cocking, R. R., & Chipman, S. (1983). *Conceptual issues related to mathematics achievement of language minority children.* Washington, DC: National Institute of Education.

Cohen, A. D. (1975a). Assessing language maintenance in Spanish speaking communities in the southwest. In E. Hernández-Chávez, A. D. Cohen, & A. F. Beltramo (Eds.), *El lenguaje de los chicanos* (pp. 202–215). Arlington, VA: Center for Applied Linguistics.

Cohen, A. D. (1975b). *A sociolinguistic approach to bilingual education: Experiments in the American southwest.* Rowley, MA: Newbury House.

Cohen, A. D. (1976). The case for partial or total immersion education. In A. Simões, Jr. (Ed.), *The bilingual child* (pp. 65–89). New York: Academic Press.

Cohen, A. D. (1979a). Bilingual education for a bilingual community: Some insights gained from research. In R. V. Padilla (Ed.), *Ethnoperspectives in bilingual education research, Vol. 1: Bilingual education and public policy in the United States* (pp. 245–259). Ypsilanti, MI: Eastern Michigan University.

Cohen, A. D. (1979b). Second language testing. In M. Celce-Murcía & L. McIntosh (Eds.), *Teaching English as a second or foreign language* (pp. 331–360). Rowley, MA: Newbury House.

Cohen, A. D. (1980a). *Describing bilingual education classrooms: The role of the teacher in evaluation.* Rosslyn, VA: National Clearinghouse for Bilingual Education.

Cohen, A. D. (1980b). *Testing language ability in the classroom.* Rowley, MA: Newbury House.

Cohen, A. D. (1983). Researching bilingualism in the classroom. In A. W. Miracle, Jr. (Ed.), *Bilingualism: Social issues and policy implications* (pp. 133–148). Athens, GA: University of Georgia Press.

Cohen, A. D., Bruck, M., & Rodríguez-Brown, F. V. (1979). *Bilingual education series, No. 6: Evaluating evaluation.* Arlington, VA: Center for Applied Linguistics.

Cohen, A. D., & Laosa, L. M. (1976). Second language instruction: Some research considerations. *Journal of Curriculum Studies, 8,* 149–165.

Cole, M., & Means, B. (1981). *Comparative studies of how people think: An introduction.* Cambridge, MA: Harvard University Press.

Cole, M., & Scribner, S. (1974). *Culture and thought: A psychological introduction.* New York: Wiley.

Coleman, J. S. (1966). *Equality of educational opportunity.* Washington, DC: U.S. Department of Health, Education, and Welfare.

College Entrance Examination Board. (1977). *On further examination: Report of the advisory panel on the Scholastic Aptitude Test score decline.* New York: Author.

Collier, J. (1973). *Alaskan Eskimo education: A film analysis of cultural confrontation in the schools.* New York: Holt, Rinehart & Winston.

Collier, V. P. (1980). A sociological case study of bilingual education and its effects on the schools and the community (Doctoral dissertation, University of Southern California). *Dissertation Abstracts International, 41,* 2481A.

Comer, J. P. (1980). *School power: Implications for an intervention project.* New York: Free Press.

Condon, J. C., & Yousef, F. S. (1975). *An introduction to intercultural communication.* Indianapolis: Bobbs-Merrill.

Crawford-Lange, L. M., & Lange, D. L. (1984). Doing the unthinkable in the second-language classroom: A process for the integration of language and culture. In T. V. Higgs (Ed.), *Teaching for proficiency, the organizing principle* (pp. 139–177). Lincolnwood, IL: National Textbook Company.

Critchlow. D. E. (1974). *Dos Amigos Verbal Language Scales.* San Rafael, CA: Academic Therapy Publications.

Cruz, N., Jr. (1979a). Parent Advisory Councils serving Spanish-English bilingual projects under ESEA Title VII. In *Working with the bilingual community* (pp. 37–44). Rosslyn, VA: National Clearinghouse for Bilingual Education.

Cruz, N., Jr. (1979b). Roles, functions, and compliance of Parent Advisory Councils serving Spanish-English bilingual projects funded under ESEA Title VII. In R. V. Padilla (Ed.), *Ethnoperspectives in bilingual education research, Vol. 1: Bilingual education and public policy in the United States* (pp. 281–294). Ypsilanti, MI: Eastern Michigan University.

Cuéllar, J. B. (1980). A model of Chicano culture for bilingual education. In R. V. Padilla (Ed.), *Ethnoperspectives in bilingual education research, Vol. 2: Theory in bilingual education* (pp. 179–204). Ypsilanti, MI: Eastern Michigan University.

Cummins, J. (1976). The influence of bilingualism on cognitive growth: A synthesis of research findings and explanatory hypothesis. *Working Papers on Bilingualism,* No. 9 (pp. 1–43). Toronto: Ontario Institute for Studies in Education.

Cummins, J. (1979a). Cognitive/academic language proficiency, linguistic interdependence, the optimal age question, and some other matters. *Working Papers on Bilingualism,* No. 19 (pp. 197–205). Toronto: Ontario Institute for Studies in Education.

Cummins, J. (1979b). Linguistic interdependence and the educational development of bilingual children. *Review of Educational Research, 49,* 222–251.

Cummins, J. (1980). The entry and exit fallacy in bilingual education. *NABE Journal, 4*(3), 25–59.

Cummins, J. (1981a). Four misconceptions about language proficiency in bilingual education. *NABE Journal, 5*(3), 31–45.

Cummins, J. (1981b). The role of primary language development in promoting educational success for language minority students. In California State Department of Education, *Schooling and language minority students: A theoretical framework* (pp. 3–49). Los Angeles: National Evaluation, Dissemination, and Assessment Center, California State University, Los Angeles.

Cummins, J. (1982). Tests, achievement, and bilingual students. *Focus,* No. 9. Rosslyn, VA: National Clearinghouse for Bilingual Education.

Curran, C. A. (1976). *Counseling-Learning in second languages.* Apple River, IL: Apple River Press.

Dasen, P. (Ed.). (1977). *Piagetian psychology: Cross-cultural contributions.* New York: Gardner Press.

Dasen, P., & Heron, A. (1981). Cross-cultural tests of Piaget's theory. In H. C. Triandis & A. Heron (Eds.), *Handbook of cross-cultural psychology: Developmental psychology* (Vol. 4, pp. 295–341). Boston: Allyn & Bacon.

Davies, D. (Ed.) (1981). *Communities and their schools.* New York: McGraw-Hill.

Davis, A., & Eels, K. (1953). *Davis-Eels Test of General Intelligence or Problem Solving Ability.* New York: World Book Company.

Davis, K. J., & Klausmeier, H. (1970). Cognitive style and concept identification as a function of complexity and training procedures. *Journal of Educational Psychology, 61,* 423–430.

De Avila, E. A. (1978). *Research on cognitive styles with language minority children: Summary of pilot study design and data analysis.* Austin, TX: Southwest Educational Development Laboratory.

De Avila, E. A., & Duncan, S. E. (1979a). Bilingualism and the metaset. *NABE Journal, 3*(2), 1–20.

De Avila, E. A., & Duncan, S. E. (1979b). A few thoughts about language assessment: The Lau decision reconsidered. In H. T. Trueba & C. Barnett-Mizrahi (Eds.), *Bilingual multicultural education and the professional* (pp. 441–453). Rowley, MA: Newbury House.

De Avila, E. A., & Duncan, S. E. (1980). The language minority child: A psychological, linguistic, and social analysis. In J. Alatis (Ed.), *Georgetown University Round Table on Languages and Linguistics 1980: Current issues in bilingual education* (pp. 104–137). Washington, DC: Georgetown University Press.

De Avila, E. A., & Havassy, B. (1978). The testing of minority children: A neo-Piagetian approach. In H. LaFontaine, B. Persky, & L. Golubchick (Eds.), *Bilingual education* (pp. 381–384). Wayne, NJ: Avery Publishing.

De Luca, F. P. (1976). Research in science education. *News, Notes, and Quotes: Newsletter of Phi Delta Kappan, 20*(6), 3.

Deutsch, M. (1965). The role of social class in language development and cognition. *American Journal of Orthopsychiatry, 35,* 78–87.

de Villiers, P. A., & de Villiers, J. G. (1979). *Early language.* Cambridge, MA: Harvard University Press.

Diana v. California State Board of Education, No. C-70-37 R.F.P. (N.D. Cal., February 3, 1970).

Díaz, R. M. (1983). Thought and two languages: The impact of bilingualism on cognitive development. In E. W. Gordon (Ed.), *Review of research in education* (Vol. 10, pp. 23–54). Washington, DC: American Educational Research Association.

Diebold, A. R. (1961). Incipient bilingualism. *Language, 37,* 97–112.

Diebold, A. R. (1968). The consequences of early bilingualism on cognitive development and personality formation. In E. Norbeck, D. Price-Williams, & W. McCord (Eds.), *The Study of Personality* (pp. 218–245). New York: Holt, Rinehart & Winston.

Dieterich, T. G., & Freeman, C. (1979). *Language in education series, No. 23: A linguistic guide to English proficiency testing in schools.* Arlington, VA: Center for Applied Linguistics.

Donaldson, M. (1978). *Children's minds.* Glasgow: Collins.

Dow, P. B. (1972). If you were a baboon, how would your mother know you were hungry? *Natural History, 81,* 2, 22–25.

Dulay, H., & Burt, M. (1973). Should we teach children syntax? *Language Learning, 23,* 245–258.

Dulay, H., & Burt, M. (1978a). From research to method in bilingual education. In J. E. Alatis (Ed.), *Georgetown University Round Table on Languages and Linguistics 1978: International dimensions of bilingual education* (pp. 551–575). Washington, DC: Georgetown University Press.

Dulay, H., & Burt, M. (1978b). *Why bilingual education? A summary of research findings* (2nd ed.). San Francisco: Bloomsbury West.

Dulay, H, & Burt, M. (1980). The relative proficiency of limited English proficient students. In J. Alatis (Ed.), *Georgetown University Round Table on Languages and Linguistics 1980: Current issues in bilingual education* (pp. 181–200). Washington, DC: Georgetown University Press.

Dulay, H., Burt, M., & Krashen, S. (1982). *Language two.* New York: Oxford University Press.

Duncan, S. E., & De Avila, E. A. (1977). *Language Assessment Scales.* Larkspur, CA: De Avila, Duncan, & Associates.

Duncan, S. E., & De Avila, E. A. (1979). Bilingualism and cognition: Some recent findings. *NABE Journal, 4*(1), 15–50.

Education Development Center. (1969). *Man: A course of study.* Washington, DC: Curriculum Development Associates.

Educational Testing Service. (1970). *Manual for Peace Corps language testers.* Princeton, NJ: Author.

Engle, P. L. (1975). *Bilingual education series, No. 3: The use of vernacular languages in education: Language medium in early school years for minority language groups.* Arlington, VA: Center for Applied Linguistics.

Epstein, N. (1977a, June 5). The bilingual battle: Should Washington finance ethnic identities? *The Washington Post,* pp. C1, C4.

Epstein, N. (1977b). *Language, ethnicity, and the schools: Policy alternatives for bilingual-bicultural education.* Washington, DC: Institute for Educational Leadership, George Washington University.

Erickson, F. (1981). Some approaches to inquiry in school-community ethnography. In H. T. Trueba, G. P. Guthrie, & K. H. Au (Eds.), *Culture and the bilingual classroom* (pp. 17–35). Rowley, MA: Newbury House.

Erickson, J. G., & Omark, D. R. (Eds.). (1981). *Communication assessment of the bilingual bicultural child: Issues and guidelines.* Baltimore: University Park Press.

Evans, A. M. (1984). *Federal education programs serving students with limited proficiency in the English language.* Washington, DC: Congressional Research Service, Library of Congress.

Evans v. Buchanan, 416 F. Supp. 328 (D. Del. 1976).

Ferguson, C. A. (1959). Diglossia. *Word, 15,* 325–340.

Figueroa, R. A. (1980). Intersection of special education and bilingual education. In J. Alatis (Ed.), *Georgetown University Round Table on Languages and Linguistics 1980: Current issues in bilingual education* (pp. 147–161). Washington, DC: Georgetown University Press.

Fishman, J. A. (1966a). The implications of bilingualism for language teaching and language learning. In A. Valdman (Ed.), *Trends in language teaching*. New York: McGraw-Hill.

Fishman, J. A. (1966b). *Language loyalty in the United States*. The Hague: Mouton.

Fishman, J. A. (1976). *Bilingual education: An international sociological perspective*. Rowley, MA: Newbury House.

Fishman, J. A. (1977). The social science perspective. In *Bilingual education: Current perspectives, Vol. 1: Social Science* (pp. 1–52). Arlington, VA: Center for Applied Linguistics.

Fishman, J. A. (1980a). Bilingual education in the United States under ethnic community auspices. In J. Alatis (Ed.), *Georgetown University Round Table on Languages and Linguistics 1980: Current issues in bilingual education* (pp. 8–13). Washington, DC: Georgetown University Press.

Fishman, J. A. (1980b). Ethnocultural dimensions in the acquisition and retention of biliteracy. *Basic Writing, 3*(1), 48–61.

Fishman, J. A., & Lovas, J. (1970). Bilingual education in sociolinguistic perspective. *TESOL Quarterly, 4,* 215–222.

Flanders, N. A. (1970). *Analyzing teacher behavior*. Reading, MA: Addison-Wesley.

Flores, P., & Hendricks, S. (1984, February). *Raising children whose linguistic and cultural background is different from the common school setting*. Paper presented at the Alaska Bilingual Multicultural Education Conference, Anchorage.

Floyd, M. B. (1981). Language variation in southwest Spanish and its relation to pedagogical issues. In G. Valdés, A. G. Lozano, & R. García-Moya (Eds.), *Teaching Spanish to the Hispanic bilingual: Issues, aims, and methods* (pp. 30–45). New York: Teachers College Press.

Foley, B., & Pomann, H. (1981). *Lifelines*. New York: Regents.

Franklin, V. P. (1983). Ethos and education: The impact of educational activities on minority ethnic identity in the United States. In E. W. Gordon (Ed.), *Review of Research in Education* (Vol. 10, pp. 3–21). Washington, DC: American Educational Research Association.

Fredrickson, C. K., & Wick, J. W. (1976). *Short Test of Linguistic Skills*. Chicago: Department of Research and Evaluation, Chicago Board of Education.

Freire, P. (1970). *Pedagogy of the oppressed*. New York: Seabury Press.

Freire, P. (1981). The people speak their word: Learning to read and write in São Tomé and Principe. *Harvard Educational Review, 51,* 27–30.

Gaarder, A. B. (1971, November). *Language maintenance or language shift: The prospect for Spanish in the United States.* Paper presented at the Child Language Conference, Chicago.

Gaarder, A. B. (1978). Bilingual education: Central questions and concerns. In H. LaFontaine, B. Persky, & L. H. Golubchick (Eds.), *Bilingual education* (pp. 33–38). Wayne, NJ: Avery Publishing.

Gallimore, R., Boggs, J. W., & Jordan, C. (1974). *Culture, behavior, and education: A study of Hawaiian-Americans.* Beverly Hills: Sage Publications.

Galyean, B. (1977). A confluent design for language teaching. *TESOL Quarterly, 11,* 143–156.

Gamboa, R. (1980). Cultures, communities, courts, and educational change. In R. V. Padilla (Ed.), *Ethnoperspectives in bilingual education research, Vol. 2: Theory in bilingual education* (pp. 234–249). Ypsilanti, MI: Eastern Michigan University.

García, J. O. (1979). Bilingual education program fiscal accountability. In R. V. Padilla (Ed.), *Ethnoperspectives in bilingual education research, Vol. 1: Bilingual education and public policy in the United States* (pp. 229–244). Ypsilanti, MI: Eastern Michigan University.

Gardner, R. C., & Lambert, W. E. (1972). *The role of attitudes and motivation in second language learning.* Rowley, MA: Newbury House.

Gattegno, C. (1976). *The common sense of teaching foreign languages.* New York: Educational Solutions.

Gay, G. (1978). Viewing the pluralistic classroom as a cultural microcosm. *Educational Research Quarterly, 2*(4), 45–59.

Gay, J., & Cole, M. (1967). *The new mathematics and an old culture.* New York: Holt, Rinehart & Winston.

Geertz, C. (1973). *The interpretation of cultures.* New York: Basic Books.

Genesee, F. (1982). Psycholinguistic foundations of language assessment. In S. S. Seidner (Ed.), *Issues of language assessment, Vol. 1: Foundations and research* (pp. 31–35). Evanston, IL: Illinois State Board of Education.

Genishi, C. (1978). Language use in a kindergarten program for maintenance of bilingualism. In H. LaFontaine, B. Persky, & L. H. Golubchick (Eds.), *Bilingual education* (pp. 185–190). Wayne, NJ: Avery Publishing.

Ginsburg, H. (1978). Poor children, African mathematics, and the problem of schooling. *Educational Research Quarterly, 2*(4), 26–44.

Ginsburg, H. (1981). Social class and racial influences on early mathematical thinking. *SRCD Monographs* #193, *46*(6).

Glazer, N. (1981). Ethnicity and education: Some hard questions. *Phi Delta Kappan, 62,* 386–389.

González, E., & Lezama, J. (1976). The dual language model: A practical approach to bilingual education. In J. E. Alatis & K. Twaddell (Eds.), *English as a second language in bilingual education* (pp. 105–112). Washington, DC: Teachers of English to Speakers of Other Languages.

González, G., & Maez, L. F. (1980). To switch or not to switch: The role of code-switching in the elementary bilingual classroom. In R. V. Padilla (Ed.), *Ethnoperspectives in bilingual education research, Vol. 2: Theory in bilingual education* (pp. 125–135). Ypsilanti, MI: Eastern Michigan University.

González, J. M. (1975). Coming of age in bilingual/bicultural education: A historical perspective. *Inequality in Education, 19,* 5–17.

González, J. M. (1979a). *Bilingual education in the integrated school: Some social and pedagogical factors.* Rosslyn, VA: National Clearinghouse for Bilingual Education.

González, J. M. (1979b, May 7). *The future of bilingual program evaluation.* Address delivered to the National Association for Bilingual Education, Seattle, WA.

González, J. M. (1980, March 17). *A look at the 1970s and projections for the 1980s.* Address delivered to the Forum on Bilingual Education, Washington, DC.

Goodman, K. S., & Goodman, Y. M. (1976, April 13). *Learning to read is natural.* Paper presented at the Conference on Theory and Practice of Beginning Reading Instruction, Pittsburgh, PA.

Goodman, K., Goodman, Y., & Flores, B. (1979). *Reading in the bilingual classroom: Literacy and biliteracy.* Rosslyn, VA: National Clearinghouse for Bilingual Education.

Graham, C. (1975). *Jazz chants.* New York: Oxford University Press.

Gray, T. (1983). *Bilingual education legislation: A state perspective 1983.* Unpublished mimeo. Washington, DC: Center for Applied Linguistics.

Gray, T. (1984, April 27). *A comparative evaluation of immersion and foreign language programs.* Paper presented at the American Educational Research Association, New Orleans, LA.

Gray, T., Convery, S., & Fox, K. (1981). *Bilingual education series, No. 9: The current status of bilingual education legislation: An update.* Washington, DC: Center for Applied Linguistics.

Gray, T., & Potter, L. (1981). Student Placement System. *NABE Journal, 5*(3), 105–124.

Grimsley, E. (Ed.). (1983, May 13). With forked tongue. *Richmond Times-Dispatch,* p. A11.

Guskin, J. T. (1976). What the child brings and what the school expects: First and second language learning and teaching in bilingual-bicultural education. In A.

Simões, Jr. (Ed.), *The bilingual child* (pp. 237–252). New York: Academic Press.

Guskin, J. T. (1981, April). *Bilingual education community study: Implementing bilingual education in an urban midwestern context.* Paper presented at the American Educational Research Association, Los Angeles.

Guthrie, L. F., & Hall, W. S. (1983). Continuity/discontinuity in the function and use of language. In E. W. Gordon (Ed.), *Review of Research in Education* (Vol. 10, pp. 55–77). Washington, DC: American Educational Research Association.

Guzmán, J. (1978). Community conflict: A case study of the implementation of a bilingual education program (Doctoral dissertation, Oregon State University). *Dissertation Abstracts International, 39,* 1465A.

Hall, E. J., & Costinett, S. (1971). *Orientation in American English.* Washington, DC: Institute of Modern Languages.

Hall, E. T. (1959). *The silent language.* New York: Doubleday.

Hall, E. T. (1976). *Beyond culture.* New York: Anchor Press.

Halliday, M. A. K., & Strevens, P. (1964). *The linguistic sciences and language teaching.* London: Longmans, Green.

Halverson, C. (1979). Individual and cultural determinants of self-directed learning ability: Straddling an instructional dilemma. In D. Della-Dora and L. Blanchard (Eds.), *Moving toward self-directed learning* (pp. 53–65). Alexandria, VA: Association for Supervision and Curriculum Development.

Handlin, O. (1951). *The uprooted: The epic story of the great migration that made the American people.* Boston: Little, Brown.

Hansegård, N. E. (1968). *Tvåspråkighet eller halvspråkighet.* (Bilingualism or semilingualism?) Stockholm: Aldus/Bonniers.

Hansen-Krening, N. (1981). Language experience for the bilingual child. In *Proceedings of the Eighth Annual International Bilingual Bicultural Education Conference* (pp. 193–202). Rosslyn, VA: National Clearinghouse for Bilingual Education.

Hansen-Krening, N. (1982). *Language experiences for all students.* Reading, MA: Addison-Wesley.

Hatch, E. R. (1977). Second language learning. In *Bilingual education: Current perspectives, Vol. 2: Linguistics* (pp. 60–86). Arlington, VA: Center for Applied Linguistics.

Haugen, E. (1969). *The Norwegian language in America: A study in bilingual behavior* (2nd ed.). Bloomington, IN: Indiana University Press.

Havighurst, R. J. (1978). Structural aspects of education and cultural pluralism. *Educational Research Quarterly, 2*(4), 5–19.

Hechinger, F. M. (1977). The American culture as educator. In K. H. Hansen

(Ed.), *Beyond the school: What else educates?* (pp. 1–7). Washington, DC: Council of Chief State School Officers.

Hechinger, F. M. (1978). Political issues in education: Reflections and directions. In W. I. Israel (Ed.), *Political issues in education* (pp. 127–135). Washington, DC: Council of Chief State School Officers.

Heller, C. S. (1968). *Mexican-American youth: Forgotten youth at the crossroads.* New York: Random House.

Herbert, C. H. (1977). *Basic Inventory of Natural Language.* San Bernardino, CA: CHECpoint Systems.

Hernández-Chávez, E. (1977). Meaningful bilingual-bicultural education: A fairytale. *NABE Journal, 1*(3), 49–54.

Hernández-Chávez, E., Burt, M., & Dulay, H. (1978). Language dominance and proficiency testing: Some general considerations. *NABE Journal, 3*(1), 41–54.

Herrnstein, R. J. (1971). I.Q. *The Atlantic, 228*(3), 43–64.

Herschenhorn, S. (1979). Teaching listening comprehension using live language. In M. Celce-Murcía & L. McIntosh (Eds.), *Teaching English as a second or foreign language* (pp. 65–73). Rowley, MA: Newbury House.

Hill, J. E. (1972). *The educational sciences.* Bloomfield Hills, MI: Oakland Community College Press.

Hoffman, D., & Rich, S. (1983, August 14). Bilingual instruction endorsed. *The Washington Post,* pp. A1, A7.

Hooker, C. P. (1978). Issues in school desegregation litigation. In C. P. Hooker (Ed.), *The courts and education* (Part I, pp. 84–115). Chicago: University of Chicago Press.

Hsu, F. L. K. (1969). *The study of literate civilizations.* New York: Holt, Rinehart & Winston.

Hymes, D. (1979). Ethnographic monitoring. In E. J. Brière (Ed.), *Language development in a bilingual setting* (pp. 73–88). Los Angeles: National Evaluation, Dissemination, and Assessment Center, California State University, Los Angeles.

Iiams, T. M. (1976). Assessing the scholastic achievement and cognitive development of bilingual and monolingual children. In A. Simões, Jr. (Ed.), *The bilingual child* (pp. 253–265). New York: Academic Press.

Ilpola, P. (1979). Australian suomalainen arvostettu: Kieliolotkin kohentumassa (The Finns in Australia rated highly). *Suomi Silta, 2,* 8–9.

Ilyin, D. (1976). *Ilyin Oral Interview.* Rowley, MA: Newbury House.

Jackson, G., & Cosca, C. (1974). The inequality of educational opportunity in the southwest: An observational study of ethnically mixed classrooms. *American Educational Research Journal, 10,* 219–229.

Jackson, P. W. (1968). *Life in classrooms.* New York: Holt, Rinehart & Winston.

Jacobson, R. (1979). Can bilingual teaching techniques reflect bilingual community behaviors? In R. V. Padilla (Ed.), *Ethnoperspectives in bilingual education research, Vol. 1: Bilingual education and public policy in the United States* (pp. 483–497). Ypsilanti, MI: Eastern Michigan University.

Jacobson, R. (1981). The implementation of a bilingual instruction model: The *new* concurrent approach. In R. V. Padilla (Ed.), *Ethnoperspectives in bilingual education research, Vol. 3: Bilingual education technology* (pp. 14–29). Ypsilanti, MI: Eastern Michigan University.

James, P. (1975). *James Language Dominance Test* (2nd ed.). Austin, TX: Learning Concepts.

Jensen, A. R. (1969). How much can we boost I.Q. and scholastic achievement? *Harvard Educational Review, 39,* 1–123.

Jensen, A. R. (1974). How biased are culture-loaded tests? *Genetic Psychology Monographs, 90,* 185–244.

Jensen, A. R. (1980). *Bias in mental testing.* New York: Free Press.

Johnson, P. (1981). Effects on reading comprehension of language complexity and cultural background of a text. *TESOL Quarterly, 15,* 169–181.

Johnson, P. (1982). Effects on reading comprehension of building background knowledge. *TESOL Quarterly, 16,* 503–516.

Jones, R. L., & Spolsky, B. (Eds.). (1975). *Testing language proficiency.* Arlington, VA: Center for Applied Linguistics.

Joos, M. (1962). The five clocks. *International Journal of Applied Linguistics, 28*(22), Part 2V.

Jordan, C. (1977, November). *A multidisciplinary approach to research in education: The Kamehameha Early Education Program* (Technical Report No. 81), Symposium delivered at the American Anthropological Association, Houston.

Jordan, C. (1984). Cultural compatibility and the education of Hawaiian children: Implications for mainland educators. *Educational Research Quarterly, 8*(4), 59–71.

Kaufman, A. S., & Kaufman, N. L. (1983). *Kaufman Assessment Battery for Children.* Circle Pines, MN: American Guidance Service.

Keller, G. D., & Van Hooft, K. S. (1982). A chronology of bilingualism and bilingual education in the United States. In J. A. Fishman & G. D. Keller (Eds.), *Bilingual education for Hispanic students in the United States* (pp. 3–19). New York: Teachers College Press.

Kennedy, G. (1972). The language of tests for young children. In B. Spolsky (Ed.), *The language education of minority children* (pp. 164–181). Rowley, MA: Newbury House.

Kessler, C., & Quinn, M. E. (1980). Positive effects of bilingualism on science problem-solving abilities. In J. Alatis (Ed.), *Georgetown University Round*

Table on Languages and Linguistics 1980: Current issues in bilingual education (pp. 295–308). Washington, DC: Georgetown University Press.

Kimball, S. T. (1974). *Culture and the educative process.* New York: Teachers College Press.

Kirsch, J. (1981). *Tests and testing for bilingual children: A bibliography of literature.* Rosslyn, VA: National Clearinghouse for Bilingual Education.

Kjolseth, R. (1972). Bilingual education programs in the United States: For assimilation or pluralism? In B. Spolsky (Ed.), *The language education of minority children* (pp. 94–121). Rowley, MA: Newbury House.

Kleinfeld, J. S. (1979). *Eskimo school on the Andreafsky: A study of effective bicultural education.* New York: Praeger.

Klineberg, O. (1935). *Race differences.* New York: Harper.

Kloss, H. (1977). *The American bilingual tradition.* Rowley, MA: Newbury House.

Krashen, S. D. (1981). *Second language acquisition and second language learning.* Oxford: Pergamon Press.

Krashen, S. D. (1982). *Principles and practices in second language acquisition.* Oxford: Pergamon Press.

Krashen, S. D., Long, M. A., & Scarcella, R. C. (1979). Age, rate, and eventual attainment in second language acquisition. *TESOL Quarterly, 13,* 573–582.

Kroeber, A. L., & Kluckhohn, C. (1963). *Culture: A critical review of concepts and definitions.* New York: Vintage Books.

Kuhn, T. S. (1970). *The structure of scientific revolutions* (2nd ed.). Chicago: University of Chicago Press.

Kumar, V. K., & Treadwell, T. W. (1982, March). *"Culture-fairness" in testing.* Paper presented at the American Educational Research Association, New York.

Labor letter: A special news report on people and their jobs in offices, fields, and factories. (1980, September 2). *The Wall Street Journal,* p. 1.

Lado, R. (1961). *Language testing.* London: Longmans, Green.

Lado, R. (1982). Developmental reading in two languages. *NABE Journal, 6,* 99–110.

Lado, R., Hanson, I., & D'Emilio, T. (1980). Biliteracy for bilingual children by grade 1: The SED Center Preschool Reading Project, Phase 1. In J. E. Alatis (Ed.), *Georgetown University Round Table on Languages and Linguistics 1980: Current issues in bilingual education* (pp. 162–167). Washington, DC: Georgetown University Press.

Lambert, W. E. (1980). The two faces of bilingual education. *Focus,* No. 3. Rosslyn, VA: National Clearinghouse for Bilingual Education.

Lambert, W. E. (1984). An overview of issues in immersion education. In California State Department of Education, *Studies on immersion education: A collection for U.S. educators* (pp. 8–30). Sacramento, CA: Author.

Lambert, W. E., & Klineberg, O. (1967). *Children's views of foreign peoples.* New York: Appleton-Century-Crofts.

Lancy, D. F. (1983). *Cross-cultural studies in cognition and mathematics.* New York: Academic Press.

Lange, D. L., & Clifford, R. T. (1980). *Language in education series, No. 24: Testing in foreign languages, ESL, and bilingual education, 1966–1979: A select, annotated ERIC bibliography.* Arlington, VA: Center for Applied Linguistics.

Lareau, A., & Benson, C. (1984). The economics of home/school relationships: A cautionary note. *Phi Delta Kappan, 65,* 401–404.

Latin American Music Review. (1980–1984). Austin, TX: University of Texas Press.

Lau v. Nichols, 414 U.S. 563 (1974).

Leakey, R. E., & Lewin, R. (1977). *Origins.* New York: E. P. Dutton.

LeCompte, M. D. (1981). The procrustean bed: Public schools, management systems, and minority students. In H. T. Trueba, G. P. Guthrie, & K. H. Au (Eds.), *Culture and the bilingual classroom* (pp. 178–195). Rowley, MA: Newbury House.

Legarreta, D. (1977). Language choice in bilingual classrooms. *TESOL Quarterly, 11,* 9–16.

Legarreta, D. (1979). The effects of program models on language acquisition by Spanish speaking children. *TESOL Quarterly, 13,* 521–534.

Legarreta-Marcaida, D. (1981). Effective use of the primary language in the classroom. In California State Department of Education, *Schooling and language minority students: A theoretical framework* (pp. 83–116). Los Angeles: National Evaluation, Dissemination, and Assessment Center, California State University, Los Angeles.

Leibowitz, A. H. (1971). *Educational policy and political acceptance: The imposition of English as the language of instruction in American schools.* Washington, DC: Center for Applied Linguistics.

Leibowitz, A. H. (1980). *The Bilingual Education Act: A legislative analysis.* Rosslyn, VA: National Clearinghouse for Bilingual Education.

Leibowitz, A. H. (1982). *Federal recognition of the rights of minority language groups.* Rosslyn, VA: National Clearinghouse for Bilingual Education.

Lemlech, J. K. (1984). *Curriculum and instructional methods for the elementary school.* New York: Macmillan.

Levie, D. R., & Adelman, M. B. (1982). *Beyond language: Intercultural communication for English as a second language.* Englewood Cliffs, NJ: Prentice-Hall.

Levy, G. (1970). *Ghetto school: Class warfare in an elementary school.* Indianapolis: Bobbs-Merrill.

Lewis, E. G. (1972). *Multilingualism in the Soviet Union.* The Hague: Mouton.

Lewis, E. G. (1978). Types of bilingual communities. In J. Alatis (Ed.), *Georgetown University Round Table on Languages and Linguistics 1978: International dimensions of bilingual education* (pp. 19–34). Washington, DC: Georgetown University Press.

Lewis, O. (1966). The culture of poverty. *Scientific American, 115*(16), 19–25.

Longstreet, W. S. (1978). *Aspects of ethnicity.* New York: Teachers College Press.

Lovett, C. J. (1980). Bilingual education: What role for mathematics teaching? *Arithmetic Teacher, 27*(8), 14–17.

Lovett, C. J., & Snyder, T. (Eds.). (1979). *Resources for teaching mathematics in bilingual classrooms.* Columbus, OH: ERIC Clearinghouse for Science, Mathematics, and Environmental Education, Ohio State University.

Lozanov, G. (1979). *Suggestology and outlines of suggestopedy.* New York: Gordon and Breach.

Lyons, J. J. (1983, January). Bilingual education: The past and the new year: A report from Washington. *NABE News, 6*(3), 1, 5–6, 11–12, 14–15.

Macbeth, D. R. (1974). The extent to which pupils manipulate materials, and attainment of process skills in elementary school science. *Journal of Research in Science Teaching, 77,* 45–52.

Mace-Matluck, B. J. (1982). *Literacy instruction in bilingual settings: A synthesis of current research.* Los Alamitos, CA: National Center for Bilingual Research.

MacKenzie, J. P. (1974, January 22). English aid in schools ordered. *The Washington Post,* pp. A1, A4.

Mackey, W. F. (1962). The description of bilingualism. *Canada Journal of Linguistics, 7,* 51–85.

Mackey, W. F. (1970). A typology of bilingual education. In T. Andersson & M. Boyer (Eds.), *Bilingual schooling in the United States* (1st ed., Vol. 2). Washington, DC: Government Printing Office.

Mackey, W. F. (1972). *Bilingual education in a binational school.* Rowley, MA: Newbury House.

Mackey, W. F., & Beebe, V. N. (1977). *Bilingual schools for a bicultural community: Miami's adaptation to the Cuban refugees.* Rowley, MA: Newbury House.

Macnamara, J. (1967). The bilingual's performance: A psychological overview. *Journal of Social Issues, 23,* 58–77.

Madsen, W. (1964). *Mexican-Americans of south Texas.* New York: Holt, Rinehart & Winston.

Maeroff, G. I. (1982). *Don't blame the kids: The trouble with America's public schools.* New York: McGraw-Hill.

Manna, S. Y. (1975). *An inquiry into community attitudes towards bilingual-bicultural education.* Unpublished master's thesis, University of California, Los Angeles.

Martin, A. V. (1982). Concept relationships: Helping the beginning student read English. In M. Hines & W. Rutherford (Eds.), *On TESOL '81* (pp. 97–104). Washington, DC: Teachers of English to Speakers of Other Languages.

Martínez, P. E. (1981, May). *Home environment and academic achievement: There is a correlation.* Paper presented at the National Association for Bilingual Education, Boston.

McCollum, P. A. (1981). Concepts in bilingualism and their relationship to language assessment. In J. G. Erickson & D. R. Omark (Eds.), *Communication assessment of the bilingual bicultural child: Issues and guidelines* (pp. 25–41). Baltimore: University Park Press.

McDermott, R. P., & Gospodinoff, K. (1981). Social contexts for ethnic borders and school failure. In H. T. Trueba, G. P. Guthrie, & K. H. Au (Eds.), *Culture and the bilingual classroom* (pp. 212–232). Rowley, MA: Newbury House.

McFee, J., & Degge, R. (1977). *Art, culture, and environment: A catalyst for teaching.* Belmont, CA: Wadsworth.

Mead, M. (1963). Socialization and enculturation. *Current Anthropology, 4,* 184–188.

Mead, M. (1978). *Culture and commitment* (rev. ed.). New York: Anchor Press.

Meadowcroft, J., & Foley, D. E. (1978). Life in a changing multi-ethnic school: Anglo teachers and their views of Mexican children. In H. LaFontaine, B. Persky, & L. Golubchick (Eds.), *Bilingual education* (pp. 84–88). Wayne, NJ: Avery Publishing.

Mehan, H. (1981). Ethnography of bilingual education. In H. T. Trueba, G. P. Guthrie, & K. H. Au (Eds.), *Culture and the bilingual classroom* (pp. 36–55). Rowley, MA: Newbury House.

Mell, C. L. (1982). The performance of Alaska native, black, and white seventh graders on three divergent structure of intellect factors (Doctoral dissertation, University of Southern California). *Dissertation Abstracts International, 43,* 1411A.

Mercer, J. R. (1979). *System of Multicultural Pluralistic Assessment.* New York: Psychological Corporation.

Mettler, S. (1983). Exercising language options: Speech into writing. *TESOL Newsletter, 17*(5), 1, 3–4.

Milk, R. D. (1982). Language use in bilingual classrooms: Two case studies. In M. Hines & W. Rutherford (Eds.), *On TESOL '81* (pp. 181–191). Washington, DC: Teachers of English to Speakers of Other Languages.

Mitchell, J. V., Jr. (Ed.). (1983). *Tests in print III: An index to tests, test reviews, and the literature on specific tests.* Lincoln, NE: University of Nebraska Press.

Mizell, M. H. (1979). Maintaining parent interest in Title I parent advisory councils. *The Urban Review, 11*(2), 81–87.

Mohatt, G., & Erickson, F. (1981). Cultural differences in teaching styles in an Odawa school: A sociolinguistic approach. In H. T. Trueba, G. P. Guthrie, & K. H. Au (Eds.), *Culture and the bilingual classroom* (pp. 105–119). Rowley, MA: Newbury House.

Moll, L. C. (1981). The microethnographic study of bilingual schooling. In R. V. Padilla (Ed.), *Ethnoperspectives in bilingual education research, Vol. 3: Bilingual education technology* (pp. 430–446). Ypsilanti, MI: Eastern Michigan University.

Moore, A. (1967). *Realities of the urban classroom.* New York: Doubleday.

Morgan v. Kerrigan, 401 F. Supp. 216 (D. Mass. 1975), *aff'd,* 523 F.2d 917 (1st Cir. 1976).

Morine-Dershimer, G. (1983). Instructional strategy and the "creation" of classroom status. *American Educational Research Journal, 20,* 645–662.

Moskowitz, G. (1978). *Caring and sharing in the foreign language class: A sourcebook on humanistic techniques.* Rowley, MA: Newbury House.

Murphy, R. C. (1982). *Wet and wild: A bilingual supplementary marine education curriculum guide for teachers, grades K–6.* Los Angeles: National Evaluation, Dissemination, and Assessment Center, California State University, Los Angeles.

Muscatine, A. (1980, September 19). Hispanic leaders cheer as Carter defends bilingual education. *The Washington Star,* p. A1.

National Advisory Council for Bilingual Education. (1978–79). *The fourth annual report.* Rosslyn, VA: InterAmerica Research Associates.

National Advisory Council for Bilingual Education. (1980–81). *The prospects for bilingual education in the nation: The fifth annual report.* Rosslyn, VA: National Clearinghouse for Bilingual Education.

National Advisory Council for Bilingual Education. (1981–82). *The sixth annual report.* Rosslyn, VA: National Clearinghouse for Bilingual Education.

National Clearinghouse for Bilingual Education. (1979). *Working with the bilingual community.* Rosslyn, VA: Author.

National Clearinghouse for Bilingual Education. (1982a). *Guide to U.S. government departments and agencies, states, and private foundations that provide information and assistance to American Indians.* Rosslyn, VA: Author.

National Clearinghouse for Bilingual Education. (1982b). *Information packet on refugee resources.* Rosslyn, VA: Author.

National Clearinghouse for Bilingual Education. (1983). *Exploring strategies for developing a cohesive national direction toward language education in the United States.* Rosslyn, VA: Author.

National Clearinghouse for Bilingual Education. (n.d.). *Information packet: Parent and community involvement in bilingual education.* Rosslyn, VA: Author.

National Science Foundation. (1980). *Science education databook.* Washington, DC: Author.

Nielson, C. R. (1981). *Communication games for English as a second language.* Eugene, OR: Chinkapin Press.

Ochoa, A. M. (1979). Parental participation in bilingual education. In *Working with the bilingual community* (pp. 45–87). Rosslyn, VA: National Clearinghouse for Bilingual Education.

Ogbu, J. U. (1974). *The next generation: An ethnography of education in an urban neighborhood.* New York: Academic Press.

Ogbu, J. U. (1978). *Minority education and caste: The American system in cross-cultural perspective.* New York: Academic Press.

Oller, J. W., Jr. (1979). *Language tests at school.* London: Longman.

Oller, J. W., Jr., & Perkins, K. (1978). *Language in education: Testing the tests.* Rowley, MA: Newbury House.

Omark, D. R. (1981). Pragmatics and ethological techniques for the observational assessment of children's communicative abilities. In J. G. Erickson & D. R. Omark (Eds.), *Communication assessment of the bilingual bicultural child* (pp. 249–284). Baltimore: University Park Press.

Ortiz, A. A., & Yates, J. R. (1983). Incidence of exceptionality among Hispanics: Implications for manpower planning. *NABE Journal, 7*(3), 41–53.

Osman, A. H. (Ed.). (1983). Summary of legislation introduced in the 97th Congress of importance to JNCL/CLOIS (Joint National Committee for Languages/Council for Languages and Other International Studies) member organizations. *TESOL Newsletter, 17*(2), 5, 7–8.

Osman, A. H., & McConochie, J. (1979). *If you feel like singing: American folksongs and accompanying activities for students of English.* New York: Longman.

Otheguy, R. (1982). Thinking about bilingual education. A critical appraisal. *Harvard Educational Review, 52,* 301–314.

Ovando, C. J. (Ed.). (1978a). Cultural pluralism: Educational concepts, conflicts, and consequences [Special issue]. *Educational Research Quarterly, 2*(4).

Ovando, C. J. (1978b). Female and male Latino college aspirations: Implications for pluralistic education. *Educational Research Quarterly, 2*(4), 106–122.

Ovando, C. J. (1978c). Political issues in bilingual/bilcultural education. In W. I. Israel (Ed.), *Political issues in education* (pp. 101–115). Washington, DC: The Council of Chief State School Officers.

Ovando, C. J. (1983). Bilingual/bicultural education: Its legacy and its future. *Phi Delta Kappan, 64,* 564–568.

Ovando, C. J. (Ed.). (1984). Culture, language, and education in Alaska, Canada, Hawaii, Guam, Puerto Rico, Australia, and New Zealand [Special issue]. *Educational Research Quarterly, 8*(4).

Owen, D. (1983, May). The last days of ETS. *Harper's,* pp. 21–37.

Oxford, R., Pol, L., López, D., Stupp, P., Gendell, M., & Peng, S. (1981). Projections of non-English language background and limited English proficient persons in the United States to the year 2000: Educational planning in the demographic context. *NABE Journal, 5*(3), 1–30.

Padilla, R. V. (Ed.). (1979). *Ethnoperspectives in bilingual education research, Vol. 1: Bilingual education and public policy in the United States.* Ypsilanti, MI: Eastern Michigan University.

Paulston, C. B. (1976). *Teaching English to Speakers of Other Languages in the United States, 1975: A dipstick paper.* Washington, DC: Teachers of English to Speakers of Other Languages.

Paulston, C. B., & Bruder, M. N. (1976). *Teaching English as a second language: Techniques and procedures.* Cambridge, MA: Winthrop Publishers.

Peal, E., & Lambert, W. E. (1962). The relation of bilingualism to intelligence. *Psychological Monographs, 76,* No. 546.

Peñalosa, F. (1980). Chicano bilingualism and the world system. In R. V. Padilla (Ed.), *Ethnoperspectives in bilingual education research, Vol. 2: Theory in bilingual education* (pp. 3–17). Ypsilanti, MI: Eastern Michigan University.

Peng, S. S., Owings, J. A., & Fetters, W. B. (1984). *School experiences and performance of Asian American high school students.* Washington, DC: National Center for Education Statistics, U.S. Department of Education.

Peshkin, A. (1978). *Growing up American: Schooling and the survival of community.* Chicago: University of Chicago Press.

Peshkin, A. (1982). The researcher and subjectivity: Reflections on an ethnography of school and community. In G. Spindler (Ed.), *Doing the ethnography of schooling* (pp. 48–67). New York: Holt, Rinehart & Winston.

Philips, S. U. (1983). *The invisible culture: Communication in classroom and community on the Warm Springs Indian Reservation.* New York: Longman.

Piaget, J. (1929). *The child's conception of the world.* London: Routledge & Kegan Paul.

Piaget, J. (1954). *The construction of reality in the child.* New York: Basic Books.

Piaget, J. (1966). *The origins of intelligence in children.* New York: International Universities Press. (Original work published 1954).

Pifer, A. (1979). *Bilingual education and the Hispanic challenge.* New York: Annual Report of the Carnegie Corporation of New York.

Plann, S. (1977). Acquiring a second language in an immersion classroom. In D. Brown, C. Yorio, & R. Crymes (Eds.), *On TESOL '77* (pp. 213–225). Washington, DC: Teachers of English to Speakers of Other Languages.

Plata, M. (1982). *Assessment, placement, and programming of bilingual exceptional pupils: A practical approach.* Reston, VA: ERIC Clearinghouse on Handicapped and Gifted Children, Council for Exceptional Children.

Pletcher, B. P., Locks, N. A., Reynolds, D. F., & Sisson, B. G. (1978). *A guide to assessment instruments for limited English speaking students.* New York: Santillana.

Polgar, S. (1960). Biculturation of Mesquakie teenage boys. *American Anthropologist, 62,* 217–235.

Pope, J. (1977, November 7). Can a state learn French? *Mais oui,* a Louisianan believes. *The Washington Post,* p. A6.

Porter, S. (1978, August 11). Bilinguality is job insurance. *The Washington Star.* From "Your money's worth," courtesy of Field Newspaper Syndicate.

Porteus, S. D. (1937). *Primitive intelligence and environment.* New York: Macmillan.

Predaris, T. G. (1982). *Guide to state education agencies: 1981–82.* Rosslyn, VA: National Clearinghouse for Bilingual Education.

Prehm, H. J. (1966). Concept learning in culturally disadvantaged children as a function of verbal pretraining. *Exceptional Children, 321,* 599–604.

President's Commission for a National Agenda for the Eighties. (1980). *A national agenda for the eighties.* Washington, DC: U.S. Government Printing Office.

President's Commission on Foreign Language and International Studies. (1979). *Strength through wisdom: A critique of U.S. capability.* Washington, DC: U.S. Government Printing Office.

El proyecto Padres de Babel. (1980). *CABE Newsletter, 4*(5), 3.

Ramírez, A. G. (1980). Language in bilingual classrooms. *NABE Journal, 4*(3), 61–79.

Ramírez, M., & Castañeda, A. (1974). *Cultural democracy, bicognitive development, and education.* New York: Academic Press.

Read, J., Spolsky, B., & Neundorf, A. (1976). Socioeconomic implications of bilingual education on the Navajo reservation. In A. Simoes, Jr. (Ed.), *The Bilingual Child* (pp. 133–141). New York: Academic Press.

Reid, T. R., & Epstein, N. (1981, February 3). Administration scraps bilingual education rules. *The Washington Post,* pp. A1, A8.

Ricklefs, R. (1972, December 15). 'See Pepín Run': Bilingual instruction for minority pupils grows, stirs dispute. *The Wall Street Journal,* p. 1.

Ringawa, M. (1980). Cultural pedagogy: The effects of teacher attitudes and needs in selected bilingual bicultural education environments. In R. V. Padilla (Ed.), *Ethnoperspectives in bilingual education research, Vol. 2: Theory in bilingual education* (pp. 347–371). Ypsilanti, MI: Eastern Michigan University.

Ríos v. Read, 73 F.R.D. 589 (E.D.N.Y. 1977), 480 F. Supp. 14 (E.D.N.Y. 1978).

Rodríguez, A. M. (1980). Empirically defining competencies for effective bilingual teachers: A preliminary study. In R. V. Padilla (Ed.), *Ethnoperspectives in bilingual education research, Vol. 2: Theory in bilingual education* (pp. 372–387). Ypsilanti, MI: Eastern Michigan University.

Rodríguez, R. (1979). Citizen participation in ESEA Title VII programs. In R. V. Padilla (Ed.), *Ethnoperspectives in bilingual education research, Vol. 1: Bilingual education and public policy in the United States* (pp. 260–280). Ypsilanti, MI: Eastern Michigan University.

Rosier, P., & Farella, M. (1976). Bilingual education at Rock Point: Some early results. *TESOL Quarterly, 10,* 379–388.

Rosier, P., & Holm, W. (1980). *Bilingual education series, No. 8: The Rock Point experience: A longitudinal study of a Navajo school program.* Washington, DC: Center for Applied Linguistics.

Ross, E. A. (1914). *The old world in the new.* New York: Century Company.

Rotberg, I. C. (1982). Some legal and research considerations in establishing federal policy in bilingual education. *Harvard Educational Review, 52,* 149–168.

Rowe, M. B. (1974). Wait-time and reward as instructional variables, their influence on language, logic, and fate control. *Journal of Research in Science Teaching, 77,* 81–94, 291–308.

Ryan, W. (1971). *Blaming the victim.* New York: Pantheon Books.

Samovar, L. A., & Porter, R. E. (1972). *Intercultural communication: A reader.* Belmont, CA: Wadsworth.

Sancho, A. R. (1979). Parent and community involvement: Issues and recommendations. In H. T. Trueba & C. Barnett-Mizrahi (Eds.), *Bilingual multicultural education and the professional* (pp. 467–472). Rowley, MA: Newbury House.

Sandoval, J. (1979). The WISC-R and internal evidence of test bias with minority groups. *Journal of Consulting and Clinical Psychology, 47,* 919–927.

Santelices, A. C. (1981, May). *Actitudes de los padres hacia la educación bilingüe en una comunidad chicana.* Paper presented at the National Association for Bilingual Education, Boston.

Saravia-Shore, M. (1974). *The content analysis of 125 Title VII bilingual programs funded in 1969 and 1970.* New York: Bilingual Education Applied Research Unit, Project BEST, New York City Bilingual Consortium, Hunter College Division.

Saravia-Shore, M. (1979). An ethnographic evaluation/research model for bilingual programs. In R. V. Padilla (Ed.), *Ethnoperspectives in bilingual education research, Vol. 1: Bilingual education and public policy in the United States* (pp. 328–348). Ypsilanti, MI: Eastern Michigan University.

Savage, D. G. (1982, January 7). Math, science teacher shortage grows. *Los Angeles Times,* p. A1.

Savignon, S. J. (1972). *Communicative competence: An experiment in foreign-language teaching.* Philadelphia: Center for Curriculum Development.

Savignon, S. J. (1982). *Communicative competence: Theory and classroom practice.* Reading, MA: Addison-Wesley.

Saville-Troike, M. (1973). *Bilingual education series, No. 2: Bilingual children: A resource document.* Arlington, VA: Center for Applied Linguistics.

Saville-Troike, M. (1978). *A guide to culture in the classroom.* Rosslyn, VA: National Clearinghouse for Bilingual Education.

Saville-Troike, M. (1980). Cross-cultural communication in the classroom. In J. Alatis (Ed.), *Georgetown University Round Table on Languages and Linguistics 1980: Current issues in bilingual education* (pp. 348–355). Washington, DC.: Georgetown University Press.

Sax, G. (1980). *Principles of educational and psychological measurement and evaluation* (2nd ed.). Belmont, CA: Wadsworth.

Saxe, G. B. (1983). *Linking language with mathematics achievement: Problems and prospects.* Washington, DC: National Institute of Education.

Saxe, G. B., & Posner, J. (1983). The development of numerical cognition: Cross-cultural perspectives. In H. P. Ginsburg (Ed.), *The development of mathematical thinking* (pp. 291–317). New York: Academic Press.

Schafer, L. (1982). Native cultural contexts and formal education. In R. Barnhardt (Ed.), *Cross-cultural issues in Alaskan education* (Vol. 2, pp. 93–105). Fairbanks, AK: University of Alaska.

Schneider, S. G. (1976). *Revolution, reaction, or reform: The 1974 Bilingual Education Act.* New York: Las Américas.

Schorr, B. (1983, November 30). Grade-school project helps Hispanic pupils learn quickly. *The Wall Street Journal,* p. 1.

Secretary Bell encourages study of non-English languages in challenge to the states. (1981). *Forum, 4*(10), 1.

Seeley, D. S. (1984). Educational partnership and the dilemmas of school reform. *Phi Delta Kappan, 65,* 383–388.

Seelye, H. N. (1974). *Teaching culture: Strategies for foreign language educators.* Skokie, IL: National Textbook Company.

Seelye, H. N., & Wasilewski, J. (1979). Social competency development in multicultural students. LaGrange, IL: International Resource Development.

Seidner, S. S. (Ed.). (1982). *Issues of language assessment, Vol. 1: Foundations and research*. Evanston, IL: Illinois State Board of Education.

Seidner, S. S. (Ed.). (1983). *Issues of language assessment, Vol. 2: Language assessment and curriculum planning*. Evanston, IL: Illinois State Board of Education.

Serna v. Portales Municipal Schools, 351 F. Supp. 1279 (D.N.M. 1972), *aff'd*, 499 F.2d 1147 (10th Cir. 1974).

Sharp, L. (1952). Steel axes for stone age Australians. In E. Spicer (Ed.), *Human problems in technological change*. New York: Wiley.

Sheils, M., McGee, H., Harper, C. J., & Boyd, F. V. (1977, February 7). Teaching in English-plus. *Newsweek*, pp. 64–65.

Shuy, R. (1970). Some language and cultural differences in a theory of reading. In D. V. Gunderson (Ed.), *Language and reading*. Arlington, VA: Center for Applied Linguistics.

Sills, D. L. (Ed.). (1968). *International Encyclopedia of the Social Sciences* (Vol. 1). New York: Macmillan.

Silverman, R. J., Noa, J. K., & Russell, R. H. (1976). *Oral language tests for bilingual students: An evaluation of language dominance and proficiency instruments*. Portland, OR: Northwest Regional Educational Laboratory.

Simeone, W. E. (1982). *A history of Alaskan Athapaskans*. Anchorage, AK: Alaska Historical Commission.

Skutnabb-Kangas, T. (1979). *Language in the process of cultural assimilation and structural incorporation of linguistic minorities*. Rosslyn, VA: National Clearinghouse for Bilingual Education.

Skutnabb-Kangas, T., & Toukomaa, P. (1976). *Teaching migrant children's mother tongue and learning the language of the host country in the context of the socio-cultural situation of the migrant family*. Helsinki: Finnish National Commission for UNESCO.

Slaughter, J., & Bennett, A. (1981). *A sociolinguistic/discourse approach to the description of the communicative competence of linguistic minority children*. Paper presented at the Language Proficiency Assessment Symposium. Rosslyn, VA: InterAmerica Research Associates.

Smith, W. L., & Wiprud, H. R. (1983). Cultural diversity and advanced technology: A potentially symbiotic relationship in the context of the community. In D. H. Schoeny & L. E. Decker (Eds.), *Community, educational, and social impact perspectives* (pp. 175–190). Charlottesville, VA: University of Virginia.

Snow, C. E., & Ferguson, C. A. (Eds.). (1977). *Talking to children: Language input and acquisition*. London: Cambridge University Press.

Social Science Research Council. (1954). Acculturation: An exploratory formulation. *American Anthropologist, 56*, 973–1102.

Solá, D. F. (1980). FLEX: Cultural autonomy as a criterion in bilingual education. In R. V. Padilla (Ed.), *Ethnoperspectives in bilingual education research, Vol. 2: Theory in bilingual education* (pp. 205–217). Ypsilanti, MI: Eastern Michigan University.

Sowell, T. (1981). *Ethnic America: A history.* New York: Basic Books.

Spindler, G. (Ed.). (1982). *Doing the ethnography of schooling: Educational anthropology in action.* New York: Holt, Rinehart & Winston.

Spiridakis, J. N. (1981). Diagnosing the learning styles of bilingual students and prescribing appropriate instruction. In R. V. Padilla (Ed.), *Ethnoperspectives in bilingual education research, Vol. 3: Bilingual education technology* (pp. 307–320). Ypsilanti, MI: Eastern Michigan University.

Spolsky, B. (1977). The establishment of language education policy in multilingual societies. In B. Spolsky & R. L. Cooper (Eds.), *Frontiers of bilingual education* (pp. 1–21). Rowley, MA: Newbury House.

Spolsky, B. (1978a). Bilingual education in the United States. In J. E. Alatis (Ed.), *Georgetown University Round Table on Languages and Linguistics 1978: International dimensions of bilingual education* (pp. 268–284). Washington, DC: Georgetown University Press.

Spolsky, B. (1978b). Language and bicultural education. *Educational Research Quarterly, 2*(4), 20–25.

Spolsky, B., & Cooper, R. L. (Eds.). (1978). *Case studies in bilingual education.* Rowley, MA: Newbury House.

Staton, J. (1983). Dialogue journals: A new tool for teaching communication. *ERIC Clearinghouse on Languages and Linguistics News Bulletin, 6,* 1–2, 6–7.

Stern, H. H. (Ed.). (1963). *Foreign languages in primary education: The teaching of foreign or second languages to younger children.* Hamburg: International Studies in Education, UNESCO Institute for Education.

Stevick, E. W. (1976). *Memory, meaning, and method.* Rowley, MA: Newbury House.

Stevick, E. W. (1980). *Teaching languages: A way and ways.* Rowley, MA: Newbury House.

Stevick, E. W. (1982). *Teaching and learning languages.* Cambridge: Cambridge University Press.

Stewart, E. C. (1972). *American cultural patterns: A cross-cultural perspective.* Pittsburgh: University of Pittsburgh Regional Council for International Education.

Suárez, M. (1973). El hoyo. In L. O. Salina & L. Faderman (Eds.), *From the barrio: A Chicano anthology* (pp. 101–102). San Francisco: Canfield Press.

Swain, M. (1978). Bilingual education for the English-speaking Canadian. In J.

Alatis (Ed.), *Georgetown University Round Table on Languages and Linguistics 1978: International dimensions of bilingual education* (pp. 141–154). Washington, DC: Georgetown University Press.

Swain, M., & Canale, M. (1982). The role of grammar in a communicative approach to second language teaching and testing. In S. S. Seidner (Ed.), *Issues of language assessment, Vol. 1: Foundations and research* (pp. 45–52). Evanston, IL: Illinois State Board of Education.

Swain, M., & Lapkin, S. (1981). *Bilingual education in Ontario: A decade of research*. Toronto: Ontario Institute for Studies in Education.

System Development Corporation. (1981). *Preliminary report in the study of parental involvement in four federal education programs*. Santa Monica, CA: Author.

Teachers of English to Speakers of Other Languages. (1976). *Position paper on the role of English as a second language in bilingual education*. Washington, DC: Author.

Teachers of English to Speakers of Other Languages. (1979). *TESOL statement on statewide programs of competency testing*. Washington, DC: Author.

Teitelbaum, H., & Hiller, R. J. (1977a). Bilingual education: The legal mandate. *Harvard Educational Review, 47,* 138–170.

Teitelbaum, H., & Hiller, R. J. (1977b). The legal perspective. In *Bilingual education: Current perspectives, Vol. 3: Law* (pp. 1–64). Arlington, VA: Center for Applied Linguistics.

Teitelbaum, H., & Hiller, R. J. (1978). Trends in bilingual education and the law. In H. LaFontaine, B. Persky, & L. Golubchick (Eds.), *Bilingual education* (pp. 43–47). Wayne, NJ: Avery Publishing Group.

Terrell, T. D. (1977). A natural approach to second language acquisition and learning. *Modern Language Journal, 41,* 325–337.

Terrell, T. D. (1981). The natural approach in bilingual education. In California State Department of Education, *Schooling and language minority students: A theoretical framework* (pp. 117–146). Los Angeles: Evaluation, Dissemination, and Assessment Center, California State University, Los Angeles.

Terrell, T. D., & Krashen, S. D. (1983). *The natural approach: Language acquisition in the classroom*. Oxford: Pergamon Press.

Tharp, R. G., Jordan, C., Speidel, G. E., Au, K. H., Klein, T. W., Calkins, R P., Sloat, K. C. M., & Gallimore, R. (in press). Product and process in applied developmental research: Education and the children of a minority. In M. E. Lamb, L. Brown, & B. Rogoff (Eds.), *Advances in developmental psychology*. Hillsdale, NJ: Lawrence Erlbaum Associates.

Thernstrom, S., Orlov, A., & Handlin, O. (1980). *Harvard encyclopedia of American ethnic groups*. Cambridge, MA: Harvard University Press.

Thomas, L. (1975). *The lives of a cell*. Toronto: Bantam Books.

Thomas, W. P. (1980). *Incremental effects of ESEA Title I resources on student achievement* (Doctoral dissertation, Virginia Polytechnic Institute and State University). *Dissertation Abstracts International, 41,* 1945A. (University Microfilms No. 8024018).

Thonis, E. W. (1981). Reading instruction for language minority students. In California State Department of Education, *Schooling and language minority students: A theoretical framework.* Los Angeles: Evaluation, Dissemination, and Assessment Center, California State University, Los Angeles.

Tiedt, P. L., & Tiedt, I. M. (1979). *Multicultural teaching: A handbook of activities, information, and resources.* Boston: Allyn & Bacon.

Timpane, M. (1984). Business has rediscovered the public schools. *Phi Delta Kappan, 65,* 389–392.

Tirrell, P. B. (1981, December). *Innovative teaching in anthropology: New approaches for new students.* Paper presented at the American Anthropological Association, Los Angeles.

Tobeluk v. Lind, No. 72-2450 (3rd Judicial District, Anchorage; Superior Court, Alaska, 1976).

Toch, T. (1982). SAT scores improve slightly for the first time in 19 years. *Education Week, 11*(4), 1.

Troike, R. D. (1978). Research evidence for the effectiveness of bilingual education. *NABE Journal, 3*(1), 13–24.

Troike, R. D. (1982). Zeno's paradox and language assessment. In S. S. Seidner (Ed.), *Issues of language assessment, Vol. 1: Foundations and research* (pp. 3–5). Evanston, IL: Illinois State Board of Education.

Trueba, H. T. (1979). The Mexican-American family: The use of life history materials. In H. T. Trueba & C. Barnett-Mizrahi (Eds.), *Bilingual multicultural education and the professional* (pp. 149–156). Rowley, MA: Newbury House.

Trueba, H. T., & Barnett-Mizrahi, C. (Eds.). (1979). *Bilingual multicultural education and the professional: From theory to practice.* Rowley, MA: Newbury House.

Trueba, H. T., Guthrie, G. P., & Au, K. H. (Eds.). (1981). *Culture and the bilingual classroom: Studies in classroom ethnography.* Rowley, MA: Newbury House.

Trueba, H. T., & Wright, P. G. (1981). On ethnographic studies and multicultural education. *NABE Journal, 5*(2), 29–56.

Trujillo, A., & Zachman, J. M. (1981). Toward the practice of culturally relevant teaching. In R. V. Padilla (Ed.), *Ethnoperspectives in bilingual education research, Vol. 3: Bilingual education technology* (pp. 30–48). Ypsilanti, MI: Eastern Michigan University.

Tsang, S. L. (1982). Asian American education. In H. E. Mitzel, J. H. Best, & W.

Rabinowitz (Eds.), *Encyclopedia of educational research* (Vol. 1, pp. 171–173). New York: The Free Press.

Tucker, G. R. (1980). Implications for U.S. bilingual education: Evidence from Canadian research. *Focus*, No. 2. Rosslyn, VA: National Clearinghouse for Bilingual Education.

Tucker, G. R. (1983). Integrative remarks. In *Exploring strategies for developing a cohesive national direction toward language education in the United States* (pp. 1–5). Rosslyn, VA: National Clearinghouse for Bilingual Education.

Tyack, D. B. (1974). *The one best system: A history of American urban education.* Cambridge, MA: Harvard University Press.

Tyack, D. B. (1981). Governance and goals: Historical perspectives on public education. In D. Davies (Ed.), *Communities and their schools* (pp. 11–31). New York: McGraw-Hill.

Ulibarri, D. M., Spencer, M. L., & Rivas, G. A. (1981). Language proficiency and academic achievement: A study of language proficiency tests and their relationship to school ratings as predictors of academic achievement. *NABE Journal, 5*(3), 47–80.

United States Commission on Civil Rights. (1975). *A better chance to learn: Bilingual-bicultural education.* Washington, DC: U.S. Government Printing Office.

United States Office for Civil Rights. (1970, May 25). *Memorandum to school districts with more than five percent national origin–minority group children,* from J. Stanley Pottinger, Director. Washington, DC: U.S. Department of Health, Education, and Welfare.

United States Office for Civil Rights. (1975). *Remedies available for eliminating past educational practices ruled unlawful under Lau v. Nichols.* Washington, DC: U.S. Department of Health, Education, and Welfare.

United States Office of Education. (1971). *Programs under the Bilingual Education Act: Manual for project applicants and grantees.* Washington, DC: Author.

U.S. v. State of Texas, 342 F. Supp. 24 (E.D. Tex. 1971), *aff'd,* 466 F.2d 518 (5th Cir. 1972).

U.S. v. State of Texas, Civ. No. 73-3301 (W.D. Tex., August 1, 1973).

U.S. v. State of Texas, 506 F. Supp. 405 (E.D. Tex. 1981), *rev'd,* 680 F.2d 356 (5th Cir. 1982).

Valdés-Fallis, G. (1978). *Language in education series, No. 4: Code switching and the classroom teacher.* Arlington, VA: Center for Applied Linguistics.

Valdés, G. (1981). Pedagogical implications of teaching Spanish to the Spanish-speaking in the United States. In G. Valdés, A. G. Lozano, & R. García-Moya (Eds.), *Teaching Spanish to the Hispanic bilingual: Issues, aims, and methods* (pp. 3–20). New York: Teachers College Press.

Valdés, G., Lozano, A. G., & García-Moya, R. (Eds.). (1981). *Teaching Spanish to the Hispanic bilingual: Issues, aims, and methods.* New York: Teachers College Press.

Valencia, A. (1976). Bilingual/bicultural education: A prospective model in multicultural America. In J. E. Alatis & K. Twaddell (Eds.), *English as a second language in bilingual education* (pp. 301–312). Washington, DC: Teachers of English to Speakers of Other Languages.

Valencia, A. (1981). Cognitive styles and related determinants: A reference for bilingual teachers. *NABE Journal, 5*(2), 57–68.

Valentine, C. A. (1968). *Culture and poverty.* Chicago: University of Chicago Press.

Valentine, C. A. (1971). Deficit, difference, and bicultural models of Afro-American behavior. *Harvard Educational Review, 42,* 137–157.

Ventriglia, L. (1982). *Conversations of Miguel and María: How children learn a second language: Implications for classroom teaching.* Reading, MA: Addison-Wesley.

Vonnegut, K. (1974). Afterword. In M. Thomas (Ed.), *Free to be you and me* (p. 139). New York: McGraw-Hill.

Vygotsky, L. S. (1962). *Thought and language.* Cambridge, MA: Massachusetts Institute of Technology Press.

Vygotsky, L. S. (1978). *Mind and society.* Cambridge, MA: Harvard University Press.

Wabaunsee, A. J. (1977). Native American viewpoint. In *Bilingual education: Current perspectives, Vol. 3: Law* (pp. 65–70). Arlington, VA: Center for Applied Linguistics.

Wald, B. (1982). On assessing the oral language ability of limited-English proficient students: The linguistic bases of the noncomparability of different language proficiency assessment measures. In S. S. Seidner (Ed.), *Issues of language assessment, Vol. 1: Foundations and research* (pp. 117–124). Evanston, IL: Illinois State Board of Education.

Wallerstein, N. (1983). *Language and culture in conflict: Problem-posing in the ESL classroom.* Reading, MA: Addison-Wesley.

Warden, J. W. (1979). *Citizen participation: What others say . . . What others do . . . .* Charlottesville, VA: Mid-Atlantic Center for Community Education, School of Education, University of Virginia.

Waserstein, A. (1975). Organizing for bilingual education: One community's experience. *Inequality in education, 19,* 23–30.

Weinreich, U. (1953). *Languages in contact: Findings and problems.* New York: Linguistic Circle of New York.

West, E. (1972). *Family of man.* Minneapolis, MN: Selective Educational Equipment.

Whorf, B. J. (1956). *Language, thought, and reality*. Cambridge, MA: Massachusetts Institute of Technology Press.

Wilkins, D. A. (1976). *Notional syllabuses*. Oxford: Oxford University Press.

Williams, R. L. (1972). *The Black Intelligence Test of Cultural Homogeneity-100: A culture specific test*. Bethesda, MD: ERIC Document Reproduction Service. (ERIC No. ED 070 799).

Winn-Bell Olsen, J. E. (1978). *Communication starters and other activities for the ESL classroom*. San Francisco: The Alemany Press.

Witkin, H. A. (1967). A cognitive-style approach to cross-cultural research. *International Journal of Psychology, 6*, 4–87.

Witkin, H., Lewis, B., Hertzman, M., Machover, K., Meissner, P. B., & Wapner, S. (1972). *Personality through perception: An experimental and clinical study*. Westport, CT: Greenwood Press.

Wong-Fillmore, L. (1980). *Language learning through bilingual instruction*. University of California, Berkeley: Unpublished mimeo.

Woodcock, R. W., & Johnson, M. B. (1977). *Woodcock-Johnson Psychoeducational Battery*. Allen, TX: DLM Teaching Resources Corporation.

Woodford, P. (1982). Foreign language and bilingual assessment: Issues approaches. In S. S. Seidner (Ed.), *Issues of language assessment, Vol. 1: Foundations and research* (pp. 101–107). Evanston, IL: Illinois State Board of Education.

Yao, K. Y. B. (1979). Teaching science to bilingual children. *NABE Journal, 3*(3), 71–76.

York, K. H. (1979). Parent/community involvement in the Mississippi Choctaw bilingual education program. In *Working with the bilingual community* (pp. 29–36). Rosslyn, VA: National Clearinghouse for Bilingual Education.

Zirkel, P. A. (1977). The legal vicissitudes of bilingual education. *Phi Delta Kappan, 58*, 409–411.

Zirkel, P. A. (1979). A method for determining and depicting language dominance. In H. T. Trueba & C. Barnett-Mizrahi (Eds.), *Bilingual multicultural education and the professional* (pp. 383–390). Rowley, MA: Newbury House.

Zirkel, P. A., & Greene, J. F. (1976). Cultural Attitude Scales: A step toward determining whether the programs are bicultural as well as bilingual. In A. Simões, Jr. (Ed.), *The bilingual child* (pp. 3–16). New York: Academic Press.

Zoref, L., & Williams, P. (1980). A look at content bias in IQ tests. *Journal of Educational Measurement, 17*, 313–322.

INDEX

Acculturation, 108–109
"Acquisition" vs. "learning" of language, 59–61
Additive bilingualism, 64–65
Adult-education programs, 30
Advisory councils, parent, 292–295
Alaska:
  cultural relativism, perspective in, 121
Alternate-language approach in bilingual classroom,
    84–86
  in teaching mathematics and science, 209
Alternative ESL programs, 44
American Council on the Teaching of Foreign
    Languages (ACTFL), 51
American Educational Research Association (AERA),
    51
American Indians (see Native Americans)
"Americanization" policy toward immigrants, 24
Amish, 127
Analytic thinking skills, 161–162
Anthropological view of culture, 102–105
"Approach" to teaching language, definition of, 71
Archeology, teaching of, 221
Art in the bilingual and ESL classroom, 92, 184–187
Arvizu v. Waco Independent School District, 35–36
Asian-Pacific Americans, test scores among, 192–194
Aspira of New York v. Board of Education of the City
    of New York, 36
Assessment, 223–261
  instruments for, 251–256
    discrete-point language tests, 251–253
    pragmatic and integrative language tests, 254–
      255
    pragmatic tests combined with discrete-point
      tests, 253–254
    references on tests, 255–256
  issues in, 239–251
    bilingual special education, 246–248
    bilingualism, intelligence, and IQ tests, 243–246

Assessment, issues in (Cont.):
    cultural bias, 248–251
    language assessment, 229–231, 239–243
  purposes of, 224–239
    diagnostic prescriptive process, 232–235
    exit criteria, 235–236
    Lau Remedies, testing implications of, 225–229
    placement testing, 229–232
    program evaluation, 236–239
    teacher-constructed tests, 256–261
    vs. test, distinction between, 224–225
Assimilation of immigrants:
  cultural, 108–109
  and melting pot, 266, 271
  in nineteenth century, 24
Astronomy, teaching of, 220
Athapaskan Indians, 104, 121
Attitudinal assessment, 237–238
Attribute blocks, 211
Audiolingual (aural-oral) method of teaching L$_2$, 72–
    73, 90, 91

Bafa-Bafa, 173
Basic interpersonal communicative skills (BICS), 38–
    39, 63–64, 77, 204–205, 228, 241
Basic Inventory of Natural Language, 253
BEMSCs (Bilingual Education Multifunctional
    Support Centers), 28, 30, 48, 49
BICS (see Basic interpersonal communicative skills)
Biculturalism, 107–110
Bidialectalism, 70
Bilingual-bicultural education, 2n.
  (See also Bilingual-education programs)
Bilingual classroom (see Classroom, bilingual,
    methods of teaching in a)
Bilingual desegregation grants (1981–1984), 47
Bilingual education:
  future of, 23

Bilingual education (*Cont.*):
  in the nineteenth century, 24
  politics of (*see* Politics of bilingual education)
  resources in (*see* Resources in bilingual education
      and ESL)
  (*See also* Bilingual-education programs)
Bilingual Education Act of 1968 (Title VII of the
    Elementary and Secondary Education Act),
    26–28, 292
  amendments of 1974 and 1978, 27, 228, 292
  funding of, 26–27
  purposes of, 27
  support services and, 46–50
  training provisions in, 27–28
Bilingual Education Multifunctional Support Centers
    (BEMSCs), 28, 30, 48, 49
Bilingual-education programs:
  components of, 1–3
  definition of, 1
  evaluation of, 236–239
    attitudinal assessment, 237–238
    longitudinal studies, 238–239
    naturalistic evaluation, 238
    norm-referenced tests, 236–237
    (*See also* Assessment)
  federal funding of, 26–30, 47
  models for (*see* Models for bilingual-education
      programs)
  range of students in, 3–4
Bilingual Education Service Centers (BESCs), 28, 49
Bilingual-education teachers, state certification of,
    32–34
Bilingual Syntax Measure, 253, 254
Bilingual vocational training, 47
Bilingualism:
  additive vs. subtractive, 64–65
  definitions of, 66–67
  intelligence and, 243–244
Biliteracy, 94–95
  (*See also* Reading in L_1 and L_2, teaching)
Black English, 69
Black Intelligence Test of Cultural Homogeneity, 249
Blacks:
  Moynihan Report and, 115
  test scores among, 192, 193, 249
Block grants under ESEA, 29
Boehm Test of Basic Concepts, 252
Bradley v. Milliken, 36
Brigance Inventory of Early Development, 247
Brigance Inventory of Essential Skills, 247
Brown v. Board of Education of Topeka, 271–272

California:
  court decisions involving, 34–35, 245, 247
California State Department of Education, 1, 13, 43,
    55, 239
CALP (*see* Cognitive-academic language proficiency)
Cambodian-Americans, 122

Canada, bilingual education in, 42–43
  longitudinal studies of, 238
Caretaker speech, 59, 62–63
Cassettes, use of, 184
Castañeda v. Pickard, 36
Center for Applied Linguistics (CAL), 151
  headquarters of, 52
  services provided by, 51–52
Center for Bilingual Education, Northwest Regional
    Educational Laboratory, 255
Center for Science in the Public Interest, 99
Certification standards, state, for bilingual and ESL
    teachers, 32–34
Chamorros, 5
Chicago Latino Institute, Parent Leadership Training
    Program, 295
Chicanos (*see* Mexican-Americans)
Children, language acquisition by (*see* Language,
    acquisition of)
Children's literature, 97
Choctaw bilingual program, Mississippi, 305
*Cintron v. Brentwood Union Free School District
    Board of Education*, 36, 273
Civil Rights Act of 1964, 26
  Title IV, 30, 50
  Title VI, 225–226
Classroom, bilingual, methods of teaching in a, 80–
    90
  balance of two languages, 82–90
    alternate-language approaches, 84–86
    code-switching approach, 86–90
    concurrent approach, 82–84
    preview-review approach, 84
  program models, types, and design, 81–82
Clearinghouse (*see* National Clearinghouse for
    Bilingual Education)
Cloze tests, 242, 258–259
Code-switching:
  in bilingual classroom, 86–90
  definition of, 86–87
  intersentential, 87
  intrasentential, 87
  principal patterns of, 88–89
  "regressive", 87
  "Spanglish", 131
Cofigurative cultural transmission, 127
Cognitive-academic language proficiency (CALP),
    39, 63–64, 77, 97, 204–205, 228, 241, 246
Cognitive approach to L_2, 73–74, 90
"Cognitive deficit" theories, 196
Cognitive skills:
  monolingualism vs. bilingualism, 243–244
  research on development of, 195–206
Cognitive style:
  assessment of, 234–235
  and cultural background, research on, 133–138
Cognitive theory of culture, 143–144
College Entrance Examination Board, 191
  SAT scores and, 191–194

Color words, 198
Communicative competence, assessment of, 241–242
Community and school, interaction between, 263–308
    development and types of ethnic communities, 265–271
        characteristics of immigrant and indigenous communities, 267–271
        chronology of the status of ethnic communities, 266–267
    involvement by community, 289–308
        legislation for community participation, 291–292
        models and suggestions for, 300–308
        parents as mutual partners, 295–300
    legal cases, 271–274
    organization efforts, community, 274–276
    profiles of communities, 276–289
        informal community description and reflection, 283–289
        language use in the community, 277–280
        social relationship between school and community, 280–283
    teacher's reflections on the community, 286–288
Community Input Process for Curriculum Development, 303
Community Language Learning (CLL) of L_2, 75–76
Community-oriented tasks, use of, 92
Community school concept, 306–307
Composition tests, 259
Compound bilinguals, definition of, 82
Concerts (*see* Music)
Concrete operational stages of development, 197, 198
Concurrent approach in bilingual classroom, 82–84
    in teaching mathematics and science, 208–209
Congress (*see* Legislation, federal)
Constructive pluralism, 111, 267, 271
Consumer education, resources in, 171–172
Consumer skills, teaching writing and reading skills involving, 99
Context-embedded communicative proficiency (*see* Basic interpersonal communicative skills)
Context-reduced communicative proficiency (*see* Cognitive-academic language proficiency)
Contrastive analysis hypothesis, 65
Coordinate bilinguals, definition of, 82
Coral Way Elementary School, Miami, 26
Council on Anthropology and Education of the American Anthropological Association, 51
    1978 resolution on the role of culture in educational planning, 149
Court decisions on bilingual education, 34–37, 245, 247, 271–274
Criterion-referenced tests, 233–234
Cross-cultural education (*see* Multicultural education)
Cross-cultural research on cognition, 195–206
    and developmental stage theory, 196–200
Cuauhtemoc Home-Centered Bilingual Preschool, Redwood City, California, 299
Cuban Refugee Act, 26

Cuban refugees, 25–26
Cuisenaire rods, use of, 74, 212
Cultural awareness, instructional approaches to, 159–169
    interdisciplinary framework, 159–164
        MACOS, 162–164, 169
    teachers and students as cultural researchers, 164–169
    simulated cultural exercises, 165–169
Cultural background, cognitive style and, research on, 133–138
Cultural bias in assessment instruments, 248–251
    empirical research on, 250–251
    illustrations, 249
    IQ tests, 244
    item content, 248–249
    language of instructions, 249–250
    socialization, 249
    testing situation, 250
"Cultural deficit", 114–117
"Cultural deprivation", 114–117
Cultural difference, language variation and, 132–133
Cultural exercises, simulated, 165–169
    culture assimilators, 166
    culture capsules, 166
    culture clusters, 166
    minidramas, 166
Cultural mismatch, home-school, 132–133, 147–148
Cultural pluralism, 110–113
Cultural relativity, 119–121
Cultural researchers, students and teachers as, 164–169
Cultural stereotypes, 121, 124
Cultural transmission, 126–129
    cofigurative, 127
    postfigurative, 127
    prefigurative, 127–128
Culture, 101–152
    anthropological view of, 102–103
    biculturalism, 107–110
    in bilingual education program, 2
    "deficit, cultural", 114–117
    definitional problems, 101–102
    "deprivation, cultural", 114–117
    ethnicity, acquisition of, 126–129
    ethnocentrism, 119–121
    home-school mismatch, 132–133, 147–148
    language variation, 129–133
    marked and unmarked languages and cultures, 117–118
    pluralism, cultural, 110–113
    popular views of, 105–107
    relativity, cultural, 119–121
    research on education and, 133–149
        cognitive styles and cultural background, 133–138
        social interaction, 138–149
    role of, in shaping students, 5–6
    "set-of-traits" approach to, 106–107

Culture (*Cont.*):
  socioeconomic status and cultural background,
    124–126
  stereotypes, 121–124
  and teaching mathematics and science, 206–221
  transmission, cultural, 126–129
  Western civilization outlook on, 105–106
Culture assimilators, 166
Culture capsules, 166
Culture clusters, 166
Culture of poverty, 115
Czech, use of, in nineteenth-century classes, 24

Danish, use of, in nineteenth-century classes, 24
Defensive pluralism, 266, 271
"Deficit, cultural", 114–117
Del Pueblo Community School Project, Denver,
    Colorado, 299
"Deprivation, cultural", 114–117
Desegregation, school, legislation for, 30
Developmental stages theory, 196–200
Diagnostic-prescriptive process in assessment, 232–
    235
Dialects, 68–70
Dialogue journals, 98–99
Diana v. California State Board of Education, 245,
    247
Dictation tests, 242, 258
Diglossia, 278
Direct method of teaching L_2, 72
Discourse competence, assessment of, 240–241
Discrete-point testing in language assessment, 239–
    240, 251–253
  combined with pragmatic tests, 253–254
Discrimination, emotional adjustment to school and,
    10
Dos Amigos Verbal Language Scales, 252
Dutch, use of, in nineteenth-century classes, 24

East-West Center, Honolulu, Hawaii, 173
EDACs (*see* Evaluation, Dissemination, and
    Assessment Centers)
Education, previous, influence of, on students in
    bilingual-education programs, 7–9
Education Amendments of 1972, Title IV (Indian
    Education Act), 30
Education Consolidation and Improvement Act, 29
Education Development Center, 162, 169
Education of All Handicapped Children Act of 1975
    (P.L. 94-142), 29, 245–248
Educational cognitive styles (ECS) model, 135–136
Educational Research Quarterly, 149–150
Educational Resources Information Center (ERIC)
    Clearinghouse for Science, Mathematics, and
    Environmental Education, 215–216
Elementary and Secondary Education Act of 1965
    (ESEA), 29, 291–292
  Title VII (*see* Bilingual Education Act of 1968)
Elementary school (*see* Primary school)
Emergency School Aid Act, 29

Emotional adjustment to school, 9–11
English as a foreign language (EFL), 45
English as a second language (ESL), 2–4
  assessment (*see* Assessment)
  content-area, 44–45
  definition of, 2
  development of, in 1950s–1960s, 25
  funding for, 29
  in mathematics and science classes, 210–214
  models for, 44–45
  resources in (*see* Resources in bilingual education
    and ESL)
  social studies classes, 157–158
  state certification standards, 32–34
  (*See also* Second language)
English-dominant students in bilingual-education
    programs, 3–4, 14, 40–43
English for speakers of other languages (ESOL), 158
Enrichment bilingual education (*see* Two-way
    enrichment bilingual education model)
Equal Educational Opportunities Act of 1974, 35, 37
ERIC (Educational Resources Information Center)
    Clearinghouse for Science, Mathematics, and
    Environmental Education, 215–216
Eskimos, 109–110
ESL (*see* English as a second language)
ESL clusters, 44
ESL pullout programs, 44
Essay tests, 259
Ethnic communities, chronology of status of, 266–
    267
  (*See also* Community and school, interaction
    between)
Ethnic discrimination, adjustment to school and, 10
Ethnic Heritage Act, 29
Ethnic-language private schools, 281–282
Ethnicity:
  vs. acculturation or assimilation, 109
  acquisition of, 126–129
  mass media and, 129
  scholastic vs. culturally inherited, 129
  situational, 109
  of teachers, influence of, 142
  (*See also* Culture)
Ethnocentrism, 119 121
Ethnographic approach to educational research, 139–
    147
Ethnographic observation in assessment, 238
Evaluation, Dissemination, and Assessment Centers
    (EDACs), 28, 216
  services provided by, 47–48
  social studies materials from, 170
Evans v. Buchanan, 36
Exit criteria in assessment, 235–236
Extracurricular activities, music in, 182–183

Federal funding for bilingual education, 26–30, 47
Federal legislation:
  for bilingual education and ESL, 1, 26–30
    (*See also* Bilingual Education Act of 1968)

Federal legislation (*Cont.*):
  for community participation in education, 291–295
Field independence, 134–135
  assessment of, 234–235
Field sensitivity, 134–135, 137
  assessment of, 234–235
Films, use of, in social studies classes, 173–175
First language (*see* Primary language)
Folktales, use of, in teaching literacy, 99
Foreign-language instruction:
  lack of, in the United States, 24–25
  in nineteenth-century schools, 24
Foreign languages in the elementary school (FLES),
  45
Foreign Service Institute Oral Interview, 254
Formal operational stage of development, 197–198
Forum, 23, 46, 47, 51
Freewriting, 99
French, use of, in nineteenth-century classes, 24
Funding, federal, for bilingual education, 26–30, 47

Games, use of, in teaching language skills, 92
German, use of, in nineteenth-century classes, 24
Grammar-translation method of teaching L_2, 71–72,
  90
Grammatical competence, assessment of, 240
Grants:
  for bilingual desegregation, 47
  to school districts for bilingual education, 47
  training, 47
  (*See also* Federal funding for bilingual education)

Hawaii:
  KEEP research in, 146
  social interaction research in, 142–143
Headstart, 196, 292
High-Intensity Language Training (HILT), 44, 158
Higher Education Act, 30
Hispanics:
  IQ tests for, 245
  stereotypes about, 121
  test scores in mathematics and sciences among,
    192, 193
  (*See also specific groups, for example:* Mexican-
    Americans)
Home background of students, 4–9
  previous schooling experience, 7–9
  role of culture, 5–6
    (*See also* Culture)
  social context, 6–7
    (*See also* Community and school, interaction
      between)
Home-school mismatch, 132–133, 147–148
  (*See also* Social interaction)
Hutterites, 127

IHEs (Institutions of Higher Education), 49
Illiteracy in upper grades, 96–97
Ilyin Oral Interview, 254

Immersion bilingual-education model, 42–44, 55, 72,
  238–239
Immigrant communities, characteristics of, 267–270
Immigration:
  assimilation programs in the nineteenth century, 24
  cultural assimilation of immigrants, 108–109
  and melting pot, 266, 271
  and population growth, 112
India, caste system in, 119
Indian Education Act, 30
Indians (*see* Native Americans)
Indigenous minorities, characteristics of, 270
Input hypothesis of language acquisition, 62–63
Inquiry-based science, 192
Institute for Cultural Pluralism, 302–303
Institutions of Higher Education (IHE), 49
Integrative tests of communicative competence, 242,
  254–255, 258–259
Intelligence:
  bilingualism and, 243–244
  cultural expressions of, 168–169
  tests of, 244–245, 249
Interdisciplinary approach:
  to cultural awareness, 159–164
  in teaching mathematics and science, 216–221
Intuitive thinking skills, 161–162
Iñupiak, 13–14
IQ tests, 244–245, 249
Italian, use of, in nineteenth-century classes, 24

James Language Dominance Test, 251–252
Japanese, 199
Joint National Committee for Languages (JNCL), 30
Journals, dialogue, 98–99
Judicial decisions on bilingual education, 34–37,
  245, 247, 271–274

Kamehameha Early Education Program (KEEP), 146
Kamehameha Education Research Institute, 142–143,
  146
Kaufman Assessment Battery for Children (K-ABC),
  247
Kpelle tribe, 202

L_1 (*see* Primary language)
L_2 (*see* Second language)
Laissez faire pluralism, 267, 271
Language, 57–100
  acquisition of, research in, 58–67
    acquisition-learning distinction, 59–61
    additive vs. subtractive bilingualism, 64–65
    BICS (*see* Basic interpersonal communicative
      skills)
    CALP (*see* Cognitive-academic language
      proficiency)
    definitions of bilingualism, 66–67
    first- and second-language acquisition by child,
      58–59
    influence of L_1 on L_2, 65–66
    input hypothesis, 62–63

Language, acquisition of, research in (*Cont.*):
 socioaffective filter, 63
 threshold hypothesis, 64–65
assessment (*see* Language assessment)
bilingual classroom (*see* Classroom, bilingual,
  methods of teaching in a)
community use of, 277–280
and cultural values, interplay between, 124
language skills (*see* Language skills, teaching of)
marked and unmarked, 117–118
native language arts, 67–70
 (*See also* Primary language)
and scientific worldview, 203–206
second, methods of teaching, 70–80
 (*See also* Second language)
in teaching of mathematics and science, 206–221
variation in, and home-school mismatch, 129–133
Language aptitude testing, 231–232
Language assessment, 229–231, 239–243
communicative competence, 240–241
 integrative and pragmatic tests of, 242, 254–
  255, 258–259
discrete-point tests, 239–240, 251–254
informal assessment, 239
observation, 242–243
Language Assessment Scales, 253–254
Language skills, teaching of, 90–99
and art, 187
curriculum materials, 70
listening and speaking, 91–92
and mathematics skills, relationship between, 207
music, use in, 179–181
and placement testing, 230
in primary school, 156
reading in L_1 and L_2, 92–98
 beginning reading methods, 95–96
 preliterate students in the upper grades, 96–97
 strategies, 97–98
relationship between the four skills, 90–91
writing strategies, 98–99
Latinos (*see* Hispanics)
Lau v. Nichols, 34–36, 53, 226, 235, 272, 273
Lau Centers (National Origin Desegregation
  Assistance Centers), 30, 35, 50, 227
Lau Remedies, 35, 36, 50, 225–229, 236
"Learning" vs. "acquisition" of language, 59–61
Legal cases (*see* Court decisions on bilingual
  education)
Legislation, federal:
for bilingual education and ESL, 26–30
for community participation in education, 291–295
Limited-English proficiency (LEP), 1, 4
and emotional adjustment to school, 9–11
and linguistic challenge of school, 11–14
in 1974 amendments to Bilingual Education Act of
  1968, 27
number of students, 3
Limited-English-speaking ability (LES), 27
Linguistic components of language, 229–230

"Linguistic deficit", 132
Linguistic difference, 132
Listening skills, teaching of, 91–92
Longitudinal studies in program evaluation, 238–239
Los Angeles, East, 1968 Chicano student walkout,
  263–264

MACOS (*Man: A Course of Study*) program, 162–
  164, 169
Magazines, use of, in teaching social studies, 171
Maintenance bilingual-education model, 39–40, 42,
  81, 82
in teaching social studies, 157, 172
Man: A Course of Study (MACOS) program, 162–
  164, 169
Maps, use of, in teaching social studies, 170–171
Marked and unmarked languages and cultures, 117–
  118
Matching tests, 257
Materials Development Centers (MDCs), 28, 70
services provided by, 48–49
Mathematics, teaching of, 191–221
achievement status of students, 191–195
alternate-language approach, 209
cognitive and cross-cultural research, 195–206
 "cognitive deficit" framework, 196
 developmental universals, 196–200
 inferences for teaching, 200–206
concurrent approach, 208–209
home context, use of, 202–203
human and material resources, 214–216
interdisciplinary approach, 216–221
language, scientific worldview, and L_2
  competencies, 203–206
language and culture in the classroom, 206–221
natural competencies of students, 201–202
preview-review approach, 209–210
in primary school, 156
second-language development, 210–214
MDCs (*see* Materials Development Centers)
Media, use of, in teaching social studies, 171, 173–
  175
Melting pot, 266, 271
Memorization in teaching L_2, 73
Mesquakie Indians, 109
"Method" of teaching language, definition of, 71
 (*See also* Teaching methods)
Mexican-Americans:
"cultural deprivation/deficit" studies of, 116
East Los Angeles school walkout (1968), 263–264
field sensitivity among, 134
SAT scores among, 193, 194
Miami, bilingual education in, 26
Microethnographic research, 139–141, 144–145, 147
Migrant Education, 196
funding of programs, 29
Milwaukee, community organization in, 274–275
"Mim-mem" in teaching L_2, 73

Mimicry in teaching L_2, 73
Minidramas, 166
Models for programs, 37–46
　application to the classroom, 81–82
　English as a foreign language, 45
　English as a second language, 44–45
　foreign languages in the elementary school, 45–46
　immersion bilingual education, 42–43
　maintenance bilingual education, 39–40
　"structured immersion," 44
　transitional bilingual education, 38–39
　transitional-maintenance dichotomy, eliminating the, 42
　two-way enrichment bilingual education, 40–42
Morgan v. Kerrigan, 36
Moynihan Report, 115
Multicultural education, 159–169
　art appreciation in, 186–187
　interdisciplinary framework, 159–164
　teachers and students as cultural researchers, 164–169
　teaching mathematics and science, 216–221
　(*See also* Social studies, teaching)
Multiple-choice tests, 257–258
Music, 175–184
　caveats on misuse of, 177–179
　in classroom events, 176–177
　in extracurricular activities, 182–183
　learning objectives for musical experiences, 179–182
　resources, 183–184
　in teaching language skills, 92
Mutual Problem-Solving Tasks, 255
Myths, use of, in teaching literacy, 99

NABE Journal, 50, 216
NABE News, 23
National Advisory Council for Bilingual Education (NACBE), 23, 31, 50, 53
National Assessment of Educational Progress in Science, 192
National Association for Asian and Pacific American Education (NAAPAE), 51
National Association for Bilingual Education (NABE), 50–51
National Association for Vietnamese-American Education (NAVAE), 51
National Center for Bilingual Research (NCBR), 28, 49
National Clearinghouse for Bilingual Education (NCBE), 23, 29, 30, 43, 46–47, 54, 147, 309
　address and phone of, 46
　founding of, 28
　functions of, 28, 46–47
National Defense Education Act of 1958 (NDEA), 24–25, 30, 191
National Indian Bilingual Center, Tempe, Arizona, 30

National Indian Education Association (NIEA), 51
National Institute of Education (NIE), 47
National Origin Desegregation Assistance Centers (Lau Centers), 30, 35, 50, 227
National Public Radio, 183
National Puerto Rican Task Force on Educational Policy, 303–304
National Science Foundation, 191, 192
National Security and Economic Growth through Foreign-Language Improvement Act of 1983, 30
Native Americans:
　bilingual-education programs conceived and controlled by, 291
　educational legislation for, 30
　research on education of, 141–142
　SAT scores among, 193, 194
　test scores in mathematics and science among, 192, 193
Native language (*see* Primary language)
Natural Approach to teaching L_2, 76–77
Naturalistic evaluation, 238
Navajo Rough Rock Demonstration School, Arizona, 291, 296
NCBE (*see* National Clearinghouse for Bilingual Education)
NCBR (National Center for Bilingual Research), 28, 49
New math, 192
New York:
　court decisions involving, 36
Newspapers, use of, in teaching social studies, 171
Nonverbal communication, 5, 138–149, 173, 245
Norm-referenced tests, 236–237
Norwegian, use of, in nineteenth century classes, 24
Notional-functional syllabus for L_2, 78–80
Numbers, cultural symbolism of, 206

OBEMLA (*see* Office of Bilingual Education and Minority Languages Affairs)
Observation in language assessment, 242–243
Office for Civil Rights (*see* U.S. Office for Civil Rights)
Office of Bilingual Education and Minority Languages Affairs (OBEMLA):
　funding by, 27–28, 47
　programs administered by, 29–30
　services provided by, 47
Omnibus Budget Reconciliation Act, 27
One-way vs. two-way bilingual education, 40
Ontario Science Centre, Toronto, 220–221
Oral language proficiency tests, 251–256
Oral production tests, 258
Oral skills, teaching of, 91–92
Otavalo Indians, 280–281

Padres de Babel, 303
Parent advisory councils, 292–295

Parents, roles for, in community-school relations, 295–300
 (*See also* Community and school, interaction between)
Periodicals, use of, in teaching social studies, 171
Personnel, provisions in BEA of 1968 for training of, 27–28
Phonics, 95–98
Piagetian developmental theory, 128, 129, 137–138, 196–201
Placement testing, 229–232
Pluralism, 110–113, 266–267
 constructive, 111
 stable, 109
Polish, use of, in nineteenth-century classes, 24
Politics of bilingual education, 21–37
 court decisions, 34–37, 245, 247, 271–274
 federal legislation, 26–30
  (*See also* Bilingual Education Act of 1968)
 state certification, 32–34
 state legislation, 31–32
Postfigurative cultural transmission, 127
Poverty, culture of, 115
Pragmatic tests of communicative competence, 242, 254–255, 258–259
 combined with discrete-point tests, 253–254
Prefigurative cultural transmission, 127–128
Preliterate students in the upper grades, 96–97
Preoperational stage of development, 197
President's Commission for a National Agenda for the Eighties, 112
President's Commission on Foreign Language and International Studies, 42
Preview-review approach in the bilingual classroom, 84
 in teaching mathematics and science, 209–210
Primary language (L₁), 1
 acquisition of, in the child, 58–59
 acquisition-learning distinction, 59–60
 BICS (*see* Basic interpersonal communicative skills)
 CALP (*see* Cognitive-academic language proficiency)
 caretaker speech, 62
 curricular materials, 70
 dialects, 68–70
 in immersion bilingual education, 43
 influence on L₂, 65–66
 IQ test administration in, 245
 proficiency in, 13
  for placement assessment, 231
 reading in, teaching, 92–98
 standard, 68–70
 subtractive vs. additive bilingualism, 64–65
 teaching, 67–68
  reading, 92–98
 threshold hypothesis, 245–246
 use of, in teaching L₂, 72–76
Primary school:
 L₂ methods for, 77
 social studies in, 155–156

Private, nonprofit organizations, research services for bilingual-education and ESL programs provided by, 51–52
Problem-solving activities, use of, 92
Productive Language Assessment Tasks, 255
Professional organizations, services for bilingual-education and ESL programs provided by, 50–51
Public Law 94-142 (*see* Education of All Handicapped Children Act of 1975)
Puerto Ricans, SAT scores among, 193, 194
Puerto Rico, bilingualism in, 42*n*.

Question-answering tests, 242

Racial discrimination, effect of, on emotional adjustment to school, 10
Rafa-Rafa, 173
Reading in L₁ and L₂, teaching of, 92–98
 analytic approaches, 95–96
 beginning methods, 95–96
 eclectic approaches, 95, 96
 preliterate students in the upper grades, 96–97
 strategies, 97–98
 synthetic approaches, 95
Reagan administration policies on bilingual education, 27–29, 44, 227–228
Records (LP), use of, 184
Refugee Act of 1980, 29
Refugee Assistance Amendments of 1982, 29
Religion, role of, in shaping students, 5
Research:
 in bilingual education, funding for, 28
 in culture and education, 133–149
 in language acquisition, 58–67
Resources in bilingual education and ESL, 46–52
 private, nonprofit organizations, 51–52
 professional organizations, 50–51
 teaching: mathematics and science, 214–216
  music, 183–184
  social studies, 169–175
 Title VII support services, 46–50
Ríos v. Read, 36, 273
Role-playing activities, use of, 92

Sandhi variation, 91
Savignon Communicative Competence Tests, 254
Schema theory, 137–138
Scholastic Aptitude Test (SAT), 191–194, 224
School and community, interaction between (*see* Community and school, interaction between)
School districts, grants to (1981–1984), 47
Schooling, previous, influence of, on students in bilingual programs, 7–9
Science, teaching of, 191–221
 achievement status of students, 191–195
 alternate-language approach, 209
 cognition and cross-cultural research, 195–206
  "cognitive deficit" framework, 196
  developmental universals, 196–200
  inferences for teaching, 200–206
 concurrent approach, 208–209

Science, teaching of (*Cont.*):
  home context, use of, 202–203
  human and material resources, 214–216
  interdisciplinary approach, 216–221
  language, scientific worldview, and L_2
    competencies, 203–206
  language and culture in the classroom, 206–221
  natural competencies of students, 201–202
  preview-review approach, 209–210
  second-language development, 210–214
Science Curriculum Improvement Study, 220
Scientific concepts, learning of, 199
Scientific worldview, language and, 203–206
Second language (L_2), 1
  acquisition of, in the child, 58–59
    socioaffective filter, 63
  acquisition-learning distinction, 60–61
  additive vs. subtractive bilingualism, 64–65
  BICS (*see* Basic interpersonal communicative
    skills)
  CALP (*see* Cognitive-academic language
    proficiency)
  in immersion bilingual education, 43
  influence of L_1 on, 65–66
  input hypothesis, 62–63
  methods of teaching, 70–80
    audiolingual method, 72–73, 90, 91
    cognitive approach, 73–74, 90
    Community Language Learning, 75–76
    direct method, 72
    distinguishing between "approach," "method,"
      and "technique," 71
    grammar-translation method, 71–72, 90
    Natural Approach, 76–77
    for primary school, 77
    Silent Way, 74–75
    Suggestopedia (Suggestology), 75
    syllabus organization, 77–80
    Total Physical Response, 76
  reading in, teaching, 92–98
  scientific worldview and competency in, 203–206
  syllabus organization, 77–80
    notional-functional, 78–80
    situational, 78
    structural, 78
  in teaching mathematics and science, 210–214
  threshold hypothesis, 64–65, 245–246
  (*See also* English as a second language)
"Semilingualism", 131–132, 246
Sensorimotor stage of development, 197
Serna v. Portales Municipal Schools, 36, 272–273
"Set-of-traits" approach to culture, 106–107
Sex role stereotypes, 122
Short Test of Linguistic Skills, 252
SIETAR (Society for Intercultural Education,
  Training, and Research), 51, 173
Significant Bilingual Instructional Features study,
  146–147
Silent Way in teaching L_2, 74–75
Situational ethnicity, 109
Situational syllabus for L_2, 78

Social interaction, research on, 138–149
Social Science Research Council, 109
Social studies, teaching of, 153–175
  classroom structural variations, 155–158
    elementary-level bilingual self-contained
      classrooms, 155–156
    ESL social studies classes, 157–158
    secondary-level bilingual social studies, 156–157
  framework for, 153–155
    as citizenship transmission, 154
    as reflective inquiry, 154
    as social science, 154
  instructional approaches to cultural awareness,
    159–169
    interdisciplinary framework, 159–164
    teachers and students as cultural researchers,
      164–169
  music, use in, 181
  resources, 169–175
    in consumer education, 171–172
    electronic media and films, 171, 173–175
    maps, 170–171
    newspapers, 171
    periodicals, 171
    for a problem-posing curriculum, 172–173
    TV, 171, 173–175
Society for Intercultural Education, Training, and
  Research (SIETAR), 51, 173
Socioaffective filter in L_2 acquisition, 63
Socioeconomic status (SES):
  and culture, 124–126
  and previous schooling, 8–9
  role of, in shaping students, 6–7
Sociolinguistic competence, assessment of, 240
Sociolinguistic components of language, 230
Songs, use of, in the classroom, 177–184
Southwest Regional Laboratory for Educational
  Research and Development, Student
  Placement System, 256
Spanish:
  standard language, 69
  use of, in turn-of-the-century classes, 24
Spanish Education Development Center, Washington,
  D.C., 94–95
Speaking skills, teaching, 91–92
  use of music in, 180
Special education, 29, 246–248
Spoken language vs. written language, 91–92
Standard language, 68–70
Star Power, 173
State certification standards for bilingual and ESL
  teachers, 32–34
State legislation for bilingual and ESL education, 31–
  32
Stereotypes, cultural, 121–124
"Structural immersion" model, 44
Structural syllabus for L_2, 78
Students in bilingual-education programs:
  adjustment to school, 9–14
    emotional challenge, 9–11
    linguistic challenge, 11–14

Students in bilingual-education programs (*Cont.*):
  discovering, 15–19
  home background of, 4–9
  range of, 3–4
Submersion vs. immersion bilingual education, 25, 43
Subtractive bilingualism, 13
  vs. additive, 64–65
  threshold hypothesis, 64–65
Suggestopedia (Suggestology) in teaching L_2, 75
Support services, funding for (1981–1984), 47
Swedish, use of, in nineteenth-century classes, 24
Syllabus organization, second-language, 77–80
  notional-functional, 78–80
  situational, 78
  structural, 78
System Development Corporation, 293
System of Multicultural Pluralistic Assessment (SOMPA), 247

Teacher-constructed tests, 232–233, 256–259
  cloze procedure, 258–259
  dictation, 258
  multiple-choice tests, 257–258
  objectives, 257
  oral production tests, 258
  true-false and matching tests, 257
  writing tasks, 259
Teacher Corps, 30
Teachers, state certification standards for bilingual and ESL, 32–34
Teachers of English to Speakers of Other Languages (TESOL), 2, 259–261
  establishment of, 25
  headquarters of, 51
  services provided by, 51
  statewide programs of competency testing, statement on, 259–261
Teaching methods:
  primary language, 67–70
  second language, 70–80
  (*See also* Classroom, bilingual, methods of teaching in a; Language skills, teaching; Second language, methods of teaching)
"Technique" of teaching, definition of, 71
TESOL (*see* Teachers of English to Speakers of Other Languages)
TESOL Newsletter, 23
TESOL Quarterly, 51, 216
Test of Auditory Comprehension of Language, 252
Tests:
  vs. assessment, distinction between, 224–225
  (*See also* Assessment)
  commercial, 232–233
  criterion-referenced, 233–234
  cultural bias in, 248–251
  dictation, 258

Tests (*Cont.*):
  discrete-point, 239–240, 251–253
  integrative, 242, 254–255, 258–259
  IQ, 244–245, 249
  matching, 257
  multiple-choice, 257–258
  norm-referenced, 236–237
  oral production, 258
  pragmatic, 242, 254–255, 258–259
  standardized, 233–234
  teacher-constructed, 232–233, 256–259
  true-false, 257
Texas:
  court decisions involving, 35–37
Threshold hypothesis, 64–65, 245–246
Title VII of the Elementary and Secondary Education Act (*see* Bilingual Education Act of 1968)
Tobeluk v. Lind, 272
Total Physical Response in teaching L_2, 76
Training grants (1981–1984), 47
Transitional bilingual-education model, 38–39
  eliminating the transitional-maintenance dichotomy, 42
  in teaching social studies, 156–157, 172
True-false tests, 257
TV, use of, in teaching social studies, 171, 173–175
Two-way enrichment bilingual-education model, 40–42
  application to the classroom, 81, 82
  in teaching social studies, 156, 157

U.S. v. State of Texas, 35–37
U.S. Commission on Civil Rights, 53, 126, 138, 141, 142, 295
U.S. Department of Education, 47
  "High School and Beyond" study, 192
U.S. Office for Civil Rights (OCR), 35, 225–227
U.S. Office of Education, 2, 35

Values, role of, in shaping students, 5
  (*See also* Culture)
Variety in language, 68–70, 129–133
Videotapes, use of, in teaching social studies, 173–175
Vocabulary enhancement, use of music in, 180
Vocational Education Act, 30

Warm Springs Indian Reservation, Oregon, 141
Washington, D.C., community organization in, 275–276
Western civilization outlook on culture, 105–106
Woodcock-Johnson Psycho-Educational Battery, 247–248
Worldview, language and, 203
Writing skills, teaching, 98–99
Writing tasks, 259
Written language vs. spoken language, 91–92

ABOUT THE AUTHORS

CARLOS J. OVANDO is associate professor of education and director of the Bilingual/Multicultural specialization at the School of Education of the University of Alaska, Anchorage. Having emigrated from Nicaragua to the United States, he was first introduced to the English language at the age of 16 and is now bilingual. He later earned an M.A. and M.A.T. in Spanish and Latin American Studies and a Ph.D. in Curriculum and Instruction from Indiana University.

VIRGINIA P. COLLIER is the associate director of the Center for Bilingual/Multicultural/ESL Teacher Preparation at George Mason University in Fairfax, Virginia. She has 14 years' experience in the field of bilingual education and ESL. Dr. Collier received her Ph.D. in Intercultural Education with a specialization in Bilingual Education and Linguistics from the University of Southern California.